The Blue Economy
Version 2.0

The Work is published
in association with

Development Alternatives

THE CLUB OF ROME | INDIAN NATIONAL ASSOCIATION

UNEP
United Nations Environment Programme

The BLUE Economy

AUTHOR:

GUNTER PAULI is a born entrepreneur whose scope of initiatives spans business, culture, science and education. In 1994, with the support of the Japanese government and the United Nations University, he launched an initiative to design an economic framework and business model that converts all waste, including emissions, into a value-added cascade, modelled on ecosystems. In 2004, he launched a research project identifying the innovations that will shift business towards higher levels of competitiveness and sustainability, while generating millions of jobs through the creation of a platform for entrepreneurship. In early 2010, he personally directed a two-year initiative that each week for 100 weeks presented another business model to inspire entrepreneurs to translate these opportunities into worldwide business initiatives. Pauli is the author of 17 books published in 21 languages, and of 36 fables that bring science and entrepreneurship to children at an early age. *The Blue Economy / Version 2.0* outlines how to go beyond green, generating multiple cash flows, reducing risk and embracing break-throughs that shift the business model to a competitive framework where entrepreneurs respond to local needs with what is locally available.

A REPORT TO THE CLUB OF ROME

The Blue Economy

Version 2.0

200 Projects Implemented

US$ 4 Billion Invested

3 Million Jobs Created

GUNTER PAULI

ACADEMIC FOUNDATION

NEW DELHI

www.academicfoundation.org

First published in 2015
by

ACADEMIC FOUNDATION
4772-73 / 23 Bharat Ram Road, (23 Ansari Road),
Darya Ganj, New Delhi - 110 002 (India).
Phones : 23245001 / 02 / 03 / 04.
Fax : +91-11-23245005.
E-mail : books@academicfoundation.com
www.academicfoundation.org

in association with
Development Alternatives

Disclaimer:
The findings/views/opinions expressed in this book are solely those of the author and do not necessarily reflect the views of the publisher.

Cataloging in Publication Data--DK
Courtesy: D.K. Agencies (P) Ltd. <docinfo@dkagencies.com>

Pauli, Gunter A.
The blue economy version 2.0: 200 Projects Implemented, US$ 4 Billion Invested, 3 Million Jobs Created / Gunter Pauli.
p. cm.
Includes bibliographical references (p.).
ISBN 9789332701519

1. Natural resources. 2. Sustainable development. I. Title.
II. Title: Blue economy : ten years, hundred innovations, hundred million jobs.

DDC 333.7 23

Typeset by Italics India, New Delhi.

Printed and bound by The Book Mint, New Delhi.
www.thebookmint.in

Praise for The Blue Economy

Over the past 30 years as I have built up the computer industry around ACER, Dr Pauli has introduced me to many creative ideas, especially through his Zero Emissions Research and Initiatives (ZERI) organisation. He has devoted himself for decades to theoretical development as well as practical application of zero emission concepts. The ideas he puts forth in *The Blue Economy* represent a sustainable and competitive business framework based on innovations that offer investors and society financial, social, and environmental benefits. Such opportunities to achieve sustainability, parity, and profitability are not only inviting, but tremendously compelling too.

— STAN SHIH
Founder, ACER Computers (Taiwan)

Gunter Pauli masterfully elucidates examples from nature that can help us solve our sustainability problems. There are refreshing and competitive options to artificial, chemical, and technological fixes and their unintended toxic consequences.

— YVON CHOUINARD
Owner, Patagonia, Inc. (USA)

Gunter Pauli is a visionary entrepreneur who is able to help us create a *Blue Economy* based on respecting the Earth's ecosystems and humankind. His book is destined to be the bible of this new economy, meant for all of us who are working to build a better world.

— CHRISTIAN COURTIN-CLARINS
Chairman, Clarins (France)

Our current economic crisis is also a crisis of ethics and values, which has led to the enrichment of a few and the disempowerment of many. *The Blue Economy* advocates for a new economy, one led by innovation and creativity to cultivate the next generation of social entrepreneurship. We are in need of such an economy and no one is better placed than Gunter Pauli to offer this to the world.

— WENDY LUHABE
Co-founder, WITHHOLD Investment Corporation

Gunter's new work, *The Blue Economy*, presents excellent innovative ideas with practical applications that will help entrepreneurs and consumers to significantly impact the economies of the world, while earning money, generating jobs, and protecting the environment. In envisioning the future, Gunter continues to be an optimist. I am one too. As you read *The Blue Economy*, you will be introduced to these ideas and their concrete applications. Don't miss it and recommend it to your friends.

— PROF HEITOR GURGULINO DE SOUZA (BRAZIL)
Rector, UN University, Tokyo, Japan (1987-1997)
President, World Academy of Arts and Sciences

Ultimately, our civilisation will survive if we are able to emulate nature. *The Blue Economy* illumines the way.

— LESTER R. BROWN
President, Earth Policy Institute (USA)
Author, Plan B 4.0: Mobilizing to Save Civilization

Although I know too little of ecology, the rich ideas and inspirations set forth in *The Blue Economy* are worthy of our greatest attention.

— ELIE WIESEL
1986 Nobel Peace Laureate

The Blue Economy shows us that by securing materials and aligning production schemes as nature does, many problems of environmental degradation and pollution would disappear. However, economic policy and core business models largely ignore integrated solutions. Future economic models would do well to take into account the strategic advantage of a portfolio of innovations based on nature and physics. That will be a tall order, but Gunter Pauli's book, with its rich presentation of how nature and economy can and must collaborate, convincingly shows the way.

— ANDERS WIJKMAN
Member, Swedish Royal Academy of Sciences
European Parliament (1999-2009)
Co-president of the Club of Rome

The Blue Economy is an exceptional vision of what is truly possible in the context of a sustainable economy. Gunter Pauli has worked tirelessly for many years to put substance to the promise of a Blue Economy. His book is the fascinating result of true dedication towards unlocking the potential for sustainability that is universally practiced in Nature's ecosystems. As investment managers, we always seek great, unique ideas that can make money while solving the world's greatest challenges. I would urge anyone who is interested in going beyond shallow notions of sustainable business to read this book and be inspired by the real opportunity we now have to create a truly enduring and sustainable economic system based on Nature's profound wisdom.

— COLIN M. LE DUC
Partner, Generation Investment Management LLP (London)

Gunter Pauli is an inspired and visionary entrepreneur. He is the kind of business leader and educator the world needs. His concepts and ideas for creating sustainable business and social enterprises are based on a deep understanding of ecosystems. This book belongs in the library of every university, business school, and entrepreneur who wants to make a difference in the world today.

— HAZEL HENDERSON
Author, Ethical Markets: Growing the Green Economy
President, Ethical Markets Media (USA and Brazil)

Gunter Pauli has formulated an entrepreneurial business model that can respond to basic needs, build social capital, and achieve sustainability. His current economic development work with READ in Bhutan is focused on introducing a portfolio of the innovations described in this book as tools to improve the National Happiness Index and foster environmental and social entrepreneurship. Given the mission of the Social Venture Network, his message in *The Blue Economy* is certain to resonate with a growing community of business and social leaders.

— OMER L. RAINS
Chairman, Rural Education & Development (READ)
Global Director, Marshall Plan Venture Capital Fund

Japan was among the first to support Gunter Pauli's early work with zero emissions. I am certain that the innovative approaches he describes in *The Blue Economy* will give the entire world a powerful engine for a new kind of economy.

— PROF KIYOSHI KUROKAWA, M.D.
Special Science Advisor to the Prime Minister of Japan (2006-2008)
President, Science Council of Japan (2003-2006)

The Blue Economy fosters our transition from a product-based economy to a system-based economy. Such a cultural leap requires all of us to see—and move beyond—the connections that have gone into an oblivious core business strategy subject to market tyranny.

— DR CATIA BASTIOLI
President, Novamont SpA (Italia)
European Innovator of the Year (2007)

As a species, we have evolved in interdependence, formulating the tools for brilliant co-existence. The novel ideas and breathtaking concepts presented in *The Blue Economy* resonate with our deepest knowing. We are led to recognise that Nature devises systems perfectly suited to continuance. The model of cascading energy and nutrients from one kingdom of nature to the next offers us a necessary paradigm that allows us to envision our place in nature's congruence.

— AMY MCCONNELL FRANKLIN, PH.D, M.ED., M.P.H.
Emotional Intelligence Education Consultant and Lecturer;
Author, Choose to Change

The Blue Economy holds a special place on my desk—front and center. In my 30 years of working for a sustainable future, it is rare to come across a book with such a high level of both intellectual rigour AND joyful wonder. I consider both essential. Gunter Pauli's insights and extraordinary breadth of solution-oriented scenarios can make your head spin and your heart beat fast. As a student of systems thinking and design, the 100 innovations described fill me with a sense of hope and thrill me with the possibilities for a future I'll be happy to leave to upcoming generations.

— KRIS HOLSTROM
Regional Sustainability Coordinator, The New Community Coalition
Colorado organic farmer

The Blue Economy reveals, through the eyes of an economist, a panoply of technological innovations based in nature. It shows us that environmental sustainability and company profitability are far from mutually exclusive.

— ANDREW PARKER
PhD, Research Leader, London Natural History Museum &
Green Templeton College, Oxford University; Blue Economy Innovator

From the GREEN (initiative)
Jump into THE BLUE (economy)
Your RED (balance sheet) becomes BLACK (wealth)!
With the true dynamic of GAIA (naturally . . .)

— TOMOYO NONAKA
Chairwoman, Gaia Initiatve
CEO, Sanyo Electric Group (Japan) (2005-2008)

The Blue Economy approach holds the promise of accelerated integrated and inclusive growth that can offer sustainable poverty eradication and prosperity for all. It takes us beyond the constraints imposed by traditional economic thinking that has held us captive to trade-offs and sequencing of development interventions that assume that "the poor will always be with us." *The Blue Economy* leverages poor people's assets and energies, involves them in the value creation chain and stops the leakage of value to outsiders, thus promoting virtuous cycles of effort, savings and investment of people in their own development.

— DR MAMPHELA RAMPHELE, M.D.
Non-violent freedom activist during Apartheid Regime in South Africa
Former Managing Director of the World Bank (2000-2004)
Former Vice-Chancellor of the University of Cape Town (1996-2000)
Trustee of the Nelson Mandela Children's Fund

Contents

Dedication

Let us not demand more of the Earth.
Let us do more with what the Earth provides.

— *G.P.*

The endeavour to grasp new insights to design creative and innovative business models that offer an inclusive growth is anything but a solitary exercise. While this book was written by one person, the impulses, energy, and support emerged from a diverse network, ranging from old friends, close family, and surprising new arrivals. The opportunity to travel the world and meet pioneers offers a platform for dialogue that can never be matched by high speed internet or videoconferencing. I had the privilege of visiting China for the first time in 1980 and have returned so often that I lost count. The meetings with Dr Li Wenhua, Member of the Chinese Academy of Sciences, Prof Li Kangmin, one of the founders of the Asia Pacific Regional Training Center for Integrated Fish Farming, and Prof Dr Chang Shuting, who masterminded through science the mushroom industry in China are just a few of the inspiration I got from China.

The intellectual supports from Ashok Khosla, Anders Wijkman, and Heitor Gurgulino de Souza, who have been fellow co-inspirators and members of the Club of Rome, have offered structures for debate. From the beginning, they provided generous support for this endeavour to identify real breakthroughs beyond "green" batteries and corn-based plastics. Jorge Reynolds, whom I have had the privilege to follow and work with over a quarter of a century, provided first-hand and deeper insight as to how single discoveries into the functioning of the whale heart could impact society beyond the health of heart patients. His inventions provide a fresh look at how innovative advances in health care could provide breakthroughs for planetary health and simultaneously build a competitive industry, in effect achieving a powerful and deliberate synchronicity. Jorge is also part of a small nucleus of individuals who witnessed Paolo Lugari's emerging dream at Las Gaviotas, which used the powers of symbiosis in natural ecosystems to heal centuries of thoughtless human abuse of the land.

The technical and innumerable pages of listings of what nature and ecosystems accomplish, gathered with painstaking effort, came to life only when scientists like Joanna Aizenberg, Andrew Parker, Peter Steinberg, Christer Swedin, and Jorge Alberto Vieira Costa, plumbed the depths of their insights and described opportunities with passion and clarity. These efforts, complemented with the entrepreneurial pragmatism of Curt Hallberg, Emile Ishida, Fritz Vollrath, and Catia Bastioli, provided a wealth of content that helped establish the vision and the foundation for ideas that stand at the core of this book.

When I subsequently contemplated the work of systems integrators like Paolo Lugari (Gaviotas), Father Godfrey Nzamujo, John Todd, and Anders Nyquist, I realised the tremendous power of bundling these technologies into systems and business models to achieve something that is economically viable, eminently natural, quite complex, yet very simple. I knew that their energy had set me on track toward something truly worthwhile. Without the generosity of time offered by over a hundred scientists and entrepreneurs, I would never have had their perspective for my goals to describe how adapting the logic of ecosystems to economic models can generate sustainable livelihood and provide the basic needs of all.

Then, there is the energy to pursue this endeavour against all odds. When my partners of the moment abandoned larger goals and chose to control intellectual property for personal benefit, it was the ethical leadership of my mentor, Elie Wiesel, that helped direct my focus to the greater good. It permitted me to drop the excessively romantic view of each species that had diverted my attention from the real power of ecosystems and the vast portfolio of entrepreneurial opportunities. Within that changing world, my wife, Katherina, provided the greatest support. Her unconditional backing helped me realise the importance of discarding the superficial calculations of idealised businesses in favour of a vision of systemic job generation that could redefine competitiveness and offer a new economic framework to a global population.

Several organisations around the world invited me to share emerging insights, engage dialogues, focus proposals, and prioritise the cases. Addressing Bioneers at the Bay (Massachusetts, USA, organised by the Marion Institute); the governing council of United Nations Environment Programme (UNEP) in Nairobi, Kenya; the COP on Biodiversity in Bonn, Germany; the Industry Leaders' Summit in New Delhi, India; bankers and farmers at ABSA in Stellenbosch, South Africa; Al Gore's Expert Panel on Solutions for Climate Change in New York, USA; the GLOBE Meeting at the G8 in Tokyo, Japan, the LIFT Conference in Marseilles, France; the Annual Congress of Engineers (ANPEI) in Brazil; the APEC CEO Summit in Singapore; the General Assembly of UNIDO in Vienna, Austria; and the 2009 Annual Meeting of the Club of Rome in Amsterdam, Netherlands, are some of the valuable exchanges that enriched my insights.

However the greatest insights were gained by implementing projects across the board. I could never have imagined that over such a short time span, nearly 200 projects would have mobilised in excess of €4 billion and would have generated 3 million jobs. There is no doubt in my mind, that the hard facts and the real numbers of these innovations that are translated into businesses, not only compete but even outcompete by every parameter. Moreover, this offers an inclusive growth, reaching the unreached and responding to the needs of all on Earth, not only the human species, but also the 100 million others that make up this magnificent biodiversity we seldom understand its importance.

In 1979, Aurelio Peccei, founder of the Club of Rome and a personal mentor, invited me to attend the annual meeting of the Club in Salzburg, Austria. Three decades later, members of the Club had considered the first edition of this book worthy of being named a Report to the Club of Rome, in the rich tradition of milestone publications like *Limits to Growth* and *Factor Four*. It is a humbling honour. Thus, it is with deep gratitude that I undertake to merit these expectations. My deepest wish is to fully contribute to the vision and the shaping of sustainable society articulated by the founding fathers of the Club of Rome. This new, updated and expanded edition hopefully demonstrates how far we have been able to go beyond our own dreams.

There are many people who have been key to making certain that this book came to be; but perhaps the most momentous inspiration have been my children, opening wide my eyes and making me look positively into the future, reawakening that fundamental feeling that parents have a responsibility to create an environment that is conducive to a better future. It is reality in the making as described throughout the chapters of *The Blue Economy*. This is what offers hope.

Note for the 2.0 Edition

Five years have gone by and the core of this book has been translated in more than 30 languages. However, what is most encouraging is that this book has inspired hundreds of initiatives. The number of mushroom farms evolved from rural initiatives to urban programs (+1,500 on record), and the maggot farming of Benin, now has duplications in South Africa, Colombia, even in Wales and the Netherlands (a dozen on record). The stone paper concept has already been converted in 2013 into a full-scale production in Shenyang (China), and the biorefinery in Italy was inaugurated in June 2014. The size and scope of the initiatives are going beyond the original content of the Blue Economy, hence the need to publish a fresh, updated, improved, expanded, and fundamentally novel version: *The Blue Economy 2.0*.

Hout Bay, South Africa on 31 August 2014.

Foreword

The central goal for most economies today has to be to generate goods and services that meet the basic needs of all, create jobs and income to enable people to buy these goods and services, and to do all these without transgressing the planetary boundaries. Today's economic approaches do neither adequately. They must now be transformed to nurture the integrity of our communities and their local economies and also maintain the stability of our climate systems and the health of our biodiversity and ecosystems. In other words, we have now to go beyond the "brown economy", based as it is on massive extraction of natural resources, particularly on excessive use of fossil fuels, and inordinate production of wastes and pollution.

The first step on this path was, over the past few decades, to adopt a "green economy" approach to deal particularly with the undesirable waste streams and pollution. The green economy has proved its value and is now championed in many countries and companies as a basic goal for their activities. But it has become increasingly apparent that this is not enough to deal with the issues of overconsumption of resources and gross inequity in societies, and in any case was widely seen to entail higher costs and lower satisfactions. The term, green economy has not yet been able to shed its connotation of an economy that requires some degree of sacrifice.

To overcome this perception and to develop an even more fundamental, transformational approach, the concept of "Blue Economy" was pioneered by Zero Emissions Research Initiative (ZERI) and its founder Dr Gunter Pauli, whose philosophy and practical contributions form the bulk of this book.

The modern formal sector of most growing economies is not capable of creating the number of workplaces and jobs needed by the increasing workforce. The capital costs of industrial production systems are too high and their gestation periods too long. Besides, their technology is specifically designed to replace labour by machines, to decreate jobs and not to create them. With continued emphasis on large industries, we cannot but expect the numbers of unemployed to grow over time.

There are, of course, sectors for which the economies of scale only work with large, mechanised units. These probably include steel making, oil refining and automobile manufacture. But the economics of most industries can be commercially viable, even at quite small scales. If the full costs of the processes and resources used in manufacturing and delivering products is taken into account, and no subsidies are allowed for energy, transportation, financial and other services, small scale production can become positively competitive.

In any case, only small and micro enterprises can do what needs to be done on the job front. What is more, they can also accelerate economic growth, not only at the local level, but also for the nation as a whole. Their return on investment is usually much higher than for a large industry and, needing only small amounts of capital for each unit, they can proliferate much faster.

The ideas this book explores offer some of the most tantalising prospects for realising a low carbon, resource-efficient, and competitive economy in the 21st century. They largely depend on allowing nature to do the work it does best: innovate, manufacture, use and recycle—over and over, for the longest of times. In fact, nature is truly remarkable in the no-fuss way it makes the most complex and worthwhile things under ordinary conditions, without the need of elaborate factories and machines, without elaborate supply chains and without leaving behind any waste.

Using nature to do some of our work for us, and learning from nature how to do our other work more efficiently is one of the smartest moves modern economies can make. As a result, not only can we gain more things of value to households and the community and satisfy our basic needs, but also create new kinds of meaningful jobs. Used in the right way, nature offers us solutions that not only can make our lives a great deal better, but also help us reclaim some of the ground lost to the massive environmental destruction that humankind has wrought on our poor beleaguered planet.

The natural world, in all its splendour and diversity, has already solved many of the sustainability challenges humanity faces in ingenious, unexpected, and even counterintuitive ways. If humans could only unravel the fascinating chemistry, processes, structures, and designs that organisms—from bacteria and mollusks to reptiles and mammals—have evolved and tested over millennia, perhaps then we would have new and transformational solutions to the many challenges faced by a planet of seven billion people, rising to over nine billion by 2050.

Gunter Pauli's book, *The Blue Economy*, opens the door to this fresh, forward-looking field. The pioneering advances it profiles will quickly persuade business and government leaders to explore and develop the cutting-edge sciences at the foundation of these new developments. It highlights the innovative work of many scientists and practitioners working in many parts of the world, creating solutions that could revolutionise the way a wide variety of things are produced and consumed.

The Blue Economy demonstrates that we can find ways of utilising physics, chemistry, and biology with renewable materials and sustainable practices just as ecosystems do. This is no longer the realm of science-fiction; it is actually happening here and now. With appropriate policies to support research and development, with promotional strategies delivered through market mechanisms, these materials and methods offer abundant opportunities for accelerating adaptation to pressing global issues.

The biodiversity and ecosystems that underpin our mega-trillion dollar economy by providing essential services at the local, regional, and global level contribute a sizable fraction of the total value added by the economy. Many ecosystem species and processes hold clues for potentially significant achievements in the production of medicine, food crops, biofuels, and low-energy materials. These could prove to be essential for societal measures so as to mitigate or adapt to climate change. Such achievements will certainly be needed to catalyse new sustainable businesses and industries to provide decent, sustainable jobs. For the 100 odd innovations described, *The Blue Economy* estimates an employment potential of 100 million jobs. The plausibility of this estimate is enhanced by the fact that there are presently more people employed in renewable energies than in the oil and gas industries combined, and that investment in wind, solar, and geothermal power generation exceeds that made in new fossil fuel power plants.

The United Nations forecasts that by 2025, 1.8 billion people will be living in countries or regions suffering from water scarcity. Two-third of the world's population could be living with conditions of water stress. Meanwhile, climate change is expected to aggravate water problems via more extreme weather events. Consider a water-collecting system modelled after that of the Namib Desert beetle. This resourceful creature lives in a location that receives a mere half inch of rain a year, yet it can harvest water from the fogs that blow in gales across the desert several mornings each month.

Researchers have recently designed a surface that is inspired by the water-attracting bumps and water-shedding valleys of scales on this beetle's wings. These scales allow the insect to collect and funnel water droplets that are thinner than a human hair. Trials have been conducted to capture water vapour from cooling towers by using a technique modelled after the beetle's skill. Initial tests have shown that this film invention can recover 10 per cent of the water lost. This lowers energy bills for nearby buildings by reducing the heat island effect. An estimated 50,000 new water-cooling towers are erected annually and each large system loses over 500 million litres of water per day. Thus, a savings of even 10 per cent is significant. Other researchers are adapting the beetle's water collection system to develop tents that collect their own water, as well as surfaces that will mix reagents for lab-on-a-chip applications. Twenty people are employed on this fledgling development, but the true world-wide potential might be as many as 100,000 new jobs.

The Blue Economy cites a project in Benin where a novel farming and food-processing system emulates the way an ecosystem cascades nutrients. Animal wastes from the slaughterhouse are processed in a maggot farm to feed fish and quail; biogas provides electricity; and plants purify water. The project is a microcosm of the Blue Economy. For the same Dollar or Rupee generated, it produces income, livelihoods, and food security while recycling and re-using wastes. To date, 250 people are employed. There is a potential of 500,000 jobs if this cascading model were used in every African *abattoir*, and five million jobs worldwide.

It has been nearly 70 years since Swiss engineer George de Mestral, having examined the natural hooks of burdock seeds that stubbornly attached to his clothes while on a countryside stroll, came up with an invention we know as "Velcro™". More recently, buildings such as a shopping centre in Zimbabwe, a hospital in Colombia, a school in Sweden, and the Zoological Society of London are cooled by structures inspired by termite mounds. Meanwhile, engineering schools around the world are racing to develop far more efficient solar power based on the molecules and processes of photosynthesis. What *The Blue Economy* emphasises is the vast potential of such innovations. It spotlights the tipping point inherent in the immense number of such breakthroughs currently in the laboratory, under development, or being commercialised.

In the final section of this edition of the book, 10 case studies are presented of projects carried out in India by the social enterprise, Development Alternatives, the South Asia affiliate of ZERI. These are intended to illustrate the range of innovative interventions that can help create a blue economy, extending from use of natural processes for agricultural and industrial processes to the design of small but viable enterprises capable of meeting local basic needs and employment goals. The concepts are applicable in a developing economy, just as well as in an industrialised one.

The world has been racked by food, fuel, environmental, financial, and economic crises. Ecosystem and biodiversity loss has led to an emerging climate crisis and a looming natural-resource calamity. A Blue Economy, able to deal systematically with these many challenges, and ready to seize the manifest multiple opportunities, is now essential. Our Earth has always been our greatest resource, and this book cites 100 new reasons why investing in both local and global ecosystem sustainability is even more valid and central today. If we follow the logic of nature, we can create a foundation for societal sea change and economic transformation that manifests from the ground up.

Leonardo da Vinci neatly summed up the power of ecosystems and nature's material efficiency in his *Codex Atlanticus*:

> Everything comes from everything; everything is made of everything; everything turns into everything, for all that exists in the elements is made of these elements.

Ashok Khosla

Chairman, Development Alternatives
Co-Chair, International Resource Panel
President, International Union for Conservation of Nature (IUCN), 2008-12
President, Club of Rome, 2005-12

Preface

If we teach our children only what we know, they can never do better than we do.

— *GP*

In the 1980s when I read the books of Lester Brown and his team at the Worldwatch Institute, I had the urge to make available to everyone this wealth of data concerning global environmental issues. The onslaught of negative statistics and trend analyses, based on data assembled in Washington DC, showed only a few positive lights on the horizon. Consequently, I created a dedicated publishing company to bring the *State of the World and Vital Signs* to a recalcitrant listener: the business community in Europe. As an entrepreneur who had established half a dozen companies by then, I was also a concerned citizen. In the early 1990s with the arrival of my two sons, Carl-Olaf and Laurenz-Frederik, a reflection crossed my mind as happens with so many young fathers and mothers: we want to leave the world to our children in a better condition than we received it from our parents. As my first son will graduate from high school nearly two decades later, I must confess it seems a Herculean task.

However, as life matures and wrinkles unveil deep concerns, we cannot simply remain concerned citizens, worried about the future, sorry about every error. Rather we must regroup and find ways to create the foundation on which we can allow the next generation to surpass our achievements. Perhaps the greatest freedom we can offer our children is to allow them to think differently and, more importantly, to act differently. It is therefore helpful to reflect on what we can bequeath future generations as a structure for positive thinking and a platform for concrete action. This is perhaps the greatest challenge.

The bad news is not merely about the health of our planet. For the first time in decades, we are realising that the economic system is also crumbling.

As an early member of the Club of Rome, which is the informal gathering of concerned policymakers, scholars, business leaders, and international civil servants, I know all too well the importance of sounding a wake-up call. The *Limits to Growth* report put forth by the Club of Rome clearly delineated the vicious cycle of population explosion, environmental degradation, unbridled industrial growth, and collapse of ethical standards. As a publisher of the Worldwatch *State of the World* in selected European languages, and as an avid participant in the Club of Rome for three decades, I could never separate the negative conclusions from the need for positive action.

I began working with Ecover, a small Europe-based producer of biodegradable cleaning products. When even the largest manufacturers adopted our biodegradable ingredient—the fatty acids of palm oil—as an industry standard replacement for petrochemical surfactants, it dramatically increased demand for this alternative. This spurred many harvesters, especially in Indonesia, to replace vast swathes of rainforest with palm tree farms. In destroying the rainforest, much of the habitat for the orangutan was also lost. Thus, I learned to my chagrin that biodegradability and renewability do not equate with sustainability.

In my first article on the subject, published in Seoul, Korea in 1991, I exhorted the industry to emulate the efficiency of ecosystems. The wisdom of an ecosystem is not just that it provides services like fresh water and clean air, replenishment of topsoil, balanced control of bacteria, and a never-ending evolutionary pathway, always searching for better solutions and higher efficiencies. Ecosystems are also an inspiration for changing our highly wasteful production and consumption model. The article suggested that sustainability is only foreseeable when our system eliminates the concept of waste, and starts cascading nutrients and energy as nature does.

After the disenchanting experience with Ecover, I was challenged by Prof Dr Heitor Gurgulino de Souza, the Rector of the United Nations

University hosted by the Japanese government, to model an economic system that generated no waste and no emissions, yet created jobs, contributed social capital, and did not entail a higher cost. I accepted this challenge three years before the Kyoto Protocol was approved. Thus I had the opportunity to imagine, from an academic ivory tower, how we could emulate the productive and evolutionary interactions of natural ecosystems where waste for one is food for another. Following three years of research, and in cooperation with the United Nations Development Programme (UNDP), the ZERI Foundation was established in Switzerland with its sole objective to implement pioneering cases that could demonstrate a scientifically feasible and economically viable model of production and consumption. This single institution was converted after the World Expo 2000 into a network of foundations, membership organisations and even companies, dedicated to making it happen.

Celebrating two decades of pioneering around the world, we are strengthened to pursue this quest for an economic model that could inspire entrepreneurs to put humanity in general, and its production and consumption in particular, on a viable and sustainable path. At the outset of this search, I had the opportunity to work with Fritjof Capra to edit the book, *Steering Businesses towards Sustainability*. This project triggered a deluge of ideas. I realised that my search for a next generation of business opportunities was based on the conviction that if I could portray the models I envisioned, it might inspire others to become entrepreneurs. I pondered over innovations that could be bundled into a system for functioning in society the way ecosystems do, clustering innovations developed by diverse players, making more efficient use of all existing, unfailing forces described by the laws of physics for which there are no exceptions.

Over a period of five years since the publication, I met with more inventors and entrepreneurs in all four corners of the world. I held dozens of meetings with financial analysts, business reporters, and corporate strategy academics. We joined the inauguration of splendid initiatives. This helped sharpen the logic. A team undertook a complete reassessment of all the successes and failures before us and examined dynamics of the current economic model's demise in the light of the innovations we had cataloged. We spotted the phoenix of new growth, even double-digit growth, that seemed to shift the logic of short-term results and bonuses to one that gives a world constrained by limited resources the ability to respond to people's basic needs with the available.

I saw a clear model emerging that could offer entrepreneurs around the world a unique window of opportunity to change the dominant business paradigm driven by cutting costs and economies of scale. It was not about cloning and genetic manipulation, protected by patents that appear closer to bio-piracy than actual innovation. It was about the pervasive logic and sensibility of inclusive growth. This book goes beyond the innovations and drew inspiration from the ability of ecosystems to always evolve to higher levels of efficiency with readily available resources, to cascade nutrients and energy, to leave nothing to waste, to utilise the abilities of all contributors, and to respond to the basic needs of all. This book demonstrates how business can respond to the basic needs, provided it changes its logic from cutting costs to generating value.

Such insights into a new business logic have crystallised into the underpinnings of this book, allowing me to establish the framework for a Blue Economy and to realise that the current economic upheaval is a blessing in disguise. It may be that we are finally calling a halt to the unrealistic consumerism that has propelled the economy into insurmountable debt. Exhorting consumers to spend more is a stereotype of the blind logic that cajoles citizens to buy their way out of crisis by indebting all of us as well as subsequent generations, beyond our capacity to ever repay. It is also clear that with mounting youth unemployment, the traditional call for austerity in order to redress broken balance sheets offers no solution. This unconscionable approach siphons the entire world's liquidity into an elite that wants to make more money with money, denying credit for everyone else. Such actions are at the base of a bankrupt economic model, a Red Economy model that borrows—from nature, from humanity, from the commons of all—with no thought of repayment beyond postponement to the future. Insatiable economies of scale callously search for ever lower marginal costs for each additional unit manufactured, making dismissive abstraction of all unintended consequences. The financial crisis of 2008 stemmed from bankers and corporate decision-makers embarking on a merger and acquisition frenzy, leveraging assets and amassing such enormous debt that the growth became self-defeating. Such is the tale of an "In-the-Red" (debt) Economy that failed.

In comparison, a Green Economy model has required companies to invest more and consumers to pay more, to achieve the same, or even less, while preserving the environment. While this was already a challenge during the heyday of economic growth, it is a solution that has little chance in a time of economic downturn. The Green Economy, in spite of much goodwill and effort, has not achieved the viability so greatly desired. Is that a surprise? How many can appreciate a green economy where everything that is good for you and the environment is expensive? Can you agree on an economy where what is bad for you and damages nature is cheap? Who invented such a misnomer of a market economy?

If we shift the spectrum, we see that a Blue Economy addresses the issues of sustainability that go beyond mere preservation. A Blue Economy engages regeneration. We might say that the Blue Economy is about ensuring that ecosystems can maintain their evolutionary path so as to benefit from nature's endless flow of creativity, adaptation and abundance.

It is the young at heart who will seize upon the entrepreneurial opportunities that emulate ecosystems and cascade energy and resources to add value and generate multiple exchange benefits, translating them into income and employment. When we implement the concepts of a Blue Economy, the decisions of millions of actors can supersede the dirigisme of a few market makers, monopolistic companies, or state controls, and eventually a powerful new social and economic structure manifests. Only the engagement and commitment of citizens is will change the rules of the game and bring about a real shift. At a moment in history where peak oil and peak food are clearly hovering, we can draw practical ideas and inspiration from ecosystems as we witness their ability to apply creativity and evolution in overcoming challenges to survival. This book aims to contribute to the design of a new economic model that is not only capable of responding to the needs of all, but also converts the artificial construct called scarcity into a sense of sufficiency and even of abundance.

While the waste of material resources exemplified by modern landfills and incinerators is to be deplored, that of human resources is absolutely unacceptable. When the numbers of unemployed youth oscillate between 50 per cent in industrialised countries like Spain and Greece, and over 90 per cent in communities under siege like Palestine, it is easy to imagine what it means to our global society if its leaders consider the next generation useless—or even worse, if the young and disadvantaged consider themselves useless. It is indicative of a system in severe decline, a society in extreme crisis, underscored by mounting statistics of violence, criminality, terrorism, drug abuse, illegal immigration, relinquished education, and the deplorable treatment of populations or communities already at risk or underserved.

Abdel Salam al-Majali, who served as President of Jordan University as well as Prime Minister, and now President of the Islamic World Academy of Sciences, once said to me, "Expose—do not impose." If our aim is to create a better world for all, not just a fuller bank account for a few, if we are prepared to counter risk with gain, then thoughtful considerations, based on solid science and documented illustrative cases, can help us envision and achieve it. A strong platform for entrepreneurship could emulate the success of ecosystems in eliminating waste and achieving full employment and productive capacity. Multiple small initiatives around the world could provide the basis for new entrepreneurial opportunities that would encourage the shift to a macro-economic system. Instead of deferment as policymakers reach agreement, the direction we take is to expose individuals everywhere to the open-source opportunities provided by nature.

It is amazing how little natural logic works in modern society. To cool a building, air-conditioning experts pump cold air "up"? To clean water, we dump chemicals in it to kill all life? Greenhouses heat the air, not the roots? We pay upwards of $100 per kilowatt hour for electricity provided by a battery that intoxicates our environment? When we drink a cup of coffee, we give value to only 0.2 per cent of the biomass, while the rest is left to rot, generating methane gas, or stressing earthworms, who suffer as much from the neurotoxin called caffeine as we do. A hundred thousand tons of titanium, mined and processed at high temperature, are flung into landfills when we discard our disposable razors. We cut millions of trees to whet our appetite to print and write, and then we recycle it consume more water than we use to flush toilets? Humanity makes excessive use of energy, emits greenhouse gases beyond reason, and causes havoc in the environment. It is hardly surprised that we face climate change and an acidification of oceans while depleting topsoil beyond repair. Indeed, the only excuse for what we do and the way we do it is that we are ignorant about unintended consequences. Once we know, we not only have the clarity needed to change, we are also empowered to consciously make it happen.

Chido Govera, an orphan who lost her mother at the age of seven and never knew her father, turned immediately from a young girl to the head of her family with the responsibility to provide food for her grandmother and little brother. Although such tragedy is real, it is far too common. There are millions of people, many of them women and children, who must tolerate abuse to guarantee a semblance of food, water and shelter. As someone who quickly learned how to survive for years on nothing more than a bowl of peanuts a day, Chido also quickly learned to appreciate the generative capacity of ecosystems, the power of a creative mind ready to persevere against all odds. In Africa, these natural systems have been pillaged by the irresponsible farming of settlers who brought their traditions from temperate climates with four seasons, whose techniques not only denuded the land of its natural vegetation, but drastically eroded the rich topsoil too. Yet Chido does not judge the errors of the past. She has grasped the opportunity to redefine the potential of coffee-crop agro-waste to achieve food and livelihood security for herself and her fellow orphans in Zimbabwe. Given food and livelihood security, abuse—both of young girls and of natural systems—can be eliminated. Chido's vision is to accomplish this in her lifetime.

What more do you expect to achieve in your lifetime? Do you mind waiting to answer until you have read this book?

1

Timeless Resources

Some dream to escape reality.
Some dream to change reality forever.

— *SOICHIRO HONDA*

This book is about adopting a new awareness that it is not so very difficult, provided we are prepared to leave modern Western habits behind and are ready to embrace new ones often founded in the wisdom of Nature and the grand traditions that surround us. It is a wake-up call to those of us who feel that the chances are simply too unique to let pass by. The opportunities before us will make a difference—now. It must be now. Ecology and sustainability are concepts that planted the early seeds of green thinking. Such ideas taught us to appreciate the use of sustainable materials in our structures and products. Though we have begun to understand the importance of sustainable processes, few know how to make these economically viable and competitive on the market. If we begin to understand and utilise nature's brilliance, economy, and simplicity, we can emulate the functionality embedded in that logic and achieve a success unrivaled by current globalised industries. We have to change the way we think and do business.

Physics and Practicality

Ours is a physical universe. All life, and all matter that surrounds us, perform in accord with the very predictable laws of physics. The vital relationship of the laws and theories of physics to the essential conditions of how we produce, consume, and survive are not given much attention in today's physics classroom. Yet it is in observing the basics of physics that we realise how minute shifts in pressure, temperature and moisture content create outstanding products that in their elegance, simplicity, and effectiveness far outshine the results of genetic modification. Instead of manipulating the biology of life, let us find inspiration in the ways that nature utilises physics.

From the first nanosecond of creation, our universe, our world and ultimately our species' evolution have been influenced and shaped by the dominant forces of temperature and pressure. Within the framework of fundamental physical forces—gravity, electromagnetism, and weak and strong nuclear forces—our Earth's species underwent interactions and reactions, translating their evolutionary experience into remarkable diversity. Ecosystems developed that are shared by millions of unique species operating within the realms of physics and biochemistry and evolving biologically.

It is amazing how everything in nature learned to use physics to advantage. Perhaps this is due to the fact that, unlike language grammars or biology, there are no exceptions to the rules of physics. The sun rises every morning, apples drop from the tree after its particles defied the law of gravity, and low and high pressure fields cause wind. When it comes to chemistry, it all depends on temperature, pressure, and a catalyst. And, as the progeny-bearing male seahorse demonstrates, when it comes to biology, there is always an exception to the rule. Actually, observing the 100 million plus species that populate this Earth, everything seems to be an exception.

Scientists posit that for the past several billion years, all life on Earth has evolved and adapted in relatively stable ambient water and air temperatures and pressures. Every living species has learned to work with what is locally available. Shaped by the inevitable laws of physics, every species that has navigated millions of years of evolution has learned how to solve challenges to survival, simply by using what they have and doing what they do best.

When a human infant is born, the pathway to individual life includes the experience of tremendous pressure, passing through a narrow 10 centimetre opening to the air-breathing world. The child's shoulders and chest are compressed so that all liquid is expelled from the lungs. By emptying the lungs, the first breath of air can be taken.

This pressure is an indispensable preparation for life, evoking a sense of stress and providing a contrast that permits savouring the beauty of arrival on Earth. It is similar with all life. When a butterfly leaves its cocoon, a patient observer will see how hard it must struggle, even for hours, to complete its transformation into a beautiful winged creature. Early scientific observers, cutting the cocoon to facilitate the butterfly's emergence from its tight protective shell, found that it could not fly, and in fact died moments after its painless birth. Thus pressure can be seen as ushering in life, catalysing the complex dynamics of form and function, from pulling muscles, to the beating of the heart pumping blood, to the animation of all the joints and the inhalation and exhalation of breath.

It seems that crisis is another form of pressure that is capable of energising us to reach for new solutions. Likewise, it reminds us to savor the beauty of living.

Wasting Away

After a billion years of species evolution, mankind alone seeks to control nature's dynamic balance of life guided by physics. We harnessed energy to use at will—at first fire, then fossil fuels and nuclear power. We exploited and shaped matter to our invention, often achieving the remarkable, sometimes less so. Yet the achievements of our industrial age also brought a strain on the carrying capacity of our planet. The profligate generation and consumption of energy has brought us things no one desires, and has destroyed or compromised much of what natural systems contributed over millennia. We find ourselves at a crossroads where we must examine the choices for our future. Are we to live in harmony with our Earth and its species, or will we continue our consumptive and destructive flagrancies? Will we learn to peacefully and productively cohabit or will we extinguish ourselves, as we have already begun to extinguish so many other species, drowning in our unproductive excesses and volumes of waste?

Nearly all the hundred thousand different molecules that comprise petroleum are taken up in the process of synthesising fuel, plastics, building materials, or any of the myriad petrochemical products in daily use. Yet, the concomitant waste stream that accompanies this masterful achievement is everywhere to be seen. No longer hidden, we now see the environmental costs entailed in the extraction and refining of petroleum, the dramatic impact on climate change caused by the release of carbon into the atmosphere, and the tremendous burden of waste accumulated from petroleum-derived products. The creation of covalently bound molecules that made plastics possible has surely been a remarkable innovation. Yet the chemical processes that synthesise plastics, requiring careful management of pressure and temperature as well as the administration of catalysts, result in products composed of super molecules that degrade only with difficulty. There are massive islands of accumulated plastics slowly degrading in a vast area of the Pacific Ocean. Small particles now mix with beach sand and clog the intestinal track of fishes, which mistake these particles for plankton. Massive landfills overflow with discarded junk of these same stubbornly fixated petroleum polymers. Think of it: a single-use water container made of plastic can remain intact in a landfill for hundreds, if not thousands of years while its functional service in a human's life is not more than a couple of hours! Surely we can do much better.

Much of our agriculturally based production creates a similarly excessive stream of waste. A brewery uses only the starch from the barley, and discards the remains. Rice is farmed only for its kernel, and the rest, especially the straw and the husks, are simply waste. Corn is farmed solely for the seeds that become feed, plastics, or fuels. Since all three applications compete for the same little kernel, demand sends the price of corn spiraling upward. Many people in developing Latin American countries can no longer afford the cost of *arepas* or tortillas, basic foodstuffs to stave off hunger and starvation. Then there is coffee, farmed only for its berries, with the rest left to rot; or the production of sugar from cane, using only the 17 per cent sugar content, while the rest is burned. Trees logged for making paper only use the cellulose; over 70 per cent of the tree is chemically burnt as waste. The methane released from untreated decomposing dairy manure tops the list for greenhouse gas emissions. Whenever we do not know what to do with a 'waste', we 'discard' it; often we burn it destroying its potential forever. That is antithetical to the way natural ecosystems operate.

Most of our industries generate massive amounts of waste. For every ton of municipal solid waste, there are 71 tons produced from mining, manufacturing, and product distribution. We have nuclear waste, soil laced with heavy metals, chromium-contaminated groundwater, and landfills bursting with cast-off plastic containers. The residues of our consumption are buried in highly centralised areas and are burned when the volume accumulates. It is misleading to claim that burning waste generates energy. Much of the waste that is incinerated is merely reduced in volume because burning cuts the moisture content. Most of the components remain, except for water, and often these left-overs are more toxic.

It is estimated that the total amount spent in the US each year just to transport waste to landfills reaches a staggering US$50 billion. If we add to this the cost of collecting, hauling, sorting, and disposing waste from construction, agriculture, mining, and industry, the price tops an incredible US$1 trillion. This means that the money wasted on waste every year is more than the 2009 stimulus package for the entire US economy, when the world economy was on the brink of collapse. This amount is more than the massive deficits undertaken by European governments to pump comparable amounts of cash into ailing banks. While these trillions count as productive activity in the national accounts, it is clear that waste management is a non-productive activity. The jobs generated should never be classified as green jobs. The use of land for waste storage is not productive. The toxic seepage and containment costs are unacceptable, and are billed to society as a whole—an externalised cost that corporations are not required to deduct from profit margins.

This prevailing economic model has fueled two centuries of an unending cycle of growth, consumption and disposal, feeding an insatiable appetite for material wealth for which societies have accumulated more debt than can ever be repaid. We reached all too eagerly for the easy credit offered by banks to buy what we often did not need. Meanwhile massive and critical demands, especially those of peoples living in developing nations, have gone unmet. World demand has grown beyond the Earth's ability to provide potable water and a daily meal for far too many families. Despite the gains we have made, our present means are not capable of responding to the needs of all. Our material lifestyles and desires require ever-larger levels of energy production that use fossil fuels, coal, nuclear power, and even photovoltaics (which require copious energy inputs) and windmills (which need electricity to power up). We can—we must—do better.

Over the past decade, there have been calls by prominent environmentalists and economists for industrialised nations to dramatically reduce their material intensity. Prior even to these voices, the call for more material efficiency was admirably articulated in Ernst Ulrich von Weizsäcker's books, *Factor Four (1998)*, *Factor Five (2009)*, and *Bankrupting Nature (2012)* by Anders Wijkman and Johan Rockström, which became Reports to the Club of Rome. William Rees' concept of an "ecological footprint", offering a calculable means for evaluating human demand in the context of renewable ecological capacity, entered the professional lexicon and expressed our excessive use of materials in an easily understood metaphor.

If our habits remain unchanged, we will need more than one additional Earth to sustain our present production and consumption level and to hold the accumulation of waste that we have nowhere else to dump. The economy is not crumbling simply because of the disintegration of financial markets where mythical money flowed. Our economy is stressed because our material world operates on the basis of physical resources we lack, and waste we cannot hide. Perhaps the first change we should make is to stop producing and consuming things we do not really need thereby preventing unwanted waste, especially waste that is toxic to ourselves and our fellow beings on this planet.

How to Welcome Waste

With any luck, what we will realise is that making waste is not the problem we must solve. If a living species does not generate waste, it is most likely dead, or at least very ill. The problem we have, and that we must address, is that we waste the waste we create. Consider that the conversion of waste into nutrients both requires and generates energy. While we are always looking for sources of energy for commercial and home applications, ecosystems never need to be wired. No member of an ecosystem needs fossil fuel or a connection to the grid to achieve output; nor is waste an outcome in natural systems. In nature, the waste of one process is always a nutrient, a material, or a source of energy for another. Everything stays in the nutrient stream. Thus the solution not only to the environmental challenges of pollution, but to the economic challenges of scarcity, may be found in the application of models we can observe in a natural ecosystem. Perhaps we can turn dilemma into solution by broadening our perspective and abandoning the concept of waste.

With green chemistry, polymers derived from petroleum were replaced with polymers derived from natural raw materials as varied as starch, amino acids, sugar, lignin, cellulose, and many more. We can now acknowledge that not only the product, but the whole process can be inspired by natural systems. Rather than accomplishing substitution of a toxic component or ingredient with a less polluting one, if we emulate how natural ecosystems utilise everything and continue to generate value, we will in effect achieve sustainable systems that provide jobs and outperform waste-spewing industries. This means that the resultant product, whether a natural colour, a building material, or a water repellent surface, can not only be manufactured in recognition of its interplay with the environment, but can attain economic success and garner appreciable market share.

Unique solutions perfected by desert insects, spiders, thistles and sea algae can replace toxic products that are standard today with products that are manufactured with truly renewable materials and means. Such solutions are important because they can noticeably improve our daily lives while reducing levels of toxic pollutants. Toxin-spewing, inefficient, old-model industries will lose competitiveness and thus their ability to employ. Ideally, the whole cycle of production, consumption, and post-consumption becomes sustainable, better industry starts to convert costs into income, and liabilities into assets. This is what will permit the fundamental shift to a Blue Economy. The first step is to search for ways to convert waste into contribution, and to identify inputs that are widely, locally and cheaply available because they are of little or no value to anyone else in the system. That is how nature works.

Under the chairmanship of Hiroyuki Fujimura, Japan's Ebara Corporation embarked in the 1990s on a quest for a 'zero emissions' strategy that would leave nothing to waste. Everything—even waste—was to generate value. Ebara funded and supported Prof Yoshihito Shirai at the Kyushu Institute of Technology to pursue solutions for plastics manufacturing using the logic of cascading nutrients and energy. Shirai and his staff developed a process that uses a fungus to convert starch collected from restaurant food waste into polylactic acid (PLA) at nearly ambient temperature. In effect, they devised a way to make plastics from kitchen waste! Although the raw materials are agricultural and renewable, they never draw down the supply of a staple food the way that corn used for biofuel or biodegradable plastic has done. Nor does the waste end up in a landfill, where it emits methane gas.

Industry leaders have the opportunity to accomplish similar successes in the area of biodegradable soaps and detergents. Sugar-derived surfactants (alkyl-polyglucoses), which are mainly used in the pharmaceutical industry, offer an ideal alternative to soaps made from palm oil. Another option would be to use d-Limonene, an extract of citrus fruit peels after pressing out the juice, ideal as a substitute for diverse harsh cleaning agents. If industry could forego the use of chemicals and waxes to preserve fruits stored for months or shipped over long distances, such 'waste' from the production of juice could be used for animal feed or as a source of pectin (a gelling agent), and could be given greater value as a truly green biodegradable soap.

Paper manufacture has a comparable option. Cellulose and lignin are traditionally processed with alkali-sulphates. This traditional wood separation process chemically burns everything, but cellulose so that the fibres used in commerce are the sole output. The residue, known as black liquor, is incinerated. Prof Janis Gravitis from the Wood Chemistry Research Institute in Riga, Latvia, has studied alternative processes for paper production, including the creation of a biorefinery to extract for commercial use all the components of a tree, from cellulose, to hemi-cellulose, lignin, and lipids. Once scientists and industrial engineers begin to design processes that cascade nutrients, so that the waste from one is a readily available raw material for another, we are closer to achieving whole systems design.

Now it is even possible to produce paper from rocks. China invented paper and now 2,000 years later, China reinvented paper. Crushed stones from mining operations are reconditioned to make paper, blending in a small percentage of plastics, decreasing the pressure on landfills while eliminating rock refuse deposits. There is no need for water, and rock paper repels moisture making it possible to read a book in the rain. William Liang, the co-founder of the Tainan-based Lung Meng Technology company launched its innovation in 2010, after nearly 20 years of research and development. The first factory was inaugurated in 2013 in Benxi City (Shenyang) in China. This could change the face of mining forever. Since stone paper can be recycled indefinitely without the use of water, this will change the face of paper remarkably. This breakthrough potentially relieves millions of hectares of land earmarked for trees that can now we dedicated to farming more food.

Given the availability of new alternatives without the drawbacks of harmful side-effects or toxic by-products, it is time to motivate the scientists and entrepreneurs to embrace such sustainable manufacturing processes and design the new business models that generate value, instead of searching solely for the cheap price and higher margin. Industry and commerce require our encouragement to recognise the business opportunity embedded in such an approach, while realising as well the value of supporting environments that are health-promoting and conducive to life.

Achieving Abundance

While skeptics may argue that modeling from natural ecosystems can only succeed against all odds, in reality these systems are designed such that it is actually difficult to fail. Natural systems provide fascinating operational models of efficient production and consumption. Although it is often an individual species we most admire and lyrically describe, it is ecosystems, with great diversity around the world, that demonstrate efficient ways to respond to everyone's basic needs with what is locally available.

This is a fundamental principle for the Blue Economy that contrasts to the current episode of economic history where we have designed a system based on what we do not have. Stop and reflect: every ecosystem has achieved a state of self-sufficiency. Although we may initially perceive scarcity, a closer look shows that abundance and diversity are the reality. The greater the abundance generated, the more that can be achieved with less, and the greater the biodiversity that emerges. Ecosystems do not evolve towards monopolies with few dominant players. Ecosystems only work with what they have, and always generate more with the sun as the main source of power. Ecosystems more closely exhibit the market conditions proposed by Adam Smith, the founder of modern economics: thousands of players fine-tuning their actions as if an invisible hand were directing them to the best allocation and use of resources.

Engineers and agronomists who might reject a whole systems model as unrealistic are unacquainted with the remarkable projects that have already achieved effective outcomes. Output is high, with low material input; energy consumption is low; and in most cases the system produces more than is needed. Health enhancement, food security, topsoil and potable water, are additional—and not inconsequential—benefits. Cascading nutrients and energy from one species to another in a continuous cycle and within a framework provided by physics is demonstrably applied in an industrial context.

Highly productive Blue Economy industries, capable of generating employment for all, are on the horizon. They are based on how nature uses physics and biochemistry to build harmoniously functioning whole systems, cascading abundantly, transforming effortlessly, and cycling efficiently without waste or energy loss. These forces not only determined the parameters of life on Earth, but also helped shape life itself. As we move from a linear perception to seeing a cyclic, regenerative model, we too can shape our behaviours and practices to assure that everyone's basic needs are met and that our blue planet Earth, with all its inhabitants, progresses towards an optimum future.

2

The Power of Pragmatism

Doing less bad—is bad!

— G.P.

The onslaught of bad news about the environment, poverty, unemployment, human rights abuses and the inaction of policymakers, combined with the usual business approach of corporations, leaves many concerned citizens baffled. The data before us are clear: climate change is advancing, and there is no chance to absorb the hundreds of millions of unemployed youth while competitiveness of most nations around the world continues to erode. The only solution economists imagine to all the problems and the wrongs is growth driven by more consumption, for which citizens are expected to accumulate more debt.

Immense of time and effort as spent on the analysis of all available information. While many desperately search for alternative solutions, there is not one, or a few that seem capable of reversing the negative trends. There is a blind belief in one solution: growth and those nations that lack growth should first pass through a period of austerity. Every expert approaches the bulk of information from her or his perspective framed in a clear silo, robbing the world of the knowledge that is required to create a vision indispensable to design a fresh and effective pathway forward. This chapter attempts to open our minds.

The lack of comprehensive knowledge of how economic and social systems operate leaves no space for the wisdom urgently needed to mobilise the best minds and the committed individuals in order to evolve from analyses of the unfolding dramas to a pragmatic portfolio of initiatives. In my view, too much effort is reserved to analyse the problems, to theorise solutions and fiercely debate these options considering the prevailing theory as a dogma. Hardly anyone focuses on the demonstration on the ground that it is possible to outcompete the present growth model by performing better—even according to their parameters of success.

A recent exchange with Prof Anders Wijkman, co-president of the Club of Rome and one of the thought leaders in policy design towards sustainability, it became clear that few people have realised that analysis and theory, concept development and case studies cannot make a dent in the present negative trends, unless there is a fundamental shift in the business model. We should evolve from the logic of economies of scale and cost cutting towards a society that uses what it has, responds first to basic needs of all, circulates the newly gained purchasing power in the local communities and generates capital, especially social capital and strengthens the Commons.

Blind Belief in Growth

While we can imagine many shifts and models, there is one factor that determines the corporate world's culture and *modus vivendi*: the focus on core business and the unfettered belief in growth ad infinitum. Whatever is imagined, from tax policies, to international conventions, and new innovations to recycling programs, it will all fail to steer society towards an environmentally and socially competitive model, unless we overhaul the business model itself. While I very much appreciate the efforts made by many thought leaders, like Walter Stahel, Michael Braungart and Ellen McPherson, and I believe in the best of their intentions and those of many others, all their valuable proposals remain trapped in the logic of the Master of Business Administration (MBA): make more money.

The millions of students aspiring for a better financial reward thanks to their investment in an MBA diploma, hardly realise that they are all learning the same business models that were once conceived at the world famous Harvard Business School. The MBA is as much a product of economies of scale and standardisation as the industries they are supposed to manage in the future. Everything is translated into financial results, market share, economies of scale and ranking. This dominating model prescribes that you sell what you produce and that growth combined with market dominance will not only offer the best return on investment to the shareholders, it will even align performance through the management of rewards and bonuses. And if the company is faced with pollution scandals or social problems, then the system will do its best to cut pollution and reduce the social injustice. We know that doing less bad simply is no good. Business needs to embrace the opportunities to perform in a better manner.

This prevailing business model that has guided the corporate world is framed by a simple logic: compete on the basis of price and quality. This core adagio has been translated into the theory and the practice of the economies of scale, with an unrelenting search for ever lower marginal costs through standardisation, leading to a dramatic concentration of production with only a few corporate leaders determining the market standards. The obsession to cut costs, especially the reduction of labour input, has lead to a logic that when companies merge and subsequently lay off thousands of workers, the listed enterprises are immediately rewarded by the stock exchange with a higher share valuation.

The sheer size of these mega-mergers leads companies to focus on their core business only building on their core competence, eliminating all outside activity through outsourcing and a strict discipline known as supply chain management. Let there be no doubt: companies are on a permanent search for low cost and are continuously sacrificing quality in order to ensure growth through multiple consecutive sales. And if this strategy needs to be pursued through the design of service models, whereby the product is not sold but leased, then the suppliers succeed in locking in the customer on long-term basis to their technology. In this manner, the new service strategy generates more profit and a secure cash flow over the years.

The logic of free trade enhanced the rapid globalisation of fewer players through the adoption of this business model, driven by the quest for ever lower costs. People are forced to buy 3 refrigerators over 25 years, saving 30 per cent on the first one and 50% on the third one, not realising that over a quarter of a century, double the amount of disposable income has been spent on imported cheaper goods than on the 'good old local manufacturer' who produced white goods that lasted 25 years. This not only implied the loss of the local industry; it is also a loss of ongoing maintenance services, a deterioration of resource efficiency consuming three times more material, forcing on society the cost of dismantling and disposing that causes a permanent loss of cash flowing through local industries and communities.

The sales and marketing strategies have successfully blinded the customer with a lower price and the promise of the latest innovation, even better energy efficiency not realising that in the end, this strategy leads to the predictable collapse of local industries. Worse, the money that used to circulate in the local economy are now channelled outside the community, leading to a deceleration of local development, a loss of competitiveness and an increase of unemployment. This cycle drains more purchasing power out of the community. Consequently, the notion of 'under-developing nations' emerges.

The Urgent Shift

The core shift in the business model is to go beyond this relentless cost-cutting drive and to embrace a business strategy that aims to generate more value with locally available resources. This fundamental shift requires companies to get out of the straight jacket to only focus on one product portfolio. The acceptance of this novel—yet easily understood strategy—is a major challenge, since it is fundamentally different from what MBA aspirants have been trained to pursue as the pathway to success.

The upside is that this new business model offers opportunities to generate multiple revenues with resources that are within the immediate reach of enterprise and entrepreneur. The surprise is that when one generates several income streams from available resources, then one can extract its business from the hard game of world market prices! Imagine, farmers and miners are able to look at the flashing numbers on their Bloomberg screen and relax: it is only an indication of one of their revenue streams and does not decide on life and death anymore. This new local production and consumption system must be organised locally and connected through networks spanning the globe.

How often are farmers or small scale manufacturers booted out of the market by overseas huge competitors who can beat prices including transport from the other side of the globe, and also find a ready partnership with large distributors who are indifferent to the generation of local purchasing power? What would the remedy be? Is liberation of the labour market an option? It is quite obvious that if the workers' compensation is reduced to a fraction that it is today, then the European social security as presently operated will put every nation into default. Is the reduction of social security an option? While economists and industrialists join in to call for a more flexible labour market, there is a firm limitation imposed on migration in Europe, North America and Japan.

The call for 'flexible labour markets' is a covert slogan that in reality demands to cut labour costs and social security across the board in order to become more competitive. The elaborate assessment and the ranking of competitiveness of nations is determined on the basis of this core business logic where the overall cost/quality balance decides the position of a country and its industries. While this competitive game is successfully played by less than 1 per cent of the largest corporations in the world, the remaining 99 per cent have hardly any chance of survival. As a result, consumers are increasingly purchasing globally sourced materials, food and energy provided by a few players who control capital. Europe seems to have accepted the inevitable demise of its social system and imagines solutions that are based on 'more of the same', like the free trade agreement with the United States (US), claiming to create a level playing field for 800 million consumers while imposing strict austerity measures on the nation state. The contraction of the economy forces people to look

Figure 2.1
How Globalisation Reduces Cost and Quality

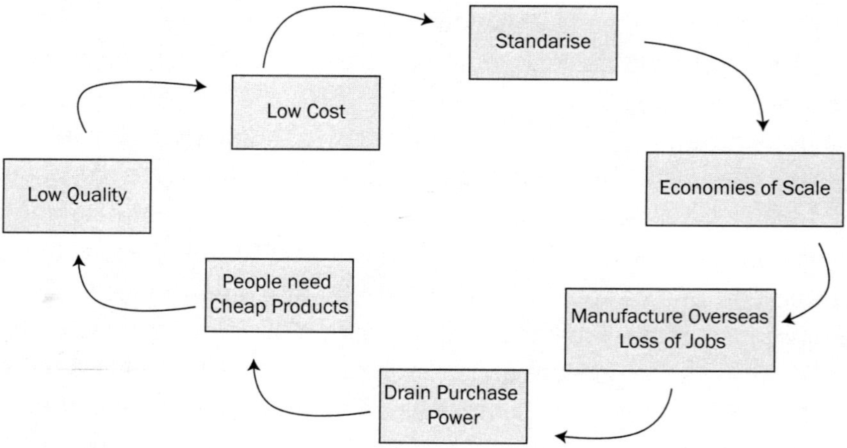

Source: Author.

for cheaper products, along with lower quality and low costs, and the vicious circle has been initiated.

Use Local First

The new business model which we have tested in over 100 sectors of the economy will generate not only more value locally, but will also secure circulation of more money locally. Better: it creates corridors of double-digit growth in areas of high unemployment and poverty, and out competes the present globalised model in return on investment, cash flow, poverty alleviation, and the capacity to respond to basic needs including jobs without the need for subsidies. Governments can now dedicate time and effort to ensure a level playing field.

We cannot stress enough upon the difficulty to pursue a smart and inclusive growth strategy in any region or nation when cash is permanently being drained out of the economy. When the primary and the secondary sectors are not capable of competing with the prices dictated by the international market, then the hard-earned income leaves the local economy, engendering an unemployment

Figure 2.2

How to Generate Local Double Digit Growth

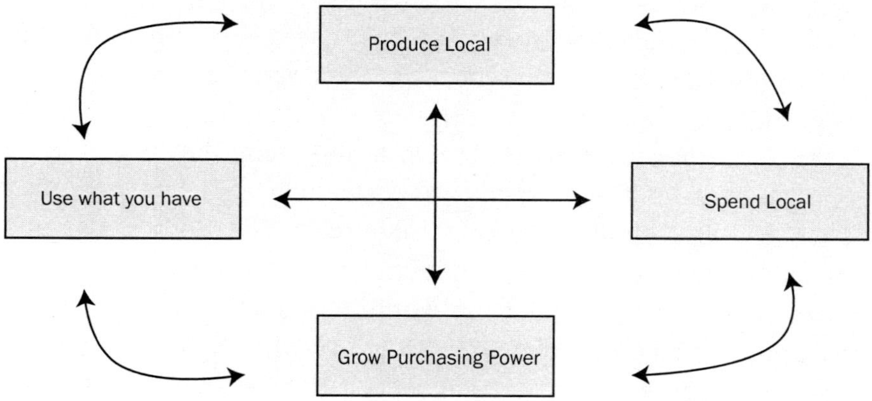

Source: Author.

and economic contraction that has become characteristic of the majority of Europe and Japan (and other nations). The only way to reverse the trend of high unemployment and the downward spiral of economic development is to ensure that available resources are used to generate greater value, thereby creating more money for being circulated through local businesses. While this logic goes against the prevailing dogma of free trade at the macro-economic level, and the dogma that one must search for ever lower costs at the micro-level, based on our experience on the ground, we see a clear strategy on the way to relieve societies out of the poverty and unemployment trap.

Traditional economics promote competitiveness in another way, that is to dramatically reduce cost of labour, even to embrace social dumping and saddle the government with health care, unemployment compensation and pension costs which translates into an untenable increase of government debt, which is followed up by a long period of austerity in order to keep the tax burden that is already too high for a dwindling working population within limits. Let us not forget that global corporations do not pay taxes, and therefore the burden is squarely and solely on shoulders of the citizens. Now if we accept that the increase in government expenditure, and the widening of the government deficit beyond the 3 per cent of GDP (gross domestic product) are not options to embrace, then there is an urgent need to change the rules of the game because the present correction to the misguided spending has only been austerity.

Thus, the first and foremost rule of the game that needs to be changed is the shift from 'ever lower costs' to 'ever higher generation of value' with locally available resources. The Zero Emissions Research Initiative (ZERI) Foundation, which is in reality a network of organisations throughout the world, has demonstrated through study and practice that this shift is not only viable, but also can be implemented short term. We have seen the mobilisation of €4 billion in capital and the implementation of +100 projects that generated 3 million jobs, and have embraced this logic with such ease. The pursuit of value—and not the urge to cut costs—very quickly brings additional products and services to the local market, which can also and quite easily outcompete the internationally traded merchandise. This puts the local economy into a growth spiral that goes beyond overconsumption of scarce resources. This is counter-intuitive, yet easy to explain.

The Cascading of Benefits

China is the leading supplier of photovoltaic (PV) panels to the world. The cost per unit has dropped so low that it is within cents of competing with traditional sources of fossil fuels. However, an innovative technology from Sweden permits the combination of energy from the PV, with hot and cold water generated by the capillary tubes inside a sandwich of PV. This is a thicker panel that is presently strong enough to be the roof, provided the base is heat resistant, instead of being put on a roof. The basic structure is ideally made from recycled heat resistant plastics offering again more jobs since this partly substitutes aluminum that was globally mined, processed and sourced. The cascading of benefits continues as water is presently stored at high temperature, not only killing bacteria, but also storing energy and replacing the batteries that all too often make renewables uncompetitive. The break even of local assembly is reached with only 200 units per month sold. The combination of all these benefits translates into a cost per kilowatt hour that is a fraction of PV solar. This is not a game of beating the Chinese PV makers on cost, it concerns winning the competitive game by generating so greater value! It is not surprising that in 2014, Solarus won the innovation prize for process industries in China!

The coffee case has been at the core of our work for the past 20 years. The recent developments amply demonstrate that this internationally traded commodity has a tremendous growth potential that goes way beyond a cup of coffee. Both at the farm and in the city, coffee waste can be converted to a substrate for mushrooms. The spent substrate, the left-over after harvesting the mushrooms can be converted to animal feed, generating three revenues instead of one. Now the cost of protein (mushroom and animal feed) is lower than that of imported food and feed. Moreover, this generates local jobs and local income. Then again, this program has been dismissed as too little too late, we need to remind ourselves that the worldwide volume of coffee waste surpasses 10 million tons—good for 10 million tons of mushrooms and 4 million tons of animal feed, all produced locally. There are new biochemical industries that have emerged extracting complex molecules of molecules extracted from post-consumer coffee waste and selling UV (ultraviolet) protection and odour control. If one could earn the same per ton of coffee as one can make with trading soy as feed today, then the triple income stream adds another US$14 billion to the coffee economy; a cash that not only comes in, but also that stays within the local communities! Now the same can be done for tea.

Any Change is Hard

Large corporations have great difficulty in embracing this multiple revenue model, incapable of explaining to the financial analysts on the stock exchange their shift from a core business to a multiple cash flow model beyond the established market model. This situation is exemplified by Nestlé's response to the opportunity of mushroom farming on sterile coffee ground from the instant coffee factories. Indeed, the largest coffee processing company in the world, with an guesstimated 3 millions tons of waste, decided to recover energy from coffee waste, reducing its reliance on fossil fuel. Whereas the generation of power from waste figures prominently in sustainability reports outlining the performance of this food group to cut its carbon emissions; it inscribes itself into the traditional logic of cutting costs. This case would be celebrated in the traditional business logic and repeated at international fora as a successful case of the green economy. And it is a major step forward. Waste that was needed to be discarded at a cost, now generates power and adds to the bottom line. This fits perfectly in the prevailing business model where the company demonstrates its social and environmental responsibility by 'doing less bad', 'The Circular Economy' and 'The Triple Bottom Line'! Would it be possible to convert this strategy from 'doing less bad' to one that is 'doing more good'?

Imagine that Nestlé would have shifted from the 'cost cutting' to the 'value generation' model. The financial, social and ecological benefits from burning a few million tons of coffee waste would look very pale compared to the total value realised for business and society through the generation of healthy food at low cost (edible mushrooms offer a healthy nutrition), or the provision of feed for animals that now rely on impact of soy from Brazil, or the conversion of slaughterhouse waste. One need not to be an experienced economist to quickly calculate the impact of mushrooms and feed on the local economy. The internal opposition to the proposal cites that, firstly, mushrooms are not one of Nestlé's businesses. Secondly, we often hear in the grapevine that mushrooms are not part of our daily diet. Our response is that hamburgers and corn flakes were not part of the daily food intake either. Nestlé has determined it is not in the mushroom nor in the animal feed business, rather it is only in the coffee business. Therefore, Nestlé will not pursue this chance to add a few billion dollars in turnover. I wonder if we should ask the opinion of the shareholders?

Figure 2.3
Heading ?

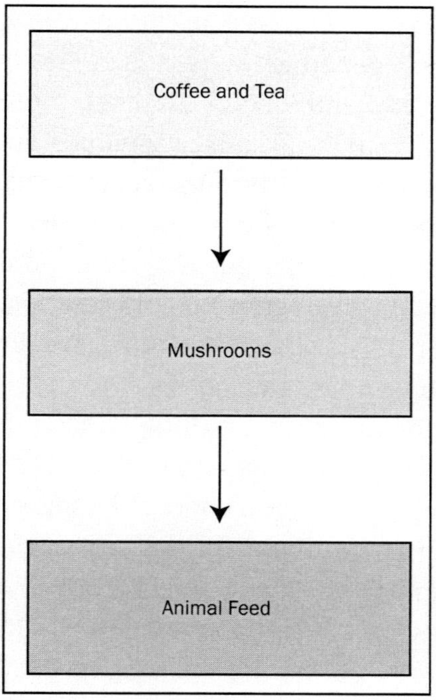

Source: Author.

We realise that companies are not prepared to embrace this new inclusive growth business model, and the millions of MBAs who leave the thousands of business schools around the world are all impregnated with the same logic, streamlining competition with the search for cost cutting as the safe way to improve cash flow. This imposes a tight discipline on the supply chain enforcing strict adherence to the financial objectives outlined in budgets, reducing the number of suppliers and putting the screws on downward price negotiations. The successful implementation of these numbers cast in budgets and forecasts determines the management's bonuses. This secures that everyone performs as is expected. Whatever insensitivity to the hard social and environmental realities that emerge as unintended consequences perceived by society, is then quickly overcome through corporate social responsibility programs, which project the company as a responsible citizen even when it just reneged on the opportunity to generate thousands of jobs and provide millions of tons of quality food and feed at low cost, thereby stimulating the local economy with readily available resources and helping to stamp hunger out of this world—not through genetic modification that puts seeds and profits in the hands of a few producers in the world.

We need to shift from the present model to an inclusive growth model—imagine double-digit growth in the corridors of unemployment, hunger and poverty. That can never be achieved through massive additional taxation on citizens nor by a forceful austerity program throwing thousands out of job, cutting pension plans and reducing health care programs. Time has come to accept that the only way forward is to change the way we conduct business. This approach will require more than one economist who is preaching to the converted. It requires a minimum winning coalition ready to demonstrate on the market that a new model can outcompete whatever has dominated the logic so far. After all, we are not against anyone or anything, we are rather in favour of better, much better indeed.

3

Emulating Ecosystems

Motanai (Waste not, want not).

— *JAPANESE PROVERB*

A vibrant economy is essential to sustainability. The reverse is also true. Without true sustainability, no economy can continue to function. With that in mind, perhaps it will not surprise you to learn, as you will while reading this book, that a solution to our current economic malaise lies in understanding and applying the logic of ecosystems. Nature demonstrates true economy—and true sustainability—all the time. If we were to develop our economies following nature, we could use energy and resources efficiently and without waste, and create hundreds of millions of jobs. Did it ever occur that in nature everyone contributes to the best of their abilities and no one is employed or relegated to a kindergarten or a retirement home? Ecosystem models offer the keys to abundance, and the means to share the same. An economic system inspired by ecosystems would work with what is locally available, such as naturally recurring energy resources that express the laws of physics first and foremost. Physics describes the underlying forces that are dynamically utilised by every species on earth. This insight is the pathway to sustainability. Transforming the current economic downcycle by emulating the logic modelled in ecosystems will allow us to meet basic needs and create a true economy—a Blue Economy, an economy of abundance.

Emulating the functional and material efficiency of ecosystems and natural habitats is a pragmatic way to achieve sustainability and high resource efficiency, while remaining competitive and generating added value. Cascading nutrients and energy is another ecosystem elegance that we would do well to emulate. It is nature's method for transforming apparent scarcity to sufficiency, and ultimately to abundance. We can picture a cascade as a waterfall, as a flow of nutrients that requires no power source, merely the force of gravity. It offers a visual metaphor to help us comprehend ways in which nutrients are transported from the species of one biological kingdom to another, for the benefit of all. Absorbed minerals feed microorganisms, microorganisms feed plants, and plants feed other species, with the waste of one being nourishment for another. Cascading energy and nutrients leads to sustainability by way of reducing or eliminating external inputs such as energy and by eliminating waste and its cost, not just as pollution but also as inefficient use of materials.

Around the world there are successful and well-established examples of entrepreneurship that illustrate how a Blue Economy can not only benefit the land but also its inhabitants, with the result that food security, livelihood security, and contributory occupations become available to all. We can look to the remarkable transformation of the Vichada savannah in Colombia accomplished by Paolo Lugari at Las Gaviotas. We can study a project for West African food and livelihood security established in Benin by Father Godfrey Nzamujo. We can follow the vision of Håkan Ahlsten and the citizens of Gotland to sustain and renew their land and culture; or the efforts of Picuris Pueblo in converting small diameter wood from a fire hazard to raw materials for an integrated biosystem that sustainably generates jobs, food, fuel, and construction materials. Moreover, we should not forget the pioneering efforts of Javier Morales and citizens of the island El Hierro, part of the Canary Islands, to turn water and energy sustainable and abundant stimulating the local economy creating economic growth on a remote Spanish island, while the rest of the country is suffering. These have in common the emulation of nature's nutrient cascade and utilisation of energy sources that function according to the laws of physics. Besides that each achieves food and energy security while generating multiple benefits, including positive cash flow, reduction of material intensity, and energy savings. These are competitive communities that are not against globalisation; rather, they have designed and managed a production and consumption model that is comparatively better.

Plenitude from Paucity

When Paolo Lugari proposed regenerating the Vichada savannah in Colombia into the rainforest it once was, no one considered it possible based on prevailing science of the time. A track of savannah on the Western side of the Orinoco River was worthless. The pH was low, the water was not drinkable, and there was no easy land, water, or air access. Who would purchase even an acre? The land was obtained through land grants, which cost approximately US$2.50 per acre. Lugari persevered, planting with neither experience nor funding, using a creative approach to regenerate the dry, despoiled savannah and transforming it into a haven of lush tropical biodiversity. Now, a quarter-century later, Lugari welcomes visitors to 20,000 acres of restored rainforest. He and his team discovered that the symbiosis between mycorrhizal fungi and the Caribbean pine tree not only secured the survival of 92 per cent of the seedlings planted, but also changed physical attributes of the region. How?

When inoculated with the fungus *Pisolithus tinctorius*, the small Caribbean pine tree *Pinus caribaea* creates a discrete shaded space protecting the soil, seeds and shoots from the sun's ultraviolet rays. Although the heat stress remains high, contributing to a thick carpet of pine needle droppings, the pine tree grows to maturity because it is well nourished by the fungus. This carpet improves moisture content of the soil, simultaneously trapping producers of humus, which would otherwise wash away in the torrential rains that characterise the climate at least three months per year.

Importantly, this debris cover also moderates the temperature of the soil. When rain falls on a hot soil, it cannot penetrate even the porous surface and thus more readily causes erosion. It is like pouring cold oil on a hot frying pan. When rain falls on a cooler soil, it is more likely to be absorbed into the ground. Thus, the increase in soil permeability caused by inversion of the temperature differential between the rain and topsoil creates an environment for new seeds to gain hold. As the emerging forest grows, diversity flourishes and rain becomes more abundant. The dry savannah with poor drinking water and overly acidic soil has now become not just a forest, but a rainforest abundant in potable water, with a richer soil ideal for flourishing plant life.

A Japanese film crew, arrived in Gaviotas to record the regeneration of the tropical rainforest what few believed could ever happen. While filming they observed clouds approach and float above the savannah. The moment these clouds drifted over the forest's cooler sphere, the crew was amazed to experience the refreshing rain that began to fall. Indeed, the green forest is fresher than the heat-absorbing plains. Thus, when the surface is cool, the clouds drop their moisture owing to the lower dew point. Leaving behind 450 years of slash-and-burn agriculture and the cultivation of invasive grasses used as cattle fodder, Las Gaviotas enfolded fungi and trees in elegant symbiosis, creating the conditions that revived an entire forest.

Despite these stunning meteorological and soil shifts, perhaps the most highly touted result of all has been an equally stunning increase in land value. Land that produces is one that has value. Over a 21-year period, the value of each acre of savannah converted to rainforest, measured solely on the values of potable water, harvestable food, industrial output, renewable energy, fuel for mobility and available livelihood, increased as much as 3,000-fold. Before restoration, people in the region around Las Gaviotas had no chance of employment. They suffered from gastrointestinal diseases, could not obtain safe drinking water, and lacked reasonably available medical care. Just one generation later, water is a commons distributed nearly for free. The sale of surplus water to the rich in Bogotá, who are prepared to pay the same price as that for a bottle of imported San Pellegrino or Evian water, provides Las Gaviotas with an important cash flow.

Inspired by its healthy cash flow, its portfolio of technologies licenced worldwide, its generous wages, and its contributions to the local community of 2,000 inhabitants, William B. Harrison Jr., the Chairman of JP Morgan, championed the expansion of Las Gaviotas from 20,000 to 250,000 acres. Based on JP Morgan's Emerging Markets analysis, he offered Alvaro Uribe, the President of Colombia, a US$300 million investment package. Such an expanded initiative could generate an estimated 100,000 jobs over the next decade, while offsetting the carbon emissions of countries like Belgium and the Netherlands.

Where government services and traditional business never benefitted the local population, one man's vision and his seminal work met the people's needs. This accomplishment of social and environmental care taking, embracing the ideals of entrepreneurship, achieved success by emulating the natural processes of ecosystems. The success of Las Gaviotas illustrates that it is the interplay of pressure, temperature, surface tension, conductivity, magnetism, and so much more that makes the wind blow and the trees grow. Once we understand the dynamic connections and interactions of nature's interwoven tapestries, whole new approaches will unfold, and genetic manipulation and drip irrigation will seem antiquated.

Food Security in Africa

The Songhai Center in West Africa, located in Porto Novo, the capital city of Benin, was created and is run by Father Godfrey Nzamujo, a Dominican priest. In 1984, the same year that Paolo Lugari launched his Las Gaviotas reforestation scheme, Father Nzamujo undertook a program to reverse hunger and provide food for Africans. It began on a few acres of swampland granted by Benin's former president. Today, a quarter-century later, it has travelled full circle from environmental degradation to an impressive endorsement of the possibilities for African food and livelihood security.

Under Father Nzamujo's guidance, Songhai developed a logical system for cascading nutrients and energy to achieve remarkable outcomes. Waste water (both gray and black) from toilets, washing, and all animal and human waste is collected in a three chambered digester. Chopped water hyacinth, a local invasive aquatic plant, is added. In the digester, the combined biomass produces methane, providing energy for local use. After mineralisation, the remaining material becomes feed for zooplankton, phytoplankton and benthos, which in turn feed fish in the aquaculture project. The digester designed facilitates a high level of curing and gas production, imitating the acid-alkaline switch our body uses to restrain detrimental bacteria. The pH evolves from acidic in the digester to a highly alkaline form in the neighbouring algae ponds. Anaerobic bacteria, complemented by sunlight, aid the powerful transformation of carbon dioxide into oxygen by micro-algae, and complete the natural systems design that eliminates pathogens. Prof George Chan from Mauritius, who dedicated his life to the design of such integrated farming and waste management systems, would be proud of the outcomes.

Songhai faced another major hygienic challenge: flies. Although chemical spraying was considered, this could not be recommended in a food-producing environment that aspired to gain an organic label. The strategy pursued by Father Nzamujo was extraordinary. He turned to maggots, the larvae of flies, to solve the problem.

All slaughterhouse waste at Songhai is collected in a special area where hundreds of small, barely hand-width deep cement squares are completely surrounded by canals patrolled by carp. The open area is covered with a huge net so that birds cannot enter. The mesh is just large enough for hungry flies to pass through. Flies thrive on the castoffs of slaughter—ones that cannot be turned into edible product. This feast for flies turns the area into a massive maggot farm, with a production capacity of nearly one ton of maggots per month. Yet, there is not one fly to be spotted anywhere else at the center. All the flies converge on what is for them a delectable soup of nutrients, gorging themselves and laying larvae in abundance. Water is then sprinkled over the half-digested waste, so that the maggots float to the surface, to be easily harvested.

What can you do with maggots? The primary local economic use is as an inexpensive feed for fish and quail. Both quail eggs and fish contribute to good nutrition and food security. However, it is the maggot enzymes that offer an even greater potential for economic value. They have medicinal properties that are proven to heal wounds by stimulating the growth of fibroblast cells. How do you extract the enzymes while reserving the live maggots as feed for fish and quail?

A brilliantly simple solution: maggots regurgitate when they are immersed in salt water!

Here is another case of elegant ecosystems design. Father Nzamujo's initial goal was to reduce disease by finding a natural means of eliminating flies. That solution in turn provided the enzymes that effectively accomplish natural healing. While the biology and biochemistry of maggots clearly demonstrates medicinal properties, a new hypothesis proposes that these enzymes generate a barely measurable electrical pulse, undetected because there is no appropriate instrumentation. This pulse stimulates cell regeneration and promotes healing. Maggots have learned how to apply the laws of physics (electricity and magnetism) as a stimulus for healing.

Maggot treatment is approved by governments worldwide, especially for diabetic patients. The purified version—without the maggots—gained a fast-track regulatory approval with the support of the British National Health Services (NHS). This is most welcome, since the main cause of amputations in Africa is untreated wounds. David and Jason Drew raised millions of dollars to recreate this business model in north of Cape Town in the old agricultural research centre of Elsenburg, owned by the University of Stellenbosch. Their company, AgriProtein aims to replace fish protein with maggots, reducing the stress on the oceans and by 2014 have surpassed the production capacity of Songhai. The National University of Colombia based on Bogotá, is pursuing this health and business opportunity under the leadership of Hilderman Pedraza Vargas, a medical doctor who uses the saliva to treat victims of land mines. By 2015, over a dozen new businesses have stared and simulations indicate that the emerging industry not only substitutes fish protein from stressed oceans, but also can generate in Africa at least 500,000 additional jobs while improving the hygiene.

An Island Afloat a Dream

Nearly a millennium ago, the greatest merchants of Florence and Russia built churches and warehouses on Gotland, a small but remarkable island in the centre of the Baltic Sea. Arriving in Visby, the capital city, leaves a lasting impression on visitors. The large stone wall that surrounds the city encompasses not only the historic buildings and cathedrals, but generations of tradition.

As the 21st century arrived, the island's inhabitants struggled to find ways to prosper in a globalised world economy. It seemed that tourism was the only option. Indeed, with just under a million visitors annually, tourism is the largest contributor to Gotland's economy. During the summer holidays, the local population grows 10 times in size, only to implode for rest of the year.

Yet it was the wish of its citizens to create a future for their land, and particularly for succeeding generations who would otherwise leave the island as soon as possible. Their vision was to design a sustainable community, in harmony with the resources of the land, juxtaposed against the background of its great historic accomplishments, and its recognition by UNESCO as a World Heritage city. At the invitation of Prof Dr Carl-Göran Hedén, a member of the Swedish Royal Academy of Sciences, the community undertook an envisioning exercise that gathered together students, bankers, policymakers, researchers, and businessmen to seek solutions.

Any observer looking for development opportunities other than tourism will immediately focus on the countryside. Dotted with picturesque churches and domiciles, the agricultural landscape has been lovingly shaped throughout the centuries. When sugar beets were introduced 100 years ago, they were significantly successful to create a new industry. Lacking appropriate economies of scale, the sugar mill closed as globalisation consolidated. There was little incentive to pursue agriculture, except carrots. Famous for their sandy look, carrots from Gotland acquire a superior taste in the island's alkaline soil. Although producing carrots was not a problem, selling them from middle of the Baltic Sea was a challenge. Furthermore, it was common for grocery store purveyors to reject a substantial portion of the harvest that did not meet their rigorous shape conformation standards.

The citizens evolved an innovative approach that took advantage of this natural cascading of nutrients, while generating value and jobs. Håkan Ahlsten, the local banker, liked the idea of manufacturing a simple product: oven-fresh carrot cakes. With such ready access to fresh and abundant raw material, a carrot cake enterprise was impossible to ignore. Agreement was reached, and a delicious carrot cake recipe was quickly developed. Baked, then frozen, the Gotland cakes gained high demand throughout Sweden and as far overseas as Singapore and Hong Kong. In five years, employment at the local bakery jumped from a mere 5 to 30.

The next major initiative was precipitated by the desire to achieve better market value by utilising the entire harvest. Mr Yngve Andersson, another of Gotland's upstanding citizens, invested in the design and construction of a carrot-sorting centre where nearly the entire island's harvest could be stored, sorted, and processed using sophisticated machinery. The massive harvest was machine-sorted into specific categories. Every variety was individually packaged, from baby carrots, to long, thin carrots, to stronger and shorter carrots, to odd-shaped roots. Surprisingly, cleaned and packaged baby carrots, which were formerly considered too small to have any market value, could be sold for four times more than standard carrots. The largest carrots are not packaged but become carrot juice, a very profitable niche market. Interestingly, the largest carrots produce the most juice—as much as 40 per cent more by volume. The shredded carrot pulp, rather than becoming waste, is an ideal pig feed.

Carrot sorting to generate higher value from the existing harvest posed major challenges. The machinery could only cope with processing the entire harvest if the total volume were distributed over the entire year, rather than concentrated in the six-week harvest season. However, processing the harvest over 12 months required an investment in cooling the warehouse to a constant temperature of 32 °F. When the economic persuasion of better price supported the feasibility of this undertaking, the next challenge was meeting the operation's now dramatic energy requirements.

With the figures before him, Mr Yngve Andersson decided to take the risk of exclusively powering the facility with wind energy. The entire operation—warehousing, sorting, processing, packaging, selling into market segments, including deep-frozen carrot cakes—is entirely powered by wind energy. The capital investment in wind energy was easily recovered from international sales. The total estimated direct and indirect employment sums to 250 jobs. Rethinking carrots generated jobs, cut costs, and successfully pointed the Gotlanders to a progressive path for job generation and livelihood security.

Finding value in what is locally available creates sustainable and competitive industries that can influence economies, even when they are located on an isolated island in the Baltic Sea. To the islander's credit, this is not their only initiative. Other breakthroughs demonstrate Gotland's pioneering spirit. Carrots are the most impressive case, but the combination of beer and bread is just as commendable. The Gotland Brewery supplies excellent beer to the local population. The spent grain left from the brewing process is shipped to the local bakery, Eskelunds Hembageri AB, where it is made into bread—another fine example of turning waste from one process into raw material for another. By using locally available resources, cascading nutrients, and encouraging entrepreneurs to implement competitive ideas, the citizens of Gotland are years ahead of their peers. This model has been emulated dozens of times by beer brewers in Germany, the US and Japan.

A Progressive Pueblo

Raging forest fires often make the news. Each year wild fires devastate vast ecosystems in the western US. The New Mexico Bureau of Land Management obtained a grant from the federal government to pay for the removal of small diameter wood (up to seven inches) from the lands of Picuris Pueblo. Whether burned or dumped in a landfill, this cleared debris would contribute to the atmospheric carbon load. Lynda Taylor and Robert Haspel proposed an alternative, and worked with the Picuris Pueblo elders to design a solution that cascades nutrients and energy in harmony with Pueblo customs.

Removal of the small diameter wood and reduction of forest fire risk was quickly accomplished. The bulk of the cut wood was dried, then placed in recycled 40-foot shipping containers and subjected to an incomplete combustion process by containing the fumes, thus converting the wood to charcoal. However, to honor Pueblo tradition it was necessary to eliminate the equipment tracks left in the forest by the brush-clearing vehicles. Mulch made from the small diameter wood was inoculated with a native mushroom spore, then spread on the equipment tracks. Remarkably, just two years later, no tracks were to be found. The mushrooms are gathered as food by tribal members, while the mushroom substrate and waste, rich in amino acids, serve as feedstock for the Sam family bison herd. With a sufficiency of livestock feed and ongoing support from Taylor and Haspel, the Sam family locally supplies buffalo meat to commercial markets.

What started as an effort to reduce the risk of fire became an integrated biosystem generating jobs, food, fuel, and construction materials, while replacing chemicals and gasoline. The Picuris Pueblo experience is an example of economic development based on natural systems, using what is locally available and building on the traditions of Native Americans.

When we replace old standards with something completely different that cascades nutrients and energy, an entirely new economic paradigm emerges. Remarkable solutions arise from reinterpreting the nature and function of energy and nutrients, allowing us to achieve greater resource efficiency, to build competitive local industries, thereby and to adopt innovations that generate jobs and create added value. This is how ecosystems evolve to ever more efficient systems, requiring ever less energy expenditure for diverse species. It is an all-inclusive cascade that leads to abundance at every level.

Bagasse: Sweet Solution

The massive volumes of agro-waste that our food industry produces can be deftly handled by mirroring ecosystems. Take the case of sugar mainly sourced from cane. The sugar content of cane is around 10-15 per cent. Thus, each ton of sugar produced accounts for only a small portion of its source biomass. The rest, waste known as bagasse, is typically incinerated. Natural systems seldom use fire as a source of energy, whereas we humans use fire all the time. Burning bagasse provides a cheap and available fuel source, but the only component that really supplies energy is the lignin. The rest, composed of hemicellulose and cellulose, creates major carbon emissions when burned because these substances incinerate without contributing useful heat.

Were we to use bagasse to produce paper, paper products, and cardboard, as has commenced on a small scale, it would clearly be a better outcome. Even though this tropical fibre does not fit the current supply chain management model, which is based on massive worldwide plantings of pine and eucalyptus, a quick calculation produces some astonishing figures. At the annual rate of 15 to 30 tons per acre, bagasse provides 100 to 200 tons of fibre in the 7 years that the fastest growing pine trees takes to reach maturity. In terms of fibre, sugar cane handily tops the volume produced by trees from temperate climates.

Hence, we begin to see how we can use what is renewably generated while building viable clusters of industries. It is our adherence to a wasteful industrial logic that uses only the sugar in sugar cane and burns the bagasse, at the high cost of damaging levels of carbon emissions. It is the same allegiance to short-sighted accounting that causes us to extract only the cellulose from pine trees to manufacture paper and waste the remaining 70-80 per cent of the tree. There are many other examples. The harvesting of coffee beans leaves a staggering 99.8 per cent of the total biomass as waste. The latest studies on solid municipal waste in the US indicate that for each dollar spent on handling household waste in landfills, US$70 per ton is spent dealing with that from agriculture, mining, and industry!

Imagine that we produced food like the rest of nature, cascading through living kingdoms from plants to mushrooms to animals to bacteria to algae, and back again in different directions and combinations according to specific habitat. The only energy sources needed are light and gravity, which are readily and freely available! Here are the glimmerings of a new economy, rooted in robust models that provide with nutrients, and generate food, habitat, employment, energy and currency in renewable ways.

An Island in the Sun

The Canary Islands of Spain are one of the most popular tourist destinations. One of the islands, El Hierro, never felt for developing its coast with high rise buildings offering tourists sunshine for the rest of the year. It suffers a chronicle water shortage and over the past centuries, thousands of islanders have emigrated since the lack of water threatened livelihood of the whole community. When the Spanish government considered building a radar installation, generating jobs through military expenditures, the population voted against the motion. However, the project woke up the citizens and the vision emerged to turn the island self-sufficient in energy and water. The vision was clear, but the pathway to reality was blurred.

It was Javier Morales, the vice-mayor of the island who realised that every year nearly US$10 million of hard earned cash was needed to purchase fuel so as to drive the generators. Most of the power was reserved for producing desalinated water. He conceived the idea to use 10 years of guaranteed expenses in order to mobilise the capital to invest in a US$100 million renewable energy program. It took Juan Manuel Quintero, the chief executive and key engineer of Gorgona del Vieuto, the power and water company. It took 17 years to translate the vision into a reality; but by 2014 the island was able to generate electricity from wind and the excess power is used to pump water more than 700 metres higher into an old volcanic basin. When there is no wind, hydropower from wind secures the energy needed. The excess power is used to desalinate at marginal cost. Now the islanders have double the amount of water at half the cost. Such a gain stimulates the local economy. The slaughter house was re-opened; the cheese and yoghurt factory converts all goat and sheep's milk to higher value products, organic bananas and pineapples increase the food pallet and all waste oils are converted to biofuel. The economy thrives, employment is low, and the young who were tempted to emigrate now find that this island offers what they want: a challenge and a change to make a difference.

Clearly, it is not only effective but essential for governmental and industrial leadership to seize the moment. At the same time, a new economic model will only succeed if it fosters grass-roots business initiatives. This is where the capacity to inspire the uninspired, to reach the unreached, the opportunity to work communally with ones who often are neither considered nor given a chance, offers the core perceptual shift for ways to make a difference in this world. Empowering young people, especially those in global pockets of unemployment and poverty, can create enormous economic impact. The constructs of scarcity are unappealing to those who must endure it. If you are without a job, hungry, abused or frail, sustenance is more than polite conversation. It is a matter of immediate survival. If we operate the way natural systems do, it is entirely possible to create more jobs while increasing productivity and improving resource efficiency. You will never hear of unemployed trees, fish, maggots or mushrooms!

How can we achieve abundance as a society? How can we continuously obtain renewable sources for food, shelter, livelihood, and well-being? In mirroring the successful methods found in natural ecosystems, we can begin to choose models with a generous scope, a propensity to cascade, a goal of planetary and species stewardship, and a future of perpetuity. Therein is true economy. As we begin to grasp the fullness of this paradigm, the image of a Blue Economy rises like a phoenix from the ashes of economic instability caused by a blind commitment to globalisation, while cutting costs, drawing strength and inspiration from nature.

4

Nature's Resource Efficiency

> Nature uses the longest threads to weave her patterns.
> Each small piece of her fabric
> reveals the organisation of the entire tapestry.
>
> — *RICHARD FEYNMAN*

Structure and Flow

Simple and pragmatic approaches to indoor comfort are lessons we can learn from the physics of moving water and air, as well as from the elegantly simple methods perfected by species as varied as the termite, the zebra, the Namibian desert beetle, and the mussel. If we follow this new framework, we can achieve more with less energy and ensure better health conditions than ever imagined. We can even eliminate components and products that are considered indispensable in modern construction. How is that possible?

Buildings that are entirely closed and fully insulated to reduce energy consumption have little chance to self-regulate. Air pumps are required to push controlled air volumes through the building to maintain the occupants' comfort. Unfortunately, closed buildings accumulate humidity; especially in the basement (moist air is heavier and moves downward). Bedrooms are heated with dry air that burdens our respiratory systems, while dust particles accumulate from the ample use of electronic equipment. Many of these particles are electrostatic. Mites proliferate in the carpets because triple-glazed windows with an ultraviolet filter provide them the best-ever breeding ground.

Dust mites are microscopic relatives of the spider. These tiny creatures live by eating the detritus of a building's occupants. The dust mite is a common culprit in dermatological and respiratory allergies, such as eczema and asthma. Removing mites requires harsh chemistry, which may circulate for months in a closed building, along with the volatile organic chemicals that compose most furniture and carpet glues. This is not how one might imagine an energy-efficient 'ecological' building! Although we may have a 30 per cent energy savings, or even a 100 per cent passive house—in fact all power can be generated by solar cells—the costly use of chemicals and the stress to our immune systems are unintended side effects. On the other hand, if energy-efficient building design included solutions with a proven track record, benchmarked for millions of years by species living in a similar habitat, then we would notice a radical difference in appearance of healthy buildings and ways in which their systems functioned. Indeed, healthy buildings can be doubly efficient by reducing both energy and health care costs, requiring less risk to build capital and securing a better return on investment. How?

Termites: The Masters of Flow

The first farmers on Earth were termites and ants. Perhaps as early as 100 million years ago, termites responded to the need to survive changing weather conditions. Their successful adaptation involved a greenhouse-like farming system. They perfected a method whereby the nest's internal temperature and humidity was under their full control, permitting efficient harvesting of fungi which is the termites' primary food. They successfully achieved food security and evolved from hunter-gatherers to domiciled species, well before homo sapiens evolved.

This admirable master of temperature, humidity, and atmospheric pressure follows the laws of physics as well as the application of complex mathematics to engineer farming and construction. Termites have perfected the design of chimneys where air warms and predictably rises, creating a pressure differential within the nest below. Since the nest is connected to its ambient surroundings by tiny underground tunnels, the outside air flows into the nest to equalise the air pressure. This precisely illustrates Newton's Third Law of Motion: "For every action there is an equal and opposite reaction." However, since the air that flows through underground tunnels is within a narrow temperature range that is kept stable by that of the deeper soil, humidity and temperature of the exterior determines the amount of moisture remaining in the air that enters the greenhouse nest. Termites know how to calculate and construct their nests anywhere in the world, in any climate, securing ideal growth conditions for the rich white mycelium that is their principal source of nourishment.

Swedish architect, Bengt Warne observed termites in Zimbabwe in the late 1950s. His original drawings of termite mound airflows, published in *På Akacians Villkor: att bugga och bo i samklang med naturen (On the Conditions of the Acacia: to build and live in harmony with nature, 1993)*, look simple but are challenging to adapt to modern architectural purposes. It took another brilliant Swedish architect, Anders Nyquist, to develop mathematical formulas that codified Warne's insights in a model that makes present automated climate control systems obsolete. Based on studies of termite architecture, Nyquist discovered that energy-saving buildings can be designed that can warming or cool when needed, providing comfort without locking inhabitants into an airtight and heavily insulated room, where air cannot flow, and harmful bacteria and microbes readily proliferate. In such a space, when one person sneezes, everyone catches cold. This cannot be the purpose of saving energy!

The Laggarberg School in Timrå, just outside Sundsvall, Sweden, was Nyquist's design adaptation of the genius that both termites in nature and ancient civilizations throughout history have used to keep warm or stay cool without guzzling energy or using elaborate chemical insulation to keep heat out or freshness in. A system of vents and channels achieves air conduction that moderates temperatures and maintains freshness. The air is fresh all year around and when one child sneezes, no one else does. Fresh air offers an exit for dust and charged particles. The students are the healthiest in the nation, as measured by days lost due to illness, and are amongst the best academically. What happens when parents learn that children are smart and healthy in this public school? Families would like to move in the neighborhood, the only way to secure entry into the classes. And what happens to real estate prices when people move in droves? Land value increases owing to a strategy to emulate nature's design.

The termite's skills are exceptionally instructive, even though the insect is subject to obliteration around the world for its supposedly voracious appetite for wood. Were we to consider that termites are traditionally responsible for the long-term fertilisation of the soil, we might have less animosity and greater appreciation for them. In fact, typically 15 per cent of the Earth's vegetation becomes the nutrient source for the fungi that termites consume. The decomposing debris produces heat that warms them in the winter, while enriching the deep soil for decades and centuries to come.

From the termite, we can learn ways to continuously refresh the air in a building without heating or cooling. If the air is refreshed, there will be less risk of a building developing what is known as sick building syndrome, where stagnant, microbe-laden, stifled air is trapped inside and which in turn leads to illness as a result of fungal and microbial contamination. In the termite's world, this same system controls humidity, which determines productivity of the fungus on which termites rely for nutrients. The termite's airflow system precisely and permanently secures 86° F and 61 per cent humidity. The only variable that the termites do not control is water. If heavy rains flood the land, the nest can be inundated. This stressful environment is the signal for the Termitomycis mushroom—a gourmet delicacy even for humans—to ensure survival by reproducing. Also, the termite queen knows how to carry spores to safety in her mouth in order to start farming at a new nest.

It is fitting that the first multi-story building emulating the ingenious work of termites was erected in Harare, the capital city of Zimbabwe. The Eastgate Shopping and Office Centre, a 10-floor edifice designed in the late 1980s by Mike Pearce, a local architect, is heated and cooled solely by natural airflows. The economics of this innovative system are convincing. Eliminating the space between floors used for air ducts drops the break-even point from 55 to 46 per cent, essentially adding an extra floor in the same elevation while reducing investment costs (in this case, a savings of US$3.5 million), and brings down operational expenses by 10 to 15 per cent. Banks fund construction projects that can demonstrate lower risk and better returns, while requiring less capital and offering better rental rates to occupants. Sustainable features such as low cost, maintenance free, and passive air conduction, instead of expensive mechanical air conditioning, also attract financing options.

Why Do Zebras Have Black and White Stripes?

The zebra offers an additional insight into technologies that would reduce or in some cases even eliminate the need for insulation in many parts of the world, through control of surface temperature. The zebra is capable of reducing its surface temperature by 17.5° F with air currents generated by the interplay of its black and white stripes. Here is another ingenious distillation of the laws of physics that is taught at school, but perhaps not well understood in practical application. Although architectural design looks for moderation of temperature through the heat-reflective properties of white, the case of the zebra would argue that buildings should rather be painted black and white. We know that the colour white reflects the sun, thereby reducing heat. The colour black absorbs the sun, thus increasing surface temperature. The air above the white stripes is thus cooler than that above the black stripes. The heated air above the black stripes rises, creating a pressure differential with the higher air pressure above the white stripes. This generates micro-sized air currents that cool the surface without mechanical ventilation. Does this make a notable difference? Can this be commercially developed?

A Daiwa House office building in Sendai, Japan, also designed by Anders Nyquist, capitalises on this interplay of black and white, while exploiting the wisdom of termites. While controlling surface temperature on the exterior of the building, the interplay between oppositely coloured surfaces decreases the building's indoor temperature in summer by 8.5° F. By extrapolation, we can see that the mere physical effects of black and white surfaces reduce interior temperatures, saving an estimated 20 per cent in energy usage. Although not as impressive as the zebra's 17.5° F, we humans have been at it for only a few decades, while the zebra has mastered the technique over hundreds of thousands of years. The low and high pressures are levelled, owing to micro-gusts of wind. Instead of insulating the interior, the interplay of physics removes heat from the exterior, reducing the need for polyurethane (with fire retardants) or glass fibre on the interior. Actually, the zebra has an insulating layer of fat only under its black stripes, since the tissue below the white stripes does not need it. It makes sense; it saves materials; it is very simple. It never stops working as long as there is interplay of black and white, which is guaranteed as long as the sun shines and the laws of physics apply. The zebra has an added advantage: no mosquitos will land on its skin, since the turbulence in the air deprives them of a safe approach. Ever considered black and white stripes to keep mosquitos away?

Aiming to save energy, architects today recommend insulation on the inside of a building and beneath the roof to block the transfer of heat or cold. Builders typically use polyurethane chemicals, or glass fibres produced with mined materials and processed at high energy cost, to insulate indoors from the outdoors. The zebra displays ways in which taking advantage of the predictable laws of physics to reduce heat or cold at the exterior can translate to less need for chemical products or expensive heating and cooling installations. This interplay based on pressure and temperature requires no additional expense and works all the time. Indeed, the laws of physics have no exceptions.

A Desert of Plenty

The dark colouration and extraordinary life span of *Welwitschia mirabilis*, a desert plant species, give us further cause to consider that white alone may offer only short term comfort with regard to beating the heat. The Namib Desert has been arid for at least 55 million years and is believed to be the oldest desert in the world. A grasshopper accidentally jumping from a stone into desert sand would scorch and die in only a few minutes. In this water-starved environment, with only one rainfall every seven years, the Welwitschia not only survives, but with an estimated life span of 2,000 years or more, seems to hold the record as the oldest living plant on earth. The Welwitschia mastered the capture of dew on its two leaves to near perfection, as well as the ability to source moisture from two metres deep.

Lighter colours reflect sunlight and reduce heat absorption at the surface. While humans value cooler temperatures, these have a disadvantage in a desert setting. In the desert the main target is not coolness, but rather decreasing the dew point so that a minute quantity of moisture can be predictably captured. A cooler surface increases the dew point and thus reduces the quantity of moisture available for harvest each morning. Darker colours induce a lower dew point in the early morning with a warmer surface and a cooler air. This would imply greater heat absorption during the day, except that plants and beetles can conduct heat away. Members of this desert ecosystem survive by soughting to heat reduction achieved through ventilation and conduction, another demonstration of the ecological use of physical principles.

The Namib Desert is also home to a large array of lichens. These are actually not a plant species, but rather a symbiosis or composite of two organisms, namely a fungus and an alga. The fungus functions as the body and harvests water for the lichen as a whole from morning and evening fog. By photosynthesis, the alga produces the nutrients required for survival. Although their mycelium may be barely two cells thick, these lichen are perhaps the best miners in the world with the ability to penetrate seemingly solid stone.

"However, is that possible?", we may ask. Our logic to penetrating rock has been shaped by Alfred Nobel, who invented the chemical reaction known as 'dynamite,' which is our only current means of extracting mineral ores from deep within the earth. Humanity takes recourse in chemistry, while natural systems first exploit physics. Lichens do not use dynamite; actually nothing in nature would use such an excessive and destructive force. The microscopic size of the lichen's mycelium allows it to easily navigate the spaces between rock crystals. When a magnesium atom is found, it is moved to the surface for plant, bird, or animal life to partake. As a result of the lichen's fine and precise mining technique, Namib fauna and flora gain access to the trace minerals needed to function in this delicate environment. The contribution of each species ensures survival for all those living within this framework of temperature, moisture and light.

Beetles for Water

The *Onymacris plana*, a beetle also indigenous to the Namib Desert, is not simply dark, but intensely black. It achieves better dew-point management results than plants in the same habitat by using heat conductivity with the addition of another physical effect: extreme hydrophobia. At first, a desert beetle's capacity to repel water may seem as irrelevant as windshield wipers on a submarine. However, the careful analysis undertaken by UK scientist, Andrew Parker reveals that microscopically small drops of dew form each morning as soon as the sun tips over the horizon. These droplets are rapidly rejected from the hydrophobic (water-fearing) wing surface of the beetle or the leaf surface of the plant before they evaporate. The minute droplets of rejected water are collected on extremely hydrophilic (water-loving) patches around the beetle's wings. This interplay of hydrophobic and hydrophilic surfaces assures the Namibian desert beetle an ample daily water supply, sufficient in fact to shower and to drink. Curiously, this system of water and temperature control is counter-intuitive: black facilitates survivability in the hottest climate and water-repellent surfaces secure drinking water.

Sophisticated Sticking

Geckos do not mind a storm. They are unmoved by almost anything, effortlessly adhering to surfaces wet or dry, rough or smooth. The gecko uses attractive and repulsive intermolecular electrostatic forces called van der Waals, named after the Dutch physicist who first scientifically identified them. Amazing! Things stick together because of the underlying physics! One day, innovative products inspired by the intermolecular manipulations of the gecko can compete with Velcro™, which is itself inspired by the hooks on cocklebur seeds that have applied a 'sticking without glue' solution for ages past. We might even suggest that the geckos and cockleburs have greater sophistication when it comes to 'sticking' than, say, mussels. Geckos and cockleburs use physics first, guiding their biology to grow cells that achieve the desired performance. Mussels rely on chemistry. This does not mean that mussels do poorly by relying on a chemical solution. In fact, they are a remarkable inspiration for ways to replace the toxins that chemical engineers have heretofore developed for several commercial adhesives.

Mussels are constantly battered by waves. As a consequence, they have perfected a glue to attach themselves to rocks. They have learned how to build such great elasticity into their water-resistant glue, so that even the strongest surf will not detach them. Kaichang Li from Oregon State University (USA) studied the resin that mussels produce and applied his research conclusions to develop a commercial glue that Columbia Forest Products uses to replace formaldehyde-based epoxies, the standard glue for particle fibreboard. Indoor air quality is markedly better when formaldehyde is not a component of the building materials.

When market leaders use green chemistry to replace toxic chemistry by putting nature-inspired innovations into their products, they achieve profitability concomitant with sustainability. Thus, while we admire the gecko and the cocklebur for elegant use of only physical forces without the need for chemistry, we give the mussel all our respect for teaching us how to eliminate toxins from our homes, schools and offices.

Vortexes as Bactericides

Natural systems don't solve problems with a shower of harsh chemicals. There are a few well-publicised biological exceptions, such as aggressive snakes, toxic frogs, venomous spiders and deadly mushrooms. However, their toxicity is nearly always directed against another species, hardly ever members of the same family;

although the black widow spider is a notorious exception to the rule, as is always found in biology. Prior to reverting to any form of deadly chemistry, and certainly chemistry that could be mutagenic or carcinogenic to members of the same family, natural species apply the forces of physics. Where living species, especially fauna and flora, are an easy inspiration for humans from poetry to technologies, the inanimate part of nature also has lessons to share.

Have you ever wondered how rivers cleanse themselves? They use physics and the nutrient needs of two diverse families of bacteria. The pervasive movement of a river allows continuous creation of vortices in the water. A vortex increases pressure at the core of its swirl to the point that nano-scale pressure and friction rupture bacterial membranes. Bacteria are thus rendered into nutrients for other species further downstream to enjoy. These finely-distributed nutrients, combined with spaces enriched with dissolved oxygen and areas where air is eliminated from the water, allow bacteria and micro-algae to mineralise any excess biomass quickly and efficiently. At the same time, this shift from spaces rich with dissolved air to those vacant of air makes it impossible for detrimental aerobic bacteria to flourish.

The power of the vortex, induced merely by flowing water abiding the laws of gravity, is among the most impressive demonstrations we have studied. Have you ever seen a river flow in a straight line? What might be the logic in a river's meanderings? Curiously, modern industrial engineers design everything in straight lines with 90° turns. Yet, the famed 20th century Viennese artist-designer-architect, Friedensreich Hundertwasser once declared, "The rigid straight line is fundamentally alien to humanity, life, and the whole of creation."

Viktor Schauberger, a brilliant Austrian inventor and the founder of implosion technology, spent much of his career as a forester. He observed that the dual vertical and horizontal swirl of river vortices caused solids to deposit in the center of the river bed, while eroding the rock and soil along the banks. One of his early design breakthroughs was a log transport system that curved as a river does, allowing logs to pass without jamming or blocking. Remarkable!

Straight transportation systems block, meandering ones flow. Straightened rivers accumulate sediment and meandering rivers provide fresh, clean water!

Swedish innovators, Curt Hallberg and Morten Oveson developed a non-linear mathematical model that made the power of any vortex predictable. With developing vortex technology, we can now replace polluting chemical solutions with physical one. The potential energy savings from vortex technology, and an increased understanding of the natural geometry of a vortex, makes way for a plethora of opportunities for businesses and societies. If we combine these insights with hydrophobic and hydrophilic checkered rooftops borrowed from the Namibian beetle, we can reduce energy and material consumption, as well as generate water on the top of a building. From there, it can follow the law of gravity and flow into the premises. With vortex technology, the same gray water that washes clothes on the tenth floor can be reused a floor or two below, thus reducing the water wasted by a factor of 5-10.

The Swedish startup company, Watreco, offers a device that uses their patented Vortex Process Technology® to eliminate air from water. This is an attractive proposal for anyone meaning to produce or maintain large amounts of ice. When you produce ice, you freeze both water and air. Air is an insulator. The energy needed to freeze and maintain the ice in hockey rinks and ice arenas, for example, is thus dependent on the amount of air the water contains. As the vortex technology eliminates the air, the energy savings (up to 43% according to Ohio State University trials) is a positive contribution. It reduces costs and decreases the input to climate change by eliminating the greenhouse gases from ice making that are produced by 100,000 kW hours per year of electrical generation.

What clinches it from a business standpoint, however, is that the ice produced from the vortex water is crystal clear, permitting advertising displays placed underneath to be highly visible. Ice normally cracks under the weight of the hockey players, since the air bubbles cause imperfect ice crystal formation. With air removed, the ice remains clear even under the weight of the crisscrossing players.

Surely advertisers with diminished budgets would comprehend the added advantage of their logo easily viewable on sports broadcasts. Then again, perhaps advertisers could even be motivated to foot the bill. This could be a strategic new business tactic: advertisers paying for energy-saving devices!

The income generated by additional advertising revenues is a multiple of the energy savings and can be measured by multiple means. While substantial sums might be contracted with large hockey league sponsors around the world, at thousands of smaller ice rinks the use of vortex technology to clarify the ice can generate additional revenue and reduce the pressure on local government budgets. Interestingly, the town-owned ice rink in Telluride, Colorado, is second only to their water treatment plant as the biggest energy consumer in town. The town recently purchased a vortex system for their ice rink. They enjoyed greatly reduced energy costs starting in 2010, once the system was fully installed. Elsewhere, the city of Malmö, Sweden, quickly realised this savings/earnings potential and installed a full system of ice-making using vortex technology. David Henderson, head coach of France's men's national ice hockey team, reports on his teams' evaluation of the vortex-produced crystal-clear ice:

> Elite players have been unanimous in their praise of the improvement of ice quality in regards to hardness and durability. The ice has also become more transparent, which leads to a second major improvement: the visibility of on-ice publicity for the sponsors.

Value created by such extrapolations of physics is enormous, and far outpaces investment costs. It actually makes the energy savings seem like an added benefit! A simple technology created a new competitive edge in advertising that at first glance had nothing to do with air, energy or ice. There are an estimated 16,000 indoor ice rinks around the world. The total savings in electrical expenditures could reach approximately US$200 million per year, if all were to adopt this technology. Better yet, the costs would be well below the first year's savings.

Natural Ways to Avoid Fire and Flame

Asbestos was once appreciated as a naturally-occurring mineral fibre that provided roofing and insulation that did not burn. Unfortunately, it was conclusively identified as a carcinogen. Yet decades after incontrovertible scientific and medical studies have proven this beyond any doubt, asbestos remains available on the market. Even more ironically, countries like Canada that pride themselves on a progressive approach to sustainability still permit open-pit asbestos mining in the 21st century.

Both Europe and the US have sharply restricted the use of asbestos. A few billion-dollar out-of-court settlements suppressed industry's appetite to pursue its use. However, there is another side to the coin. Legislation around the world mandates the use of fire and flame retardants in many things, for example, children's clothing, car seats, interior textiles, airplanes, and office furniture. The quest for a family of chemicals that lowers the possibility of fire from cigarette butts or candles has stimulated the development of bromine and halogen-based chemicals. These fire and flame retardants work. The only inconvenience is that they also seem to cause cancer. Worse, mammals in the Arctic accumulate these fire retardants in their fatty tissues in general and their reproductive organs in particular. Everyone agrees that these chemicals find their way to the Arctic. However, since no one can explain the pathway by which they arrive, there is no verifiable link to bromine and halogen-based products. Thus, no legal responsibility can be assigned. Industry will continue to manufacture and sell these products.

Will consumers continue to ignore the havoc caused by the dumping and incineration of halogens and bromines? Scientists wonder if polar bears will become extinct more quickly from chemically-induced infertility or from habitat disruption through climate change. A few substitutes like phosphorus-based retardants have been introduced to the market; however, industry claims that there is no substitute for the effectiveness of bromine.

Mats Nilsson, a scientist and the founder of the Swedish firm, Trulstech Innovation, has developed a portfolio of gels and powders made from abundantly available food-grade ingredients that he calls Molecular Heat Eaters (MHE). The product is successfully commercialised through Deflamo AB, based in Malmö (Sweden). This makes sense. Our bodies have a unique capability to manage heat and oxygen. If heat is channeled away from a fuel source, and if oxygen is converted into carbon dioxide, there is no risk of fire. Most chemistry students learn this as the Krebs Cycle. This is a worthwhile substitution: replace carcinogenic chemicals that have a negative impact on our health with food-grade materials that are available in abundance at comparable prices. Imagine the competitive advantage of Nilsson's fire and flame retardants. It is no longer necessary to choose between immediate death by fire or slow death by cancer! We can replace products that destroy life with those that promote life. The biochemicals needed for Nilsson's inventions could be derived from grape pomace, a by-product of wine making, or citrus peel that is waste from juice production.

These products succinctly illustrate advantages of the Blue Economy model. The crowning beauty of Nilsson's technology is that it has the potential to solve massive ecological challenges. When wildfires devastate California or Colorado, the US Forest Service rushes to spray chemicals by plane. Now, we can blanket the area with food-grade chemicals, instead of phosphorous, and secure fast relief from fire without harming to the ecosystem.

In the future, the same technology could be used to eliminate the risk of explosions in mines. Excessive concentrations of naturally-occurring methane fill mining tunnels and create underground disasters if sparks occur as the mining equipment gouges out rock. At present, mining equipment is manufactured from expensive nickel and cobalt metal alloys to reduce the risk of sparks. Using the air channels already in place to mist the mining space with food-grade fire retardants could suppress sparks and prevent explosions. This would additionally reduce the demand for cobalt and nickel mining, and the subsequent expensive processing into high-performance metals.

These advances in applied physics, physical chemistry, chemistry, and biology give us reason to believe that innovations inspired by nature are shaping a new economy. In a recent interview, Achim Steiner, Executive Director of the United Nations Environment Programme, declared, "Many technologies are in commercial use. We're not talking about theory any more; these are real results occurring in the real world and in the real market."

Unlocking Solutions

The vital relationship of the laws and theories of physics to the basic conditions of ways we produce, consume, and survive are not given much attention in today's physics classrooms. Yet, it is in observing the basics of physics that we realise how minute shifts in pressure, temperature, and moisture content create outstanding products and processes that far outshine the results of genetic modification with their artfulness, precision and effectiveness. Instead of manipulating the biology of life, we can find inspiration in the ways that nature uses physics.

Quick, one-off solutions don't appear to be resolving the complex problems that we confront, both in our individual domiciles and our greater domicile, our Earth. Successful future industries will re-examine the basics of science and seek inspiration for innovative solutions that apply physics first and chemistry second. If we consider the underlying forces and the systemic conditions that predict the results prescribed by physics, then we will understand why chemistry in nature differs markedly from one that dominates our lives presently. The few molecules retained in natural products and production processes reflect the best possible use of physics. The gecko and the mussel demonstrate two sticking systems, each of which performs within clear physical parameters. While green chemistry and even sustainable biology are important goals, we need to look more deeply in order to grasp the forces that determined both. Whenever possible, Blue Economy models follow the physics. Such a different approach is unmatched by market leaders.

This may well be the logic that we need to pursue in an era of economic crisis. Instead of using chemistry—traditional or green—nature shows us ways to eliminate chemistry. We need to go beyond the closed loop, recycling everything. We need to eliminate many components from the loop, which can be achieved by application of physics. Green chemistry and sustainable biology face the challenges of obtaining funds and navigating lengthy approval processes required by the government authorities of developed nations. Such drawbacks hamper the rapid business reconfigurations required by economic crises. The market's competitive framework needs encouragement to help fast-track procedural regulatory requirements as new insights unfold from our observation and implementation of what nature achieves.

Imagine the impact such innovations can have on building design. There are nearly dozens of breakthroughs that could be utilised in homes, offices and factories. Buildings that use these technologies are first and foremost healthier for their occupants. The additional benefit, as demonstrated by Renzo Piano's Centre Pompidou in Paris, France, together with Richard Rogers and Gianfranco Franchini, is that everyone who has the chance to explore such a building sees the elegant application of the laws of physics. As we adopt the principles of a Blue Economy, our use of non-renewable resources can dwindle to just a fraction of what it once was, requiring less investment and less cost. Now imagine that we apply these innovations and creative business models to cities. Then real smart cities and real eco-cities would emerge.

A Blue Economy goes beyond efficiency and better return on investment. Much of what we believe we need is entirely unnecessary, and can be replaced by products and methods that are better and simpler than those most widely used today. Perhaps something, made from chemistry can be replaced by nothing, an effect owing to physics. Rather than adversely effecting our economy, these alternatives can make it stronger, freeing up material resources and currency, empowering us to respond to the needs of all. Thus with a bundled portfolio of innovations based on pragmatic solutions to critical issues that have already been faced and solved by many species on Earth, we can redefine the competitive model. Such insights can help solve many of the sustainability challenges faced while giving power and precedence to entrepreneurs. When we create pathways for strengthening our capacity to respond to the basic needs of all—water, food, health care, housing and energy—with what is readily available, we are building an openly sourced Blue Economy from the ground up.

The few insights shared here, such as, dew point management through the interplay of colour, heat conductivity and hydrophilia, put us on track for new thought patterns. The design of a building or home need no longer be about saving energy. Instead it can be about replacing old ideas like polyurethane with new ideas beyond insulation. This is a refreshing approach. The growth economy was always driven by consuming and investing more. Here, a reduction in consumption provides a stimulus to the economy, whereby a material or a process that uses a harsh chemical solution is replaced by a solution that utilises merely the properties of physics.

Something ... is replaced by ... nothing. This sets the tone for our emerging model of the Blue Economy.

5

Leading the Way for Market Leaders

> Today we have a temporary aberration called "industrial capitalism" which is inadvertently liquidating its two most important sources of capital—the natural world and properly functioning societies.
> No sensible capitalist would do that.
>
> — *AMORY LOVINS*

Oak from Seed

By 2014, the innovations showcased here have generated an estimated three million jobs. While this is encouraging, it is a mere trickle for a world that needs a vast river of one billion new jobs. Where the bailout of defunct industries and financial institutions may be money down the drain, investments made in innovations that are part of a systemic portfolio can provide the catalytic effect the world economy urgently needs. Even someone without business experience and only a grasp of the fundamental principles of a Blue Economy can have an entrepreneurial chance to succeed. If a new solution requires less expenditure or energy, or if multiple income opportunities are available, then start-up capital or micro-investments may be all the encouragement needed to make it happen.

Crisis generates a unique degree of freedom to innovate, and a window of opportunity to fast track businesses that meet basic needs, where the status quo has no interest to act and no chance to succeed. The ventures we contemplate may be once-in-a-lifetime opportunities to reorient our economy. In inner city, rural and peri-urban environments, in the North and South, East and West, we have a chance to introduce innovations and business models that respond better to our economic needs than 200 years of industrial progress.

In the last two months of 2008 alone, the worldwide financial crisis caused an estimated net loss of 50 million jobs in the emerging nations. A continuing crisis could push another 200 million people into extreme poverty. The International Labor Organization (ILO) reports that the number of working poor could reach 1.4 billion, or become half the working population of the world's developing countries. Spain and Greece's youth must tolerate in 2014 that nearly 60 per cent of their friends under 26 has no job. Even if economic growth were to pick up and maintain itself for years to come, never could the present model absorb such an offer of human capital. How do we condone such travesty? How can we abide such loss of human potential? It is with a sense of urgency that we focus on the solutions that can make a difference in the lives of many. Achieving livelihood security means individuals can obtain food, shelter and comfort, provide for their families, and experience a measure of dignity and satisfaction from the contribution of their labour. Innovations that emulate nature's cascading effect can offer an invitation to a greater and more abundant future, thriving with diversity. The jobs potentially created may well be counted in the hundreds of millions.

New Possibilities, New Perspectives

We might compare the current economic upheaval that has gripped the world to what nature accomplishes with volcanic eruptions and tornadoes. Although such natural disasters wreak destruction and cause tragic loss of life, such extreme, out-of-bounds situations also restore the prevalence of ambient conditions. They are the exceptions that confirm the rule. Besides putting whole systems under enormous stress, these exceptions also provide an opening for new possibilities and new solutions where none were evident before.

In economic terms, when disruption occurs at such a fundamental level, a completely new pathway to the market becomes available. Innovations that can emulate nature's cascading effect and that make use of the laws of physics have the chance to succeed because they have little to gain from existing business models. They simply do not compete by the same rules. Batteries are replaced by no batteries; medical devices, surgery and pharmaceuticals are replaced with none of the above! Instead of dealing constantly with waste, the residues of production are used to realise greater income than that generated by the core business of another totally unrelated business. In essence, this is why now, more than at any time in recent history, we have the opportunity to generate millions of jobs while moving away from scarcity, pollution and waste. Furthermore, there are so many resources readily available that are not considered: thistles and nettles grow by the millions and are destroyed since these are labelled a week. Thousands of people in hundreds of countries will intuitively grasp the principles and realise the opportunities in what lies before them. Their work will cascade and conjoin with the work of others and create opportunities for even greater numbers of people. This fundamentally rooted approach emulates nature's models. Such innovations are benchmarked, and the solutions are real.

These opportunities are tied to the reality that the use of non-renewable resources is a weakness. The use of toxic components is an even greater weakness. Failing to use or even destroying resources not considered part of the core business definition are lost opportunities and significant weaknesses. Shedding thousands of jobs does not promote customer loyalty; resisting change and receiving government bail-outs are simply other forms of energy wasted. They engender no confidence and have no chance of long-term success. Paying excessive bonuses to top management undermines any grain of loyalty that might have survived.

For the past two decades, prominent and eloquent scholars, academics and leaders have lectured on and presented many of the breakthroughs described in this book. Introduced by various researchers and with various names, examples of nature technology have been put forth around the world. Many brilliant and enthusiastic researchers and innovators have contributed to growth and interest in the field. As the first awareness of nature technology achieved international prominence, research dollars were allocated to study innovations that could direct business towards sustainability. The media reported these innovations in stories accompanied by marvelous photographs and films. Televised presentations all found large and appreciative audiences eager to know of the next fascinating flora or fauna performance unimagined by humans.

Yet top business management remained disaffected. With the exception of a few cases, notably in Germany and Japan, market leaders fell short of adopting or promoting any of these technologies. Industry barely paid lip service to the possibilities and hardly responded to proposals. Business executives attended presentations that outlined these marvelous opportunities and voiced their enthusiasm. Yet they returned to their offices to continue business as usual. At Vice-President Al Gore's Expert Panel on Solutions for Climate Change held in New York in January 2008, it was common to hear that although venture capital had its antennas directed towards nature technology, most of the proposed innovations were simply "too different to get traction on the ground." Perhaps this is true, because these innovations essentially alter the current business model, and business experts unwilling or unable to adapt will have little understanding and little in common with the emerging approaches.

If we are serious about designing a new economic model richly inspired by natural solutions that have evolved over time, then it is not enough to attend lectures, read reports, watch colourful documentaries and contemplate connections. There is a major hurdle that must be surmounted to move from talk to action. The key is to achieve a competitive and strategic positioning of these innovations by vigorous operators in an open economy, thereby mapping a pathway within the competitive environment from discovery, to understanding the science, to replacing the present unhealthy and unsustainable production and consumption model with something better.

How do we transform our present socio-economic downturn and our present economic system that is woefully in need of improvements, into a system that promotes life, strengthens resilience, relies on what is available, builds on sustainable practices, works with the flow of physics, offers innumerable opportunities to learn, adapts to changing conditions, responds to basic needs, builds community, instills a sense of responsibility beyond oneself, generates jobs, creates multiple revenues, and provides challenges? We risk that our children will confront the same mistakes we have endured: wars waged, human rights violated, worldwide hunger and poverty rampant, as society at large remains distracted and disengaged. There is a need to encourage the freedom to improve, the liberty to rethink and re-imagine, as well as to find solutions that are just, equitable and stabilising. Whether theirs are fresh young faces in posh Manhattan preschools, or faces streaked by grime and hardship in the favelas of Ecuador, the new generation is easily inspired by opportunities that are alive and present around them. Why are our business leaders missing out? Are there enough entrepreneurs to transform our economic systems so that as a society we can move beyond behaviours of consuming more and exhausting the resources available to us?

Certainly, the wealth of innovations before us provides an impetus to this urgently needed economic shift. Imagine an economy without a scarcity syndrome. Imagine an economy that evolves to sufficiency, where moments of stress catalyse us to abundance, where the abiding impetus is to realise ever more creative ways to stimulate innovation. Imagine an economy that encourages new generations to greater success than their parents achieved—greater even than their parents could imagine.

Getting Out of the Box

Although applying the cascading model may be most attractive to innovative business organisations with broader and stronger social missions, the opportunity to generate jobs in the new economy will not be based on the time and motion studies that has brought to us 19th and 20th century labour productivity. New job generation opportunities will emerge from 'eco'-facture, not 'manu'-facture. The new industries that emerge will utilise processes that conform to the same physical rules as that of nature.

Harsh chemicals, refined metals, and other polluting and non-renewable materials will be replaced by solutions derived through simple physics—gravity, pressure and temperature. Eco-facture will replace energy-intensive and toxic processes with ambient temperature operations that make use of natural variations of pressure and other principles of physics to produce goods. Waste will become a resource. Locally available materials will be incorporated into the materials stream. Market standards will be transformed, and creative ideas will take precedence over stagnant business norms where the status quo rules out changes to revenue streams.

Many companies even today operate under established management school doctrine that does not encourage thinking 'out of the box'. This is a model that cleaves to five management principles outlined below. In actuality these principles can be a hindrance to progress, and even antithetical to a model that can deliver the means we need to meet the present critical needs. Our challenge is not only to get out of the box, but to find a way to work with the landscape of these management principles, while replacing old limitations with new opportunities.

Many years ago, Mr Soichiro Honda, founder of Honda Motor Company, was asked if he had run a business analysis based on the strengths and weaknesses of his own company and those of his competitors when considering whether to evolve from a motorbike manufacturer to an automobile producer. He responded, "If our team had run that business analysis, we would never have ventured into the car business." He quickly added, "I simply made a list of weaknesses of the world's biggest carmakers—and that list was quite long," he concluded with a smile. He did go on to become one of Japan's reknowed carmakers.

MANAGEMENT PRINCIPLE 1: CORE BUSINESS DEFINED BY CORE COMPETENCE

Graduates of modern business schools follow the axiom that any initiative must subject itself to a thorough business analysis, producing detailed reports and mapping out clear-cut strategies for how to succeed and how to fend off major competitive forces. Corporate CEOs (chief executive officers) and managers are trained and expected to operate within well-defined fields that have clear parameters for success. If a company is not competitive, it is not viable. Achieving market share means consumers must repeatedly buy a product when offered at the perceived ideal combination of cost and quality. However, once mainstreamed, this model resists change and often excuses collateral damage to the environment and even to society at large. The blinders of a core business approach can even disconnect managers from social ethics, creating a moral double standard. Remarkably, business often concludes that doing less bad equates to doing good.

The concepts of core business and core competence have dominated management directives for the past half century. If a new approach emerges that falls outside the scope of a core competence, it is extremely difficult for management to accept. Furthermore, a new technology cannot be brought to the market solely on the basis of core competencies. Even though a market leader may be persuaded that a new technology is an opportunity to gain competitive edge and market share, there is no guarantee will be approved for development. Often these new fields are more easily engaged by entrepreneurs outside of so-called market leaders. The shift in technological platforms and the need for new competencies liberate a start-up company from requiring any previous experience in the industry.

Take the case of the pacemaker. For 50 years, this surgically implanted medical device has been the solution to irregularities in cardiac rhythm. The pacemaker is powered by a battery located near the collarbone. Our current stress-filled lifestyles insure that millions of pacemakers—at a minimum cost of US$50,000 each—will be needed in the years to come. While everyone is focusing on developing more efficient batteries, the next generation of cardiac rhythm solutions requires neither surgery nor battery. The cost of this new intervention technology could be as low as US$500 dollars; that of the nanotubes is not more than a few dollars.

The introduction of a nanotube conductor that channels electrical current from healthy tissue to afflicted areas of the heart was inspired by studying the channels of cells that provide conductivity around and through the heart of a whale. This is a knowledge base that is foreign to pacemaker manufacturers. No mainstream medical technology company has the foundation on which to build this new business. This innovation requires a conductor, carbon tubes, communication capabilities, natural energy sources and chip designs. Such a retooling implies a deep chasm of unknown factors, making market leaders disinclined to invest. This sort of disruptive technology would further require new staff, components and business planning, comparable to the creation of an entirely new business division. Most challenging of all, adopting such an innovative approach could very well undermine the lucrative income stream enjoyed by medical equipment companies.

Who would venture into the unknown, particularly during a recession? Industry giants, like Boston Scientific or Medtronic, are not apt to lead the way. If a top business executive has made the decision to acquire, at great expense, a gadget with guaranteed revenue potential from a proven and successful technology, why would they promote research funding or approve an investment that would undermine it? Who would accelerate the shift to this non-surgical approach when the revenues generated would be only a fraction of the cash flow each operation generates for the whole medical system, including surgeons, anesthesiologists, pharmaceutical companies and battery makers? The answer is obvious: no one who benefits from the market today. This creates the technological and institutional lock-in, blocking real innovations from market entry. The well-being of client, and the lower cost to insurance companies are not served by this blockage. Yet, Dr Jorge Reynolds succeeded by 2013 to have two prototypes inserted in dogs and have these under surveillance at Medtronic. While this is not a full-fledged animal testing program, it is a first attempt to get the notion of a battery-free world into the minds of greatest scientific instrumentation companies in the world.

Another example is the innovative use of the physical properties of vortexes. Currently, industries that desalinate, de-scale, and purify water depend on chemistry and reverse osmosis. Chemicals like chlorine kill bacteria, other acids de-scale, and a pressure of up to 800 PSI separates salt from seawater to create potable water. New technology is benchmarked that utilises mounting pressure in a vortex to convert calcite to aragonite. Ever higher vortex pressure ruptures bacterial cell membranes, while the increased water density naturally achieves 39° F, thus expelling salt, leaving the centre of water flow pure and clean. This is a fundamentally different approach than that taken by market leaders, although some market leaders, such as Nitto Denko, Siemens, and General Motors (GE), may be ready to pursue these new developments. It requires not only forward thinking, but the appetite to master the challenges of new technology and the willingness to learn new competences.

MANAGEMENT PRINCIPLE 2: SUPPLY CHAIN MANAGEMENT

Supply chain management involves the oversight of materials, financial transactions and market delivery as products move from harvest or collection, to manufacture and later to consumption. Even though a market leader may be persuaded that a new technology is an opportunity to gain competitive edge and market share, there is no guarantee this innovation will be approved for development. It must fit a manufacturing and distribution system—a supply chain—that predates the innovation and can carry the breakthrough to the end consumer. The strategic management team must make sure that research ideas make sense to marketing and manufacturing.

Many activities within a company need to converge around the introduction of new technologies and emerging product portfolios. Lack of a joint commitment from all departments, especially finance, supply chain management and marketing, could unleash overt and covert conflicts based on personal interests ranging from career plans and year-end performance bonuses, to corporate policies such as depreciation rules, tax planning, and quarterly earnings targets. In the end, these conflicts often undermine any innovation strategy. There are in fact remarkable innovations described herein that perfectly fit an existing supply chain model. Nevertheless, developing market share is a challenge that requires enormous fortitude and perseverance.

Here we would take the example of vaccines that traditionally require a complete cold-chain from production to transportation, delivery, and storage at the dispensing medical facility. The supply chain management is based on strict temperature control. If one link in the chain fails, the spoiled vaccines must be discarded and replaced. In developing countries, where access to refrigeration often depends on an irregular electrical power supply, the solution has been to invest in solar- or propane-powered refrigeration in order to eliminate the risk of spoiling vaccines. Yet viable innovative solutions are available.

Thermo-stabilising technology inspired by the resurrection fern (*Polypodium polypodioides*) and a microscopic invertebrate, the *Tardigrada*, or water bear, has been developed by Bruce Roser and his venture companies, Biostability and StablePharma. They offer a freeze-drying system using tardigrades for preserving vaccines, applying this innovation with off-the-shelf equipment. This could handily facilitate a speedy integration of the innovation into the supply chain.

Mats Nilsson's fire and flame retardants, made of natural food-grade ingredients, have successfully integrated the supply chain for use in particle board (for furniture or housing), polyurethane (widely used in cars and homes), and carpet fibres (for offices, homes and airplanes). There are hundreds of additional applications that need to be developed. Even though he can offer these non-toxic chemicals in gel or powder form, bonding with the materials to be treated requires minor adjustments for each application. The research to make this possible takes time and money. Treating materials as varied as latex, nylon and cellulose requires a detailed understanding of ways to bond the food-grade retardants with the production processes for different materials. Lack of major investment funding has so far compromised Nilsson's ability to complete the necessary research and make the bonding specifications that each material and process requires. Need we wait decades before halogen and bromine toxins have been replaced by Krebs Cycle inspired molecules? Perhaps a clear preference expressed by consumers would encourage the world's largest homebuilders to test, approve and utilise this product. One can hope that mainstream companies, like Albemarle, Chematur or BASF, would be ready to move forward with such breakthroughs.

MANAGEMENT PRINCIPLE 3: OUTSOURCING

Innovations that succeed in meeting core competence and supply-chain management requirements must also fit with the management principle of outsourcing. Outsourcing is the process of subcontracting to third-party companies so that management can dedicate time, people, and resources to its core competence. This requires more than the mere adoption of a new technology by corporate management. The company must act as change agent for all its suppliers and subcontractors. If Daiwa House (Japan), the world's largest homebuilder, decided to replace the fire retardant chemicals they currently use, it would require developing and testing distinct product variations for each field of application, approval from industry regulators, determination of new adoption specifications, and coordination with the procedures of over 600 suppliers and subcontractors. That would be a significant task.

When this innovative flame retardant does not contribute additional revenue, but only better indoor air quality, then the shift of one technology to another during an economic downturn diverts significant management attention from its perceived core responsibilities—securing sales and improving cash flow. The will to change would of necessity come from some greater sense of allegiance to health and the environment than that given to ingrained management principles.

Another technology based on the Fibonacci sequence demonstrates proven energy efficiencies that could save computer server companies millions by cooling their servers with natural geometry. Overheated computers and game consoles like the X-box from Microsoft are a well-known problem. The noise generated by ventilators is a nuisance. Naturalist Jay Harman, while working with the Australian Department of Fisheries and Wildlife, observed the flow geometries of ocean and air currents. His observations led him to formulate what he terms the "Streamlining Principle", which translates nature's flow efficiencies into streamlined design geometries. What he learned from the nautilus shell and kudu horn significantly improves the performance, output, and energy usage of a wide range of fluid-handling mechanical movements while reducing noise. He founded Pax Scientific in 1997 and raised capital through the sale of sub-licenses since the proof that this technology saves energy is beyond debate. Yet, not one of his applications has been successfully mainstreamed. The delays he and his team face are in accessing supply chain management, responding to fast turn-around cycles in the computer industry, and coordinating with the computer industry's worldwide outsourcing. The patents accumulate and the revenue from advances on sub-licenses continues to provide the cash for further research. But to close the first mega-sale, a fourth obstacle must be overcome: the seal of approval of the vice-president for finance.

MANAGEMENT PRINCIPLE 4: CASH FLOW IS KING

Even though new products may reduce costs by saving money or energy, while simultaneously benefitting the environment, they may not automatically produce sales. In standard business practice, improved margins are great because they generate additional cash with which new investment can be funded. But shelf space is expensive for consumer goods, and fast-moving consumer products, heavily advertised in the media, imply that the cash flows faster. In the current economic downturn, giant international companies with a wide portfolio of products are dramatically reducing the number of their offerings and brands, limiting their catalogue to products that have the fastest turnaround and not necessarily the highest profit margin. The overall cash flow is considerably greater on a product with daily sales and a 5 per cent margin, as opposed to a 50 per cent margin on a product that sells only once a month. Just-in-time

(JIT) inventory turnover eliminates holding products in a warehouse, freeing the capital locked in stored consumer or industrial goods. Fast-turnover goods are attractive to investors and shareholders, especially industries that manufacture and deliver basic necessities like food- and health-related products, not as subject to up-and-down economic cycles.

Another aftermath of the financial crunch is that credit is hard to get. When a technology like Watreco's vortex-based device to remove air from water might save 10-12 per cent of energy usage, corporate financial management will conclude that this reduction in energy cost does not justify committing scarce cash. The money spent on marketing and manufacture may take years to recoup, and that is sufficient to derail a purchase decision. Innovations providing energy savings of even 20-30 per cent are unlikely to be adopted during an economic downturn. The idea of securing investments out of the savings offered is part of an unacceptable model. Innovations must offer more than energy savings; simply costing less and saving more is not good enough. Market leaders are confident to make the necessary capital investment, only when more additional revenue can be assured.

Innovations have been constrained to cutting costs. This must be complemented by a portfolio of balance sheet, profit and loss, and cash flow operations that convince the Vice President, Finance, of validity of the proposal. When the concept of paper making from crushed stones was scientifically demonstrated, it did not take long for mining companies to adopt the technology, even though the core business is far to be found. Converting rock refuse and dried tailings from mines into raw materials for rock paper that requires no water in its production had the immediate approval since it cuts down the capital expenditure and the long-term risk of a mine. The elimination of the need to build a deposit or a dam reduces that for cash up front by 25 per cent, thus rendering the project easier to finance with lower risk. The acceptance is viable since the innovation generates multiple cash flows (ore and paper), which speeds up decision making.

MANAGEMENT PRINCIPLE 5: CROWDING OUT

Even when the corporate strategist, the supply chain manager, and the finance director have endorsed an innovation, the marketing team remains to be swayed. Inventors and innovators must develop a unique selling proposition that gets a product on the shelf and into the catalogue, while successfully communicating its story to prospective consumers. In an atmosphere of concern about scarcity, the on-the-shelf reality is that everyone operates in a market characterised by oversupply. Our present variety and choice of consumer products is aptly described by the French proverb: l'embarras du choix. In other words, 'an embarrassment of riches'.

With so many alternatives, success is not a given even when a new product is better and cheaper. The first difficulty is getting attention and the next is attracting purchasing dollars. This is mainly due to the fact that established market leaders pursue a strategy known as 'crowding out'. This means that a product based on the same technology is made available with minor variations, absorbing all the possible shelf space, or responding to slightly different industrial requirements. The idea is to give buyers the sense that they have exactly what they need, thereby leaving little room for a new arrival.

Products and services are standardised; production and distribution are streamlined and simplified. Diversity is reduced to marketing gimmicks and packaging design—whatever is underneath is nearly the same everywhere. There is essentially only one diesel engine on the world market, although it is used by a dozen carmakers. The electric motors for home appliances are nearly identical everywhere in the world. Such manufacturing processes universally consolidate market share into the hands of a few whose goals is economies of scale: producing more of the same at an ever lower marginal cost. Once an item is mainstreamed, the associated and secure money flows inhibit and discourage change.

The adhesive products market superbly illustrates this dilemma. There are hundreds of glue and sticking solutions on the market, dominated by giant companies such as 3M. Henkel, a German company, markets adhesion products derived from plant starch. In effect, the market is inundated with solutions. The world demand for adhesives and sealants approaches US$50 billion in annual sales. The adhesives and sealants sector in Europe alone invests US$200 million in research and development each year. This is a huge market with immense research power concentrated in the hands of a few who already have such high number of products that it is difficult for a new one, however creative and however appealing, to build a niche and crowd others off the shelves, gain space in the sales catalogues, or acquire the attention of buyers. An article in *Time Magazine* or *The Economist* may provide some visibility, but as long as there is no actual accompanying order form, it will make little difference. Despite the many solutions that could some day replace the unsustainable products now for sale, present market leaders are disinclined to endorse such change.

This brings up another aspect to developing and maintaining market share that can threaten or obliterate a product on its path to the mainstream market. 'Suffocation' can preempt the necessity for crowding out. Once a new product starts selling in a niche market, and is perceived as a threat to the market standard, the giants of industry may act to acquire the emerging business and its patented technologies. The inventor will be offered a favourable buyout, and the new technology may simply be buried, never reaching consumers, simply because it disrupts an existing cash flow and profit margin.

The Downside of the Upside

So Many Solutions, So Little Time

Over and above the range of synthetic solutions already competing in the market, there are numerous known innovations inspired by natural systems. The gecko is the popular new arrival, while Velcro™ has successfully created a multi-million dollar niche of its own. The paper wasp native to central Europe has pincers that enable it to break down wood mechanically (physics first). It then eats these pieces and mixes them with aqueous digestive juices. This chemically shortens the length of the fibres. On drying, water evaporates, the cellulose fibres form a mat, and the adhesive hardens. The nest is ready.

In contrast to paper wasps that use a water-based adhesive, the one used by honey bees for comb building contains wax. Wax is a liquid at a bee's body temperature. Only on cooling does it solidify and adhere. Bees' wax hence meets the ideal requirements for modern adhesives, it is solvent-free but can be applied as a liquid. Barnacle larvae can bond to virtually any hard marine material. The bonding is achieved through a secretion from cement glands. This secretion is a reactive adhesive possessing a high resistance to water. New adhesive is constantly secreted to ensure that the bond remains intact.

Such competition in the glue and adhesion sector alone illustrates that opportunities using natural solutions abound. Thus, even an alert management team can face difficulty choosing the innovation to support. Where do you start if your research department has hardly any biologists or biochemists, and the marketing and production strategies remain bound by the straightjacket of core business based on core competence? The only way forward is to redesign the business model and go beyond the mere substitution of one technology with another.

Greenwashing

While many of us would consider ourselves positive and pro-active, consumer enthusiasm and the desire of concerned citizens to contribute to solutions for sustainability can end up as an obstacle to embarking on real change. In our quest for green solutions, we are keen to quickly embrace what seems an obvious path towards sustainability, even though in reality it may not be such a good idea after all. In 2006, Europe rushed to promote biofuels, only to realise that this sudden massive demand for raw materials, spurred by consumers wishing to buy green fuels, would affect the availability of corn grown for food. Instead of maize corn for human consumption, farmers planted field corn—suitable for livestock or biofuel manufacture. Prices for this staple food increased, making food security in the developing world even more difficult to achieve. The rush to secure corn supplies helped the world's largest traders and processors of agricultural output achieve record profits, yet it caused enormous hardship elsewhere. The United Nations (UN) issued a warning, and corn and palm oil were discouraged as biofuel sources.

Similarly, we rightly question the sense of biodegradable soaps made of fatty acids derived from palm trees planted on denuded land where rain forests once stood. We ponder over the rationale of consuming delectable shiitake mushrooms cultivated from felled oak forests in China. If we can be mindful of the larger picture, we can avoid embracing an obvious solution too readily only to later discover compromising harm.

The conversion to biodegradable soaps in Europe and America destroyed the habitat of the orangutan. When ecologically minded companies developed a line of biodegradable soaps derived from the fatty acids of palm oil trees, their success in securing market share incited the major market players to follow suit. To meet burgeoning international demand, millions of acres of rainforest were cut down and replaced by cultivated palm oil trees. Such unintended harm is a hard way to learn that biodegradable does not equate to sustainable. Green solutions that put the livelihood of the poor and the life of primates at risk are morally and ethically unacceptable, and are merely another form of greenwashing. As long as we are ignorant about the impact, it is an unintended consequence. The moment we realise the same, it turns into collateral damage, and that cannot be condoned under any circumstance.

Green solutions that have toxic inputs or processes and unintended side effects should not be in line for sustainability awards. It is irrational to congratulate for doing less harm, especially when the damage is inflicted upon the whole ecosystem that supports life. The ethically correct choice is to achieve greater benefit, not create less damage. Substituting asbestos with halogen- and bromine-based fire retardants, for example, does not offer a real solution. A less toxic solution is toxic nevertheless. We must seek out solutions that neither pollute our food chain nor our personal environment. We can adjust our thinking and neighten our ambitions. The argument that a little toxin load does no harm relies on the pretense that something proven detrimental, mutagenic, or carcinogenic can be tolerated in minute quantities. There is no such diagnosis as 'a little bit of cancer'—you either have cancer, or you don't! The same applies to the notion of making as much money as possible by whatever means, then reserving some of that gain to do something special for society. Such a compensation game is unethical, although unfortunately widely played.

The inability to see connections beyond the obvious is a major challenge we must surmount when designing the Blue Economy. Several innovations have succumbed to flawed or short-sighted processes. A new molecule for controlling bacteria promoted by Peter Steinberg (Australia) used toxic solvents in the production of the synthetic analogue. The first hydrophobic/hydrophilic sheets manufactured by QinetiQ (UK) to capture dew in the desert used a chemistry that created a potential health hazard for workers and consumers. Compact fluorescent lighting pioneered by Osram (Germany) provides major energy savings and is widely accepted by consumers, yet the mercury used in manufacture is a toxin. It is released into the environment when the light bulbs are discarded and not recycled. We cannot with a clear conscience defend saving energy, while releasing mercury into the ecosystem. I am not here to accuse, rather I am writing this book to demonstrate that everyone can do much better.

From 20,000 to 100,000,000

When the markets soften and margins are under pressure, it may be that the last thing desired by established management is anyone in the research or product design departments to promote a creative new idea inspired by nature. Within this context, it is a challenge to introduce innovations, even those with many applications. While we may lament the difficulties in convincing market leaders of this brilliance, we may more reasonably be delighted that such innovations will generate numerous entrepreneurial ventures and sustainability based jobs. The inaction of today's market leaders may turn them into the dinosaurs of tomorrow, leaving tremendous opportunities for those who are ready to change the rules of the game. Of course, it is possible that mainstream management may be convinced to think out of the box. We all know from our own experience that in desperate times, you are more willing to try a new approach. After all, why do 99 per cent of the men diagnosed with lung cancer stop smoking? And, why did they not stop before?

Re-imagining the future requires entrepreneurs in science, social affairs, business, environment and culture. It requires with drawing from an economy where the engine of growth is indebtedness loaded upon our children and grandchildren, squandering those future generations' material resources. Perhaps now, as we continue to voice our desire for change, having witnessed the tsunami-like destruction wrought by greed, lies and blindness, we may find that government, business and industry are ready to alter their perceptions and allocate the resources to support and develop a Blue Economy. Perhaps now, they can move forward with the will to respond to all needs with what we have and what we can share with those who have not.

6

Nature's MBA (Master of Brilliant Adaptations)

How strange that Nature does not knock, and yet does not intrude!

— *EMILY DICKINSON*

An MBA (Master of Business Administration) degree confers a status to the holder that makes them desirable as business managers and leaders. They have learned to analyse transactions and interactions that help pinpoint cost reduction for labour and raw materials, maximise cash flow, increase market share, and fine-tune supply chain management. Unfortunately these experts, who are the present dominant business leaders, seem on the verge of disconnection from the habitats and inhabitants of our planet. Worse, their narrow focus on one core business blinds them from recognising viable opportunities outside their sphere of business or knowledge. Our production and consumption schemes are outdated, incapable of responding to the basic needs of all. They must either evolve or be replaced by ones that thrive by functioning harmoniously with all life, promoting diversity, and fairly ensuring food, shelter, health, and livelihood for everyone. It is with this conclusion that we turn our admiration and attention to nature's MBA—Master of Brilliant Adaptations.

Ecosystems offer tremendous inspiration for devising economic models capable of responding to the needs of all. Natural systems always change, always evolve. That is their power and their beauty. When we attend to nature's MBA, we can begin to realise ways to integrate innovations into multifaceted models cascading nutrients and energy, supplying energy from integrated and renewable sources, designing structures that capture and utilise what is minute and transform it into what is grand, into networks that become so efficient that nothing is wasted and we have a net energy gain.

Industry is resistant to continuous change. Predictability is the name of the game. The model of core business and core competence pursues productivity in a manner that actually inhibits the natural path of evolution and change. This is, in fact, the logic by which industry arrives at solutions based on standardisation and genetic manipulation. Once you know how to alter genes, you believe you know how to predict outcomes. Where industry leaders prefer a predictable production system that uses harsh chemistry to stabilise molecules forever, and apply genetic modifications that stifle natural evolutionary tendencies, natural systems offer a different solution. Water is the solvent; molecular bonds are temporary to permit high biodegradability for natural feedstocks and high stability for mineral feedstocks, so that molecules can be combined over and over again. Genetic modifications naturally occur in the realm of bacteria as this is part of their evolutionary pathway; every other form of life is very slow to adopt genetic variations.

These differing frameworks explain why natural systems are always changing, unlike the industrial systems. To avoid change and to provide more of the same, industrial systems create global standards that apply everywhere, under the pretext that this reduces costs. In contrast, ecosystems source everything locally. They satisfy their needs with what is readily available. Since ecosystems thrive on local biodiversity, standardisation is of little use. After all, biodiversity is based on—as the word implies—diversity while enjoying a stable presence of minerals that can never be destroyed, only transformed in different combinations. This helps elucidate why new business models based on bundled portfolios of innovations will be implemented through thousands of entrepreneurs, each of whom will find their niche and chance, making best use of the local conditions. Industry's desire is to control and standardise, to merge and expand on the imaginary curve of economies of scale, thereby externalising all costs outside their narrow focus. The fact that only a few varieties of tomatoes and potatoes are commercialised, while there are hundreds of varieties, and that our main crops are primarily wheat, corn and soy monocultures, makes it evident why soils are depleted and disease infestations meet little resistance, thus requiring a constant search for new genetics. This is self-defeating.

On observing nature, we see that ecosystems evolve towards ever-higher levels of efficiency and diversity, owing to contributions from all players. A 500-year-old cedar tree and a majestic bear may be the most remarkable inhabitants we notice while hiking the Rocky Mountains, but a closer look shows that millions of other species, mostly invisible to the eye, are not only contributing but are critical to the whole system. Evolution implies a constant trend towards greater efficiency and greater diversity. So may it be with our new economies, shaped by entrepreneurs at all levels in business, science, culture and education.

As Fritjof Capra has pointed out, ecosystems are networks made of networks. The same management principles can be observed layered within each network. Indeed, ecosystems are all about connecting, about allowing everyone to contribute to the best of their abilities, while operating within clearly defined boundaries where nutrients and energy are endlessly cascaded and the laws of physics are followed without exception. Following a cascading model and capitalising on the principles of physics helps to appropriately respond to basic needs, in every location, with is locally available resources. Instead of contrived scarcity and shortages, what we see in a Blue Economy model is abundance—of food, energy, jobs, and revenue. How many communities would oppose? Given the potential outcome, how many entrepreneurs would refuse the risk of bringing such innovations to the market?

One can also imagine what it means to have the benefit of a platform technology that replaces chemicals with purely physical effects, as the vortex has been documented to do. All can understand what it means for food security when coffee or other agro-waste turns into protein-rich mushrooms, contributes income from both the waste and the mushrooms, and then provides amino-acid rich leftovers as high-quality animal feed. We are building up social capital and eliminating abuse. Yes, when a poor family, or an orphan can provide in their own food, they will not tolerate abuse anymore, nor sell girls into rings of prostitution to survive. We are turning a globally traded commodity like coffee into a resource for food security. Food security offers people dignity. Surely, everyone can understand such value.

Empowering Entrepreneurs

The model for a Blue Economy is based on what is real. While job losses and youth unemployment are dramatic in the industrialised world, the reality to be confronted is that the present economic disarray leaves no place for the one billion new arrivals entering the labour market, especially those from developing nations. The incapacity to imagine meaningful jobs and to provide worthy challenges to a whole generation equates to telling the young that there is no future for them, that their generation is lost. Every night over a billion people go to sleep hungry. Nearly two billion have no access to safe drinking water. Worse, the current economic system is based on the bankrupt notion of scarcity where growth is funded with debt—mostly government debt—perpetually carried over to future generations who will have to contribute the taxes to cancel our debts of over-consumption. Shortages and deficiencies are considered the logical base and a necessary evil from which a more efficient allocation of resources will evolve. This same scarcity mentality also foments debate and social resistance to innovation, because it portrays such change agents as threats to job security, by proposing to replace labour with no labour.

Thus it will require creativity and inclusiveness of the entrepreneurs in science, social affairs, business, ecology, and media to move us toward a Blue Economy. Natural systems can build local entrepreneurship much as evolution embraced innovations through diversity. There may be no greater power for change than the young at heart, ready and willing to assume the risk. It requires as much clarity of purpose as it requires perseverance. Fortunately, it does not require experience in a given sector, nor a lot of money. It does require maintaining a solid ethical underpinning, and knowing how to generate cash flow against all odds.

As we have noted, innovations outlined in this book may prove hard for mainstream businesses to adopt. Big companies content with producing more of what has proven successful may lack cutting-edge competencies, or may be unwilling to commit the initial capital necessary for a new approach. This is a major advantage for committed entrepreneurs. Basing their actions on solid science and their vision on social and emotional consciousness, they can implement and develop these innovations to create waves of change that infuse every business sector, shifting entire markets towards sustainability. They will succeed by developing successful partnerships, taking advantage of institutional aggregation, and achieving market viability by garnering consumer support across a wide socio-economic stratum. Market success will stem from the availability of better products that cost less than their competition. We need to collectively prepare the next generation of leadership to understand that it is possible to create a company without money or experience; actually that is the only way fundamental innovations have found their way to the market.

A time of crisis, when market leaders are stressed and some are even on the edge of survival, is perhaps the best moment for the young and the young at heart to set their minds on a new business model. Practically speaking, there are not too many careers available when millions of jobs have been lost and well-paid jobs for graduates are the exception rather than the rule. As well, and contrary to expectation, the barriers to market entry are actually lower in a downturn. In a relatively stable economy, innovations do not easily find their way to market. However, when the entire economic framework experiences turmoil, decision-makers latch onto any object that seems stable or that stands out. A major firm may be disposed to accept products and methods with a fundamentally new or different approach.

The task of an entrepreneur is literally to coalesce something new into being, to be the carrying force that brings an idea into substance, to be the agent between thought and realisation. Yet alone, even if well funded and passionate, you are just alone. Market success depends on partnerships and teamwork. One of the ways to succeed with the introduction of these innovations is to build partnerships with change agents who have the power to influence the market and tip the balance. Innovations do not necessarily flow into the market, nor are company executives and investment bankers the only players who shape the market. Often market breakthroughs are brought about by change agents. Although numerous innovative consortia exist (consider the role of media, grass-roots activists, and NGOs [non-governmental organisations]), there are established ways to create pressure effectively.

For example, insurance companies have the pulse of today's market, tabulating trends in the world economy through the monies they must pay out when disasters occur. Insurance companies are an obvious pressure point for bringing about change in the market, especially when savings are substantial. They closely follow a wealth of statistics, which is one of their core competences. No one knows how to crunch numbers better. In fact, a decision on their part to object to business as usual is based entirely on the simple science of statistics. Insurance companies, along with consumers, institutional investors, local communities and local governments, are the stakeholders who drive decisions that stimulate innovation beyond the steady pace and comfort zone of industry.

To illustrate this, let us consider how insurance companies earn money offering fire insurance policies. When infant death by fire became a concern based on statistical data, insurance companies and industry manufacturers lobbied for the adoption of requirements specifying the use of fire and flame retardants. The risk of fire damage statistically decreases when any fire and flame retardant is used. A lower incidence of fire means an increase in industry's profit. A few decades later, if their statistics indicate an increase in male infertility, allergies, or even cancer at young age, and these figures can be scientifically linked to the fire and flame retardants in use, then the insurance industry can once again stimulate change by urging lawmakers to accept a new standard or a new solution, while restricting (even against will of the industry) the agents suspected of causing such conditions.

Insurance companies and their expert statisticians know all too well that correlation does not prove cause and effect. Rather, it is the reversal of the burden of proof that changes the business model. To achieve a secure angle, the company must demonstrate that it has considered all options and has concluded that negative effects could never occur. For change agents, it offers another lever for securing faster acceptance of breakthrough innovations. In our case in point, consider that insurers could earn multiple revenues by selling product liability policies to the makers of toxic fire retardants. If emerging evidence were to link a particular chemical to a specific illness, the liability insurance premium would increase, perhaps to a point where cost pressures would spur management to change even faster than legal guidelines dictate. The cost of insurance and the reluctance of re-insurance companies to cover the risks would force the company into action.

Insurance companies can further augment their revenue potential by integrating data from each of their separate risk businesses. This would provide a formidable base of information with obvious pathways for shifts in industry, encouraging innovations on the recommendation of insurance companies. Health insurers could link toxicity beyond the Ames Test, which assesses the mutagenic potential of chemical compounds. They could rank the chemicals suspected to cause health problems, suggesting substitutes.

Three Levels of Sustainability

All too often industry finds natural substitutes for effective but toxic products, then manufactures the natural replacements in the traditional 'heat and beat' mode that is responsible for our excessive carbon footprint. When industry finds solutions in biology, it reverts to cloning and genetic manipulation to secure 'predictable' results. Thus, the inspiration from nature to find substitute molecules for the market's standard bearers requires more than the simple shift from one molecule to another. The molecule and the manufacturing system must be inspired by natural processes to create the desired convergence toward sustainability. A Blue Economy offers a blueprint that follows physics and nature in materials selection and production methods. From this basis, it initiates a generative and regenerative cascade of implementable innovations. We thus have sustainable product, sustainable manufacture, and sustainable whole systems. In terms of business and economic benefit, this creates competitive products, competitive processes, and competitive business models that go far beyond core business practice.

Nature works at ambient temperature and pressure. Even abalone shells and spider silk, which are stronger than the bullet-proof ceramic Kevlar™, are methodically assembled—the former one layer by layer, the latter by pressure and moisture control only. The shells are made from calcium carbonate and proteins, materials that are completely locally sourced. Silk is made from protein. These processes are sustainable. The manufacturer could argue that nature produces too little, too slowly, and that industry standards require efficient, timely and predictable results. It is true that the time needed to manufacture ceramics in an oven at a temperature over 1000° is considerably less than that needed by the abalone. However, a ceramics company purchases mined materials. These mines had to be discovered. A permit was needed to exploit the resources. These materials must be shipped around the world, processed (at high pressure and high temperature to speed and standardise operations and product output) and delivered in the appropriate format. When we take these factors into account, beginning with search for the mine to the arrival of calcium carbonate at the ceramic production facilities, the time and efficiency advantage is less obvious. It is worth noting that whenever mining is part of the production process, natural systems will perform faster and at a fraction of the energy cost.

One Innovation, Multiple Revenues

The innovations described herein clearly have the potential to generate multiple revenue streams. The market turns around money; money is thus a medium of exchange. Innovations that generate more market applications have greater appeal, and are thus most likely to be embraced by established businesses and entrepreneurs. The opportunity to generate multiple revenues is a very attractive phenomenon since it mobilises parallel investments for several niche markets. This reduces the risk of innovation. Nonetheless, these are still high risk investments. The terms may not be appealing for the inventors, but the urgent need for cash might make them accept an investment agreement.

In a downturn, cash is king. Those who have billions to invest can easily set the terms of a deal. The model of a core business with a single revenue stream is often preferred by investors who want management to focus on the single most promising application. Any investor will hire MBAs to assess a new technology's chances for success. Entrepreneurial companies wishing to raise venture capital must reveal a very long list of 'things that can go wrong'. At the same time, hardened Silicon Valley venture capital companies will listen to a presentation of one innovation with dozens of possible applications. Without exception, they will ask for the one application that guarantees to gross US$100 million within three years and ask the inventors to make abstraction of all other opportunities that combined could be a multiple of the 100-million dream factory.

While risks are inherent to business, those associated with the majority of the innovations considered and reviewed in this book have been calculated, mitigated, and are found to be much lower than usual for the market. In fact, these innovations can reduce risk because they alter the business model at its core. The achievements of a platform technology where basic parameters have been successfully applied clearly reduces risk and offers potentially better returns than funding a narrowly defined niche. Such a vast potential for sales implies that investors reassess the risk in light of these multiple revenues. This is the key advantage to nearly all the top innovations we describe.

We need not look far to demonstrate this fact. For example, there are 37 known commercial applications for the vortex. There are over 20 for seaweed furanones that control the proliferation of biofilm by jamming bacterial communication (see Chapter 8). Savings are hard to miss in replacing a US$50,000 surgery with a US$500 non-surgical intervention that provides permanent heart monitoring without batteries and at a fraction of the cost. Instead of selling a pacemaker one million times per year, the medical industry can sell monitoring patches a billion times a year.

The silk polymers developed by Oxford Biomaterials (see Chapter 7) are already under development in five different companies, each with separate financing. Peter Steinberg's Australian startup developing antibacterial applications for furanones (see Chapter 8), had a comparable strategy of spinning off potential applications for agriculture, consumer, industrial, medical equipment and therapeutic markets, before its another company. Each of these in turn might raise diverse funds for mobilising niche solutions, such as anti-corrosion in oil and gas, antiperspirants or a potential cure for cystic fibrosis. All derive from the same platform technology. Watreco, the start-up company built around Curt Hallberg's mathematical interpretations of a vortex, brings solutions to the market as varied as saving energy in ice making, speeding percolation on golf greens, de-scaling pipes, and pumping air into fish farm tanks. These venture companies exemplify entrepreneurs who are ready to move businesses forward.

The power of these technologies to provide multiple cash flows through multiple applications reduces risk and dramatically increases value of the intellectual property, potentially allowing inventors to sub-license technological applications and focus on what drives their interest and simulates their curiosity. The power to overcome obstacles requires partnerships. Although inventors and marketers have different goals, a winning coalition can begin with solid leading-edge science and be build on the sharp competitive analysis of entrepreneurs. The world of risk capital is ready to finance people with good ideas. What is needed now is the capacity and willingness to bring innovations to the market.

Innovations with the potential to generate multiple revenues in diverse markets are attractive. If these cash flow generators change the business model, then businesses developing these innovations not only meet an important need, but these also will be pursued as investment and entrepreneurial opportunities.

Cascading Resources in a Community

Such innovations can empower communities to respond to their own needs, especially in societies under major stress. They offer the foundation and means to grow initiatives into movements, achieving market share despite adverse conditions. Communities that have neither money to trade nor capital to invest are often regarded as less responsive to the introduction of new ideas. Yet, the achievements of Father Godfrey Nzamujo in Benin, Chido Govera in Zimbabwe, and Paolo Lugari in Colombia demonstrate that this is not true. The design and implementation of these integrated biosystems have converted non-viable communities into economic successes where money flows and capital grows. Half of the world's human population lives in rural or agricultural settings. Developing nations with rural and agricultural populations can greatly benefit from integrated biosystems complemented with bio-refineries, such as the method of conversion used in Las Gaviotas for collecting resin from harvested trees, locally processed with renewable energies from the region into nine different products, with all waste from the process used in the production of construction materials. Integrated biosystems will also permit industrialised nations to dramatically reduce their ecological footprint and increase their material efficiency.

Real Opportunities, Real Solutions

This shift in business model that is becoming more evident and necessary develops from our growing understanding of nature's MBA—how natural systems rely on the forces of physics, rather than consuming resources of the planet and the very things needed to support survival. The impact is surprising. The results are compelling. There are vaccines that need no refrigeration, heart rhythm devices that need no surgery, vortex technologies that de-scale water pipes without chemicals, algae that defeat bacteria by deafness, or silk that cuts with razor-sharpness—the list is long! The replacement of something that is chemically toxic and clearly unsustainable with what is nothing more than a natural process may well help solve the biggest challenges of our time, while opening a window of opportunity for a portfolio of completely new products and services.

This opportunity to replace something with nothing—to replace a toxic or non-renewable material or process with one that relies merely on physics and natural processes—is particularly exciting. The capacity to reduce risk by generating more cash flow makes products and services competitive. This is where it will foster a new wave of entrepreneurship. Consequently, millions of sustainable jobs will be created, fundamentally shifting old model products and bygone production methods to innovations and processes based on the scientific understanding of already benchmarked solutions, which encourage the next generation to become innovators. The billions of years of experience accumulated in the evolution of ecosystems and species do count, when it comes to perfecting solutions and providing alternatives for different environments. These are proven solutions that evidence resilience and flexibility.

In past decades, the goal of sustainability required everyone to pay and invest more to save the environment or reduce pollution. Few were prepared or willing to adopt this means to effect that goal. Even government tax levies and fines for polluting practices did not noticeably promote stewardship. We even condone today the cleaning up of rivers in Europe using palm oil farmed on destroyed rain forests in Indonesia. And how supportive are you of an economy where everything that is good for your health and for the Earth is expensive, but for the happy few?

Now we can achieve better results and create multiple revenue sources, while building social capital and community resilience at lower costs. Those who profited in the past from poor choices can now rationalise investing in new solutions that will strengthen economies and communities from the roots upward. The driving force of success could well be thousands of entrepreneurs whose boundless enthusiasm and commitment more than compensate for any lack of capital or experience. Moreover, innovations with the greatest market success will be those that address basic needs. This is what management wizard, Peter Drucker claimed in the 1980s: "The needs of the poor are opportunities waiting for entrepreneurs."

When manufacturers choose to replace a toxic process with a less toxic alternative, they are simply 'doing less bad'. That is the option taken when billions of dollars are poured into less toxic, although longer lasting, batteries. These batteries still rely on mining, smelting, and harsh chemistry with an overwhelming majority ending up in landfills that pollute the environment, poisoning ecosystems as well as posing a long-term health hazard to us all. Many will argue that a halfway measure is at least on the right track. Yet, this is nothing short of a duplicitous moral standard. We all have the urge to do more good. Let us not accept that doing less bad is good enough. This is the basics of ethics.

Current scientific literature offers insights into thousands of possible breakthroughs inspired by ways that natural species have exhibited to solve challenges to procurement and survival. Although fewer have revealed the entirety of their process, the possibilities remain and the mysteries can be solved. We still have to understand how each breakthrough emerges in a network of networks. Time will permit us to understand and implement innovations that will dramatically shift our methods of production and consumption toward sustainability. This relies on MBAs who can design the business models that emulate Nature's Master of Brilliant Adaptations.

In the next chapters, we will further explore the framework of the Blue Economy on the basis of existing contributions and solutions that are at work presently. A Blue Economy is one that will apply the achievements of ecosystems to economic systems. Indeed, implementing a Blue Economy will ensure that human systems, in fact all living systems, can attain stability and security that will safeguard and maintain their evolutionary and regenerative path.

Table 6.1: The MBA Comparison

	Nature's MBA – Abundance	*Core Business MBA – Scarcity*
1.	Everyone has a job to do and contributes their best.	Unemployment is part of the system.
2.	Thousands of small contributors; many opportunities for entrepreneurship.	Power concentrated among a few. Multinationals rule.
3.	Everything is used: cascading of nutrients, matter and energy.	Minute parts are used. The rest is wasted, abandoned in landfills, indiscriminately incinerated.
4.	Predictable physics provides the first source of power.	First source is non-renewable fossil fuels. Climate change and acidification is guaranteed.
5.	Water is the primary solvent. Chemistry has limited, secondary use.	Heavily reliant on chemistry. Aggressive solvents are used to create covalent links.
6.	Biodiversity is time and place specific. Biology is characterised by exceptions.	Biology is cloned.
7.	Diversity flourishes and continues to evolve.	Standardised and predictable output.
8.	The constant of change is the basis of evolution.	Resistance to fundamental change. Innovative technologies are considered disruptive.
9.	Locally available,resources is put to use.	Centralised manufacture requires global sourcing.
10.	The basic needs of all are met.	Vast numbers of the population are left out even when a majority lives in wealth.
11.	With few exceptions, nearly all models are non-linear.	All calculations are linear.
12.	All materials degrade over time, but transform and reconstitute.	Covalent molecular bonding gives us components that do not degrade for centuries even millennia, even those with an one-time use.
13.	Everything is connected, evolving in symbiosis.	All is a stand-alone. Synergies are discouraged, except in finance.
14.	Clean air and water are free and abundant.	Everything can be sold for profit, even basic necessities like water.
15.	One initiative generates multiple benefits for several partners.	One project equals one cash flow, only for the progenitor and controlling partners.
16.	Risks are shared.	Risk hampers innovation.
17.	Material and energy utilisation is permanently improved; taxation does not exist.	Taxation to redistribute wealth, unsuccessfully due to tax havens.
18.	Optimise the system.	Maximise one critical success factor.
19.	Negatives are converted into positives.	Negatives are mitigated at high cost, or ignored, or passed on, unresolved, to future generations.
20.	Economies are based on scope.	Economies are based on scale.
21.	Generate value with available resources	Cut costs at all costs

7

Ethics at the Core

> **Recycling and renewables are not enough to steer society towards sustainability!**
>
> — *G.P.*

Programs to recycle are applauded and supported. The use of renewable energy is encouraged. Eating organically farmed food is hip, and the switch to vegetarianism is often considered a major step towards sustainability. While all these initiatives are taking us in the right direction, we need a society that not only embraces the circular economy, the green or blue economy, where we all evolve from recycling to upcycling, we need a society that firmly embraces core ethical and universal principles. Ethics is part of the new business model. If we wish to embrace innovative businesses that transform society and inspired by ecosystems, then ethics will have to be at the centre; otherwise we may meet material needs and abate environmental damage, but our disjointed societies will not be redressed on the basis of more efficient flows of material and energy only.

We are often confronted with the harsh realities of our short-sightedness. Biodegradable soaps that use on palm oil depend on large areas of destroyed rainforest. How can we defend cleaning up of the rivers in Europe by destroying the habitat of the orangutan in Asia? Vegetarians who promote the consumption of mushrooms certainly reduce the footprint of their protein consumption by substituting animal and animal feed with fungal protein. However, few mushroom friends realise that shiitake farmers around the world are fast destroying their oak forest in order to boost their produce. This implies that saving animals could well destroy natural forests. We very often do not realise the unintended consequences experienced and therefore we need to think in terms of connections, seeing and searching for the broader impact created, while consuming and producing as we do.

Reinventing Fishing

While we can easily be concerned about our lack of understanding and the subsequent errors, we have several engrained routines that do not allow us to fundamentally change our approach to business and the way we live. Let us take the case of fishing. We should assess a few realities of this industry with a deep ethical perspective. Firstly, we overfish, taking away too much of what can be sustainably harvested. Secondly, while fishing the fish we want, we harvest up to 70 per cent of those we do not want. While this sound quite irresponsible, our fishing techniques do not permit us to differentiate. Thirdly, we drag nets around the ocean, often scraping mile-long dragnets made from Nylon 6 at the bottom of the sea, killing life for years—even decades to come. To make matters worse, a medium-size fishing vessel will consume 250,000 tons of fuel per year, nearly always subsidised by governments. And, apart from needing energy to drag the nets, immense power is consumed to feed the compressors that drive the ice machines. Worse, these vessels (and the processing of their catch) consume more water than communities ever have access to.

While this is the standard worldwide, and the problems are well known, it is difficult to change behaviour in a world of dwindling resources. While everyone desires more of the same, it is exactly that 'more of the same' that destroys ecosystems beyond repair. And while all parties debate the harsh realities of unsustainable fishing, there is one reality that everyone overlooks: female fish with eggs! There is no cattle farmer who will send his cow for slaughter a month before a calf is to be born. There is no fruit farmer who destroys his harvest weeks before fruits are ripe. But all fishermen around the world find it normal to catch females with eggs and throw them along with all other fish on freezing ice. This is one of the most unsustainable acts of modern times, and yet it is never debated nor has any attempt been made to redress this anachronism.

So if we agree on a basic ethical position that females with offsprings should always be protected irrespective of the species, then it becomes clear that we need to change our fishing model. We cannot simply continue to catch fish and submerge it in ice. Basically, freezing temperatures lead to a rapid release of acids attempting to counteract congelation, and while this affects the taste of fish, the freezing approach requires massive energy. In addition to the unethical behaviour, the dragging of nets and the production of ice represent more than half of the energy required to operate a fishing vessel, with the balance needed for propulsion of the boat. If we eliminate the production of ice, and find another way of catching fish than with nets, then the energy requirements of any boat will shift.

The new fishing vessel design starts with a catamaran, powered by electric engines. Fishes can be caught using a combination of nets and air curtains—just like whales and dolphins do—and preserved into cold water tanks with temperatures between 2-4° C. Energy consumption drops dramatically. We could equip the boat with four fixed sails, especially designed for the currents and winds of the region, inspired by unique designs of the BMW-Oracle ship that won the Americas Cup. When there is no wind, the masts drop and convert the sails in solar panels capable of generating electricity to power engines. The goal is to quickly process all the fishes into value-added products. It is here that an innovative ecographics system permits to check each fish for eggs. A breakthrough technology, much along the same logic as pregnancy tests that is performed for decades, permits the identification of pregnant fishes. Each female with eggs is immediately released from her state of hibernation and put back into the sea water, thereby securing repopulation of the fish stock.

We often lose sight of the fact that a half-kilogram female fish can carry up to 500 eggs, whereas an one can kilogram fish can have 3,000 eggs. The magnificent sun fish, which weighs up to one tone when mature; can carry as many as 300 million eggs. Are you surprised that this fish is critically endangered when we not only catch the females, but also enjoy eating the eggs as a delicacy? This exponential growth in reproductivity is the main reason why the catching of females is so counterproductive. The experience on El Hierro in the Canary Islands (Spain) permitted to demonstrate that the protection of female fishes through creation of an United Nations Educational Scientific and Cultural Organization (UNESCO) Biosphere zone provides the opportunity to redress fish stocks within two years, offering thereafter an exponential growth in productivity and fish catch. While the fishermen of El Hierro applied the simple approach of total protection of an area known as the egg spawning area, the innovative ecographics approach permits a very targeted selection of all egg-bearing females.

The design of fishing vessels that take into account the protection of reproductive fishes will shift the logic of the business model. And, as always happens once a direction is chosen, a cascade of additional innovations emerges. A boat that requires no ice, nor power to drag nets, can operate with electric power only. When the boat is sailing with wind, it can even generate power from the woke by applying the same principle as a hybrid car, recovering energy from the brakes—now from the turbulence caused by sailing. This new vessel design is the most sustainable and while offering opportunities to cut out fuel altogether, it also creates chances to translate the subsidies associated with fuel for the fishing industry into financing for the new vessels. Indeed, every government around the world reserves state funding to support fishermen. Now if the new catamaran operates without fuel, then the subsidies committed for years to come can be converted into a net present value that takes subsidies (and corruption) out of the equation and puts renewable squarely on track.

The new designs of the vessel which checks each fish for eggs, now processes the whole catch on the boat, thus generating more revenue from filets, Omega-3, collagen and fish meal that is produced from all process left overs. This allows to conduct processing with seawater, thus saving drinking water on shore and permits the sale of the processed catch prior to landing. This system cuts down the intermediation by middlemen securing that the fishermen, who at the end of the day risk their lives generate at least double the income, and in some cases (especially owing to the Omega-3) even five times their standard revenue. A new boat benefits from a start-up funding owing to the elimination of subsidies, and enjoys lower risks, given to the generation of more income with available resources.

This breakthrough design is driven by a simple yet blunt statement when it comes to sustainability: protect the female fishes carrying eggs. It is seldom that the drive towards sustainability generates better income and more jobs, while eliminating dependence on fossil fuels. However, the most important result of this paradigm shift is that more cash is now circulating in the local economy and this generates a badly needed multiplier effect urgently needed to create growth in the local economy exploiting sustainable available resources.

Once the multiplier effect kicks in, then one sees the brain-drain back. This project has been pioneered in Morocco, a joint-venture between French and Moroccan entrepreneurs. The power of this approach is that highly qualified Moroccan engineers are keen to contribute to this innovative business development operating out of Caen (Normandy, France), and soon they will want to travel back to their motherland contributing to re-industrialisation of the economy that can even include the local construction of fishing vessels, a sector everyone had considered long gone and impossible to ever recover. It took a deep ethical shift in fishing—to protect the expecting females—to lead to the relaunch of industries we could never imagine.

The decision to move beyond reducing the negative impact, and to embark on doing good, is in the end an ethical decision. If you are ignorant about your impact, then you have unintended consequences. If you knowingly cause a negative impact, then you are responsible for collateral damage. When you know you can do good, and you refuse to do it, then it is unethical behaviour.

8

Multiple Cash Flows

> **Give me a place to stand,**
> **and I can move the Earth!**
>
> — *ARCHIMEDES*

In times of upheaval, positive minds look for solutions, wherever they can. There are always areas of growth even when the overall economy is considered to be in decline. Health care, food production, renewable energy and pollution control are four areas, where there is consensus that increased expenditures are certain even in rough times. Few markets better exemplify growth potential than the burgeoning worldwide demand for edible and medicinal mushrooms.

Ever since a middle class with purchasing power emerged in China, demand for the fruiting bodies of shiitake (*Lentinula edodes*) and other fungi has been explosive. Double-digit growth rates have been the norm for over two decades. Europe and North America are also discovering the unique nutritional and medicinal effects of several mushrooms with unfamiliar names, like Judas ear (*Auricularia auricula*), enoki (*Flamminula velutipes*), maitake (*Grifola fondosa*), or reishi (*Ganoderma lucidum*). Soon these words may well become part of our daily vocabulary just like expresso, latte, sushi, and pizza.

Demand for fungi and the number of jobs required to meet that demand has risen ever since these delicacies could be produced at will. Wu Sangong, a 13th century farmer-scientist, initiated the Chinese foray into healthy protein from fungi, one of the five kingdoms of nature. The shiitake capital of the world is Qingyuan, located in the Pearl Delta of Guangdong, China. Qingyuan is smaller than the San Francisco Bay Area, yet this region employs over 120,000 people farming shiitake mushrooms with a market value in the West of over US$1 billion. According to Prof Shuting Chang, the mushroom expert who taught for years at Chinese University of Hong Kong and has made major contributions to the international success of mushroom farming, the total export value of Chinese mushroom cultivation topped US$20 billion and supported 12 million jobs in 2012. Although for decades this has surprised Western food and population experts, fungi (*Volvariella volvacea*) grown on rice straw clearly contribute to food security for China's large population.

Harvested remains of plants, fruits and vegetables (Plant Kingdom) provide feed for chickens, ducks, pigs and fish (Animal Kingdom). This food source is complemented by protein from mushrooms (Fungi Kingdom), which prodigiously converts plant waste, especially straw, to food. Bacteria (Monera Kingdom) are also mobilised in digesters in order to convert manure to a growth medium for algae (Protoctista Kingdom) in shallow open air ponds.

Annual US demand for tropical mushrooms is barely 200 grams per person per year. Consumption in Canada is already double that amount. Hong Kong reaches an amazing 30 pounds per person per year. If US consumers were to eat only as much fungi as Canadians, this would translate into an additional US$2 billion in revenue. If the US population were to shift its food habits to match those of Hong Kong, the tropical mushroom industry would top most other businesses in the world at today's market prices for petroleum and mushrooms. The significance of this order of magnitude is that mushrooms are traditionally farmed on agricultural waste, which is widely considered a nuisance and often simply burned.

The biomasses from plant husks, cobs, or straw on which mushrooms thrive contain no protein or polysaccharides of any importance, yet mushrooms are rich in protein. Based on dry weight, some varieties of oyster mushroom compete with meat for concentration of protein as well as all the essential amino acids. Interestingly, white button mushrooms (*Agaricus bisporus*) remain the most consumed species in the West, despite containing the least protein and requiring pasteurised horse manure to grow. Some countries even import this waste from overseas to locally farm the white buttons. Imagine, we have world free trade in horse manure to produce low quality protein! This is neither a sustainable nor a competitive business model for achieving the nutrient needs of an expanding world population. The only one who makes money on promoting this business is the hardware salesman.

The interplay of natural systems is capable of securing a cascade of protein from multiple sources, and is thus free of reliance on a single source. This provides insight into ways to facilitate worldwide food security with what is locally available. Mushrooms convert plant waste into edible fruiting bodies. The portion of the fungi that remains in the substrate after harvest is mycelium, which is highly nutritious, and full of essential amino acids for animals. Animals in turn generate manure which bacteria digest, enriching the soil so as to help plants and microorganisms thrive. The cascading of nutrients from one species belonging to one kingdom to another species belonging to a separate kingdom is an ecosystems marvel. That is why there is neither starvation nor unemployment in an ecosystem. Everyone is busy contributing their best, gaining sustenance from something that was waste for another, and satisfying the basic needs of all.

The business model for the production of tropical mushrooms is simple. First, a fibrous biomass is sterilised under pressure and high temperature, although many know how to skip this process saving the energy cost. The growing medium is mostly dead or dying biological matter. Next, mushroom spores are introduced in small quantities. Since bacteria have been largely eliminated by the sterilisation process, the mycelium quickly expand into the substrate over a few weeks. Once the substrate is fully populated, a thermal or water shock is applied. This causes the fruiting bodies to emerge. Mushrooms typically reproduce quickly when their survival is threatened. What we refer to as 'mushrooms' are the offspring—the fruiting bodies.

The Chinese reuse all straw waste to grow straw mushrooms. Unfortunately, several straw crops have been genetically modified, as is the case with rice, to have short stalks and thus much less straw. Elsewhere in the world straw is burned, generating massive air pollution. Burning rice straw is a horrendous problem in Egypt, affecting upwards of 20 million people along the Nile Delta. Those who study massive population needs have yet to emulate the Chinese wisdom of converting straw into protein, and the mushroom substrate into animal feed. In fact, countries such as Egypt have adopted genetically modified short-straw rice, and have simultaneously experienced a shortfall in food security, relying on imported wheat to make up the difference. This is where we find the obvious business opportunities.

Current mushroom farming practices are not always sustainable. Where oak is used as the preferred growing medium, it is logged, shredded, and converted into a high quality growth substrate for shiitake, one of the priciest and healthiest mushrooms on the international market. The rapidly increasing demand for shiitake strains harvest capacity of oak forests throughout China.

Over the past 20 years, innovative and efficient farming of local and tropical mushrooms has evolved to a low cost, competitive, year-round business. The innovations are multiple and have led to the creation of a new business model for production and marketing. The model of mushroom farming inspired by the cascading of nutrients in ecosystems has been benchmarked in Africa, Latin America and recently in Europe. An increased Western demand for exotic mushrooms, coupled with a price trend towards greater affordability, would be critical for securing widespread adoption of this cholesterol-free, fat-free food. Increased demand would spur cultivators to search for more abundant waste materials as a growing medium. Since mushroom farming is relatively more labour intensive, this waste-to-food chain would create thousands, even millions of jobs. Entrepreneurs working locally to realise this potential would create job opportunities, particularly in areas where accessing the employment market holds greater challenge.

The Buzz about Coffee

At the turn of the 21st century, mushrooms overtook coffee as the second most widely traded commodity. Now a new opportunity is seen to emerge that will increase the value of both: mushrooms grown on coffee waste. There are two waste streams related to coffee. The bulk of the waste is generated on the farm and is known as pulp. Brewing coffee produces a second waste stream known as grounds. From the time the beans leave the farms to the moment they are done with brewing in coffee pots, 99.8 per cent ends as waste and only 0.2 per cent is ingested. While this currently contributes mightily to the waste management issues we noted earlier, there is now a positive and creative approach that cascades waste streams generated by both farms and coffee shops into nutrient streams for mushrooms. This opens up an unparalleled opportunity. The farmer earns about one-tenth of a cent on a coffee shop espresso that sells for US$3, a mark-up factor of 3,000! Given that the annual world consumption of coffee in 2011 was 139 million bags (one bag is 60 kilograms), the total biomass left to rot is a shocking 25 million tons. If the value realised from the coffee bean can be replicated or even surpassed with the potential value of waste released from coffee harvest and production, it would be a genuine bonanza.

Mushrooms grow on ligno-cellulose. The massive waste generated in the process of converting coffee from a berry on a bush to a beverage in a cup is mainly ligno-cellulose. Better yet, coffee is a hardwood, like oak. In 1992, Prof Shuting Chang, whom we had introduced earlier, demonstrated that coffee is an ideal substrate for cultivating mushrooms, especially oyster and shiitake. Even the medicinal and highly-prized reishi thrives on coffee grounds. This means that if all coffee grounds and pulp were converted to a substrate, we could add 25 million tons of protein to the world's food table.

From farm, to roaster, to consumer, the coffee bean is a perfectly monitored crop. Seldom will you find any agricultural product that is subject to more stringent quality controls. When the coffee beans are processed on the farms, the husk is fermented off, and then toasted to perfection. When coffee is brewed, hot water or steam at high temperature passes through and sterilises the ground and roasted beans. All this is to great advantage for mushroom purposes, as it simplifies the production process of mushroom farming. The steamed and wetted grounds, returned to the packages of their arrival, can be directly inoculated with mushroom spores without the added necessity of sterilisation. This would further reduce cost and readily supply local entrepreneurs. In addition, since the caffeine stimulus in the coffee grounds encourages some mushrooms to fruit faster, using grounds would generate a better cash flow than the typical mushroom farm. This corresponds perfectly with our economic ideal: less investment, more cash flow; one initiative, multiple benefits. This translates to lower cost, faster output, higher customer loyalty and better cash flow.

A venture that converts waste into a highly nutritious food that is cheaper and healthier for everyone is attractive in these challenging times. From a business perspective, the best message is that this method offers improved cash flow, which interests investors and bankers. After Prof Chang undertook the first scientific studies, Carmenza Jaramillo spent six years studying the utilisation of coffee waste to propagate fungi for CENICAFE, the research institute of the Colombian Federation of Coffee Farmers. She published more than 20 peer-reviewed scientific papers in international journals to report and document her findings. Dr Ivanka Milenkovic at the University of Belgrade scientifically analysed the use of mushroom substrate as animal feed and found no loss of meat or milk production. Clearly, this Pulp-to-Protein method has major economic benefits.

It is unfortunate that on the farms, coffee pulp is simply left to rot, often with the excuse that it is good fertiliser. Annually, 16 million tons of organic waste are left to decompose on coffee farms and in landfills, producing millions of tons of greenhouse gas. The Pulp-to-Protein approach reduces the need to harvest wood. This allows trees, particularly the hardwoods such as oak, to continue to fix carbon, which slows the adverse effects of climate change. Feeding waste back into the nutrient cycle simplifies waste management and cuts methane gas emissions from rotting biomass. The integration of mushrooms and coffee leads to a dramatic reduction of every negative. In combination, two negatives become a positive.

When we look at coffee from the perspective of global development, we realise that the use of pulp on coffee farms would offer many advantages that would offset the negative impact that has tainted this cash-crop monoculture for decades. What we see in the current model is that coffee as a cash crop provides a living for farmers and their communities only when market prices are high. The moment the price drops below a certain threshold, farmers, their families, and their communities suffer. Significant decrements in coffee prices result in the onset of poverty so severe that many *cafeteros* plow their coffee bushes into the soil, turning to subsistence farming with two cows per acre on their plot of land and little or no chance of ever making ends meet. Unable to feed his family and prepared to do anything to save them from hunger, the farmer moves with his family to a shantytown at the edge of an urban area, joining millions of others looking for jobs that pay little and offer only a bleak future.

At the end of the 20th century, Vietnam became the world's second largest exporter of coffee, creating economic havoc in many countries, particularly in Africa. However, as soon as coffee and mushrooms become a unified ecosystem, the dichotomy between cash crops and food security evaporates. We can envision a potential end to poverty in the coffee regions from a nutrient cascade, involving plants, fungi, and animals. Each pound of farm waste generates at least half a pound of protein-rich food for the farming family. As the mushroom substrate is an excellent (and free) animal feed, farmers will be able to afford and maintain livestock, which will further augment their nutrient needs and food security. It is a unique opportunity to observe how the waste of a cash crop like coffee can provide food security and many additional benefits. These farming techniques can resonate with the young, the unemployed and the disadvantaged, as well as with hardened MBAs who see an opportunity to generate cash from nothing. A decade of field experience in Zimbabwe gives us a brilliant demonstration of these benefits.

Table 8.1: Multiple Benefits of the Pulp-to-Protein Model of Coffee Waste To Mushroom Nutrient
(To Meet the United Nations Millennium Development Goals)

For Consumer and Producer		*For the Planet*	
Richer	coffee provides the ideal nutrients and growing medium for mushrooms	Low Energy	coffee grounds are sterilised, no further processing is necessary
Cleaner	both brewing and inoculation require only hot water	Less Methane	grounds used won't decompose in landfills so less greenhouse gas
Faster	caffeine makes mushrooms grow faster	Less Grazing	post-harvest substrate is a high-quality animal feed
Cheaper	raw materials are free	Less Logging	coffee is also a hardwood and an ideal substitute for oak
Healthier	mushrooms are protein-rich and cholesterol- and fat-free	Less Landfill	coffee shops waste removal costs and contribute less to landfill waste
Food Security	waste from the cash crop secures food for the region	Food Security	waste from the cash crop secures food for the region

Source: Author.

The 'Orphan Teaches Orphans' programme, started by Chido Govera who was herself orphaned at the age of 7, teaches other orphans how to grow mushrooms using locally available agricultural waste, including water hyacinth, an invasive species that proliferates throughout much of Africa. Water hyacinth has been named 'Public Enemy Number One' in Zambia, and is fought with chemicals and non-native species like the weevil beetle that is imported from Australia. Yet, one kilogram of water hyacinth can provide the nutrient base for

Table 8.2: Pulp-to-Protein to Mitigate Climate Change

Impact on Climate Change	*Progress Towards Millennium Goals*
Low energy use	Food Security
Preservation of forests	Empowerment of Women
Lower Transportation Energy Costs	Improved Childhood Health
No Landfill	Environmental Sustainability
No Methane Gas	Global Partnerships
Elimination of Charcoal Usage	Fight HIV/AIDS
Cultivation of Slow Food	Learning Self-Sufficiency

Source: Author.

up to two kilograms of mushrooms. Chido collects wild mushrooms during the rainy season and has mastered tissue culture techniques for the production of mushroom seed stock. With Chido's inspiration and guidance these orphan girls, who have suffered much, find the will and acquire the skills to build a future without abuse and provide for their livelihood and sustenance. Food security motivates many to think beyond food.

Pulp to Livelihood

Based on results in Colombia, each coffee farm undertaking mushroom cultivation could generate two new jobs. With an estimated 25 million coffee farms in 45 countries, this translates to an additional 50 million jobs worldwide, while providing food security not just for the workers but for their families as well. If we include other waste streams like straw, cobs, clippings and water hyacinth, we are quickly edging towards truly amazing numbers. The capacity to provide local food for local populations increases farm income and farm stability. Instead of expending time and money to gather a subsistence diet with only the most basic nutrients, a considerable quantity of healthful and protein-rich food as well as animal feed can be derived from mushroom production.

This is only a tributary of the cascading model of the emerging Blue Economy. It provides an economic stimulus to generate jobs in rural areas. It has the potential to become one of the engines to re-launch the world economy. If there are jobs on the farms that pay, provide food, and ensure that generations of expertise and tradition are used to their full potential, none will be tempted to leave for a bleak future in slums of the nearest metropolis. By now, thousands of village women have been trained in Zimbabwe, Ghana, Tanzania, Congo, Cameroon, South Africa and even in India using this simple methodology. Chido is presently preparing a special training center, The Future of Hope in the vicinity of Harare, the capital of Zimbabwe, to institutionalise this health and food security programme.

There are other tributaries: the creation of inner-city jobs. Worldwide, coffee grounds are produced in more than 100,000 inner-city coffee shops. From the Arab cities of the Middle East, to the *kohi shoppu* in Tokyo, to the traditional French cafés and the voracious American coffee culture, converting coffee grounds into mushrooms could mean a potential 100,000 additional jobs in urban zones. This pioneering effort has been tested and proven in Amsterdam by Jan Willem Bosmans and his start-up company, GRO Holland in cooperation with the restaurant chain, La Place, as well as in the San Francisco Bay area where Nikhil Aurora and Alex Velez decided to forego a consulting career and create their coffee/mushroom company, BTTR Ventures. Siemen Cox and Mark Slegers even converted a defunct public swimming pool into a thriving mushroom cultivation and training centre in Rotterdam. It is no surprise that by 2015, we have over 3000 mushroom farming initiatives on record. And it only has just begun! Knowing that orphans in Zimbabwe can farm mushrooms with hardly anything but local waste, the assurance of success in the city is robust.

Jobs are only sustainable if income is generated. Income is only sustained when value is added. The core of this proposition is healthy food at a lower cost and with greater availability. That part of the market will always grow because of its price elasticity—lower prices create proportionally more demand, sustaining the farmer's livelihood and expending the business. Calculations using research data and hands-on experience indicate that the income potential from cultivating mushrooms in a coffee ground substrate is vast. Considered together, and solely on the basis of coffee waste, the inner-city and farm-based production units could produce an estimated 25 million tons of additional nutrients for human consumption. This is more than half the protein provided by the entire world's fish farming. And today, we are aware that the same can be done with spent tea leaves! It is a secure revenue stream and a major resource for a global food market that is under severe stress from population explosion. Cascading nutrients and energy, not genetic modification, is what will allow us to respond to humanity's basic needs.

Waste has always been unpopular. Aside from what we contribute to the waste stream on a personal basis, massive-scale disasters have turned our attention toward nuclear waste, petroleum spills, and chlorine pollution. The branding of waste has been universally negative. Imagine now a waste that generates jobs and healthy food. This is only good news. Since coffee pulp and coffee grounds make such an ideal substrate for mushrooms, and generate all the aforcementioned benefits, it should be touted and made part of coffee's image: Coffee makes for healthy food and secure jobs. Coffee can be associated with energy efficiency, sustainable livelihood, climate change mitigation, and even nourishing food at lower prices. The social capital would be substantial and widespread. Considering that it all started from something considered waste, coffee can hardly be positioned more positively. Whose waste is it really?

It would be an admirable act of corporate social responsibility if coffee traders of the world—from Neumann Kaffee Gruppe to Nestlé Foods—were to ensure that the farms they buy from convert all on-site waste to an ideal mushroom growing medium. It would create jobs and enhance food security. If the proponents of fair trade were to provide their farmers with the technical assistance necessary for converting waste to mushrooms, with whom would farmers prefer to trade? Cascading coffee waste could become a strategic tool for positioning long-term supply contracts with farmers, importers and roasters.

To go one step further, traders and consumers who already support the organic and fair trade movements can be made aware that the real arena for fairness, the real opportunity for growth and development, can come from 99.8 per cent of the coffee harvest that has little value for those who harvest, purvey and consume the bean. Such a viewpoint goes far beyond organic and fair trade. It permits the coffee trade to embrace sustainable development to the fullest extent anyone has ever imagined. The label, organic only certifies the absence of chemical fertilisers and sprays. It does not say anything about resource efficiency. The label, Fair Trade secures a fairer reimbursement for farmers, but does not secure the added value for the environment. Few coffee drinkers actually realise how little of the biomass generated at a coffee farm is consumed, or the wastefulness associated with their consumption habits. If the traders and distributors helped foster a Pulp-to-Protein model on the farms whose beans they market, such collaboration would then bring about self-sustaining communities that experience food and livelihood security, as opposed to malnourishment and despair. What incredible potential might be redirected for benefit of the poor, the jobless, and the Earth!

The Pulp-to-Protein initiative is based on the power of ecosystems, and builds on worthy organic and fair trade initiatives. It creates value for 100 per cent of the nutrients. If fully developed in all coffee-producing communities, by turning a waste stream into an income stream, this business model could generate a staggering 1.5 million times more revenue than coffee produces today. It is in this fashion that entrepreneurs in the emerging Blue Economy will look at all waste streams, and succeed either by eliminating them or by converting them into tributaries that cascade livelihood, food security and abundance for all.

Table 8.3: The Pulp-to-Protein Machine

Jobs on the farm	1 acre farm = 2 jobs x 25 million coffee farms worldwide = 50 million jobs
Jobs in the inner cities	10-15 coffee shops = 1 farming unit = 10 jobs x 21,000 coffee shops in the U.S. + 100,000 ~ worldwide = 1.2 million jobs
Results	25 million tons of fresh protein worldwide in +45 countries 5x sales increase 2000–2010 – worldwide 51.2 million jobs

Source: Author.

Let us do the numbers together. If we are using the totality of the biomass, and not just the 0.2 per cent that ends up being ingested, then we improve the material use to factor 500. If we generate as much value added as a coffee shop in any major city does, where a cup of coffee includes 3 grams, bringing the farmer an income of one hundredth of a dollar (one cent) but is sold for US$3, then we are looking at a potential of factor 3,000. If we combine the two opportunities (factor 500 and factor 3000), then we realise that coffee has a potential revenue that is 1.5 million times the present economy.

Imagine how much better that cup of coffee would taste to the well-to-do of the world when they realise that their purchase has helped to train another coffee farming community in ways to achieve self-determination, sustainability, and food and livelihood security. The invigorating effect of coffee would be enhanced with the flavour of satisfaction, and without further expense. The consumer has the power to channel what they pay to those who do it sustainably and equitably, using locally available resources, providing food for all and empowering communities.

These mushroom cultivation programs have been field tested and fully realised from Colombia to Zimbabwe, from San Francisco to the Netherlands. The Colombian state of El Huila has over a hundred coffee-to-mushroom companies and is rapidly replacing illegal crops with nutritious food. The conclusion of all contributors is that this works. The expertise is fully prepared and readily available.

The power of a just and sustainable economic model is that it generates greater value for all stakeholders. The Pulp-to-Protein business model does not advocate investing more to save money or to recover the additional expense, but stresses on reducing costs for everyone while generating additional revenue. When waste becomes nutrient, it creates value that can be measured in jobs, cash flow and profits. Green business and fair trade are stepping stones. Economies that cascade like ecosystems achieve the goal of providing multiple benefits for diverse partners.

From Waste to Superfood

Continuing to play with the potential of our Pulp-to-Protein model, let us imagine an entrepreneurial enterprise that makes coffee and coffee consumers healthier: an infusion of medicinal mushroom with that espresso or latte. Most mushrooms are rich in protein. Reishi and shiitake are prized nutritional varieties that are also medicinal marvels. In ancient times, the wild red reishi was exclusively reserved for the Emperor of China. Although little is published in the way of clinical trials, the beneficial influence of these mushroom varieties for health conditions ranging from diabetes to hypertension is time-tested in traditional medicine. If the costs of these exotic mushrooms can be reduced using the aforementioned production system, a bit of Ganoderma in that morning cup can be offered to customers wishing for an instant immune-system booster. It would even take the acidity out of that energy drink, balance the pH naturally, and make its digestion easier.

This arithmetic is attractive for all the parties involved. Beyond the first mileposts of employment, income and nourishment, if Starbucks were to offer its worldwide customer base a healthy Ganoderma infusion for their coffee, it would initiate a massive increase in demand for the mushroom that in Japanese means "one thousands lives." If only a hundred customers each day at the 19,000 Starbucks coffee shops around the world were to order a fluff of Ganoderma in their espresso, macchiato, latte, or chai, at say US$0.50 a serving, it would annualise to an impressive additional revenue of US$365 million.

Consider further that were Starbucks to help develop the Pulp-to-Protein programme on the coffee farms and in urban areas, it can easily donate 10 per cent of their increase in revenue, or US$36.5 million dollars per year, to fund the effort. This would handily pay for itself in terms of social capital and tax-deductible expense, to say nothing of the employment, income, and nourishment made possible from a market consuming approximately two tons of Ganoderma per day. Such a sum represents US$25 per pound of mushrooms for the coffee farmer. Where the cash transfer of the total value in coffee itself is one to the farmer, and 2,999 to everyone else, for Ganoderma the terms of trade could tilt towards one for the farmer and 10 for everyone else. This would generate a net cash infusion into rural and inner-city economies, which would effectively stimulate supply and demand, build consumer confidence and social capital, and provide opportunities for jobs and education seldom seen or mentioned today.

Negative branding of waste through publicising blacklists of the world's worst polluters has caught attention of the public at large. With the Pulp-to-Protein model, we have nothing less than a complete re-branding of waste. A product negatively associated with exploitation and poverty could be transformed into a means to eradicate injustice and generate livelihood security. The chance for such a positive accomplishment comes at an opportune moment. Positive branding marks a shift in the focus of the business model. Entrepreneurs who are prepared to adapt to these business models can play a critical role in society by empowering their clients to speak with their purchasing power.

Tea as well could quickly engender a Pulp-to-Protein initiative of its own. The amount of tea biomass that is ultimately consumed in a cup of tea is only half of that from coffee, a mere one-tenth of one per cent. Fruit tree clippings are another possibility as a medium for exceptional mushroom growth. These hardwood species lack the added stimulus of caffeinated coffee grounds. They are nonetheless a quality wood that should not be incinerated as is the current practice. Ivanka Milenkovic from the University of Belgrade tested apple orchard clippings as a growth substrate for mushroom cultivation. Not even the coldness of winter seemed to slow down mushroom growth. In the field tests, goats were partaking of the substrate residue at harvest, even before scientists could establish the amino acid content. As noted earlier, bison herds in New Mexico share that appetite.

There are endless possibilities and resources. The key is simply to uncover value in waste. Water hyacinth is an ornamental plant from Latin America that creates havoc in tropical lakes, rivers and dams, proliferating on the massive flow of nutrients from soil erosion and excessively utilised fertilisers that accumulate in water bodies. Instead of trying to obliterate this invasive aquatic plant, it could be harvested and converted to a growing medium for mushrooms. Although foraging ruminants would not eat the water hyacinth itself, the mushroom substrate remaining after harvest would make an ideal feed. Merely with the waste from coffee, tea, hardwood clippings, water hyacinth, and straw, astronomical volumes of nutrients can be derived.

Ecosystems inspire us to look beyond conventional to cascading models, where waste of one becomes raw material for another. Generating multiple benefits for diverse partners is a fair and positive

Blue Economy model that evolves towards ever greater levels of efficiency with ever more diversity. This is how rainforests regenerate from depleted savannas. This is how a cash crop like coffee can not only provide food security and meet basic needs for clean water, fresh air and healthy soil, but can also substantially augment local income and social capital. Thus while 10,000 jobs today may be considered a success, there are 25 million coffee farms that can benefit from this model. Given the magnitude of possibilities, perhaps even Nestlé, a giant in the coffee trade business, might reconsider its rejection of an undertaking that seemed too far outside its core business definition. With a little vision, perhaps the greater goal of profitability, along with food security and environmental stewardship, would be sufficient.

Drink it—Eat it—Wear it

Opportunities are vast and innovation is often just around the corner, provided we are open to ideas that go beyond status quo. Grandma knew all too well that when the refrigerator had a foul smell, she should put some coffee grounds in it to resolve the problem. Jason Cheng, the founder of Singtex Corporation (Taiwan), turned that observation into a business. He produces textiles mixed when produced with a small percentage of coffee grounds, which jointly control odour and block ultra-violet rays (UV). While we knew coffee eliminates smells, its capacity to block the sun with a protection factor of 50 was a surprise. The complex processing of coffee, starting from a bush that originated in Ethiopia, to a fermentation process that was developed in Colombia, and a roasting technique that was perfected in Italy, provided this Chinese innovator with a tailor-made ingredient. Today, Singtex delivers odour-abating fibres to more than 100 textile companies, including market leaders such as Nike and Adidas, pioneers like Patagonia and innovators like Ecoalf from Spain. These synthetic fibres include 5 per cent fine coffee grounds. The coffee-enriched fabric eliminates odours, even after a good run or climb. It even holds on after multiple washes. Timberland now lines the inside of its shoes with this odour controlling tissue, attaching the label, "Drink It—Wear it".

Synthetic fibres have a value of US$1,500 per ton. Functional fibres command a premium price. Coffee waste has no value. Jason started collecting coffee grounds from the local 7-Eleven stores, but soon ran out of supply. Here is another opportunity; this time for the instant coffee makers of the world: next to the extraction unit that isolates the soluble part of coffee using steam only, there is an opportunity to set up a recycling plant for PET bottles, and process these with coffee grounds doubling the income of the factory. The Buendía instant coffee factory in Chinchiná, owned by the Cooperative of Coffee Farmers in Colombia, is seeing light at the end of the tunnel. The 20 tons of waste coffee, which today is incinerated, would double income of the factory, while responding to a pressing demand on the market.

Once we start on this pathway of cascading and identify opportunities, the innovations do not seem to stop anymore. Crises are opportunities. It now even offers the chance to imagine re-industrialising regions using waste streams that render the primary sector competitive again, providing farmers with a decent income. It is just to thank Jason Cheng for putting coffee into the textiles, knowing that the physical chemistry is so strong enough to even work after washing and drying.

9

Spinning a Silken Tale

> **When one tugs at a single thing in nature, he finds it attached to the rest of the world.**
>
> — *JOHN MUIR*

Topsoil on the Cutting Edge

Centuries ago, the Chinese confronted a growing demand for food and a limit of fertile soil. As they searched for ways to acquire additional arable farmland by regenerating topsoil, they observed and reflected on the materials and processes that natural systems used to make arid land fertile. They noted in turn how farming and animal husbandry often failed to maintain the flow of contributory elements, causing fertile land to degrade and become barren, arid soil. What they discovered and the strategy they devised not only changed the course of their civilisation, but may well enable us to use an ecosystems approach to change an economic model and thus business strategies for modern products as diverse as airplanes and razors.

The mulberry tree (*Morus alba*) thrives in most of China's typically arid soil. The mulberry leaves are eaten by the wild moth caterpillar (*Bombyx mori*)—more commonly known as the silkworm. The silkworm's droppings fall to the ground, attracting bacteria and microorganisms and quickly producing nutrients that build the soil. Over years, then centuries, and even millennia, the density of newly created, healthy topsoil increases about one millimetre each year. This equates to the annual formation of 15-25 tons per acre of organically enriched topsoil.

This natural symbiosis of caterpillars and trees and the contribution to soil fertility promised food security for an expanding population. China undertook a large-scale planting scheme. As dynasties rose and fell, soil fertility was regenerated and maintained. Previously, infertile land became productive without tilling, plowing or irrigation. Farmers intercropped with cowpeas and groundnuts. Throughout history, Middle Eastern and European countries also planted mulberry trees, and benefitted from its positive effect on soil fertility and erosion control. The Italians planted vineyard borderlands with mulberry trees so as to stem erosion on vineyard slopes, as did the Turks.

These natural methods to generate topsoil were eventually forgotten as attention was diverted from the practices of sustainable farming to commercial monoculture. A lucrative industry and enormous wealth emerged from producing one of the legendary artifacts of human culture: silk, the natural polymer spun from the silkworm's castings.

According to Chinese legend, the idea to use caterpillar castings as silk thread is attributed to Chinese Empress, Si-Ling-Chi (Lady of the Silkworm). One afternoon, as she sat under a mulberry tree to sip her tea, a cocoon fell into her cup. She noticed the strong, smooth threads of the cocoon uncoiling, and began pulling them from her cup. She was fascinated and enthralled as a thread over a thousand feet long emerged. It is said that Empress Si-Ling-Chi first developed the uses of silk for clothing and for wrapping fruits and vegetables—a proven preservation technique. Her husband, Emperor Huang Di (the famous Yellow Emperor), has been credited with the invention of methods for raising silkworms and spinning silk thread. Emperor Huang Di is also said to have taught humankind to fabricate with wood, ceramics, and metal, and to have ordered the construction of the first boats and wheeled vehicles.

As the legend implies, silk is a serendipitous discovery. It is a by-product that originally had no value compared to the strategic long-term importance of soil regeneration and fertilisation of arid land. More recently, the introduction of synthetic polymer textiles made from petrochemicals not only replaced a renewable (silk) with a non-renewable (petroleum), but also deprived intercropped farmland of millions of tons of fertiliser. The popularity of stronger and cheaper synthetic polymers decimated silk production. Consequently, the planting and care of mulberry trees became obsolete. The millennia-long tradition of regenerating topsoil fell into oblivion, since its by-product could not compete in the modern market. Worse, while plastics and polymers made inroads into every stratum of consumption, the land not only lost its source for nutrient and soil replenishment, but also required petrochemical fertilisers to boost levels of food production. This increased the energy input needed to achieve a harvest and furthered dependence on fossil fuels, while increasing greenhouse gas emissions.

A loss of topsoil today represents one of the greatest challenges to food security for the world's future population. Ethiopia, a mountainous country with highly eroded soils on steeply sloping land, loses an estimated one billion tons of topsoil a year, carried away by rain and wind. This is one reason Ethiopia always seems to be on the verge of famine, never able to accumulate enough grain reserves to provide a meaningful measure of food security. In dust storms alone, 2-3 billion tons of fine soil particles leave Africa each year, inexorably draining the continent of its fertility and biological productivity, while depositing considerable amount of dust in the Caribbean seas to cloud the waters and impact coral reefs. The farming practices brought to Africa by European colonisers are not compatible with the continent's climatic conditions.

Some farmers build the soil they sow. Most, however, simply rely on chemical fertilisers, pesticides and intensive irrigation. Using modern farming practices, from 1-10 tons of topsoil per acre are lost annually. Then again, soil losses of as much as 125 to 250 tons per acre are common. Losses of 750-1800 tons per acre due to soil runoff from a single rainfall have been recorded. When all these factors take their toll, farmers are persuaded by the promise of higher yields to consider petrochemical fertilisers and genetically modified seeds, although such promises are often short-lived or misleading.

Over a five year period, Prof George Chan extensively studied integrated farming systems around the millennia-old Chinese tradition of using mulberry trees and silkworms. He assisted farming communities in more than 70 countries to realise the practice of nutrient cascading by planting mulberry trees and introducing silkworms to build topsoil. The application of Prof Chan's topsoil-generating techniques has inspired agriculturally based industries in Namibia, Japan, Fiji, and the US to adopt their own nutrient-cascading strategies. Thus, an ancient Chinese tradition is now transforming the modern food production industry.

Silk for Carbon Capture

Natural silk contains more than 30 per cent carbon. Replacement by petrochemical fibres ends carbon fixation from silk production and from the growth of mulberry trees. As well, it ends the associated topsoil regeneration. Just this one case demonstrates that petroleum emissions are only half of the problem. The substitution of a renewable (silk) by a non-renewable (petroleum) eliminates natural carbon sinks. The ecosystem then looses efficiency since it is incapable of replenishing soil nutrients. It therefore requires additional input in the form of fertilisers. This releases more greenhouse gases, especially since nitrogen-based fertilisers are one of the biggest sources of nitrous oxide (N_2O).

According to the Intergovernmental Panel on Climate Change (IPCC), even though this gas is released in small quantities, its impact is huge. The emission of one ton of N_2O equals that of 310 tons of CO_2. Traditional farming techniques work in harmony with the delicate interconnections that characterise an ecosystem. With silk production, we see a stunning example of how these positive cycles unwind when replaced by monoculture and synthetics. The fertilisers and plastics proffered as symbols of modernity are in reality case studies of ways in which production and consumption systems devolve from sustainable to unsustainable.

Wallace Carothers, the chemical engineer who invented nylon for Dupont, could have had no idea that his petroleum-derived fibre would unravel a web of life that had harmoniously enfolded industrial production in a nutrient cascade benefitting land and agricultural cultivation over five millennia. It is fair to say that in our quest for modernity, we have demonstrated considerable ignorance concerning the impact of our inventions. How can we now expect that government and industry will be able to solve the challenge of climate change, unless they gain an understanding of the thousands of connections that can be destroyed through facile ignorance? Once we grasp the elegant interplay of physics and biochemistry in ecosystems, we can model more breakthrough innovations that open ever more possibilities for progress and sufficiency. It is up to all of us to realise the opportunities.

The Geometry of Silk

Recognition of the problem is also a key to its solution. There are hundreds of species that produce silk. Ants, wasps, bees, mussels, and spiders are among them. Only one, the Chinese silkworm, has been domesticated. Sophisticated instrumentation makes it possible to analyse at the nano-level all the different silks produced. Scientists are beginning to see how these natural polymers can outperform some of their synthetic counterparts and even some metals, such as titanium, which is considered to have the highest strength-to-weight ratio of any metal. If we can master the ways to manufacture biocompatible polymers as these other species do, under ambient conditions, with available nutrients, it then opens a new world of possibilities and a potentially virtuous cycle of soil regeneration and climate stabilisation.

While on a Smithsonian mission in Central America, a professor from Oxford University, Fritz Vollrath encountered a species of golden silk orb weaver spider (*Nephila clavipes*) that spins a one-metre diameter web of a beautiful golden colour. He was fascinated by experimental evidence suggesting that the colour served a dual purpose, both attracting prey and providing disguise. After decades of research, he came to understand silk and its remarkable qualities of resilience, strength and flexibility. He realised that the extraordinary performance of the spider's silk is due to its geometry at the nanoscale. Geometry is part of mathematics. In this case, Vollrath used it to determine how the crystalline and non-crystalline structure of silk creates variations of strength that often outcompete metals and designer plastics. By merely controlling pressure and humidity in the rear abdomen at the moment of its spinning, the golden orb spider is capable of producing seven different types of silk.

The *Nephila clavipes* web outperforms many others in terms of tensile strength and versatility under changing conditions. The extreme toughness of spider silk stems from the controlled folding during spinning of all the proteins that compose the silk. This protein folding is largely dependent on the precise extraction of water accomplished with no more than the pressure in the spider's abdomen. Prof Vollrath's comparisons between spider and insect spinning provided further insights into the extrusion processes.

Spiders have a remarkable capacity to recycle their web, reconditioning it to meet new requirements. They ingest the portions of their web that they wish to renew, converting the polymers into their original amino acids. How could we not be impressed by this performance? It models one of the best recycling programs ever designed for a polymer! How does this compare to the 'disposable' plastics of our modern life that continue to accumulate in a massive floating continent of plastic waste in the Pacific Ocean, intoxicating ocean life?

However, it is challenging to domesticate spiders. The species are aggressive. Even if such defensive behaviour were overcome, their productive output is low. They simply recycle too much, reprocessing their web into a new variety of silk adapted to the changed circumstances, with little need for additional production. These limitations compelled Vollrath to compare the structure of silk spun by the mulberry silkworm with that spun by the golden orb spider. Using the basic amino acids as building blocks, he and his Oxford team replicated the spider's recipe to structure silk from the silkworm so as to match that of the silk from the spider. The processed polymer they developed is a silk with properties identical to those that make the spider's version unique.

Prof Vollrath is engaged in the design of a systemic approach to the production of biocompatible polymers from renewable resources, very much along the lines of the original Chinese strategy for regenerating topsoil. Building on his visionary research, Vollrath has established business entities that manufacture these polymers and identify markets where these biocompatible products can outperform and underprice petroleum-based polymers and expensive metal alloys. Instead of generating collateral damage, as is the case with products spreading greenhouse gases, these products can help reconnect our economy to the original purpose of China's silk production: regeneration, renewal and abundance—of soil fertility, harvest capacity and carbon capture.

Over a century ago, the annual output of raw silk hovered around one million tons. Current production fluctuates in a range below 100,000 tons per year. With the exception of luxury fabrics such as those made by Hermès, the future market for silk will not be textile or clothing manufacture. It cannot compete in price with branded petrochemical synthetic polymers that hold greater market share in the textile industry. However, it notably outperforms (by a factor of six in price and performance) expensive metals such as stainless steel and titanium. Titanium has become the standard structural material for jet engines, spacecraft, desalination plants, medical prostheses, orthopedic implants, dental implants, sporting goods and mobile phones. Although the aerospace industry uses up the largest portion of processed titanium, consumer goods increasingly include titanium in stainless steel manufacture, as well as many products ranging from bicycle frames and jewellery to implants and prostheses.

It this context, we can spot a potential strategic shift in the business concept that could give rise to a new economic development model. The production of titanium from metal ore consumes large quantities of magnesium, chlorine and argon gas. Titanium must be welded in an inert atmosphere to protect it from contamination with oxygen, nitrogen, or hydrogen. Both the energy inputs and the use of scarce and mined resources are significant, so that the end products have high price tags. Processed and cured titanium has a high tensile strength-to-density ratio and high resistance to oxygen and seawater corrosion. Because of these desirable qualities, customers pay more and ignore the collateral damage to the environment. When we contrast a life cycle analysis of titanium with the simplicity of mulberry leaves transformed into silk, at relatively ambient temperature, and moisture, silk clearly emerges on the positive side of the sustainability index. We quickly understand how we can move these industries towards sustainability. Companies willing to take advantage of Vollrath's nanoscale insights for controlling silk's geometry will find that these biocompatible silk polymers are an ideal substitute for high-performance metals.

A Close Shave

A ubiquitous example of our unsustainable consumption is the razor used to remove hair. There are very few activities more banal than shaving. Hair grows inexorably, year in, year out. Cave paintings show that even prehistorically men scraped off unwanted hair using implements such as stones and clam shells. During the Bronze Age, humans developed the ability to forge simple metals and began to make razors from iron and bronze. Early Egyptians shaved both their beards and heads, a custom eventually adopted by the Greeks and Romans, particularly soldiers facing hand-to-hand combat: a lack of locks meant one less handhold for an enemy.

A modern shaving blade manufactured in the early 21st century uses almost 20 times less metal than the first disposable ones

Table 8.4: Pulp-to-Protein to Mitigate Climate Change

Impact on Climate Change	*Progress Towards Millennium Goals*
Low Energy Use	Food Security
Preservation of Forests	Empowerment of Women
Lower Transportation Energy Costs	Improved Childhood Health
No Landfill	Environmental Sustainability
No Methane Gas	Global Partnerships
Elimination of Charcoal Usage	Fight HIV/AIDS
Cultivation of Slow Food	Learning Self-Sufficiency

Source: Author.

introduced by King C. Gillette over a century ago. While this confirms the drive towards material efficiency, lowered cost and thus greater affordability result in less incentive to extend a product's useful life. As Gillette's strong research team increased profitability and market share, the overall volume of individual razors as well as the total weight of metal waste increased dramatically. An estimated 10 billion throw-away razors annually contribute 250,000 tons of valuable metal as waste to our landfill volume. Most unfortunately, the latest models have increased the number of blades from two to five or even six. Here we witness a rebound effect that undoes the material efficiency gains of the past 50 years.

Razor blades are exposed to high levels of moisture and must therefore be made from a special corrosion resistant steel alloy or titanium. The grade of steel must be hard enough for the blade to hold its shape, yet flexible enough for it to be processed. Carbide steel is preferred because it is made using carbon, silicon, manganese, chromium, and molybdenum, with the remainder being iron and a finishing layer of titanium. The steel is heated to temperatures of 2012° F, then hardened by quenching in water to a temperature around -94° F. The steel is tempered at 662° F. The blades are then stamped to form the appropriate cutting edge at a rate of 800-1,200 per minute. As the blade is quite small, a special metal and plastic support structure is required to hold it inside the cartridge. Similar to titanium, stainless steel is part of a production and consumption pattern that makes life unsustainable. This whole process offers only a few clean shaves and then the razor ends up in a landfill.

The shaving industry now has a choice. Rather than market growth by volume, they can turn the razor business into one that contributes to solving the environmental and employment crisis while offering something better and cheaper. A razor made of silk will cut through keratin (hair), but will not slice the skin since it rolls hundreds of fine threads over the skin surface, in effect a miniature version of a hand-pushed grass mower. The technology is here. Its fine-tuning and production are just a matter of time and money. The fact that silk can be substituted for mined ores, dramatically reducing carbon emissions and even sequestering carbon, reveals an ideal cost/benefit structure. At US$100 per pound for processed silk, each silk-blade razor would cost less than a dollar, yet its performance and feel would be equal to the latest industry versions.

Smooth as Silk

Given that the manufacturing is a trade secret, another use of unsustainable polymers has escaped consumers' attention—cosmetics. After water, polymers represent the second largest category of ingredients in cosmetics and personal care products. A diverse range of polymers are used as film-formers, fixatives, thickeners, emulsifiers, stimuli-responsive agents, conditioners, foam stabilisers, skin-feel benefitting agents, and antimicrobials. The market value of synthetic polymers is currently US$15 billion dollars and steadily growing. They have replaced many cosmetic ingredients formerly derived from natural sources. While it may be difficult to visualise how silk can replace stainless steel in razors and airplanes, our tactile association with the softness of silk makes it relatively easier to imagine how silk can be a main component of skin and hair care products. Using silk nano-technology products as substitutes for synthetic polymers can become the most promising and highly profitable direction for the cosmetic industry.

It will take only one market leader, like Clarins or Shiseido, shifting from synthetic to natural polymers in order to gather the attention of all major market players. The first application would likely be sunscreen products, since silk could provide a dual functionality. Silk polymers would give structure to the cream and dissipate ultraviolet (UV) rays. Silk could also be a biocompatible replacement for titanium in the expensive titanium oxide creams that are marketed to protect against UV exposure.

The hair colouring market is a second area where naturally produced silk nanostructures can quickly gain market share. Greeks and Romans used highly alkaline soap, boiled walnuts and henna to create different shades. Although such colour tinting products are kinder to our body, they do not retain their colouring over time.

The colouring products made from harsh chemical polymers provide more permanent hair colour. Yet, published research linking cancer to the prolonged use of hair dyes has prompted the US Food and Drug Administration to study the potential toxicity of these colouring agents. Fortunately, new insights on silk polymers have made it possible to develop biocompatible products that can obtain and hold a desired colour. Silk polymers and other biologically derived renewable raw materials could handily replace toxic hair dyes and at the same time release a cascade of positive health and ecological effects.

Biocompatible Medical Uses

Silk thread has been used worldwide for many years as a suture in intricate surgical and ophthalmological operations. It is suitable for this purpose because of its fine, soft fibres and tensile strength. It is also easy to tie, yet difficult to untie. Its protein composition makes it compatible with the human body, eliminating the need for surgical removal. Other medical applications have been commercialised: anti-hay fever masks, gauze pads, and bandages for dermatological disorders are now made from silk. The development of technology to dissolve silk fibres and make film from silk protein has opened the way for further research and development for use in artificial skin, blood vessels, tendons, and nerve regeneration, as well as contact lenses, catheters for surgical procedures and anticoagulants. All these applications exploit silk's biocompatibility and permeability.

Today when knee or spine tissue cartilage is damaged and cannot regenerate, an artificial knee made of titanium is surgically implanted. Another product being developed by Prof Vollrath and his team is a porous silk scaffold with mechanical properties that nearly match those of human fibro-cartilage. The silk scaffold is inserted in place of damaged cartilage and stimulates cell growth on its porous biocompatible surface, regenerating the cartilage using the body's immune response. A natural system with biocompatible components can successfully strengthen an existing structure, as opposed to a system with expensive and incompatible components that require immunosuppressants to overcome rejection. The world market for biocompatible devices already approaches US$20 billion annually, with an annual growth rate of over 10 per cent. Silk sutures will soon be complemented by silk-based wound dressing, replacement joints, and orthopedic implants, all stemming from insights into the functioning of natural systems.

The demand for medical devices made from silk offers a high-end proof of concept that these products are financially viable even under present economic conditions. Prof Vollrath and his team have succeeded in bringing silk-based products to market. The opportunities for these technologies to become available worldwide will substantially stimulate the demand for silk. If the research is done for products as complex as these, making razors or cosmetic ingredients from silk polymers will be easy. It is just a matter of putting our minds to it! And who will do that? Will Schick, Gillette, or a consortium of entrepreneurs transform a surprisingly unsustainable consumer product into a quality product that sequesters carbon and is as smooth as silk in performance? At its peak, 100 years ago, the annual volume of silk production had reached one million tons. If the demand for silk to make razors and cosmetics were to reach just 100,000 tons over the next 10 years, imagine its beneficial effect in relation to increased soil fertility.

Merging the Arts

China has an exceptional tradition with silk. China has an equally exceptional tradition in bamboo. Silk has been beaten by cheap nylon, bamboo weaving has been beaten by its own cheap automated mass production. Bamboo weaving has emerged as a new art, creating by hand, shapes and forms that sustain for decades if not centuries without the use of metal or glue. Now these forms are covered naturally by caterpillars working months in a row with a blanket of silk. A crib, made to measure, is now covered painstakingly by thousands of silkworms (really these are not worms but caterpillars) in their search for a safe home. Raw silk has a few unique features: it is free of virus, bacteria and fungus, offering an environment that every parent would desire for his/her baby. Then again, silk and bamboo as a stand-alone art would not stand up against the global onslaught of competition; the two combined offers a product that is unique, outcompeting whatever is presently available.

The added appeal of this approach is that it does not eliminate any industry jobs. The number of jobs potentially lost will be far outnumbered by that of new jobs created—a total of 1.5 million jobs for each 100,000 tons of additional silk harvested. Applying a sustainable model that uses silk instead of plastic is more competitive, has greater marketing appeal, generates topsoil, and cuts carbon emissions. This is the Blue Economy that we seek to bring to the centre stage of modern society.

10

From the Mighty to the Miniscule

> The sun, with all the planets revolving around it and depending on it, can still ripen a bunch of grapes as if it had nothing else in the universe to do.
>
> — *GALILEO GALILEI*

Only a Heartbeat Away

While we rightly worry about human-induced climate change, humanity is hovering between two killing fields: children dying of malnutrition from shortages of the most basic nutrients, and adults dying of malnutrition from excesses of the wrong foods. Our artificial and refined diet and our lack of exercise combine to create a terrain that lessens our quality of life and shortens our lifespan. The unconscionable truth is that we know it. Until this pattern shifts, monitoring heart disease is a foregone necessity.

Heart disease takes a higher toll of lives than any other single malady. Medical researchers have tried to address this for decades and have found ways to apply technology to create beneficial effect in helping correct heart malfunction. Dr Jorge Reynolds is one of these researchers. Having studied electronic engineering at Cambridge University and graduating in 1953, he devised a way to correct an irregular heartbeat by modulating an electric current that was sourced and transformed from a car battery and attached to two diodes connected to the heart.

Between 1954 and 1964, Prof Reynolds developed a prototype version of a pacemaker that could be placed into the heart in order to correct heart function by maintaining the beat. Even though the device was the size of a car battery on wheels and required continuous connection to the post-surgical patient, over 1,700 patients were aided by his invention. In fact, in 2013, five of these patients were still alive. His prototype pacemaker is on display at the Museum of Science and Industry in London. In the 1960s, Reynolds transferred all his patents and protocols to a third party for further development and dedicated the rest of his life to research. He was looking for a better way to get the human heart to keep working. His curiosity and research led him to study the heart functioning of other mammals. When he began to study the whale's heart and circulatory mechanism, his fascination was complete.

Energy from Whales

Long ago, the whale was a land mammal who returned to the sea, evolving into the largest and most intelligent animal living on earth. In the 18th century, the whale was sought after for its blubber. Whale oil, rendered from whale blubber, was globally harvested and traded. Its uses ranged from nighttime illumination to cooking oil. Whales were hunted to near extinction. It took another 250 years of human development for us to realise that the real marvel of a whale is not its blubber, but rather its capacity to generate 6-12 volts of electric power merely from potassium, sodium and calcium. This is remarkable since whales rely solely on krill and small fishes for their nutrition and energy. This biochemical capacity to generate electricity is a phenomenon that has been studied by Reynolds, who has non-invasively monitored the whale's heartbeat for over three decades.

Reynolds wondered how the heart of this magnificently large mammal adapted throughout its remarkable physical and physiological transformations. With each pulse, over a lifespan of approximately 80 years, and without any maintenance or intervention, the whale's heart, bathed in blubber, flows 250 gallons of blood along 100 million miles of arteries and veins. While the muscles, valves, veins, and arteries evolved over time, Reynolds pondered over ways in which the whale was able to distribute electric current to its massive physique and coordinate the pulsing rhythms at a scale 1000 times greater than the heart of its dog-like ancestor. There are no known cases of cardiac arrest among whales. Yet if our heart were to lie in so much fat, it would simply stop working.

Reynolds posed these key questions: What do we learn from this? What clues are there? No one could offer answers. He embarked on an intensive quest to learn everything he could about whale and other mammalian hearts. Wishing to record and graph the whale's heart, he designed an EKG (electrocardiogram) recorder to attach to a whale and transmit heartbeat data via satellite to his research centre in Bogotá. Although we might imagine the difficulty of designing and fabricating the machinery, and setting up electronic data transmission, the real feat was how the attachment was made. Reynolds did it by hand, one whale at a time, working from an open boat in the ocean waters. This was science on the edge!

Reynolds' career in heart research spans five decades, but his fascination is not limited to whales. He recorded ECGs from over 200 animals, some as small as a fly, as elusive as a pink dolphin in the Amazon, or as curious as a grazing iguana in the Galapagos. Today, Reynolds and his team have compiled over 10,000 whale ECGs. They used advanced sound filtration systems, originally designed for military eavesdropping, as underwater audio-phones. This greatly facilitated the research, as it eliminated the need to physically attach the equipment to a whale. The team eventually gathered such immense data that Reynolds could accurately map the functioning of a whale's heart. Further remarkable data was revealed from medical dissections performed on expired beached whales. Scientists postulate that the whale has channels of cells that appear solely dedicated to guiding electric currents in and around the heart. These currents coordinate its flow and are capable of adjusting their pathways to bypass damaged tissue.

Reynolds' curiosity drove his research far beyond observations of heartbeat. To comprehend at the molecular level how potassium, sodium and calcium combine to power electric currents without either metals or batteries, he studied the entire genesis and transformation of the whale heart beginning with its embryonic materialisation at the time of conception. He mapped his findings onto a three-dimensional virtual heart. Using off-the-shelf AutoDesk engineering software, he gave other scientists and cardiologists access to open source information that could be mapped before their eyes.

His observations made him rethink pacemaker fundamentals. By now a practically ubiquitous device prolonging millions of lives, the pacemaker replaces the natural capacity to generate electric currents with a battery-powered device that connects into the depths of the heart. Yet defects in the hundreds of thousands began to plague these devices. This pushed Reynolds to think beyond the obvious. He hesitated at first because of the simplicity of his idea. Inspired by the whale, he thought that he could recreate these cell-thin tubes to improve the distribution of current throughout the heart. He envisioned replacing the existing device he had helped invent with a nano-scale carbon tube containing the same power as a pacemaker. Instead of replacing the natural function of the heart, the tiny carbon coil would simply channel the current from healthy tissue to the damaged tissue. That was a revolutionary thought: build on the existing power generation capacity, and improved conductivity.

The second revolutionary concept was based on his realisation that the whale, all other mammals, and even the fly generate and conduct current with neither battery nor wiring. Our planet's diverse living species have learned to generate the electrical power they need using a quite extensive collection of energy sources: gravity, temperature differential, pH differential, kinetic energy from muscle movement, piezo-electrical energy from movement of the heart and blood, energy derived from CO_2, and bodily biometals. Reynolds' studies concluded that all these species' applications work and have in fact been proven over millions of years.

He designed a series of new medical devices that operate like everything else in nature—that is, without cables or a battery. He focused on how whales generate a continuous flow of electric pulses from the minuscule supply and fine coordination of chemical reactions produced with a combination of potassium, sodium, and calcium. The medical devices and bodily monitoring systems he produce, rely only on the sources of energy that exist in and around the body.

The first such application Reynolds designed, the nano-pacemaker, is a minute device of just 700 nanometres (700 millionths of a millimetre) in length that is controlled by the latest microprocessors. It takes its inspiration from the whale's conductivity channels and has proven its viability in the laboratory. However, the argument that this works successfully in whales is unconvincing for the Food and Drug Administration (IDA). The cost to develop this prototype into an FDA-approved medical device is in the range of US$100-US$500 million. Although Reynolds has limited seed money available, Medtronic offered to run and monitor animal studies of his home made prototypes.

It is easy to understand why the market leaders in pacemaker sales like Medtronic, Johnson & Johnson, and Boston Scientific, who now have their market securely captured for decades to come, would challenge this innovation. They are earning royalties on each surgery, in conjunction with the pharmaceutical industry that will supply medicine for rest of the patient's life. How would the leading pacemaker manufacturers react to an innovation that eliminates a guaranteed income of at least US$50,000 for each patient diagnosed with a treatable cardiac arrhythmia problem, and another average of US$50,000 for a lifetime supply of medicine? All this expense could be reduced to a US$500 procedure. Placement of the nano-wire is done with a catheter and requires no general anesthesia. Since patients are not likely to require any continuing medication, the total cost for insurance companies drops by a factor of 200. Insurance companies should be keenly receptive to this application.

Healthy, Battery-Free Electrical Current

Our industrial system is oriented to immense size and power. Thus, it is not surprising that the minuscule electrical charges generated by natural systems are dismissed as trivial. Self-winding watches and flashing lights in children's shoe soles are on a short list of familiar commercial applications. Yet, our heart and brain function with such micro-currents. No one is wired or carries a battery, except when a pacemaker has been surgically implanted or a hearing aid is fit into the ear. Simple, naturally generated current is adequately powerful to continuously regulate the flow of blood through our heart each day. Over a single lifetime, the energy the body produces, sourced from the core elements in food, is sufficient to lift a 40-foot shipping container from the harbour in Mumbai (India) to the top of Mt Everest!

Reynolds' research and subsequent innovations may well herald the end to our dependence on chemical batteries that load our landfills and pollute our environment. By eliminating the need for a battery, we would also be eliminating pollution and toxic waste. Batteries offer convenience, but they are a major source of demand for mined materials, and are seldom fully recycled. It is no secret that metals from batteries pollute and are health hazards. There are over 40 billion batteries manufactured and sold each year. The vast majority of smaller 'disposable' batteries just become waste. Worse, this trend is accelerating. It is one of the double-digit growth segments of the market. Even Sweden and Germany, two countries with great societal discipline, do not recycle half of what is used. Given their low cost, availability and size, these smaller batteries most often collect in landfills. It is another daily tragedy that we fail to realise the adverse impact such a tiny device has on the health of our planet and ultimately on our own health. The metals contained are indiscriminately dispersed into the ecosystem on which we depend for critical resources, like drinking water and fertile soil.

We also fail to consider the high energy cost of battery power. If we compare the cost per kilowatt hour of a battery to that of the same energy from a socket at home, most of us would be surprised to discover that we are paying 100-500 times more for battery power than for electricity in our homes. Industry analysts who have come to this realisation are now avidly searching for the most efficient battery. Billions are being spent by governments and private investors to find the longest-lasting and least-polluting battery that will provide consumers with the convenience and flexibility of electricity when required. While huge amounts of money are expended, we seem to have collectively forgotten that any battery made of metals (heavy metals) is taxing our Earth's resources beyond the capacity to sustain future demand. Worse, it increases mining and unregulated dispersal of metals into the environment. Batteries may be a convenient source of energy but the economic and environmental costs are beyond reason. It is time we design a battery-free world. Now that Medtronic has embarked on animal testing, this vision may be closer to reality than ever imagined.

A Cooler Way to Cool

For decades, medical researchers have had great success in developing vaccines to eliminate serious diseases. Unfortunately, the vaccine delivery mechanisms have not been as successful. According to estimates by the World Health Organization (WHO), only 50 per cent of all vaccines produced and sold are actually successfully administered. The lack of refrigeration at out-of-the-way points of administration means that only 50 per cent of at-risk children can be reached.

Thus, the key challenge for vaccines is preserving the cold chain. There are an estimated 6,000 solar medical refrigerators installed at medical delivery sites in developing nations. Their purpose is to keep vaccines at reliably cold temperatures. At an average cost of US$5,000 to US$7,000 per refrigeration unit, this represents a total investment in excess of US$30 million. Although photovoltaic energy is arguably a more reliable energy supply than is kerosene, there is another alternative: a nature-based delivery mechanism that substitutes both fossil and clean fuel refrigeration with *no refrigeration at all.*

Typically, when water evaporates, cells dry out. The cell membranes rupture, making reconstitution impossible. However, scientists have identified and studied a host of microorganisms as well as other simple plant and animal species that can completely dehydrate and appear to be dead, yet can survive and be restored to full biological function in less than two hours merely by contact with water. Two of these species—one a microscopic water-dwelling animal known as the water bear or tardigrade (*Hypsibius dujardini*), and the other is a species of creeping fern native to Africa and the

Americas known as the resurrection fern (*Polypodium polypodioides*)—are organisms that survive by producing high sugar concentrations in their tissues. On losing water, these special sugars solidify as if they were glass, preserving cells and tissue. When water is once again available, the glass-like sugars dissolve, allowing the cell's normal biological functioning to resume.

Bruce Roser engineered a natural process for the stabilisation of pharmaceutical products, which he is now commercialising through StablePharma in the UK. Roser's application not only eliminates the need for vaccine refrigeration, but also overcomes the challenge of supplying syringes by delivering a complete vaccination package system requiring neither cooling, nor a local water source, nor any further handling. This means a dramatically improved delivery of functional vaccines at much lower cost. The WHO estimates that potential monetary savings for the developing world are in the range of US$200-US$300 million per year. The humanitarian savings are even greater.

Not only can this technology eliminate the cold-chain delivery mechanism for vaccines, other applications using this no-refrigeration innovation may also herald the end of the supermarket frozen food department (perhaps not the ice cream!). Importantly, it is needed is the research that can devise a way to phase out dependence on perfluorocarbons (PFCs), a greenhouse gas that is currently used to suspend microparticles in vaccines. We often forget to consider why we freeze food. It is to preserve it longer without loss of taste or texture. Hence, the application of this technology potentially reaches into high-value markets like baby food, frozen foods and functional foods. Even perishable products derived from coffee, tea, fruits and meats could be brought to market using a method that has been tested in the most challenging of circumstances: delivery of viable vaccines to developing countries.

How many jobs might be created by substituting refrigeration with no-refrigeration? In the field of health services, the fact that several hundreds of millions of dollars will not be wasted on expensive energy to power refrigeration implies that uncountable millions can be used to finance other budget priorities. Estimates are that nearly 40,000-60,000 additional health care positions in developing countries can be funded with the savings, a very welcome prospect.

Direct and indirect emissions from refrigeration systems worldwide account for approximately 20 per cent of the greenhouse effect. Although the refrigeration of vaccines is only a minor component, Roser's preservation and delivery technique, teamed with other existing industrial technologies, demonstrates that an innovation inspired by tardigrades and ferns can achieve more than delivering vaccines to the children who need them most. It helps reduce carbon emissions along the way. We can be inspired by these multiple benefits.

The Furor over Furanones

The first living species on Earth was bacteria. Photosynthesis by bacteria emerged at least 2.8 billion years ago, well before plants existed. While scientists call them *monera*, we call these single celled organisms germs, bacteria, or even bugs. Bacteria are everywhere and just about everything we know finds its origin in bacteria. Our eyes, nose, ears, and tastebuds are all associated with these first living creatures. Few of us seem to recognise that we are in symbiosis with bacteria. While we like to think that our ancestors were apes, we are really nothing more than the great-great-great-great grandchildren of bacteria! Knowing that we cannot digest food without them makes it even more curious that we want to obliterate them all.

Ever since microscopes permitted us to see these nucleus-free single cell organisms, and science and industry convinced us of their evil intentions, we have been on a quest to exterminate them. If we are so determined to kill them, using the harshest versions of chemistry and antibiotics (originally based on biology of the fungus), then we find ourselves ... killing ourselves. We supposedly cleanse our bathrooms and kitchens with chemicals that are not conducive to life. Assuming that we brush our teeth twice a day, there are still probably more bacteria living in our mouth than people living on Earth. Our preoccupation with killing bacteria is a campaign that is certain to fail.

Bacteria are basic and ubiquitous forms of life that actually comprise almost 10 per cent of our bodies by weight.

Failure is certainly the result we are likely to achieve with our excessive use of bactericides. Not only are many of these chemicals linked to a higher incidence of cancer and an array of unhealthful and physiologically disruptive side-effects, our desire to eliminate these microorganisms in fact spurs them to mutate faster. Bacteria pursue genetic modifications at will since they have no nucleus. This chemically-loaded killing spree has put these tiny but mighty organisms on the evolutionary path towards super bacteria. Our immune systems, already continuously stressed by coping with increasingly ineffective chemical bactericides, and functioning without the benefit of the helpful bacteria eliminated by the same chemical overload, cannot keep up. The double whammy of chemical attack and depleted natural defense mechanisms exhausts our body's ability to respond effectively.

Since trying to kill bacteria may in fact kill us, it is worth observing how the second form of life on earth—microalgae, or protoctista, ancestor of seaweeds—adapted to bacteria, the first form of life. Considering that the ocean, from which life emerged, is literally a soup of bacteria, killing bacteria did not make sense for the newer microalgae. Had the protoctista developed a poison potent enough to kill all bacteria, it would have annihilated every other form of life, including itself.

As seaweeds started populating the oceans, they quickly found their surfaces colonised by bacteria. Bacteria slowly build a biofilm, similar to those that line our digestive system, cover our scalp, and populate our tongue. If the colony gets out of control and bacteria sense they have a quorum, they may decide to take over the host.

How did the seaweeds then cope with the need to compete and the challenge to survival? To survive as a recently arrived species, seaweeds needed to become better at mastering their environment. The *Delisea pulchra*, the red seaweed found between Tasmania and Japan, perfected a way to jam communication among bacteria. Instead of endangering their own long-term future and attempting (ineffectively) to eradicate bacteria, *Delisea pulchra* simply learned to make the bacteria temporarily deaf. It creates a small molecule, named furanone, which occupies a bacteria's receptor and makes it impossible for the bacteria to hear other bacteria of the same genus.

This is a brilliantly effective solution. Bacteria use chemicals to talk to each other. If they do not receive specific molecules, because the necessary receptors are already blocked—by a molecule from seaweed—bacteria do not have a clue where other family members are. Under these conditions, it is difficult for bacteria to form a dominant biofilm. Better even, existing biofilms disintegrate when there is no communication to coordinate joint action. If there is no biofilm, there is no danger of infection.

Scientists, Peter Steinberg and his colleague Staffan Kjelleberg, who conducted breakthrough research of the *Delisea pulchra* at the University of New South Wales in Sydney, Australia, quickly understood the value of their discovery: human-induced superbug mutations could be replaced by seaweed-inspired bacterial controls! The potential applications envisioned give them many choices of where to start.

Yet, industry roadblocks are daunting. As it applies to controlling the spread of bacteria, a broad range of industries, including private housing, commercial buildings, transport, agriculture, consumer products, medical devices and pharmaceuticals, could benefit. But a naturally occurring substance that deafens bacteria and thereby eliminates their proliferation, threatens Big Pharma's antibiotic cash cows, which seem to be prescribed at will for just about any health inconvenience. Moreover, the financial investment and approval procedures are such that actually bringing a new medical innovation to market can take years, if not decades. If it were not for lengthy and complicated government approval procedures, furanones might have replaced antibiotics and bactericides by now.

Meanwhile, other fields less burdened with approval processes are readily apparent. Consumer goods and industrial and agricultural applications represent vast potential for this significant platform technology. Consider deodorants, currently manufactured with questionably safe ingredients including titanium and zinc. Body odour is caused by bacteria feeding on perspiration. A furanone-based deodorant would result in fewer bacteria and consequently less odour.

Then there is tooth brushing, part of our daily routine. The amount of bacteria in our mouths is impressive. Although bacteria contribute to the digestive process and to our ability to taste food, bad breath and tooth decay are also caused by bacteria that feed on food residues in the mouth. If furanones were present, no bacteria-laden biofilm could form. Thus, a furanone rinse would have a major refreshing effect.

Agriculture is likewise affected by biofilms. Seeds could be protected from bacterial contamination by simply dipping them in a furanone bath. Cut flowers, which decay under a bacterial onslaught, would remain fresher for a longer span when held in furanone-infused water.

Heating and cooling systems in buildings are at risk for the creation of biofilms including the worrisome accretion of *Legionalla*. This bacterium is tough to eliminate because it lives in a host. The doses needed to kill the host expose the building's occupants to an excessive chemical burden. The alternative is to install filters and replace those regularly, further increasing handling costs and downtime. In all these applications, furanones offer a remarkable alternative to the toxic chemistry in widespread use today.

British Petroleum made the headlines in 2006 because of the leak in their Alaskan pipelines. Few people realise that the corrosion commonly affecting pipelines that transport oil, gas, or water is induced by bacteria. Every two weeks, the entire pipeline is shut down and flushed with acidic chemicals to kill the accumulation of bacterial biofilm on the interior. Since it is known that even these measures are not adequately powerful to remove all the corrosion-causing microorganisms, a pigging machine is used to scrape the surface and remove these accumulations. Perhaps, furanones trickled into the pipelines could simply and safely deal with this problem.

Reverse osmosis production of fresh water from seawater is adversely affected by the accumulation of biofilm on the membrane filters, thereby lowering their effectiveness by more than 50 per cent.

Today, just as is the case with oil and gas pipelines, entire water purification systems must be shut down to kill bacteria with chlorine. The drawback is that excessive use of chlorine chemically degrades the osmosis membranes, reducing the life of a system and increasing costs.

This handful of applications is only a fraction of the possibilities. The real future of furanone use, and Peter Steinberg's core fascination, has always been the application of his insights to pharmaceutical and medical devices. Cystic fibrosis and tuberculosis are two biofilm-based illnesses, where a colony of bacteria slowly and steadily overwhelms the host, eventually fatally. As soon as the bacterial biofilm is formed, antibiotics attain far less effectiveness. A thousandfold dosage increase is sometimes required. Imagine the impact of a seaweed-inspired synthetic analogue. As bacteria in the biofilm are rendered deaf by the furanones, individual bacteria dissipate and disintegrate since they do not sense a quorum. Ultimately, the supra-structure becomes non-functional and the individual bacteria can be more readily eliminated by the body's natural maintenance processes.

The understanding that furanones do not obliterate, but rather functionally impair detrimental bacteria, offers in itself a fresh insight as to how we could improve health and treat illness without stimulating the evolution of superbugs that defy our own immune system. If Steinberg's medical applications ever reach the market, it will break ground for hundreds of different applications. The reasoning is impeccable, the performance is demonstrable and the cost of production is likely to be competitive, since effective concentrations of furanones appear to be just tens per billion.

If we take an educated guess at evaluating the net job potential, we must consider that the production of furanones will replace the volume production of chemicals that are proven occupational and health hazards. Thus, employment in the manufacturing sector would have neither loss nor gain. Improved material efficiency can be estimated at 20-25 per cent; for example, reverse osmosis membranes and pipelines would function longer, more efficiently and with lower maintenance costs. However, the most important job generation will likely come from exploring the bacteria-defeating product possibilities of a remarkable species silently at work.

Table 10.1: Some Possible Uses of Furanones

Housing and Building	Air conditioning, Water supply
Agriculture	Fish farming, Food preservation
Industry	Food processing, Micro-electronics
Transportation	Oil and gas
Pharmaceutical	Cystic fibrosis, Tuberculosis
Medical Devices	Urinary catheters, syringes
Consumer Products	Deodorants, Mouth and tooth hygiene, skin care

Source: Author.

Miraculous Maggots

The spread of AIDS (acquired immense deficiency syndrome), malaria, and IDD (iodine deficiency disorders) throughout Africa have caught the attention of Western health experts. A number of philanthropic US foundations are aggressively funding the quest for solutions. Yet overlooked is the reality that more Africans are adversely affected by a lack of basic wound care than by these debilitating diseases. Poor wound care leads to infections, gangrene and amputations—all precursors to social marginalisation and shortened life expectancy. If a basic treatment were more widely available, especially in rural villages, subsequent larger problems would be avoided. Although it sounds incongruous, one surprising (and successful) wound care technique comes from gaining insights into how maggots incorporate hygiene.

In nature, when an animal dies and begins to decompose, flies arrive in swarms. They feast, then lay their eggs. The maggots that hatch quickly consume the rotting flesh. With the flesh consumed, there is no opportunity for bacteria to proliferate. The maggots either grow into flies, or are devoured by birds, fish or other species that have the highly acidic digestion needed to quickly absorb the 80 per cent protein content of maggots.

The use of maggots in delicate wound treatment is historically well documented. Healers in ancient Mayan culture and Australian aboriginal tribes regularly used maggots for wound healing. Napoleon's Surgeon General, Baron Dominique Larrey, reported the use of maggot treatment for wounds during France's Egyptian campaign in 1799. Hygienic conditions in war campaigns certainly left much to be desired. Maggots were an important and effective field therapy. The widespread use of maggots for wound therapy prior to World War II diminished, following Alexander Fleming's discovery of penicillin in 1928.

More recently, with the acknowledged dangers of antibiotic-resistant bacteria, medical doctors have sought to re-introduce maggot therapy. Worldwide, over 4,000 therapists in 20 countries use maggot wound therapy. Dr Stephen Britland from Bradford University (UK) pioneered research into the healing capacity of maggots. Advanced Gel Technologies (AGT) aims to complement the products developed by Biomonde, which started as a government services provider and is now one of the world's largest supplier of live maggots for wound therapy, with production in the UK, Germany and the USA. His research found that maggots do more than simply clean wounds. Maggots produce enzymes that stimulate cell growth through the release of slight electrical charges. For the maggots, even antibiotic-resistant bacteria are nothing more than competitors for food. Left to do what they do best, maggots perform exceedingly well.

However, modern hospital conditions require sterile conditions, and maggots are not traditionally associated with bacteria-free hygiene (though the same is often said of modern hospital settings). One of Britland's innovations has been to devise a way to collect the active wound-healing ingredients that maggots produce without collecting the maggots. This procedure is quite simple and not too different than what happens when we take a few gulps of salt water when swimming in the ocean—we regurgitate. Maggots are collected and then immersed in salt water to induce disgorgement. The procedure is fast, cheap and easy. This scheme, as proposed by AGT, would allow wound therapy to be accomplished using only the enzyme-rich regurgitated matter, without the disconcerting sight and sensation of maggots consuming necrotic bacteria-laden tissue.

Maggot therapy favourably compares with vacuum treatments, where leg ulcers are locally isolated in a low pressure environment to facilitate cell growth. The use of maggots for wound therapy eliminates the need for antibiotics, as no bacteria remain once the maggots eliminate the dead tissue. Antibiotic resistance thus becomes a non-factor. Clinical trial results demonstrate that maggot treatment is at par in performance with the strongest antibiotic regimens, in itself a remarkable testament.

Apart from the key benefit of healing with a low risk of infection, another major advantage is hospital cost savings for patients who are not critically ill, but nonetheless require nursing care to protect them from infection. This is of particular importance for burns or ulcers contracted by diabetic patients. When Britland's research team received funding from the British government to develop and commercialise this therapy, it was because the medical records clearly demonstrated a dramatic Health Services savings for wound care treatment. Money is saved by reducing the length of hospital stays from an average of 72 to only 14 days, heretofore often prolonged because of unhealed leg ulcers requiring amputation. The biggest expense is rearing maggots, as they dine high on the food chain and feed on meat. Fortunately, they are not particular, and will dine on any portion of carcass or slaughterhouse waste available.

Considered in the context of Africa's health care challenges, maggot therapy could greatly contribute to the successful treatment of wounds. It is a lack of treatment that causes major health problems. When wounds are not treated, ulcers remain. The WHO estimates that the lack of wound care in Africa generates as many fatalities each year as malaria. It seems this problem should be easy to resolve. However, the cost of delivering the necessary products to remote areas is high and therefore ineffective. A cascading model that utilised inexpensive raw materials, delivered output and generated cash flow and jobs could easily be configured. In fact, the system benchmarked at the Songhai Center in Benin (introduced in chapter two) demonstrates ways to accomplish the same. Maggot wound therapy could become a major health care initiative, while simultaneously generating massive numbers of jobs without imported material and equipment.

The country of Benin in Africa is a small former French colony bordering Nigeria. It has a rich history as a part of the Songhai Kingdom, which stretched across Benin and Nigeria before the French and the British imposed boundaries that severed culture and tradition. In 1985, Father Godfrey Nzamujo, a native Nigerian, undertook an ambitious plan to create an integrated farming and livestock operation that would provide food security for people of the region. Earlier, we described how he started the Songhai Center in Porto Novo, Benin. Like any farming program that includes animal husbandry and an *abattoir* or slaughterhouse, maintaining a high level of hygiene was a major challenge. What to do with the offal and the carcass portions that are not readily processed into meat and sausage? When mad cow disease swept Europe in the last decade, it was attributed to the use of animal waste as feed. European slaughterhouses were forced to incinerate all their waste. Father Nzamujo planned a different approach: feed it to the flies, as happens in nature—but in a controlled environment.

Father Nzamujo's strategy exemplifies a Chinese farming principle: if you have pests, give them the foods that they really like. Reserve a plot of land to grow their favourite nutrients and the pests will leave your crops in peace. The same applies to flies, which are always a nuisance in any food processing project. Killing flies with chemicals is like killing bacteria; it is not very effective. Their ecological function guarantees ample presence and supply.

Father Nzamujo allocated a remote site on the Songhai Center property where all slaughterhouse waste is deposited in small, square containers covered with bird nets to discourage feasting by vultures. The flies arrive and leave their eggs; the maggots hatch and grow. Harvesting is done by filling the containers with water, which causes the maggots to float to the top of the water so as to reach the air necessary for them to breathe. From there, they are easily scooped off each day and fed to quails. The quails flourish and the eggs they produce are air-exported to France where quail eggs are a highly sought-after delicacy. A portion of the maggot harvest is also used to feed fish, which in turn are netted for local consumption, and the remains contribute to soil amendments that nourish the chemical-free food crops. The Songhai Center generates organic food. According to Father Nzamujo, "That is easy in Africa, since fertilisers and pesticides are difficult to come by, and even if available they are too expensive."

Feeding maggots to fish and quail generates a lucrative return on many levels. However, regurgitated maggot enzymes that can be easily harvested and used for medical wound care generate a value that is a multiple of the whole system. It does not take a mathematician to do the arithmetic in terms of income and jobs. Considering that Africa imports most of its medical wound care supplies, the ability to utilise a locally produced resource represents huge savings. At Songhai Center, although no more than 60 pounds of enzyme can be collected on a monthly basis, their model holds promise as a major opportunity to lessen Africa's need for imported wound care materials and to make this ideal application broadly and inexpensively available to those in urgent need of treatment.

There are an estimated 15,000 *abattoirs* in Africa. Additionally, many animals are slaughtered in small villages. An estimated 200,000 villages locally process slaughtered livestock. If every *abattoir* in Africa were to complement their operation with a maggot farm, a fish farm, and a poultry farm (chickens, turkeys, quails and such), it would create an estimated 300,000-500,000 jobs in the production of maggots to provide protein-rich livestock feed and better, cheaper wound care. There would be no additional expense for raw materials. Only what is currently wasted, or what takes additional energy and effort to dispose, would be used. It would also eliminate the health risks associated with handling slaughterhouse waste. Maggot enzyme collection at this scale would be sufficient even for export. Such more extensive use would translate into unprecedented medical savings and tremendous benefit for wound care patients, who would regain health and mobility more quickly and reliably.

Benin was a first step, now others are following suit. Two brothers Jason and David Drew made their money establishing call centres in South Africa. The soldier fly and maggots made them rethink their calling in life. Jason wrote the book, *The Story of the Fly, and How It Could Save the World* (2012); and David pioneered farming maggots taking production, after experimentation on a farm in Franshoek, from the small scale 7-8 tons a month at the Songhai Centre in Benin to 100 tons a day in Elsenburg (Western Cape), in cooperation with the University of Stellenbosch. While this may sound like an awful lot of maggots, it only represents 300-400 carcasses of cows a day, a droplet in a mountain of offal.

Their mission is well articulated: for each ton of maggots, save a ton of fish meal and break out of the protein crunch. The brothers went on to create AgriProtein Ltd. in Cape Town (South Africa) and are committed to make a difference not just for the slaughterhouses in Africa, but for fish stocks around the world. Now the Drew brothers are not on their own with such ambitious missions. Hilderman Pedraza Vargas, medical doctor working with the National University of Colombia in Bogotá, has set up operations as well, and as the word spreads, dozens of small scale maggot farms will emerge throughout Africa and Latin America. The reason for success is simple: it is easy, fast, and while maggots generate income 24 hours a day, 7 days a week, you can do immense good.

Painless Injections

If maggots offered you a bit of inspiration and perhaps garnered a little of your respect, let us move on to the mosquito—another creature on most short lists of irksome pests. For some, a mosquito bite is nothing more than the cause of a bothersome itch, a micro-massage, or perhaps a nuisance. But for Tetsuya Oyauchi from Terumo, a large Japanese medical instrumentation company, and Masayuki Okano, president of a small metal-pressing company, the painless bite from a mosquito was an accomplishment that piqued their curiosity. Okano wondered, "Why do our syringes cause such pain, when mosquitoes are perfectly capable of extracting blood without any pain?"

Most people have an aversion to injections. They hurt. Anticipating the injection causes an anxiety that is almost unavoidable. A few patients will even faint. When the Terumo engineers and researchers learned what it was that allowed mosquitoes to painlessly draw their sustenance, and what it was that caused painful injections, they were stunned by the mechanical simplicity. It was about sizes and cone-shapes. The mosquito's proboscis is finer at the tip and gradually widens along its length. It was once thought that a needle's inside and outside diameters should be kept constant to transfuse medication. Making the tip diameter smaller was thought to make it harder to inject medical solutions, thus limiting how small the tip of a needle could be. But it is the cylinder-like shape of needles that causes pain.

Okano-san is known in Japan as the 'metalwork magician'. Starting with a super-thin sheet of stainless steel, Okano rolled it into a tiny tapered cylindrical cone, sealing it by welding the seam. Oyauchi used his medical engineering expertise to refine and develop what he names the Nanopass 33 Syringe. Its tip diameter is only 0.2 millimetres, 20 per cent less than previous needles. Rolling the metal into a cone with a specific contour gives the needle point its fineness. The tip can be superfine and gradually become wider, similar to the shape of the mosquito's proboscis. The problem was solved.

Terumo's patent application for a tapered injection needle and liquid-introducing implement was granted in 2004. Today hypodermic needles by Terumo are the standard for diabetic patients' daily needs. In Japan alone, there are some 600,000 diabetic patients who require daily insulin injections. Nearly 8 per cent of the American population suffers from diabetes, some 23.6 million people. Thus, the Terumo needle meets the needs of a large and appreciative customer base. By using less metal, there is also a net gain in material efficiency.

The Nanopass 33 needle received the Grand Good Design Award from the Japan Industrial Design Promotion Conference in 2005. Upon accepting the award, Okano commented: "It is fun to make something that doesn't exist in the world, and accomplish something people think can't be done." Like the case of silk, this is another example of how geometry borrowed from nature shapes products and helps solve our needs. While the Terumo needle cannot claim to have generated jobs, it has substantially reduced the pain suffered by patients needing medical injections. This puts it far ahead of the many disruptive technologies we thoughtlessly condone.

Gasless Propulsion

In nature, ecosystems first use the powers of physics without recourse to chemistry. The value of this is once more demonstrated by a significant potential application: propulsion gases. University of California researcher, Mario Molina, who with Sherwood Rowland received the Nobel Prize for their original work first published in 1974, identified propulsion gases as the cause of drastic ozone layer deterioration we now endure. Their work led to banning the infamous CFC (chlorofluorocarbon) gas and its derivates under the Montreal Protocol. Although industry offered a few new variations on propulsion gases, their use exemplifies how doing less harm is still very harmful.

Propulsion gases are commonly used for consumer applications, including misting devices for medical dosing of antihistamine or bactericide, and for cleaning and hairspray products. Mist spray technology enables droplet size, temperature and velocity to be closely controlled. Thus it has other applications, such as in the fuel-injection systems of automobile engines. More recently, the use of this chemistry has been replaced in some cases, such as hairspray, by a high pressure atomising dispenser. It is another of the fine examples demonstrating how the chemical industry found a solution that moved in the right direction, but failed to eliminate the unwanted and unplanned side-effects caused by inhaling designer chemicals. (We could note as well that patients suffering from cystic fibrosis or tuberculosis might better eliminate the biofilm of detrimental bacteria when a seaweed-inspired furanone is effectively blended with air and inhaled.)

Even though the French philosopher, Voltaire once declared, “The perfect should not stand in the way of the good,” it is timely to make a fundamental distinction between the good and the less bad. The search for a perfect solution should not stop anyone from implementing a good solution, but the search for total risk elimination should remain high on the agenda. In the case of propulsion gases, total risk elimination becomes a practical reality with the help of the bombardier beetle. It has an ability that may facilitate improved delivery of aerosolised respiratory medicines, greater automobile fuel efficiency, reduced emissions from fuel-injection systems, and even lowered risk of explosions in mines.

In nature, much has to do with nutrients and defense, or predator and prey. The bombardier beetle (*Brachinus carabidae*) is a rare evolutionary survivor. This amazing little insect has the ability to spray a stinging 100°C (212°F) liquid irritant over a distance that is 10 times its own length. This captivated the mind of Andy McIntosh, Professor of Thermodynamics and Combustion Theory at Leeds University, who was introduced to the bombardier's remarkable feats by Cornell University entymologist) Tom Eisner.

Just two centimetres long, the bombardier beetle uses its exothermic spray to defend itself against ants. The bombardier creates its spray by reacting hydroquinone with hydrogen peroxide stored in its fuel glands, producing a blast of steamy liquid. The beetle's one centimetre (0.4 in) diameter combustion chamber works rather like a pressure cooker. Once more, it is about pressure—physics—more than chemistry. The liquid in the chamber is held under pressure, a valve is opened, and flash evaporation occurs. The valve closes, the chamber refills, and the liquid heats to above the atmospheric boiling point when the chamber valve is re-opened. The beetle does this quickly and efficiently, spraying at 400-500 cycles per second. "Essentially, it is a high-force steam cavitation explosion," explains McIntosh.

This ingenious mechanical propulsion system that perfectly distributes a substance into the air at a particle size of no more than two nanometres has been modelled by scientists, who can reproduce its action at 20 cycles per second with the same throw ratio. As the bubbles in the chemical reaction of hydroquinone with hydrogen peroxide are so small, the ratio of surface area to volume administered is greatly increased, thus likewise enhancing efficiency.

Says McIntosh, "No one had ever studied the bombardier beetle from a physics and engineering perspective. At first, we did not appreciate how much we would learn from it." His new discovery has the potential to eliminate the impact of propulsion gases on the ozone layer while increasing dispensary performance. The Swedish entrepreneur, Lars Uno Larsson was enthused by this innovation and is taking it from concept, to pilot, to potential commercialisation. The innovation has found its entrepreneur. Once benchmarked, it can inspire others to pursue a wide range of applications.

Bundling Innovations

Possibilities that emerge from this examination of just a few innovations is that the combination of several of these technologies can potentially allow us to reconfigure our approach to health care. If one technology motivates us, bundling several innovations may encourage the design of a system that can impel our world towards true sustainability, and eliminate our dependence on the false comfort of chemistry that relies on non-renewable resources with unforeseen and detrimental effects. It suggests that we might rethink our approach to health and health care, to seek out and promote solutions that substitute something with nothing, that take inspiration from the physics of natural world.

To achieve this, to even work towards this goal, more contributions are needed. If the bacteria-suppressing furanones from seaweed or enzymes from maggots can be administered using a mechanical misting device inspired by the bombardier beetle, then we are truly achieving a new era of health care delivery. We will not be depositing residues and waste materials with undesirable side-effects into the ecosphere and its inhabitants. Instead, we can borrow components perfected over millions of years to achieve a functional, integrated system. The real power of evolution is not just that one species survived, but that a collaboration emerged. Multiple species fine-tuned their processes to reach symbiosis, achieving their needs and enhancing their survival.

This implies that the opportunity for entrepreneurs is not just creating new batteries or antibiotics, but in bundling innovations into sustainable systems. For businesses, for the economy itself, the employment opportunities the Blue Economy heralds point to a solid evolutionary path. The innovations of many will combine to achieve a greater whole.

What we have explored only scratches the surface of the potential. In less than a hundred years of modern scientific and technologic invention and application, we have achieved diminishing success in conquering viral and bacterial pathogens and the dangers perceived in our surrounding biota. Yet, any number of nature's time-tested solutions can inform our ability to overcome bacteria and viruses. Earthworms and barberries are producers of potent antibiotics and have resisted bacterial mutation for millions of years. The bombardier beetle, in surviving against armies of ants, deserves admiration and emulation for its exceptional capacity to outwit a species known for its superior swarm intelligence. This alone should further inspire us to respect biodiversity and ecosystems. It should motivate us to go beyond preservation of biodiversity toward ensuring that ecosystems continue to evolve without human-induced species loss. It offers a compelling logic for humanity to collaborate with evolution towards building ever more cohesive and adaptive ecosystems. Instead of learning about nature, we should start learning from nature.

Biodiversity and Health

With the loss of biodiversity comes the loss of the chance to learn from our fellow sentient species and to adapt the solutions they have invented. This is particularly the case for the gastric brooding frog or platypus frog (*Rheobatrachus silus*). Unfortunately, this species, native to Australia, did not survive excessive exposure to pesticides, herbicides, and the release of non-native species into its habitat. It could have taught us much about promoting healthy digestion and controlling bacteria. Once the mother frog had conceived, she swallowed the offspring, brooding them in her stomach until they were ready to be released into the world. This is possible through control and eradication of acidophilic bacteria and the delicate pH management of the stomach environment. The first phases of the tiny frog's life occur in an alkaline environment. If the typical gastric acidity persisted and acidophilic bacteria remained competitive, the offspring could not survive.

Our digestive health could have taken great inspiration from the *Rheobatrachus silus*. Stomach ulcers and gastric cancer have been poorly understood for decades. Extreme acidophilic bacteria were not considered the cause of these stomach diseases. Scientists, Barry Marshall and Robin Warren nonetheless identified ulcer- and cancer-causing bacteria so that the design of an appropriate cure and even a preventive treatment for high risk patients could be formulated. In 2005, both scientists were awarded the Nobel Prize in chemistry for their work. Had we the opportunity to further study the gastric brooding frog, we might have learned how to avoid the health hazards of excessive stomach acidity altogether. This knowledge was lost because we were ignorant or dismissive of the impact of our flawed systems on the life around us, which allow waste to be wasted and end up as pollution. Thousands of species are now threatened simply by such ignorance.

Our beautiful blue planet Earth, endlessly cycling in the embrace of dark cosmos and brilliant sunshine, provides us with the living conditions on which we depend not only for survival, but also for happiness. It is time to actively and consciously link our health to that of the Earth. It is time to reassess the contributions and genius of our ecosystems, and find ways to adapt natural processes and whole systems solutions to secure livelihoods and survival for all sentient living beings on this planet. Consequently we will discover, as has every other species through millions, perhaps even billions of years, new models for survivability, sustainability and abundance; models based on a Blue Economy—an economy of support and exchange—that provides more with less, and that is conducive to all life.

11

A Rainbow of Possibilities

> **The eye is the primary means whereby our understanding may most fully and abundantly appreciate the infinite works of Nature.**
>
> — *LEONARDO DA VINCI*

Light Perception

Visible light is made up of photons, which are packets of electromagnetic radiation travelling in straight lines, reflecting off objects then passing through the transparent, curved cornea into the eye. As the photons pass through the cornea and the lens, they transition from traveling through air to traveling through liquid. This liquid contains proteins with refractive properties, causing the photons to change direction and further bend to focus onto the retina, which is essentially a sheet of light-sensitive cells. This process is enhanced by adjustment of the pupil diameter to admit the right quantity of light. Specialised muscles adjust the shape of the lens to improve focus and visual flexibility. Meanwhile, muscles attached outside the eye work to keep the same focal point and to scan back and forth in a coordinated manner. Photons strike a retinal molecule, a modified form of vitamin A. Contact with an incoming photon causes the retina to react by initiating a complex biochemical cascade within the cell that ultimately generates an electrical signal sent to the brain. There, the information from millions of retinal photoreceptors is combined to provide details about contrast and colour. The upside-down images formed on both retinas are mentally combined and inverted and the resulting images are interpreted—in this case, as the words on this page.

Lenses are a key component of the art of light. These refract light, converting or diverting the beam. The earliest mechanical lenses were devised in Assyria almost 3,000 years ago. However, several of nature's fauna developed lenses hundreds of million of years ago. The octopus created thin film lenses. The brittle star produced distortion-free lenses. These two marvels of lens technology are indications that our scientific understanding of optics still has a long way to go, and a huge potential for commercial application is yet to be tapped.

New applications do find their way to the market in a most surprising manner. In Japan, dragonflies represent lightness and joy. They remind us that we are light and, if we choose to do so, we can reflect that light in powerful ways. The dragonfly's ability to generate energy through the concentration of light has garnered the attention of renewable energy researchers. Concentrated solar power (CSP) is an emerging and benchmarked industry highly dependent on subsidies. In the desert of southern Spain, over 1,000 mirrors have been positioned that reflect sunlight to superheat water in a central tower, a development and investment of Abengoa. It uses mirrors to focus sunlight onto the water much as the dragonfly does. By 2050, the solar power harvested using CSP is expected to eliminate the atmospheric release of 2.1 billion tons of CO_2. Annual CSP investments can exceed US$100 billion and create almost 2 million jobs even when the crisis in Spain causes temporary job losses since subsidies evaporated. The technology of light is likely to persist and live up to its expectations.

Ultraviolet: Light Humans Do Not See

Light does not always bring colour. There is also light from the sun that we do not see at all. Light has different wavelengths. Ultraviolet (UV) light has shorter wavelengths than visible light, having a frequency higher than what we identify as violet—hence its name. The UV light emanates at a higher frequency than the human eye can distinguish. The potentially beneficial effects of UV light exposure are well documented. It can address many skin diseases, such as psoriasis. It stimulates the production of vitamin D, which helps the body absorb calcium to maintain bone strength and lower cancer risk. It provides a natural control mechanism for mites in carpets, rugs, and upholstery. Ultraviolet light treats the water in swimming pools to control bacteria, replacing the use of chlorine, that ubiquitous (and toxic) germ killer.

There are also well-known negatives to excessive UV exposure. It may lead to skin cancer, especially since our protective ozone layer has been damaged by propulsion gases like CFC, which, as learned from the bombardier beetle, need not have been used in the first place. Consumer product marketers promote a variety of protection schemes to counter the perceived risks of excessive UV exposure. These include designer chemicals like oxybenzone, a compound that absorbs UV but is now a suspected photo-carcinogen. In the laboratory, this chemical may have low reactivity, but when illuminated by light, it gets excited and becomes potentially harmful to biological tissue. Zinc and titanium oxide, inorganic particles that reflect, scatter, and absorb UV rays, were marketed for their UV-protective properties. But recent research at the University of California Riverside indicates that these sunscreens must be reapplied every two hours to remain effective. Otherwise, they unleash free radicals causing skin cell damage that may be worse than the UV exposure! Of course, that has all changed since coffee came to the scene.

In nature, many species have adapted to prolonged exposure to UV light and are able to neutralise its effects. Of course, plants must have sunlight to drive photosynthesis. Being rooted, they cannot move into available shade when the sun is too bright. They must create protection. Many animals are also vulnerable to prolonged UV exposure. The mechanisms evolved by plants and animals to protect against these negative effects can give us resources, insight and inspiration.

The edelweiss, the unofficial national flower of Austria, has been studied in detail by the Belgian scholar, Jean Pol Vigneron. The edelweiss does not reflect UV but rather absorbs it in thousands of little hairs, avoiding tissue penetration that destroys living cells. Many lichen and fungi exist in high Arctic, Antarctic, or desert areas where

UV exposure is immense. As a result, they tend to have absorbing pigments. For instance, a novel photo-protective mycosporine has been isolated from the fungi living in symbiosis with Collema cristatum, a microalgae forming lichen. The pure isolated compound prevents UV-induced skin cell destruction when applied prior to irradiation. Certainly, some lichens show better protective traits than others. Yet this field of research is most promising because it offers simple protection, replaces toxic applications, and eliminates reliance on mined materials that require massive energy to extract and process.

Certain fruits such as apples and tomatoes are notably sensitive to ultraviolet radiation and must protect themselves. They offer a biochemical recipe that provides better protection than titanium oxide. The tomato skin is rich in lycopene, a carotenoid in the same family as beta-carotene. Lycopene has powerful antioxidant properties and provides a high level of UV protection. In fact, as the two colleagues at Café des Deux Magots now discuss, some tomatoes even do better than others in generating this protective shield.

The Evolution of Colour and Perception

The optical mechanisms for vision was first developed some 540 million years ago, during the period named Cambrian Explosion. Suddenly—in less than one million years, a short span in evolutionary terms—and for no obvious reason, a broad range and diversity of life began to flourish. Creatures took on hard body parts, shells and spines, and shapes and colours of every description. The ability to perceive and visually distinguish surrounding phenomena became a dominant force of evolution. Vision was a survival advantage for both predator and prey. Food could be more easily identified, predators could be recognised, and mates could be located. Some species evolved bright colourations and intricate patterning to blend with their environment, to warn of their power to defend, or to impress mates.

Cambrian decendants—birds, mammals, reptiles, fish, mollusks, and wonderfully iridescent beetles—have all created their own way of seeing, as well of producing colour. Poison dart frogs use conspicuous colour to tell predators that they are not good to eat. Venomous coral snakes sport rings of bright colour to advertise that they are not to be messed with. A white milk snake, which isn't poisonous and could be quite safely eaten, benefits from the coral snake's reputation simply by copying its colourations. A cuttlefish changes colour to match its background in a millisecond. A chameleon camouflaged with stripes and spots can stalk its prey without being seen.

Dr Hopi Hoekstra, Loeb Associate Professor of Natural Sciences at Harvard University, studies the genetic mechanisms at work in a species of mouse that adapts to its environment by being sand-coloured if living at the beach and dark if inland. Parrotfish are able to change their sex and appearance from female to male. Females in a group are much less colourful than the dominant male. If the male fish gets eaten, the dominant female changes her sex—and puts on brilliant colours of the male. Parrots, the birds, can see UV light. They look flamboyant to each other, even when we only see their monochromatic feathers.

Pigments are chemical substances produced by living organisms that appear as colours because they selectively absorb and reflect certain wavelengths of light. Pigments can never add to, but only subtract, wavelengths from a light source. A frog is green not because it has green pigment, but because it reflects blue light from yellow pigment. The white hairs of a polar bear or an arctic fox's winter coat are actually clear. There are neither pigments to absorb nor structures to reflect certain wavelengths. Thus, they reflect the entire spectrum, making the animal appear white.

The Cyphochilus beetle and other beetles have a highly unusual brilliantly white shell. The cyphochilus has evolved its superb whiteness on scales that are just five micrometres thick, 10 times thinner than a human hair. The random surface structure on its scales simultaneously absorbs and scatters every colour. Industrial mineral coatings, such as those used on high-quality paper, plastics, and some paints, need to be twice as thick to be as white. According to measures for whiteness and brightness, beetles are whiter and brighter than milk or the average human tooth, both of which are considerably thicker.

Many animals acquire their colouration through pigments that are metabolise. Others take in pigments through what they eat, displaying those through their skin. For example, the pink colouration of the scarlet ibis comes from its diet of crabs and shrimp that consume red algae. (Imagine if humans could generate colours simply from what we eat!) Nearly all the blue hues we see in the animal world, including the colours of the blue damselfly (*Enallagma civile*), are produced not by blue pigment, but by blue light reflected from tiny tissue structures that scatter light and often enhance it. Some species produce colour not by pigmentation but by microstructures in fur, feathers, scales, petals, or other features that reflect only certain wavelengths of light. In animals, the building material is often keratin.

Birds-of-paradise and hummingbirds have feathers that possess a stunning iridescence, a metallic sheen that is perhaps the most spectacular colour effect of all. The colour effects of the Egyptian scarab and the rainforest beetle have been copied in jewellery for millennia, but have never been industrially reproduced. Some orchids enhance their visual attractiveness by the combination and spacing of gold and silver flecks in their otherwise chemically pigmented petals. A similar effect is found in African violets. Through millions of years of trial-and-error, many organisms have perfected methods to enhance attractiveness using metallic colour effects, although no metals are involved. The underlying structures that generate these colourations vary widely from species to species. One exceptional colour producer identified and described by Andrew Parker is the sea mouse (*Polychaeta aphroditidae*). This marine animal is covered with iridescent hairs and the effect is sheer beauty.

Colour Pigmentation as Commodity

The earliest known pigments used by humans were minerals. Natural iron oxides produce a range of colours and are still discernible in cave paintings after 20 millennia or more. As early as the Middle Ages, the search for permanent and stable colours drove industry towards complex chemistry and created highly profitable businesses. Two of the first synthetic pigments were white and blue. White was made by combining lead with vinegar in the presence of CO_2. Blue pigment, known as 'blue frit', was made with calcium copper silicate derived from crushed glass coloured with a copper ore, such as malachite.

In the merchandising world of today, like the Cambrian Age of pre-history, colouration still serves as an attractant. In the contemporary case, however, bright colours and unique patterns are displayed more in the hopes of attracting a buyer than a mate. The marketing, selling and even consumption of product such as paint, ink, fabric, plastics, cosmetics and food, rely on colouration to stand out. The demand for colour is vast and growing. By 2015, total world pigment consumption will reach 9 million tons, good for a turnover of more than 24 billion dollars. This means that the average price for a ton of colour was more than US$2,600. This is four times the price for cellulose needed for paper making, or palm oil for biofuels. From a business standpoint, colour pigments are a high-end product with solid margins.

It is remarkable that humans are prepared to adorn themselves with clothing and cosmetics without ever asking about the ingredients and methods used to create the same. Today, colour pigmentation is created by cadmium, chromium, cobalt, lead, mercury, titanium, and zinc. In short, it depends on mining practices and ore processing that are far from a model of sustainability. Furthermore, the application and use of colour pigments is now highly regulated, since many have been found to be potential health hazards. Yet, none of the modern industry standards require biodegradable pigments. Nor are regulations to be found when it comes to disposing cast-off goods and their metal oxide colour components. Along with batteries, colour pigments are probably responsible for the majority of heavy metal pollution in landfills. Since these pigments were designed to last and not to fade, thus not to degrade; they can concentrate at dangerous levels of contamination. When indiscriminately dispersed into the environment, they often pollute entire ecosystems.

Colour is beautiful but it is a dirty business. From a business standpoint, the most desirable colour is white. Optical brighteners such as chlorine bleach and benzene, the market standards for 'brightening' fabric, paper and plastics, effectively produce visible white due to their very strong light absorption capabilities. These optical brighteners convert the yellowish colour from oxidation to an effect perceived by the eye as white, giving the impression of cleanliness. Clean or not, the impression is what we value. However, these optical brighteners are suspected allergens and are highly toxic. While pigments and optical brighteners may be the best we have, how can we manage this differently than the way our industrial society has done? The hope is that once we grasp the way in which light and colour shaped evolution in the past, we may be able to use nature's solutions to shape the industries of tomorrow.

Andrew Parker has identified the simple structure responsible for the iridescent colouration of species, such as hummingbirds and beetles, and understands how to produce metallic iridescent colour the way nature achieved it millions of years ago. He has challenged himself to formulate iridescent colours that can be manufactured on a commercially viable scale and produce a desirable visual effect while emulating the creative ways nature has produced colour. He rightly contends that if these vibrant and attractive colourations can be formulated using the physics and biochemistry adapted by animals and plants, it not only represents an important breakthrough, but also offers a strong marketing message that resonates with the growing segment of manufacturers and consumers seeking nontoxic and non-polluting alternatives. His goal is to establish the technical research base for a portfolio of innovations that could find applications in multiple industries. Photonic engineering may soon provide colouration results without cadmium, lead, or chromium!

The manufacturing technique may be as simple as the production of glass. If the concept proves successful, the potential is vast. The preliminary trials are convincing. The first application is for cosmetics, a sector with a unique interest in generating colours beyond those offered on the market presently. Since cosmetics are more than beauty and also embrace skin health, Parker's work has multiple facets. Companies looking to differentiate themselves with a 'fresh and natural' angle in their marketing strategies will be interested in this innovative approach. Parker's research efforts may well be a milestone in industrial development and a platform for the creation of new industries that are in true harmony with ecosystems. The only challenge remaining is organising supply.

Beyond cosmetics, there are applications such as a chemical-free coating for glassware and crystal, which have traditionally relied on lead. A novel crystal figure can be produced, if a piece of glass containing the appropriate microstructure was invisibly inserted into a crystal statue of the whole animal. It would feature spectacular flashes of colour in a more effective way than can be achieved with glass prisms. This would not only have the same visual effect as the living animal, but the effect would be based on an optical device identical to what the animal uses. The Austrian crystal maker, Swarovski has grasped the opportunity and will be the first to meet people's desire for adornment and delight working with this innovation.

Waste for One, Resource for Another

The location of a tomato processing plant is carefully chosen to minimise transportation from the farm, so that as soon as fresh tomatoes arrive, they can be converted to tomato paste. Unilever represents 6 per cent of the 40 million tons of industrially processed tomatoes, good for 2.2 million in 2012. With a high volume of tomatoes to process, there are factory waste streams for everything that is not processed and packed. The tomato skin waste generated from the said volume of tomatoes amounts to some 30,000 tons a year. If the Unilever factories were to add a subsidiary operation that produced a lycopene-based sunscreen from tomato skin waste, then the present titanium-based UV protection agents would be instantly under-priced and outmoded. The renewable available raw material would be free, and using it would actually save the tomato paste factory the expense of waste disposal.

It is true that compared to coffee, tomatoes generate much less waste. Yet, the processing residue is expelled through the wastewater treatment system, using thousands of cubic metres of water. Of the remaining solids, some 3 per cent ends up as landfill. This goes unnoticed, given that supply chain managers and corporate policy focus on short-term gain and do not search for any value from waste. To us, however, these few percentage points should be interesting indeed. In business, there is a saying that a penny saved on each product is a million added to the bottom line. However, it is a logic that is not applied once an output is considered waste. This is where ecosystems offer solid inspiration, since nature finds value in waste.

As per the ways of nature's whole systems achieving material efficiency isn't accomplished by just one process. There are always multiple functions providing multiple benefits, as tomato skins superbly illustrate. Tomato skins diverted from the waste stream are not only good as an antioxidant and for UV sunlight protection, but also form the source of a naturally derived, food-safe red colouring that could be utilised in many frozen food products ranging from packaged salmon, to strawberries, to ice cream. Thus, if tomatoes were the core business, the spin-offs in health (UV protection), personal care (cosmetics), fisheries (protein food) and ice cream (dessert) would fit them into a cascading model. Iron oxides and synthetic colour pigments derived from petroleum and mined metals are only offering one product and an unaccountable waste stream. Lycopenes are part of a cluster of utilisable materials that can be rescued from biological waste. Red lipstick made from tomato skins would have a cachet of its own. In fact, if women knew the ingredients presently used for lipstick manufacture, the tomato skin version would become irresistible.

An entrepreneurial business plan would involve developing lycopene extraction and processing technologies; knowing the lycopene extraction potential from the skins; assessing the volume of UV-protection products the market consumes and at what price; and determining the volume and price of red pigment purchased by the food industry. A tomato skin processing plant established near a tomato processing factory could sell extracted lycopene at a competitive industry price in order to be manufactured into food-safe pigment dyes and UV sunscreen products. This transformation of waste management to accelerated innovation would profitably generate local jobs, provide lower consumer prices for higher quality products, replace unsustainable business practices, and help secure health and reduce toxin exposure. Such an environmentally sound and financially secure business model can succeed on many levels. Analysing tomatoes starts sounding like processing coffee grounds. It gets interesting all the time.

From the viewpoint of cost analysis, it is considered too expensive to extract lycopenes from tomatoes for the lycopenes alone. Yet, this conclusion implies that we would waste rest of the tomato and that would not make sense, although this is exactly the way industry rationalises today. In such a narrow economic analysis, Parker's proposal to derive both colouration and UV protection from the tomato could never compete with titanium oxide in sunscreen lotions. On the other hand, if the raw material for both is derived from tomato waste, then we are in business. The generation of two value-adding derivatives (UV protection and colour pigment) from one waste stream is a much improved business proposal, collectively complementing the industrial food production. This logic is not taught in the world's best academic business schools where core business–core competence strategy is locked in with discounted cash flow analysis. Double revenue streams generated from free materials result in a much higher integrated cash flow than could be achieved by the processing of tomatoes alone.

Thus the entrepreneurial business model could also incorporate use of the tomato seed waste as well as the skin. Tomato seeds from the larger volume paste processors are either dumped in landfills or sold cheaply to cattle farmers. The nutritional value of the seeds for cattle feed is low—it is a filler, rather than a feeder. However, tomato seeds are rich in health-boosting trace elements and softening monounsaturated and polyunsaturated fatty acids. Hence, a better match of materials to market would be to turn these seeds into products that soothe our skin or nourish our bodies.

The world demand for processed tomato products—boiled, sliced and diced, canned, bottled, dried, in all its many international flavours—could also meet that for safe UV-protection products, cosmetic products, and pigment dyes from the unused tomato peels and seeds. Cascading materials in this fashion offers unique opportunities to develop promising markets, create successful applications and achieve busy factories. If these derivative processing facilities were located near the primary tomato processing centre, the transport costs would be minimal. This clustering of businesses contributes to cash flow, reduces costs and generates jobs.

The Biorefinery of the Future

Imagining ways to reintegrate waste streams into nutrient streams brings into focus the outline of a biorefinery. The concept of a biorefinery was originally developed by Prof Dr Carl-Göran Hedén, member of the Club of Rome and of the Royal Swedish Academy of Sciences. Hedén's idea of a biorefinery involved the capacity to generate more with what has already been harvested or processed. Envisioning a cascading of nutrients and materials, he devised a demonstration facility where all chemicals and catalysts were processed in a closed loop. Lignin, hemicellulose, cellulose, lipids, and essential oils were extracted from one tree. Revenues were tripled merely by eliminating waste.

In the case of the tomato, we might calculate how many jobs could be generated using the biorefinery concept. The net job generation of this initiative may be larger than expected. The Food and Agricultural Organization (FAO) of the United Nations reports that the worldwide area utilised for tomato farming is nine million acres. The world output is about 150 million tons. The USA alone produces 10 million tons. Considered entrepreneurially, we would say that the world wastes around two million tons of potential additive, pigment, and oil sources. This amount is impressive and allows us to realise that it is possible to replace metal-based pigments and UV-protectors without ever stressing the Earth to produce alternatives, and without competing for food as is the case for the corn grown to produce fuel or plastics. The earth is already producing all that is essential; we only need to use what is available.

At present, one ton of colour pigment costs an average of US$2,600. Tomato-derived natural pigment sources could be made available for roughly US$1,000 per ton, as the materials are obtained from spent product that is available for free or for the cost of local transportation. Inexpensive raw materials would make it possible to produce the pigment at a lower base cost. This new business opportunity would factor out at about US$2 billion—the value of what is wasted today, dumped in landfills, devoured by cattle that cannot digest it, and off-gassing methane pollution in the process. In Brazil (where Unilever currently has its newest processing plant), factory workers live comfortably on US$10,000 per year. We could safely state that a turnover of US$2 billion in a country like Brazil could generate possibly 100,000 jobs.

These numbers give rise to a broader debate. Prior to embarking on a guesstimate, it is important to remind ourselves of the market dynamics. If something is expensive yet desirable, demand will remain low. As the price decreases, demand will increase. Price elasticity studies show that lowering the price of highly desirable products generates a greater than proportional increase in demand. If tomato-based biochemistry were available at half the price of that used today, then it would undercut the dominant products on the market and stimulate demand. Where part of the increase would be by replacing of the non-sustainable options now available, the overall demand would also grow.

Worldwide, two million tons of tomato waste equates to only 12 per cent of the world's coffee waste. Yet thanks to our appetite for ketchup, salsa, and spaghetti sauce, this waste stream could supply every lipstick manufacturer in the world with all the colour pigments required. Colour pigments from tomato waste would provide cheaper, better, natural, and proven UV protection, while helping the women of the world enhance their beauty. Nor does this lipstick taste like tomatoes! This is the basis of the new economy that we see emerging. While it is already more than an idea, imagine what would happen if everything produced were to follow this logic. Here again is our Blue Economy—working with what we have, responding to basic needs, accomplishing greater sustainability than we ever envisioned, generating jobs, and building social capital while competing successfully in the market.

The Biorefinery Today

The idea of Prof Hedén may have been a grand vision. Now it is turning into a reality. Surprising but true: Dra. Catia Bastioli, the CEO of Novamont, the pioneer in bio-plastics opened in 2014 the first biorefinery. Based on a 1,000 patent strong portfolio of intellectual property, her team of engineers studied the infrastructure of a defunct petrochemical plant in Porto Torres, Sardinia (Italy) and concluded that a major portion of the infrastructure could be reused to process a biological feedstock. The question emerges: what feedstock is locally available? The 1.6 million strong population does not drink enough coffee to power a 360,000 tons per year facility; the farmers have long given up planting tomatoes. The Sardinians believed that tourism would provide for their livelihood. Thus, 175,000 acres of fertile land was left foul. Then in the aftermath of the 2008 financial crisis, the tourists stopped coming, worse the friendly regime in Libya crumbled a few years later in the Arab Spring and the low cost supply of fuel must now be purchased at world market prices. Bastioli's team studied all local resources and soon realised that the native artichoke thistle (*Cynara cardunculus*), which invaded the land after agriculture came to a stop, can be processed into protein, animal feed, plastics, lubricants, herbicides and elastomers. ENI, one of the top 10 petroleum groups of the world, quickly calculated that the social and environmental cost associated with the closure of their facility could now be turned into an investment.

The effect is profound. Millions that used to flow from the island into pockets of the oil supplier now enrich local farmers. Thistles are perennials, require no tilling, fertilisers, irrigation or pesticides, lowering the barrier to re-entry into the profession of agriculture. The lack of capital and of experience actually comes in handy. Farming thistles does not compare with corn. The creation of value to a 'weed' generates a multiplier of growth into the local economy, where readily available material is processed at a fraction of the capital cost, producing six revenue streams protected by two decades of fundamental research. The concept of the biorefinery now gains credibility, the fantasy turned vision now becomes reality owing to science and the preparedness to swap a certain cost of closure for an opportunity to compete in the bio-based economy. Better, Matrica, the newly established joint-venture between Novamont and ENI, offers a solution for the traditional petrochemical industry in Europe and elsewhere, which is forever deprived of low cost access to naphtha, this petroleum-based liquid that is the starting stock for most chemical derivatives. The conversion of a society processing coffee and tomatoes already seemed a major leap forward. A society benefitting from thistles processed in an old petrochemical plant really gets everyone's mind spinning. And this is only just the beginning of this emerging Blue Economy.

The gain in material and energy efficiency is impressive. The petrochemical plant processed 2.5 million tons of fuel and naphtha into 700,000 tons of chemicals. The processing of 360,000 tons of thistles give value to 350,000 tons of feed, plastics and functional chemicals. Jobs are maintained, nature is put back on its evolutionary path, and funds are available to undertake the clean-up of Europe's first petroleum cracker built in 1962. A clean piece of land, a revival of farming, a re-industrialisation and a social opportunity, while replacing non-renewable feedstock appeals to investors, civil society, the unions and the policymakers. It is seldom that innovations can build on consensus. Perhaps, the only one struggling with this new reality are the economists who have to get used to multiple benefits and chemical engineers who now embark on a blend of organic and inorganic chemistry. It is new, but fun.

If Heinz and Unilever—the giant tomato processors of the world—neglect these opportunities, then entrepreneurial partnerships will emerge like the one of Novamont with ENI, which that take science and cash flow to the next level: profit derived from converting old uncompetitive plants while responding to the basic needs of all—including a healthy blue planet on which to live—with what we have, including the thistles.

12

Envisioning New Energy Options

If you do not change direction, you may end up where you are headed.

— CHINESE PROVERB

The class of fourth grade children in Yokohama, Japan, is excited: they are getting a banana they can eat during class, and the aroma is as pleasing as the taste. The teacher also gives each of them a hardboiled egg. They are instructed to cut the banana peel into little pieces with scissors and to pulverise the eggshell. The two are mixed and a little water is added. Next, the probes of a digital voltmeter are inserted into the eggshell-banana peel paste. Everyone exclaims and claps their hands: the voltmeter registers an electrical current!

The reaction in Japan is no different in Brazil, or South Africa: adults are surprised and children are excited. Everyone wonders how it is possible. We are only familiar with modern sources of energy, such as steam generators, nuclear power stations, coal-fired electrical power plants, hydroelectric generators, and photovoltaic solar panels. Yet these forms of energy are all recent arrivals on Earth. For the previous four billion years no one relied on any of these human engineering marvels. As a result of this ingenuity, we struggle with climate change due to excessive CO_2 and face long-term societal costs for storage and containment of nuclear waste.

While we are busy getting electricity from the grid, we are unaware that our heart requires just 0.2 volts, built up by the combination of 70 millivolt charges in order to regulate the daily flow of roughly 2000 gallons of blood through all four chambers of the heart. Its power supply consists of nothing more than the biochemistry of potassium, sodium, and calcium. There are no batteries and nothing is wired. No copper is needed. Indeed, thanks to a selective diet evolved over millennia, we ingest a blend of molecules that, amongst other functions, provides a regular supply of biochemicals to make our heart, brain, and nervous system work without maintenance—hopefully measured for decades, or even longer. No power station designed by man supplies energy as reliably as the simple biochemical reactions performed within our body.

Amory Lovins, co-founder of the Rocky Mountain Institute, is among the world's most creative thinkers on energy. He has often shown that our society's centralised energy production, consisting of huge power stations with masses of wires and cables reaching like tentacles into every home, is not the ideal way to achieve a sustainable electrical supply. If we were to take time to observe the manner in which natural systems have secured a continuous supply of energy for millennia, we would realise that none of our mainstream power generators apply those principles. Indeed, the collateral damage created by our present energy scheme risks destroying the very life support systems on which we depend.

Today, it is the means of providing energy that tilts the supply equation towards trouble. The massive output of three gases—carbon dioxide (CO_2), methane (CH_4), and nitrous oxide (N_2O)—has had a pervasive impact on the thin band of breathable atmosphere that surrounds our planet. The delicately balanced atmosphere that envelops the Earth is the result of millions of years of interactions with its forest cover. Since less than 30 per cent of the original forests remains, unless we embark on massive regeneration of forests in all climates, the basis by which the atmosphere is maintained is shifting beyond repair, as Dr Paolo Lugari already outlined in 2002 on the occasion of his lecture to the scientists of Los Alamos in New Mexico (USA). The sources are known. The carbon dioxide comes mainly from burning fossil fuels, the methane from animal waste, and the nitrous oxide from applying natural gas-derived fertilisers to our agricultural crops. We have created a system much like a huge tanker ship on autopilot. It is hard to stop, takes time to change course, and has no one to make the quick decisions required to avoid collision.

The drive towards energy efficiency only started in earnest after the first petroleum crisis in 1974. The Club of Rome had warned about the vicious cycle of population explosion, increased industrial output, rising energy demand, and excessive pollution two years earlier through its report *Limits to Growth*. Yet, nearly all the current alternatives to fossil fuel have major drawbacks. None are inspired by how natural systems have resolved the issue of energy security over millions of years. Worse, most of the options being considered make no economic sense. Ultimately, we must go beyond temporary and intermediate options such as nuclear, photovoltaic, hydrogen, and wind power, and embrace solutions proven in ecosystems that continuously renew and refresh air and water.

Nations that have opted for nuclear power as their back-up energy source have committed their citizens to cover the risks, often without asking permission. Nuclear proponents should ask the world's leading insurance companies whether or not they are prepared to cover the risks without a taxpayer-funded guarantee. What they will discover is that no insurer is willing to write a policy for a nuclear energy site, unless the government agrees to accept full risk, forever! This generates neither jobs nor value. And when governments are prepared to commit to all citizens and their offsprings for generations to come, why does not the same logic apply to all other renewable energies?

Rethinking Demand-Side

In nature, most species meet their basic needs using the resources available. How can we model the same for our energy generation and consumption? If we consider how natural systems efficiently generate energy, as they have successfully done for millions of years, we might discover the means to cut demand by a factor of 10 or even 20 while offering greater accessibility. The idea emerges of a consumption system that requires much less external energy, that significantly reduces the need for mining and dramatically cuts down the pollution from carbon dioxide, methane and nitrous oxide. The new business model we envision will actually undo some of the collateral damage that has been tacitly tolerated. This is the new approach to demand-side management: intervention on the supply side. If we make better use of what is available, if we retool to achieve greater efficiency, if we learn how to produce sustainably by generating multiple benefits from the same infrastructure, it will mean that we have learned to apply physics in our daily lives. We will at last be achieving best use of our physical universe. Replacing something with nothing, and reusing waste as raw material, means we need less, and have more.

Over time, every species has adapted to refine and conserve the energy it needs to naturally heat, cool, transport, or transform. Bottlenose dolphins and whales know how to reduce drag, whereas bluefin tuna know how to conserve heat. The boxfish inspires car design with its superb efficiency. Antifreeze is naturally made by yellow mealworm beetles; the abalone produces ceramics in cold water. We can include the cold light made by squid, the hibernation chemistry of bears, solid-state energy produced by lichens, frictionless sliding accomplished by the Arabian sand lizard, water harvesting by desert beetles, and the heating and cooling systems perfected by termites. Each adaptation convincingly demonstrates that species can evolve ways to achieve maximal energy efficiency. When the contributions of each are woven into ecosystems that cascade nutrients and energy, we cannot but be in awe of their elegance and precision. Energy is never an objective on its own, it is a means to an end. Most of the time, energy brings food and water, creates housing, facilitates transport (to get food or mates) and promotes health. Ecosystems generate energy far more efficiently than our manufactured approaches. Nature teaches us that replacing 'something' with 'nothing' can bring us the surprising solutions for incorporating sustainability, and creating the industries of the future.

That is the concept: replace something with nothing, or with something so tiny and different, that it has no resemblance at all to the system replaced. This is a radically different approach to solve our energy problems. It also underscores the business model shift that is required to reduce our dependence on oil and mined materials that are refined by burning additional fossil fuels.

Recall Fritz Vollrath's silk nano-engineering. Where designer polymers—plastics—have replaced metals over the past 50 years, they have increased demand for petroleum, which is the raw material for these plastics. Here again is the opportunity to use benchmarked, tested, developed technology that mirrors nature's methods and 40 centuries of farmers' wisdom. Replacing titanium with silk would realise a dramatic reduction in the demand for steel and high performance metals, as well as the need for mining and energy consumption. Chelating bacteria are also being researched that can meet demand by recovering metals from end-of-life batteries. Instead of employing smelters that evaporate metals, chelation recovery is done at ambient temperature, using less energy.

Recall Bruce Roser's innovation using natural processes to stabilise temperature-dependent pharmaceutical products that would otherwise perish. Eliminate the need for vaccine refrigeration and we can shave US$300 million off the cost of heath care delivery in developing nations. Such a portfolio of replacing something with nothing technologies, applied to our health care delivery system and our food production systems, will further reduce energy consumption. The energy savings would be truly massive, counted not just in what would be preserved, but also what would be reused.

Recall Curt Hallberg's vortex technology. The greatest and most reliable source of energy on Earth comes from gravity. We cannot neglect the vast opportunities offered by a force that works 24 hours a day, not merely when there is sunlight. Just about every living species has adapted to this very predictable force, and uses it to optimally meet its needs. A vortex is reliably generated by gravity, and has the potential to provide potable water with a minimal expense of energy. The swirling force of the vortex, used in applications that would remove bacteria and air from water, would eliminate the need for bactericides and lower energy consumption as well.

And let us introduce Stefan Larsson, the brain behind fascinating solar systems that work north of Stockholm. Stefan used to work for Vattenfall, one of Europe's leading generators of electricity and heat, and one of the biggest wind power operators in the UK. Stefan headed their solar research and had the challenging task to design solar panels that would catch the sun even when it is only 8 degrees above the horizon. Now we reckoned that solar research is pioneered in solar-rich parts of the world. Stefan applied another logic: if you can make solar work in the north of Sweden, then it will work beyond doubt anywhere in the world. As he deployed optical effects to concentrate sun rays and light using stationary reflectors, Stefan succeeded in getting the systems to work. Then, Vattenfall decided that its future depends on nuclear and decided to close the solar research program. Stefan received the opportunity of a lifetime; he got the patents and the basics of the lab, and created with partners, Solarus.

It seemed misplaced to imagine a solar industry in Sweden but as time evolved, Stefan applied simple logic that had been overlooked by all experts—who spoiled by abundance of sun—never asked the obvious question: if solar photovoltaic (PV) works on both sides, why do we only use one side? The specialists will quickly point out that solar on top and concentrated solar on the bottom overheats the panels, and efficiency drops. Stefan had responded with a second obvious question: why don't we cool solar panels with water just the same way we do with a car engine? At the time when all PV manufacturers raced to reduce thickness of the wafer, cutting costs by reducing the core material, the idea to put water pipes inside a wafer seemed to come from an outsider, disconnected from the real solar world. Stefan insisted and built his own version relying on PV panels from Hitachi. With one-third of the wafer size, he could generate 18 per cent more electricity while generating 60-70° hot water for free. The combined efficiency of heat and power, using less energy and material, is more then double the performance of traditional panels. Who has been blinded by an abundance of sun? Need is the mother of invention.

Solar on Both Sides

Stefan had went on the surreal question: do solar panels work at night? While he had earned some credibility in the scientific world with his innovative multi-layered optical films that caught sun and light that barely rose above the horizon, he received a cold response. However, tests demonstrated that the water in the double-sided solar system actually cooled at night. Indeed, the black cells radiate all heat out into the dark space, and cold water could be harvested. Now Stefan's design offers heat, power and chill. Whereas Sweden has no need for cold water, its relevance was quickly spotted by Prof Eduard Ayensu from Ghana, a leading scientist from Africa who also worked with the World Bank. He concluded that solar cells at night can replace the refrigerator. A two cubic metre room inside a home would provide natural cooling during the hot summer days eliminating not only the investment but also the ongoing cost for power. The solar system now offers three benefits. And it only had just begun.

Water stored at more than 60° for hours is sanitised. The units offer clean water, a major contribution for health. Consequently, Stefan and his team redesigned the structural design and substituted the aluminum frame with recycled plastics. It can be adapted to serve as a roof structure; in with other words, the solar system serves as a roof and since it includes a 22.5 centimetre deep air filled space, it works like insulation in winter and summer. This remarkable adventure to capture sun in Scandinavia now emerges as a revolutionary multi-modal system that offers heat, chill, power, sanitation, roofing, insulation and kick-starts a plastics recycling industry. Stefan and his partners never imagined that they would be able to cut the cost chase with solar panels made in Sweden, but decided to share their breakthroughs with anyone prepared to start local assembly, adjusting the business model to local reality. This means that the making of solar starts looking like the farming of mushrooms on coffee.

Unlocking New Energies

It is curious that what we often describe as invention is merely what the ecosystems of our living Earth have been doing for countless eons. When Thomas Edison created the first light bulb, his original filament was bamboo, rich in naturally occurring iron. A hundred years later, these original light bulbs still work. However, contrary to common misconception, Edison did not invent electricity. It has been used in cells for billions of years. Minute differences in pH (potential hydrogen) on opposite sides of a cell membrane generate minuscule currents, often too small to measure. Electric current in natural systems never relies on mined and smelted metals, yet achieves conductivity with practically no resistance. Energy that flows through concentrated metals in a battery requires mining and generates massive pollution both in processing and post-consumption. Bamboo and whales are two species that have much to teach us about electricity and conductivity.

Nature draws on six main sources of electricity: heat, light, friction, pressure, magnetism and biochemistry. Magnetism contributes the largest portion of electrical production worldwide. Power generators, whether hydroelectric, coal, oil, methane gas, or nuclear, all use magnetism as the actual means of electrical generation. Light acting on solar panels is slowly making headway but at high cost. Electricity is generated by spinning a coil within a magnetic field. Smaller less powerful electrical current can be generated directly by heat, pressure and friction. Chemical reaction in the form of batteries is both the oldest means of producing electrical current and has had the greatest impact on our modern way of life. Biochemistry is a major source of bodily electric current and the supply basically comes along with the nutrient intake of the particular species—yet it is given no major industrial attention. The biochemical system as perfected by the electric fish is a marvel of engineering, not the least in its use of insulation.

Natural systems do not rely on any of the extreme methods that humanity has devised. In nature, fire and incineration are the exception rather than the rule. Even a 50 per cent dry matter content is not handled by burning. Humans easily resort to burning everything considered waste, even water. It is a policy dominant in agriculture, in industry, and in municipal refuse disposal. Whenever we do not know what to do with something, we burn it. Lately, experts have invented the argument that pyrolysis (chemical decomposition by heating) recovers the energy embedded in complex materials. There are even companies promoting the burning of water! Surprisingly, after funding years of study, Nestlé—the largest instant coffee processing company in the world—concluded that burning coffee waste (composed of over 80% water) was the best environmental option!

The exercise of observing natural sources of energy is inspiring. Although we may fully comprehend the law of gravity, few of us pause to question how the constituents that become apples—before these acquire form and submit themselves to the law of gravity—first defy it. It is this fresh look at the forces at work in ecosystems that provides the right state of mind to search for lasting solutions to our energy predicament.

How does the coconut fill with water? There is no pump, neither does the nut absorb rainwater. How do trees erect their massive structures? Where does osmosis in plants derive the power to trump gravitational forces, pushing nutrient-filled sap upward through their capillary network? Of course, there is interplay with surface tension and the powerful draw of the moon. It is responsible for tidal ebb and flow, another steadily predictable force in the physics of our universe. There are many forces exploited by natural systems, in great detail and at minute levels, giving all manners of life the energetic resources uniquely developed for their needs. This stands in stark contrast with the industrial solutions we have invented and financed. Modern solutions seem straightforward, yet their inherent inefficiencies are vast compared to clusters of natural energy sources. This is why we waste so much energy, and this is why we now ask, "Where are the real opportunities?"

Electricity from pH

While humans debate the values of nuclear, solar, coal, wind and photovoltaic generation, natural systems cascade their energy requirements among all contributors based on differences in pH. A tree generates electric currents from the difference between the pH of the soil and itself. Potential hydrogen is an important factor in the natural energy equation because it controls the speed of biochemical reactions. It does so by controlling the intensity of enzyme activity, as well as the speed of electricity moving through our bodies. A higher pH means a substance or solution has greater alkalinity and electrical resistance. Therefore, electricity travels slower with a higher pH. If something is acidic (lower pH), the current runs faster. A car battery is acidic. On cold days, a properly acidic battery quickly starts your car. Biochemically, what is alkaline is slow. Compare the lead-acid car battery to an alkaline flashlight battery. The flashlight battery discharges more slowly. Natural systems use this interplay constantly, without ever resorting to lead (car battery) or lithium (flashlight battery). In living species, membranes are the gates for these flows. Sometimes membranes let electrons pass rapidly, sometimes slowly; it is the management of the differential in pH levels that determines the current.

Electricity from Temperature Differential

Thermoelectricity is the conversion of temperature differential into electricity. In our new energy model, electronic equipment could draw power from the warmth of the human body. In Germany, the Fraunhofer Institute for Physical Measurement Techniques has developed a way of harnessing electricity from natural body heat. Imagine! The difference between the temperature of the human body and its surrounding, hot or cold, environment is conductive to generate electricity. Normally, a difference of several tens of degrees is considered necessary to generate sufficient electricity to nominally power electronic equipment, but the differences between the body's surface temperature and its immediate environment is only a few degrees. "Only low voltages can be produced from differences like these," explains Peter Spies, project manager at the Fraunhofer Institute. This ambient body heat differential capture device delivers roughly 200 millivolts. Electronic devices require at least one or two volts; an LED light will shine with less than one volt.

Yet, the Fraunhofer Institute engineers have found a solution. Instead of searching for ways to create more power—the standard way industry thinks—the Fraunhofer Institute engineers cleverly created circuits needing less energy—just 200 millivolts. They have built entire electronic systems that require neither an internal battery nor a connection to the grid. The system draws energy from body heat alone. Peter Spies is confident that in the future, when further improvements have been made to the switching systems, a temperature difference of only 0.5° will be sufficient to generate enough electricity to power a cell phone. This is exactly how natural systems evolved, with ever smaller currents achieving ever more until everything they needed was accomplished without waiting for a massive surge, such as a lighting strike to make things happen.

Peter Spies' breakthrough allows us to seriously consider how to liberate ourselves from the burden of the battery, metals, mining, and the massive energy required in commercial manufacture so as to produce a consumer product that will shortly occupy a landfill. In a Blue Economy, many instruments could be reconfigured to work without power from a battery to a wall socket. Nature offers endless inspiration.

Seiko, the Japanese watchmaker, marketed 500 units of the first watch powered by body temperature in 1999. Once fully charged, it operated for 10 months. It became one of the most sought-after watches ever made. The power-generating capacity depends on the air temperature and individual differences of body temperature. When worn on the wrist, the watch absorbs heat through the back case and dissipates it from front of the watch, generating power with its thermal converter. As the difference between the air temperature and the surface temperature increases, the power generation increases, and *vice-versa*. Ideally, this is the way we will be working with energy in the future.

Electricity from Gravity and Pressure

Pressure, or technically speaking, piezoelectricity, is another abundant natural source of electricity. *Piezo* is a root word from Greek that means stress. The main source of compression is of course the pressure of gravity. The weight of a tree can generate electricity from the gravitational stress on rocks in the soil. As a source of energy, stress or pressure works most efficiently with materials that have a crystalline structure. In the past, obvious resources like quartz and diamonds were utilised. Rochelle salt (made from sodium bicarbonate and potassium bitartrate) was the first material used to demonstrate piezoelectric generation. Notably, the molecular composition of salt consists of potassium and sodium, the two key biochemical components powering our heartbeat. Recent insights into piezoelectrical generation added common products like cane sugar, dry bones, silk, and even wood. As cutting-edge research explores yet uncharted paths, more sources of piezoelectricity will be discovered.

Whereas industrial uses are still undeveloped in much of the world, Japanese industry has given the commercial applications of piezoelectricity a vote of confidence. Numerous applications have nestled themselves into our daily lives without us ever realising that they operate with energy from pressure. The original television remote controls used quartz technology to convert a button pressure into an electric current. The echo-location device in cars is also based on this energy source, as is the engine that powers the autofocus of reflex cameras. Simple pressure on the small lever of a cigarette lighter is enough to create an electric spark to light the fuel. Robert Bosch, the German maker of car parts, developed the first piezoelectric fuel injection system. This is one of the factors that rendered the Volkswagen Jetta a very fuel efficient car. It outperforms the Toyota Prius, which gained fame in the USA merely by generating electric power from braking and recovering waste power from burning gasoline. Yet, the Jetta performs better!

As our understanding of piezoelectricity broadens, a new vision emerges for the design of buildings that could produce electricity using the pressure the structure exerts upon the floor. A pilot project in Torino, Italy, the city elected as the 2008 Design Capital of the World. Quartz crystals are ubiquitous in the European Alps, and could be placed under pillars on each floor of a building, generating electrical power exactly where it was most needed. In fact, this application is a direct conversion of the power of gravity. The pressure exerted by the structure is easily calculated based on gravitational force. The potential is huge because the immense weight of a building pressuring crystals can generate several megavolts, certainly sufficient to power at least the building's elevator.

Gravity is our best hope for moving our societies in general and our buildings in particular towards sustainability. Using the electrical potential of pressure is the means to realise a completely different vision of energy-emancipated houses and buildings. Recall the description of how a design based on the same principles as the Namibian beetle's water collection method could produce water on a roof and how a vortex would clean that water as gravity pulled it from floor to floor. To this, we can add electricity generated not from thin-film solar cells that power carbon fibres, but from the structure's gravitational force generating thousands of volts of piezoelectricity. Let our engineers focus on achieving this vision!

These energy insights offer ways that could draw down or eliminate the explosive demand for small batteries for hearing aids, toys, mobile and miniature devices, and cell phones. Where venture capitalists have invested billions in funding research for less polluting disposable batteries, the real investment return will be in tapping energy sources that integrate harmoniously with nature and eliminate dependence on metal extraction.

Another potential source of piezoelectricity is vibration, in particular the vibrations we call sound. Although it is a level of sound that humans do not perceive as such, scientists have long known that seismic communication is common in small animals, including spiders, scorpions, insects and a few vertebrate species, such as white-lipped frogs, kangaroo rats and golden moles. Seismic sensitivity has been observed in elephant seals—huge marine mammals. Testimonials concerning elephants clearly sensing an upcoming tsunami, breaking their chains, and running to safety, drew scientists' attention. In 1997, Caitlin O'Connell-Rodwell, a research associate at the Stanford University School of Medicine, discovered that elephants can communicate over long distances with low-pitched sounds that are barely audible to humans. She charted a bold new research direction by proposing that low-frequency elephant calls generate powerful vibrations in the ground—seismic signals that elephants can feel, and even interpret, via their sensitive trunks, knees and feet. According to O'Connell-Rodwell, the elephants communicate through the ground, and are able to discriminate very subtle vibrations through their feet.

She has conducted observations of elephant herds at the Etosha National Park in Namibia, and is applying the data collected on animal seismic sensitivity to the problem of hearing loss in humans. People with hearing impairments often develop the capacity for much greater tactile sensitivity in the auditory cortex of their brain than people with normal hearing. "We want to investigate the possibility that newborns with severe hearing loss could have their hearing improved by exposure to vibrational stimulation shortly after birth," states O'Connell-Rodwell. Elephants and hearing aids are both stimulated by sensing vibrations. Here again is one of the basic principles of physics at work—vibrations—helping to meet the changing needs of a species—creating cells in the brain to compensate for hearing impairment and sensitizing a nervous system to vibrations through hands or feet.

The most promising version of a piezoelectric power source is where the pressure created by a voice (yes! even sound creates pressure!) generates electricity. If the piezoelectric unit that converts sound pressure to electricity were in contact with your skin, both piezoelectricity and thermal electricity could power your phone. This means the more you talk, the longer you can call. We might further imagine the look and design of a hearing aid powered by the wearer's voice to which it connects, supplemented by electricity powered by body temperature. Combining these proven power sources would quickly make the lithium battery and solar cell charger obsolete. They would establish the basis for a wide array of new energy applications.

Energy from Sweat

Athletes measure their fitness and work rate through lactate levels. Lactate is naturally present in sweat when exercising vigorously. Dr Wenzhao Jia at the University of California in San Diego (USA) strips electrons from lactate with an enzyme embedded in a temporary tattoo, generating 70 microwatts per square centimetre of skin. She did not build a biobattery, she just created a permanent supply of power for a sensor that measures efficiency of the work-out combining physical data like heart rate with chemical data. Dr Jia delivered a proof of concept and produced a self-powered lactate sensor onto a tattoo paper. Since less fit people get tired faster they form more lactate, and create more power.

The device is sufficiently advanced to link this tattoo to portable gadgets, adding a capacitor to store the generated current. A digital watch needs 10 microwatts, and the batteries included are the most toxic and easily discarded ones on the market. A space of two by three millimetres is enough to generate what you need and get rid of the metals forever. These biobatteries recharge quickly, never leak toxic chemicals and the risk of explosion is nil. Of course, the most powerful argument is that it relies on the use of a renewable energy source: YOU. Is this just the fantasy of a scientists? The highly respected German Journal Angewandte Chemie published a peer group reviewed article in 2014, in which Dr Jia provides details of her method, following which she has attracted capital and entrepreneurs to make it a reality. The creation of a new product evolves from fantasy to a vision, and can only be translated into reality through science and risk taking. The opportunity to substitute billions of tiny batteries, which are the vogue of our times by using our sweat, is too inspiring to neglect.

Energy from Movement (Kinetic Energy)

Another variation of pressure is the kinetic energy generated by movement. Again, the watch industry has taken the lead on this technology. Rolex commercialised the first gravity-operated watch in 1931. It contained a small semi-circular metal device that wound the watch simply by freely moving. More recently, Seiko has introduced hundreds of variations on this theme and uses it as one of its main watch designs.

While this use of energy from movement has found a favourable market, ways in which biological systems use kinetic energy elicits our greater curiosity. Flowing blood has mass and velocity, thus it has kinetic energy. The flow of blood through our vessels would be a simple resource that could be utilised immediately. Furthermore, as the blood flows inside a vein or artery, pressure exerted against the walls of the vessel can also generate piezoelectric energy. The total energy of blood flowing within our vessels is the sum of the energies from movement and pressure. Experts might argue that such minute amounts of energy are insufficient to make a dent in the world's demand for electricity. We are reminded of the Dutch proverb, *Wie het kleine niet deert is het grote niet weerd*—if you do not appreciate the small, you do not deserve the large. Surely advances in nanotechnology will find a way to convert these two pressures to electricity.

Even as limited funding has been made available for solar research and massive amounts of venture capital are invested in developing new types of batteries, research and development of pressure- and temperature-driven electrical generation has received no support from governments, private investors, or venture capitalists. Investors seem uninterested in exploring ideas for renewable energy sources that do not require heavy metals and energy storage. The Max Planck and Frauenhofer Research Institutes are pioneering the field of renewable energy beyond the mainstream. There are as well innovators like Alan Heeger, who discovered that thin-film polymers are highly electrically conductive and can replace batteries on just about everything; and Michael Graetzel, who is pioneering ideas to produce electricity the way a leaf achieves photosynthesis.

As the February 2008 article in the Harvard Business Review noted, were we to cover the Golden Gate Bridge with thin-film solar cells, not only would it eliminate the necessity of anti-corrosion chemical applications, but also generate sufficient electricity to power much of local municipal requirements. Here again is a multi-tiered approach that takes advantage of an economy of physics and natural temperature variations to capture electricity (revenue from renewable energy) and eliminate chemical use (anti-corrosion application cost). Such approaches move us closer to zero-waste models. Now we are moving to the design of integrated business models where the combination of these innovations evolves into an ecosystem, exploiting the opportunity to substitute something with nothing (no more need for anti-corrosion, thus cutting costs) while generating additional revenue (power from a local generator that is consumed within a few kilometres range). This double whammy makes thin film solar competitive, whereas as a stand-alone technology it would be discarded as too expensive.

Physicists and farmers alike easily recognise the power of pressure and temperature. Yet, these forces are neglected in our modern debates about energy efficiency. It is for this reason that innovative energy sources open a vast trove of entrepreneurial opportunities. These technological options permit generating small amounts of energy with limited investment for local consumption. Potential applications are wide open and new markets are accessed everywhere and all the time. Even greater opportunity is open to those who bundle multiple technologies just as natural systems do, providing a reliable energy system that consistently performs with locally available resources. At this critical juncture, instead of losing focus in a debate over oil or nuclear sources, exploring innovative energy sources is a quest that should fully engage us.

CO_2 as a Source of Energy

It is impossible to conclude a chapter on innovations in energy without discussing the societal potential of CO_2. While out-of-control CO_2 emissions are roundly excoriated for contributing to climate change, we need to consider the potential of CO_2 as a valuable input to our industrial society, helping to meet basic needs. Oxygen was originally a toxin that became a pre-condition to all life. In the same sense, if we turn our mental switch from problem to opportunity,

CO_2 could well become a major contributor to a sustainable society. "How?," you may ask. One answer lies with algae.

Having lived on Earth for a billion years, algae are among the earliest of photosynthetic organisms. These single-celled species were the first to develop a nucleus and to carry the memory of life known as DNA. Algae require only CO_2, water, nutrients and sunlight to produce their own food and chemical energy through photosynthesis. Oxygen, the by-product of this photosynthesis, is abundantly released into the air and into the waters of the world's lakes, oceans and rivers. Algae are not plants, belonging rather to the kingdom of protoctista. They are tremendously efficient at capturing the power of light, and consequently are the fastest-growing species on the planet. They grow 10 times faster than sugar cane and compete with bacteria in output and proliferation. Managing algal proliferation would be like needing to mow your lawn three times a day, instead of only once every other week.

This capacity for growth renders algae an important contributor to managing climate change. Its virtues are that it gives off oxygen as it grows, it is high in oil content, and it contains high nutrient levels. The University of Minnesota Center for Biorefining has estimated that algae produce 5,000 gallons of oil per acre per year. The Brazilian team directed by Jorge Alberto Vieira Costa from the Federal University of Rio Grande do Sul at the Rio Grande Campus handily cultivates spirulina at low cost, generating 2,000 gallons of oil per acre per year. By comparison, corn yields 18 gallons, soybeans produce 48 gallons, and palm trees yield 635 gallons per acre per year. This is a result that is hard to dismiss. One of algae's other great virtues is that unlike corn-based ethanol, many strains can be grown in salt water on marginal land and can even take up carbon emissions from coal-fired power stations, and decontaminate soil.

All oil and gas extraction processes generate brackish water, an unwanted waste product. The water is often left in retention basins that leach over time into surrounding soil, rendering the land toxic and infertile for centuries. As warm water affects the habitat of aquatic life in rivers and oceans, coal-fired power stations also have retention basins for cooling water prior to discharge. These retention basins have been mandated by law, ostensibly to mitigate collateral damage to the environment. It takes only a little imagination to see that algae can be profitably farmed in these basins, thereby converting an unproductive waste receptacle into a system that attenuates CO_2, replenishes oxygen, and produces low-cost and renewable biofuel. Depending on the type of algae farmed, up to one-third is lipids, which fuels derive for oils. What we envision is one more simple yet effective way to reduce our legacy of environmental damage by returning waste to the nutrient stream, learning how to utilise available infrastructure for productive outputs. In a Blue Economy, we will solve our current challenges by doing more with what we have. Farming algae for food and biofuel is an admirable example. Dr Vieira Costa even succeeded with his team to produce polyesters from algae. It is this generation of multiple products with multiple renevues that shifts the bio from academically interesting but uncompetitive due to high cost, to entrepreneurially attractive and competitive not because are cut down to the bottom, but because so much more revenue is generated.

The National Renewable Energy Laboratory in Colorado undertook trials to document a portfolio of 300 protein-, carbohydrate-, and oil-rich algae that could produce biodiesel in the desert wastelands of New Mexico. In 1996, Jorge Alberto Vieira Costa adapted this research to help establish a project aimed at achieving food security at Mangueira Lake. Biodiesel was not the focus of his attention. The food security focus came from the needs of rice farmers in Southern Brazil who were challenged to compete on the world market without fertiliser subsidies. Joining Vieira Costa in his algae project was Professor Lucio Brusch da Fraga, a physicist by training but with a special degree in quality management.

It was a remarkable partnership. Mangueira Lake is one of the most alkaline lakes in the world; a far cry from qualifying as an environmental asset. Vieira Costa and Brusch da Fraga set out to demonstrate that it is possible to farm algae everywhere, including temperate climate zones like Southern Brazil. Once they mastered the production of algae around rice paddies in Vittoria do Palmar, on the southern tip of Brazil bordering Uruguay, they harvested the algae. It contained a high concentrate of micronutrients—what in the US is called super blue-green algae. They distributed this nutritional food source to the local underserved population around the city of Rio Grande. The social and medical delivery services, the schools, and the media lauded their success in alleviating hunger and malnutrition. Following this, they quickly realised that algae production in retention basins could accomplish more than food security. An extension of the program was explored: algae for biodiesel.

Even though Brazil only has five coal-fired power stations, compared to 3,000 in the US, they were able to run a series of industrial trials using coal-fired CO_2 exhaust in combination with algae farming to produce biofuel. Building from the ground up, Vieira Costa initiated a process similar to the Brazilian development economics that earned international acclaim for producing ethanol from sugar cane. Instead of rushing into business, Prof Vieira Costa established a research institute that undertook scientific inquiry into the typical ecosystem conditions found in Southern Brazil. He recruited a group of eager students who were progressing through undergraduate, masters, and ultimately doctoral degrees. From this institute came a strong portfolio of patents.

Vieira Costa and his team went from strength to strength, working with local biodiversity, local ecosystems, and local field experience. Their projects using Lagoa Mangueira and Laguna Morin as huge natural retention basins for algae farming have provided experience on ways to evolve from the micro scale of a rice paddy to the industrial scale of retention basins at energy generation facilities. In essence, what we see is physics supporting biology. The residues left after extracting food, biodiesel, and esters (the latter for polymers usable for cosmetics) from the algae can be converted to ethanol. Thus, what we see is a substantial increase in productivity when conjoined with other complementary technologies.

Algae and carbon dioxide live in symbiosis. Algae grow fastest with a rich supply of CO_2 and absorb this greenhouse gas like a sponge. Scaling up the industrial processes for using CO_2 to supply the algae requires blending more carbonic gases into water so that the algae are more productive, while maximising sunlight exposure and avoiding shade. The present technique for mixing air with water is like killing a fly with a sledgehammer; the effort and force is used for a small result in output. Such inefficient processes help explain why the resultant products are too expensive. Worse, the producers typically settle for the core business model—in this case, the biofuel—and discard everything else. It is no wonder that the present techniques are not commercially viable especially with petroleum prices dropping in the spring of 2015.

If we assess how to best blend air into water, we would wisely look to nature. Natural systems never use pumps or air blowers. Nature relies on the vortex. Early estimates indicate that water pressurised with air containing up to 13 per cent CO_2 could absorb up to four times more air if a vortex were used. Under the cap-and-trade scheme legislated for greenhouse gases, this is equal to generating four times more revenue with the same capital infrastructure simply by using gravitational forces! However, this is only the first improvement. The second is perhaps even more important.

Air bubbles containing carbonic gases can be distributed into the water and made available to the algae at a size that fits the algal membranes. Air bubbles that are 10 times larger, and in some bioreactors even 10,000 times larger, than the pores in the algae's membranes, render the process inefficient and uncompetitive. The oversized bubbles remain unused and end up as turbulence on surface of the water. Vortex technology permits the production of micro-bubbles tailored to membrane openings. Why eat dinner with an excavator, when forks, knives, and spoons will do? The proof that the air bubbles are small in size is that the water body acquires a milky appearance. The catalyst for the whole process is water and the energy source relies on the most dependable force on Earth: gravity. These insights permit us to design sustainable and competitive solutions.

The power of algae is that the output is not limited to lipids that can be converted to biodiesel. Once the oil is extracted, what remains is high-protein micronutrient-rich matter suitable for human as well as livestock consumption, as Prof Vieira Costa imagined from the outset. His students even discovered that the residual algal membranes are composed of pure esters, and can be converted to natural polyesters. Thus we return to the concept of an entire biorefinery, or, as the Brazilian team would name it, “a whole photo-biorefinery”—one that renewably produces as long as the sun shines, gravity works, and CO_2 is emitted. Given the low risk that any of these three factors will cease to manifest, the odds are good. The Brazilian team has now confirmed that 2 million tons of CO_2 emitted from coal-fired power stations can be converted to one million tons of algae demonstrating that there is no reason to waste carbon emissions, and there is yet another opportunity to generate more food and energy than ever imagined before.

This bundle of discoveries and innovations can help mitigate climate change, while providing energy and food, using water as the catalyst. We wonder why anyone would propose ‘sequestering’ CO_2 by pumping it deep into the oceans or into old oil wells. Such a capital-intensive venture would earn great income for the engineers, but nothing for the investors. It completely lacks economic sense, unless of course governments provide subsidies without reason. Nor would it earn profit on the sustainability ledger. ‘Out of sight, out of mind’ is old thinking. It gives us superfund sites, overflowing landfills, recreation parks atop nuclear waste storage, and other short-sighted ‘protection by separation’ follies that often result in irremediable loss and crippling damage. Despite knowing that future generations will have to pay the bill, why do it?

With food and energy as the by-products to a process that transforms algae, CO_2, water, and sunlight into biofuel, what we have is an efficient symbiosis. To crown the benefits, the process generates jobs. How many jobs? The biggest CO_2 emitters are power plants and cement factories. If 10,000 power plants from the US, Europe, China, and the developing world were to apply these technologies, they would on average require 100 jobs per facility, in sum one million jobs. This would be a marriage of the old and the new, a bridge between fossil fuel, mainly coal and renewables. The investment required to build these facilities equals the cost of 10 nuclear power stations at US$10 billion each. Would 10 nuclear power stations generate a million jobs? No! How much time would it take to put these 10 new nuclear facilities on line? At least a decade for the first one!

If we take a dispassionate look at the economic and social impact of one set of solutions *versus* another, if our debate concerns the economics, the average cost of investment, the potential jobs, and the generation of multiple benefits from health and employment from renewable fuels and natural polymers, it is clear that a nuclear power solution is unfeasible. The option of nuclear power has never been utilised by any ecosystem that promotes life. Economic and business models must now change focus to enhance life. Surely enhancing life should be the starting point of any activity humanity engages. It is not a matter of being in favour or against nuclear. Even without ever considering the obvious safety of nuclear power with accidents that will happen again and again, is not the best option on all other counts, except when you studied nuclear physics and are looking for a job.

It is surprising that our engineers seem to ignore many potential energy sources, even though these are the real power sources for all the creatures with whom we share this planet. Discoveries for how we can respond differently to our needs for energy never seem to reach the antennae of corporate policymakers and strategists who believe that bigger is better, and who are risk-averse even in times of plenty. To those industry professionals who would be quick to argue that no alternative technologies will ever power the grid, we offer the words of Maria, a young 10-year old student from Curitiba, Brazil, who heard engineers say that the power generated by banana peels and egg shells would never compete with that of nuclear fission or burning coal. Maria listened patiently and respectfully to the petroleum company director, then responded, “Well, in 25 years—when I am old—I will prove you wrong.” There is nothing better for a society than when the next generation is eager and motivated to make a difference and go for what they believe is the better.

13

Mines as Platforms of Healing

One generation plants the trees,
another gets the shade.

– *CHINESE PROVERB*

How to Restore Errors of the Past

Picture yourself at the end of a 45-minute ride outside Johannesburg, the industrial capital of all Africa. The desolate, moon-like landscape that now surrounds you could provide a perfect backdrop for the latest sci-fi movie. You are standing atop a mountain of mine tailings, rich in uranium and containing half a gram of gold per ton. You are imagining a straight line extending four kilometres (12,000 feet) upward into the air and sense the scope of the deepest mines on earth, extending four kilometres beneath your feet. While we decry the environmental havoc, we must also marvel at the engineering handiwork. Deep in the Earth's crust, the natural heat reaches nearly 130°F. Imagine the expertise it took to solve the challenge of providing air and temperate conditions to 20,000 miners working as much as 4,000 metres below the surface. Ice-making machines in the belly of the Earth are used to make the working environment tolerable. Consider again, the biggest ice-making machines in the world, powered in the heated depths of the Earth to cool the air.

The question comes immediately to mind: "Could this ever be sustainable?" Could mining companies ever conduct their operations and leave the local community better off than when they arrived? Lichens are great miners, capable of extracting specific inorganic molecules like magnesium from rocks and sharing these with all other life in the ecosystem. Bacteria selectively separate metals through chelation, but mankind alone uses brute force and harsh toxins including mercury and cyanide to acquire desirable ores. Although we may lack the knowledge and skill to undo the errors of the past, it is within our ability to do better in the future. We may not currently be capable of transforming mining into a benign operation, yet we can at least design a strategy that assuages the environmental and social pain that mining inflicts.

From atop our mountain of tailings, we are surveying one of humanity's most aggressive conceits. Armed with dynamite and consuming massive amounts of water and energy, mining operations extract minute concentrations of gold from deep within the Earth. The miners who toil in the shafts endure abject and barely tolerable living and working conditions, sending their meagre earnings home to provide for their often far away families. No one knows how many will still be alive, much less on the job, in a decade.

Mining is a risky enterprise in more ways than one. Even with the world market price for gold dropping down from record levels, there is no guarantee that the extraction of this precious metal will remain profitable in the years to come, especially if all the external and remediation costs that burden the local communities surrounding the mines were fully covered from the mining companies' existing revenue streams. When gold ore reaches the surface from deep within the South African earth, it sometimes comes with a natural complement of uranium. The tailings—what is left once the ore is extracted—are dumped above ground, forming a stark line across the horizon. The magnificent view of the surroundings is clouded, not by pollution from the city nearby, but by dust released from the uranium-laced tailings. The uranium leaches into the air and the water, exposing all animate life to potentially lethal cancers. A few watchdog organisations decry this contamination and have repeatedly pressured management to find ways to abate these high levels of risk. Sadly, because shareholders prefer a steadily upward (imaginary) progression of capital gains, any plan or cost directed towards complete abatement does not even reach the Board.

Picture the richest concentrations of gold layered beneath huge water reserves amassed on a bed of dolomite. At an energy cost of US$1.5 million dollars per day, water and air must be pumped into the shafts to provide a tolerable environment for the workers. Now, realise that the air vented from the mine shafts releases approximately 100,000 tons of methane per year. As fresh shafts are explored, the volume may even double year by year for a few decades. Apart from the impact of its effect on the atmosphere, methane is a tremendous risk factor for explosions. That is why every mining tool is expensive. They are made of copper, titanium, or beryllium because these metals do not produce explosive sparks.

Mining entails health risks and major occupational hazards. Johannesburg—Jozie as it is known to the locals—is perhaps the only major industrial city in the world that is not located alongside a river or in a coastal zone. Rather, it is built around mining sites. The massive pumping of underground water and the diversion of a river into a 30-kilometre pipeline severed local agriculture's lifeline to water. What was once the vegetable garden for the Jozie megalopolis is now scarred by mine shafts, miles of tailings and sinking surfaces. The water that is available has questionable levels of pollution that will render the soil unsuitable for food production for at least a generation, if not more. Any form of farming, especially cattle ranching in and around the mines, cannot be recommended. Still, a few families try to subsist herding their animals where there should be none. Mining executives are at pain trying to keep the poor off the land, who usher back moments after being sent off.

Geologists and biologists are learning more and more about the ways toxins are assimilated by water, air and soil. Broadleaf plants accumulate toxins in their tissues. This creates health risks, particularly the irradiation and contamination of the animal life that consumes them for food. As there is scant research and monitoring data, the statistics are unclear. Neither management nor government can obtain a full picture or a complete understanding of this complex process. As a result, anecdotal stories and brief scientific reports performed by outsiders are often based on little more than speculation.

These environmental and social realities are not the only reasons mines are under stress. While the world market price for gold has dropped from historic peaks, the cost of operation likewise has never been so exorbitant. To make matters worse, the South African electricity grid is heavily stressed: Electricity Supply Commission (ESKOM) has informed the mining industry of its inability to meet demand due to a lack of investment in capacity expansion. Thus, rising energy prices for pumping air and water are exacerbated by an uncertain electrical supply. This forces the mines to make huge investments in back-up diesel generators in order to secure safety of the underground workers and provide a habitable zone by cooling the horizontal shafts to a depth of several thousand metres. Simultaneously, energy is required to move ore from 12,000 feet below to the surface for processing. When electricity is unavailable, the mines are forced to close for a day or two of the week. How do you stimulate competitiveness under such work conditions? How do you take care of your workers when you are faced with such uncertainties?

A thorough inventory of mining's adverse impacts would necessarily include the ore-processing rubble gathered in mounds on porous soil, the uranium-filled dust clouds rising from the tailings, the desertification of land from continuous pumping of water, the sink holes caused by the same process, and the accumulation of uranium in waterways and soil. Nor could we exclude the social havoc associated with mine-site hostels for workers that are an open invitation to HIV (human immunodeficiency virus) infection and other sexually transmitted diseases. After visiting these deep mines and seeing the reality of mining life first hand, it would be easy to despair at the extent of societal and environmental degradation that is evident all around. Yet to find solutions, it helps to have a positive mindset, to learn creatively, and act decisively. In South Africa, truth and reconciliation surmounted tremendous difficulties. The way forward is not about culpability, it is about acknowledging shortcomings and designing a new business model that can simultaneously please stockholders and remediate local conditions. Advocates such as Mark Cutifani, the former CEO of Anglo Gold Ashanti and now the leader of Anglo American, are committed to pioneering a new way forward. It is not self-evident that they will succeed.

Binding the Wound to Heal

Operating a mine should be considered an intervention into the Earth's crust comparable to a surgical intervention in a human body. Even if we consider it a necessary procedure, we must bind the wound to heal. The past two centuries of mining has left many tragic legacies, some documented and some yet to surface because disclosure and restoration take time. The advent of improved instrumentation and better understanding means that less invasive and more sustainable practices can and should be introduced.

From a core business management point of view, an economic crisis requires cost reductions at every level. Realising the limitations of continuing business as usual, management must search for ways to lower expenditures. However, if we were to redefine these core business principles, if we were to turn our thinking around, we will be able to identify applicable technologies and energy-saving solutions that would lower costs and strengthen cash flow at the same time. Innovation can generate new revenues and create social capital that will support the local communities, even after the mines are exhausted. If we can save more, generate more income, remediate more environmental damage while securing additional revenue, and create more value while investing less, everyone benefits. We can convert liabilities and provisions into investments and secure that assets of no value in the balance sheet will be upgraded. What is required is for us to think outside the box of current practice.

Paper Made from Rocks

One of the largest investments of any mine is dealing with waste: rocks and tailings. Mining engineers have learned ways to create rock refuse deposits, where low pH debris is stored forever. Valleys are converted into mountains at high environmental costs. Tailings, the left-over from crushed ore, processed and void of any precious, non-ferrous or rare earth metals is also stored for eternity. This slurry is transported over large distances and pumped into a dam where it settles and is left—forever. A gold mine can well dump one billion tons of rocks and tailings over its lifetime requiring a dam of 100 metres high to hold the massive flow of waste. The permit to excavate ore always goes hand in hand with the same to dump the leftovers which will alter the landscape forever.

It is time to ask the obvious question: is anyone interested in tailings or rocks? The standard answer from the mine experts is "if there would have been a use that makes money—then we would have done this long time ago, and everyone would have by now applied the same solution." It is not that easy to get experts out of their comfort zones until the crisis bites. The drop in gold prices and the capital cost of rock deposits and tailing dams render the extraction of gold and other ores unviable. Breakthrough solutions can never be found inside the circle of ready wisdom, it must come from the outside.

China invented paper production two millennia ago. China re-invented paper in the 21st century. In 1990, Mr Shih Huei (William) Liang from Taiwan had a question: could we ever make paper without felling trees? He worked tirelessly and concluded after 12 years of research that he could blend 20 per cent recycled plastics with 80 per cent crushed stones produce a novel paper that needed no water in the making—stone paper. The pulp and paper industry was too busy finding a response to the rapid digitisation of media, so it lost sight of the arrival of a completely new competitor—a paper made from crushed waste materials. While the paper industry looked the other way, the mining companies kept on piling up their waste ignoring the revolution in the making.

While Mr Liang cracked the formula for stone paper over a decade, it took him another decade to finetune the machinery. Now Mr Liang offers mines the opportunity to convert all its rocks—crushed to dust particles of 3-5 micron—into the most sophisticated paper. The capital cost is only a fraction of a modern paper mill and the fact that no water is needed in its production makes it an ideal add-on to any primary industry. Whereas a tailing dam could absorb a billion dollars in capital, and represents a risk forever, the stone paper generates cash, eliminates the capital expenditure and reduces the risk. How long will the mines be able to argue that paper is not part of the core business? After Mr Liang inaugurated his first plant in 2008 in Taiwan, followed by improved operations and marketing, the first large scale industrial production came on stream in Benxi City, close to Shenyang (China) in September 2013 with 6 factories in total going for 1 million tons in production capacity by 2016 in China and Taiwan with two more scheduled in China. The first factory created about 1,000 jobs. However, the conversion of the rolls of paper in final products like notebooks, packaging material and labels for wine bottles generate an additional 4,000 jobs per 100,000 tons of paper produced.

The world demand for paper is expected to reach 500 million tons by 2020. Approximately half of the market is water absorbent tissue, which will continue to depend on fibres from trees. The other half, which is today tree-based but coated with polymers to resist water absorption can in one generation be based on stone paper. The one billion tons of waste around Johannesburg is only sufficient to supply the world four years of paper! This would become the biggest job machine that South Africa has seen in modern times. Thanks to the mining waste that was discarded for two centuries?

Critics rightfully ask the question about the 20 per cent polymers. The last thing needed is to upset the existing paper recycling systems, which is one of the most successful recycling programs ever. Mr Liang has worked out the solutions. First, a small amount of stone paper can be mixed with regular paper, since the tree-fibre based material is already laced with polymers. However, stone paper has the advantage of being recyclable forever. It is a mineral that cannot be destroyed, and the polymers have a half life of hundreds of years. Thus, now a real recycling business can be set-up, creating a resource efficiency that is unknown to SAPPI and Mondi, the South African market leaders for paper.

Reduced waste, lower investment, and increased revenue and jobs makes it a competitive proposal, yet the most important advantage of this technology for the Earth is that it has the potential to free up millions of acres of land now locked in for agro-forestry for food production, or the regeneration of biodiverse forests which regenerate topsoil and percolate and filter water. Who would have expected a mine to contribute to food security and biodiversity. This Blue Economy logic can losing about the most surprising designs of sustainable societies.

A Method for Methane Capture

Quite a few mines are massive producers of methane, a greenhouse gas that dramatically contributes to climate change. The volume of methane from one mine shaft is the energy equivalent of at least 30 megawatts of electrical power. Currently, it is pumped from the mine shafts into the atmosphere because it is erroneously thought that no technology can capture it at concentrations below 0.2 per cent. If this 'waste' were captured, it could generate the power that the mine must otherwise buy at 18 cents or more per kilowatt hour. Proprietary access to this naturally-occurring gas could augment a large portion of the electricity supplied by ESKOM, the highly stressed South African national energy supplier. Although nearly all methane gas from mines is lost into the atmosphere, signatories to the Kyoto Protocol can be compensated with carbon credits for methane capture or even just flaring methane at the source. The first carbon credits for flaring mine methane were issued to the South African Beatrix Mine owned by Gold Fields.

Methane is approximately 21 times more polluting than CO_2 and carbon credits are expressed in CO_2 equivalents. As such, these credits could generate US$10 million in four years, with very little investment and significant improvement of the working conditions for those underground. The payback period on the cost of installing pipes to capture and channel the methane is less than a year. Clearly, climate change protocols need not hurt your competitive market strength.

Carbon credits could be a small yet quick addition to the bottom line that could tilt a marginally producing shaft toward profitability, while contributing to social stability in the region and justifying additional safety investments within an open market. However, flaring of methane gas for carbon credits in a country that is facing energy blackouts seems an anachronism that merely scratches the surface potential. The mines have more to offer the energy market than mere carbon credits.

Even at an average concentration of just 0.1 per cent, the total volume of methane released is minimally estimated at three million tons per year. For all the shafts near Johannesburg, it could be upward of six million tons for each mine over the next 25 years. Present air purification technologies require a concentration greater than half a per cent. At least a few shafts have been identified that meet this concentration level. In fact, the concentration of methane in the air escaping the mine is often kept below 0.5 per cent by blending higher and lower concentrations. Creative engineers will surely go beyond today's market standard to make air purification effective even for much lower concentrations of methane.

A methane concentration averaging one-tenth of a per cent would make air purification potentially only marginally profitable. Even though the Clean Development Mechanism (CDM) under the Kyoto Protocol exists to create additional cash flow so as to finance such less attractive investments, a combined program that put in place vortex technology, wind turbines, heat exchangers, and potable water accessibility would provide the revenue strength necessary to carry over the air purification strategy.

MEGTEC Systems AB, a Swedish supplier of air purification technology, has installed systems that efficiently abate methane concentrations as low as 0.1 per cent without adding energy to the oxidation process. In 1983, Australia's West Cliff Collier Power Plant constructed a 1.2 megawatt power generation plant, and a second larger 12.5 megawatt plant in 1985, to utilise the methane gas content in the ventilation air. At the heart of the technology is a system capable of efficiently oxidising the extremely low methane content, while handling extremely large volumes of air—a combination typical of mine ventilation. It is important to take into account that the methane concentration is below one per cent and the project only utilises one-fifth of the entire air volume from the shaft. With the production of just 6 megawatts of electricity, the power plant reduces methane emissions equivalent to 200,000 tons of CO_2 per year.

This model demonstrates exactly how nature works with what is locally available, gathering what is useful for the task. Beneficial use can be made of even minute amounts of methane. If the giant mines outside Johannesburg were to utilise the MEGTEC or similar technology for capturing the escaping methane, they could potentially operate a 90-180 megawatt facility. This is as much as 50 per cent of their present energy needs. Even though these are merely estimates, the basic numbers are considerably attractive to warrant follow-up. Many mines could pursue this strategy, yet none do since management simply cannot break through their core business blockade. Surely someone will see the sense in capturing the methane in exchange for carbon credits, profitability, and planetary survival. It's another great opportunity waiting to be seized.

Converting Water from Cost to Revenue

Pure, clear fissure water, devoid of bacteria and exposed to the highly positive energy emitted by gold, is drawn from cracks in the deep. It is currently used to dilute highly polluted processing water to meet wastewater quality standards. We are hard put to think of any more wasteful use of pure water: to blend it with toxic water so that 'on average', it meets minimum safety standards? South Africa is suffering from a critical water shortage on top of an energy shortage. The projections for the shortfall between demand and supply are dramatic. While water for Johannesburg is pumped at great cost through pipelines from Lesotho, gold mines like the Driefontein and Kloof siphon away 100,000 cubic metres of water every day.

Rather than diluting and polluting pure water, chelating bacteria or vortex technology could easily and inexpensively separate toxins and impurities from the processed water to meet discharge standards.

Spending R10 million (Rand) per day (US$500 million per year) to pump water out of the mines and render it undrinkable is not in tune with the needs of a society suffering from a dramatic water shortage. What does make sense is shifting from the culture of cost-cutting to the mindset of generating income by responding to market demand and community needs. This equates to building social capital, which the population that was oppressed by Apartheid deserves from business and policymakers alike. Not only can the water needs of the local population be met, mining companies will also be able to operate a subsidiary enterprise providing bottled drinking water.

Owing to the hazardous presence of uranium, chelation technology would be necessary to achieve safe removal of such elements from the bottled product. In addition, mine management could easily identify those fissures without any taint of uranium and thus tap the water sources offering maximum potential revenue. The creation of a bottled water industry that at the outset sells 100,000 bottles a day is financially attractive. With just a touch of imagination, we can expand that to many other levels of profit, creating a business that provides naturally occurring high-quality drinking water for the local population, and high-end deep-earth bottled water that radiates the positive energy acquired from exposure to gold deposits. It can even include a minute health-benefiting gold flake. There are unquestionably markets for such water.

The implementation plan based on comparable experience from around the world would hardly need feasibility studies. In less that a decade, the Fiji Water Company developed from nothing to occupy a US$200 million high-margin niche in the US. In Hawaii, Japanese investors pump water from 600 metres deep, bottle it, and transport 200,000 bottles per day, selling for the Yen equivalent of US$10 per bottle in the Land of the Rising Sun. Using select distribution channels, The Environmental Research Center Las Gaviotas in Colombia freely dispenses drinking water to the local population, while profiting from selling bottled water in the capital city of Bogotá.

Water management at a mine site demonstrates how a cost can become an income. Accessing fissure water as a separate, stand-alone business would incur unrecoverable investment costs to reach the water deep in the Earth's crust. On the other hand, the mines must cover these costs to operate their core business of mining gold. By offering inexpensive and safe drinking water to the local population, mining not only turns an expense into a revenue, but also turns attention from the stigma of pollution and sink holes to a demonstration of social responsibility, thereby creating a better international reputation. Even a proverbial "gold mine" can use stronger brand equity.

Electrifying Savings

Mines need massive amounts of electricity to pump water and air, cool the shafts, produce ice, and transport ore. Huge electrical generation stations are located at the base of each mine. It is only common sense to explore opportunities that would save electrical costs. Perhaps this is the ideal environment for implementing Jay Harman's mathematical model, inspired by the nautilus, to increase energy efficiency by 20-30 per cent in ventilators and mixers, or other applications in either water or air transportation. Perhaps it is also an opportunity for Curt Hallberg's vortex technology. The ice-making machines necessary to moderate the high temperatures are placed in deep shafts and must cope with water containing vast amounts of dissolved air particles. Using Hallberg's gravity-based vortex technology to extract these air particles from the water would reliably reduce the energy costs by 10-15 per cent. However, the latest research results indicate as much as 41 per cent energy savings. Furthermore, when water and air must move up and down 4,000 metres, there is room to exploit the forces of gravity.

The mine should generate power from the drop of water, and fly wheels that were invented already during the age of Leonardo da Vinci can recover at least 70 per cent of all the energy spent to operate the elevators. If we consider other innovations based on nature's adaptive technologies, we can save even more energy and reduce the risk of explosions by introducing cold light, instead of traditional light bulbs. This would save energy and reduce the risk of explosion. In the darkest shafts of the mines, light should not be based on electricity generated with coal through the grid, or heavy fuel for the backup generators, when it can work on simple chemistry.

Power from Airflows

Just like water, airflows are by-products of the core business of mining that could easily generate additional revenue. Airflows created by a vacuum exit the mine shafts at high pressure. When a staggering 2,800 cubic metres of air is released into the atmosphere each second, we can easily comprehend how a few highly efficient windmills equipped with an anti-drag device such as that observed in whales would capture some of the power. Pumping the fresh air needed into these deep shafts generates an exhaust air stream, and the vacuum created can easily keep a dozen turbines constantly turning. Compared to the price South Africa's ESKOM must charge for electricity from the grid, the return on investment for wind-driven turbines at both the shaft inlet and the outlet exceeds 50 per cent of capital investment. Given this comparison, it would be hard to justify the investment expenditure for back-up diesel generators.

Energy Generation from Temperature and Pressure

The temperature differences generated by mine operations are another vast source of energy generation. These temperature extremes come from ice making, exhausting hot air, and transporting the ore from deep within the Earth. These become useful sources of energy simply by installing appropriately placed heat exchangers. Heat exchangers are nothing new. However, this technology has not found much application in mine except for the Mine Water Initiative undertaken in old coal mines in the Netherlands and Germany which is in operation since 2008 heating and cooling the district water for the City of Heerlen (the Netherlands). Gone are the days when electricity in South Africa was either inexpensive or even subsidised. Now the urge to embark on energy efficiencies is paramount. When we consider that nanotechnology enables us to power a cell phone with a half-degree of temperature differential, imagine what could be done with the 36° F differential found in the mines. Such an energy-generating project is already technically and commercially underway in Europe with only a 3-5 degree differential. More food for thought: at the depth of 4,000 metres, what method might be found to convert the piezoelectric potential into a power source?

Environmental Remediation

The persuasive logic of carbon credits, profitability, and remediation applies to all energy sources: wind generators, heat exchangers and methane-fueled generators. It is hard to defend leaving any stones unturned when contemplating revenue generation and cost reduction, even the production of stone paper. And, there are more options.

Gold Fields, the corporate proprietor of one of the Jozie's largest gold mines, owns an astounding 175,000 acres of surrounding land. These holdings were acquired over the years from farmers who could no longer achieve reasonable productivity due to the declining availability of water. (Recall that mining operations require tremendous amounts of water, which lowers the surrounding area's water table.) Although to their credit Gold Fields utilises some of this acreage to grow roses for commercial sale, much of the acreage can be quickly converted to biodiesel production.

South Africa has a supportive policy for biodiesel that grants producers tax exemptions. Although this is to be applauded, it also raises eyebrows since planting vegetation for ethanol production is hard to justify, when this displaces crops for human and animal consumption. A country that is struggling to feed its children needs to focus its priorities where they belong. If land that should produce food were used for biodiesel, it would increase the cost of food. This particularly affects those who live on the margins of society. Since it carries a recognised risk of uranium contamination, not all the land around the mines can be used to produce food. However, it can serve perfectly well for roses and can likewise grow crops for biodiesel production.

If 50,000 acres were put into production, within 2-4 years it would generate 100,000-120,000 tons of biofuel, depending on the species selected for biofuel production. Similarly, water-guzzling invasive tree species like eucalyptus and black wattle (*Acacia auriculiformis*) can be uprooted and replaced by plants and trees that have extractable oils and that would re-establish the water table over time. To further cascade nutrients, mushrooms can be grown on the rich biomass remaining once the oils were extracted, provided there were no measurable contamination or radiation. Alternatively, or even additionally, capturing the methane biogas escaping from the spent crops could be engineered. Unemployment rates in excess of 50 per cent of the adult population in communities around the mines could be dramatically lowered. Carbon credits alone can kickstart the initial financing for such an operation. Until recently no one thought Africa can generate carbon credits. If the mines were to exploit this biodiesel potential, they could have set the stage for a major contribution towards reducing greenhouse gases.

Turning a mine into a competitive operation that recovers farmland, makes stone paper, renews biodiversity, produces biofuels, provides jobs for the community, creates energy efficiencies using available resources and innovative technologies, and supplies water for sale as well as for the needs of local communities is a business that would qualify for brand equity. This is not a costly public relations initiative aimed at extracting community goodwill and trust. Rather, it is an approach that is part and parcel of the day-to-day management responsibility to increase cash flow by slashing expenses and improving revenues. From a manager's viewpoint, the social capital created in the process of cutting costs and generating income is simply icing on the cake. Why not? If such a systems approach became a part of management culture, the issues that have typically wasted management's time are no longer a stress factor, but a component of efficient resource use and income generation.

Chelating Complex Ores

Now we address the sensitive issue of uranium. Like it or not, uranium is often found in combination with gold. Thallium and copper are also standard by-products of ore processing. These are known as complex ores. When uranium prices sank to such a low level that extraction was no longer competitive, gold mines stopped producing uranium. Revenue turned to waste and after a few decades of release into streams, uranium accumulated in the wetlands and river beds. According to some activists, this pollution crisis is reaching dramatic proportions and the related clean-up costs could quickly run into the hundreds of millions. While the science is unclear and the costs unaccounted for, companies can discard neither the growing doubt, nor the responsibility for future and potentially significant expenditures. A publicly traded company will be forced to make loss provisions the day the Board is informed of the risks. These risks must be reported to the stock exchange authorities which immediately creates pressures on the share price. Recall that PCB and asbestos contamination were not considered problematic in the 1960s when their usage was widespread. General Electronics (GE) (USA) and ASEA Brown Boveri (ABB) (Switzerland) recently settled 1960s-era contamination-related claims for a staggering US$500 million dollars one billion respectively.

The opportunities in energy and water described above are realistic. If managers want to avoid the negative impact on their company's capitalisation brought on by declining share prices on the stock exchange, they need to respond proactively to a potential crisis from uranium pollution of the local water and soil. With such a sensitive matter, analysts typically account for the risk of a future clean-up and the subsequent media hysteria by discounting the present valuation of the shares. The shares then suffer from a strong downward trend. The time to invest in innovations that can convert problems into opportunities is well before a risk filing with the stock exchange is required.

Chelating technology has been around for a few decades. This approach to isolate precious metals and toxic compounds like uranium, thallium and lead is well proven. Chelating ligands bond with metal ions to render the metal inert. The leading provider of this process is the pioneering company Prime Separations, which brought together an expert team of engineers who built a career in Polaroid, the expert on thin film surface chemistry, to apply the chelating techniques observed in bacteria. The technology developed alongside other innovative means to recover metals, even those dispersed in minute amounts, like the capacity of the wood ear mushroom (*Auricularia auricula-judae*) to recover copper and the ability of geraniums (*Geranium spP.*) to recover lead. Their efficiency is a million-fold greater than the complex ore smelters that now process these blended ores.

Managers would do well to remember that mines exhaust the available raw materials and thus cannot operate forever. Gold deposits come to an end, as is predicted to occur within half a century. Prime Separations technology benefits the mining operations through a continuous approach towards extracting gold, uranium, thallium, and whichever other elements of the periodic table can be sold in pure form. In particular, the processing of uranium from both the tailings and the surrounding wetlands can be funded from cash reserves over the next decade or two. This would renew the land and the region for the next generation of economic activity, and avoid the fate of companies like GE and ABB, who had to pay their pollution bill 40 years after the fact.

The chelating technology learned from bacteria is not limited to recovering heavy metals and chromium IV. In geographical conditions where water is very scarce, such as gold mines in Venezuela and Burkina Faso, the of know-how Prime Separations can become a key factor in processing ore in a closed-loop water cycle. This technology renders obsolete the need to permit and build pipelines, or to truck water from nearby rivers, or to spend massive sums of money on reverse osmosis facilities and the electricity to keep them running. For new mines that are found to have available thallium, the same technology could purify the metal for sale. Purified Thallium-203 is sold for US$1,800 per kilogram by the Los Alamos National Laboratory in the USA. This is real income, stemming from continuous filtering of the tailings and sedimentation. This is real cost elimination. There will be no cleanup bill due in 40 years. Only bio-regenerated land with considerable value located proximally to a large urban market would remain. Land value was the real payoff of the Las Gaviotas project. In the case of South Africa's gold mines, we can see that augmenting land value is an appreciable way to maintain shareholder value and accrue social capital.

The chelating technology has another potential benefit: the co-habitation of artisanal and large scale mining. While large corporations abide by stricter environmental rules, small scale operations get away with the unrestricted use of mercury and cyanide. If established mining conglomerates were to make the chelation technology available, then the artisans would be happy to eliminate their deployment of toxins. The market makers of gold can vouch for the quality, refine to world market standards and most importantly eliminate the middlemen and the hardware salesmen who tend to take home the largest profit share from the artisans. While the small operations can scavenge gold deposits that are uncompetitive for large operators, the blending of innovations can make both viable. The upside for the stock exchange quoted mining group might well be the opportunity to increase turnover by 30 per cent, without the same increase in capital expenditure, while the artisans generate a better revenue and the environment benefits from a better control of deadly substances. The Blue Economy is an inclusive proposal for growth.

Mines as Biorefineries

It is an advantage that the tasks of mine management require long-term vision. There is simply no quick buck to be made when you operate a mine. The time between obtaining an exploration license, getting permission to process the ore, then selling the product is often a decade or more. The company must be prepared to invest the trust funds legally required to rehabilitate the land or to provide cash for creating a future beyond the mines. In this sense, mine management is acutely aware that the future must be imagined today. Yet the availability of 400,000 acres, only 45 minutes from downtown Johannesburg, has more potential to benefit the shareholders than has yet been realised.

Agriculture is not the only sector to facilitate multiple cash flows through the concept of bio-refineries that re-industrialise regions that have been labelled as uncompetitive in this race of globalisation. Mining can achieve the same benefits, merely by using what is locally available. If we imagine the reprocessing of tailings into stone paper and building materials under a creative financial structure that returns the landscape to its original dramatic beauty, with uranium on its way to the market instead of accumulating in the topsoil and water, then the historic and cultural wealth of the region will be an asset. That asset may well represent the investors' assessments of the ultimate value of gold mines. No one has taken the time to value these surrounding land assets. They are not even valued in the company books of account. Land holdings are considered a cost ready to be dumped on any buyer at any price. What would you pay for land that carries the risk of uranium contamination? What is the value of that land if it is pristine and beautiful?

Sometimes it takes an outsider to show what is extraordinary on your doorstep. This is the reason why the Blue Economy teams around the world perform a scan and screen with a clear dedication towards implementation of the projects that are retained as viable. If a gold and uranium mine is converted over years into a sophisticated water extraction and energy generation system, generating more jobs than ever considered viable, combined with the public display of engineering marvels that facilitated mining at 4,200 metres deep, it becomes a potential public attraction that is likely to pay for itself. Jozie is one of the most vibrant cities in Africa. Considering the cultural, natural, and industrial sites classified by United Nations Educational, Scientific and Cultural Organization (UNESCO) as World Heritage Sites, the gold mines, the natural environment, and its historical context certainly qualify for this international recognition.

The necessity for the mines to achieve a sustainable economic basis, combined with the national need to implement sound social and ecological policies and maintain adequate foreign exchange, have seldom been so potentially interconnected as are the possibilities at mining sites around Johannesburg. The probability of immediate and long-term benefit is significantly high. Some of the concepts presented are based on existing technologies, others are envisioned and need additional research. What is certain is that the same mines that was criticised in the past, and are still rightfully on the radar of governmental and non-governmental organisations today, have seldom been seen in as positive and proactive a light as we have looked at them in this chapter. They are interconnected systems, capable of contributing to society.

A mine that is a World Heritage site, that provides drinking water to the poor, that serves the top of the market with energised, gold-flaked bottled water, that generates additional revenues from stone paper and carbon credits, that slashes costs by providing a major part of its own energy needs from readily available resources, that diversifies into energy and food production providing much-needed jobs, that offers a future to communities that presently lack the vision or even ability to dream, is a company that will garner respect, admiration, appreciation, stock value, and public praise from the very first moment it begins to deal with pollution from the past.

Financial Engineering

It does not take a financial strategist to translate these opportunities into cash flow, nor a business analyst to understand the value of lower business risk compounded with improved social capital. The Blue Economy approach is based on improvements of the profit and loss accounts, strengthening of cash flow, reduction of capital and operational expenses, improvement of asset values, conversion of provisions into investments and transformation of a culture of cost reduction into that of generating additional revenues and value.

Understanding the array of opportunities is not the requirement. What is required is a shift in management culture. Attention now must be focused on only one major issue, instead upon the interconnections that extend beyond the core business. It is this shift that is likely to be the biggest challenge. The gold mine, will remain a gold mine but the multiple inputs and outputs that are so easily outsourced and framed into supply chain management must now be viewed in terms of additional cost reductions, substantial revenue improvements, long-term capital gains, improved market capitalisation, reduced business risk from strong cash flow, and a flexible company ready to risk and innovate. These qualities have always characterised the market leaders who are more often than not rewarded for their foresight and vision.

Thus the way forward is based on technological benchmarks elsewhere achieved and on progressive financial engineering applied to the real and future value of all assets. A persuasive rationale based in solid science and economic feasibility awaits the decision of the management and endorsement of the stockholders. Mining companies in Russia, China, Africa, the US and Latin America can then demonstrate that despite a regrettable history, there is a future of hope and a presence of intention.

14

Buildings Designed by Flows

> It is clear from da Vinci's notes that he saw the city as a kind of living organism in which people, material goods, food, water, and waste needed to move and flow with ease for the city to remain healthy.
>
> — *FRITJOF CAPRA, THE SCIENCE OF LEONARDO*

The Ecosystem of the Domicile

Every living system searches for shelter, from the egg nest, to the nutshell, to the algal membrane. Everything alive creates subtle borders that delineate exterior and interior. Each creature finds its unique way to achieve inner stability, to control temperature and humidity, to store reserves, and to ensure health and survival.

In recent times, the design of human shelter has undergone much transformation, although perhaps not always improvement. The physical constructs of the way we live now far exceed mere shelter. They provide the conveniences that fit our ideas of comfort and contentment. We live in an age of modernity, drifting towards *Domótica*, where progress and comfort require ever greater acquisition of electronics and robotics. For most of us, the largest share of our time is passed indoors—at home, at work, at school. We spend about eight hours a day asleep. Perhaps another eight are spent at work or at school, and the remainder commuting or absorbed in household chores and activities. The design of the buildings we inhabit for two-third of our lives should reasonably assure health and safety. Surprisingly, the key to a healthy environment is, again, potential hydrogen or pH.

The ocean, with a pH of 8.2, is the cradle of life on Earth. Ecosystems and their life-creating powers thrive in an alkaline environment. Yet much of our environment—indoors as well as outdoors—has reached a high level of acidity. Our excessive use of fossil fuels and the massive volume of carbon dioxide pumped into the atmosphere every day render the air very acidic indeed. There is no escape anywhere in the industrialised world or in any city on the globe. Those who live in rural areas or near a coastline may be less affected. If you live in a megalopolis like New York, Los Angeles, London, Paris, Sao Paolo, New Delhi, or Johannesburg, the atmospheric pH is just above 4. Remember, pH is measured on a logarithmic scale; hence, a pH measure of 5 is 10 times higher than 4 and a pH measure of 6 is 100 times greater than 4.

Consider the remarkable functioning of our digestive system. The food we ingest is taken into the stomach where the highly acidic environment quickly and safely reduces the grains, vegetables, meats, and other comestibles to their basic components. The small intestine, where the nutritive matter is absorbed and made available to the blood for transport to the organs and tissues, is also a significant component of our immune system. It requires an alkaline pH factor to optimally function. Similarly, because a bedroom is where sleep allows the body to repair and regenerate, the air should also have an alkaline pH. Starting at home, we should use our understanding of the flows of air and matter to create an environment supportive of life and health.

If you take the time to check pH of the air in your house, you will quickly realise that the air in urban areas is acid, and usually does not get better circulating from outside to inside. Unfortunately, it typically gets worse. Interior air quality is degraded by the off-gassing of almost everything inside the home or office, regardless of living on the beach or atop a breathtaking mountain range. The overall result is simply not good. What is the use of making sure that what you drink and eat offers a healthy balance of acid and alkaline when you breathe acids all day? What is worse is that you inhale acids all night as you sleep. As we power up our Blue Economy, the outside air we breathe will become less polluted and less acidic. In the meantime, the design and construction of our buildings can be such that their interiors naturally evolve to be more alkaline.

The 7 Flows of Building Design and Living Space

Architects, along with medical doctors, are potentially the most 'connected' thinkers. Yet they too are subject to a rigid compartmentalisation of knowledge. As a consequence, they conclude that acidity and alkalinity are topics for chemists. Even the most environmentally progressive architect, who has successfully built a LEED Platinum Certified building, is likely unaware of the importance of maintaining the pH factor in buildings. While physics and mathematics figure prominently in the training of architects, life sciences are left to the margin. That is regrettable, since physical structures based on solid math and biology are at the foundation of health and livelihood on Earth.

When an architect receives the specifications for a new building, the volume and surface area determine its size and functionality; for example, the number of bedrooms, the integration of a kitchen and dining room, the combination of a gymnasium and classrooms, a school solarium, or the pairing of open office space with a kitchenette. Some architects will consider the position of the sun, and propose a south-facing building in the northern hemisphere (and a north-facing building in the tropics). This is straightforward and requires neither much creative insight nor detailed scientific knowledge, or even much inspiration from ecosystems.

Physical buildings cannot be viewed as merely static esthetic structures that meet functional goals and comply with local regulations. Moreover, buildings that are constructed with renewable resources and targeted energy savings are only the first step in the context of redesign. There are seven important flows that must be brought into the design concept: air, light, water, energy, sound, matter and occupants. Each of these flows influences the dynamic balance that provides the life-promoting conditions allowing us to survive and thrive. Life enhancement is the driving force behind all these flows. Survival and health must always be the priority, particularly because we spend so much of our time indoors. The composition and functionality of our domicile determine our health, comfort and repose.

Air includes matter such as dust. Matter includes the food we eat and what is discarded, while water includes what we drink and what we use to wash away waste. Materials cover the flow of goods that contribute to the functionality and efficiency of our personal environment. These are all important components of our lifestyle and contributors to our comfort levels. Yet, it seems that we design our homes without considering such flows. Accumulated dust can make us ill. Biomass left to rot is a health hazard, and truly a waste. The water in our sewers transports effluent to holding tanks where it is chemically treated to attack accumulated bacteria. The trash generated by our packaging-obsessed consumer society bursts from innumerable landfills outside the scope of our vision or consciousness. These are all literally dead ends. Consider that a flow implies an unimpeded continuity of movement. If we were to enhance rather than obstruct our household flows, we could take advantage of a wide portfolio of innovations that would contribute to comfortable and healthful living conditions, reduced costs, and saved energy.

Natural systems always design for and with flow. Nothing evolves statically but rather by interaction, with everything around it. Insight into this fundamental design principle will reveal connections among disparate phenomena and objectives. These connections in turn leads to a bundle of solutions that natural systems have adapted and modelled for millions of years. Hence our challenge becomes how to interweave a set of parameters so as to design with these flows. In short, our challenge is to emulate ecosystems that make use of physics and locally available materials to meet basic needs and to promote greater efficiency and diversity. As we set these goals, and as architects and home designers prioritise health and comfort, it will then be possible—actually quite easy—to achieve a better balance and more open flows.

To begin, we need to know ways to design esthetically pleasing physical spaces that maintain a proper interior pH balance and allow for interplay of the seven flows. If we successfully create a design model that encompasses all these flows, then we will experience a completely new comfort level. The structure would be in tune with its environment, and would thus achieve ideal sustainability with neither extraordinary effort nor higher expense. Such buildings would be more than green; they would reflect more than energy savings from a grass roof or from certified sustainable forestry lumber. As a first priority, these structures would contribute to health and self-sufficiency by drawing from locally available resources and energy sources. They would conform to a healthy and dynamic balance between humanity and the ecosystems on which we depend for the free supply of commons, such as water and air. Such spaces would enhance life.

The first architect to realise the importance of flow as a determining principle in the design of buildings and cities was Leonardo da Vinci. His designs demonstrate a remarkable insight into multiple flows and the need to connect with the surroundings. Moreover, da Vinci imagined the design of cities based on the flows of water, waste and people. In *The Science of Leonardo*, Fritjof Capra writes:

> Leonardo's special attention to how movements would flow through his buildings was not restricted to the interiors, but included the surrounding grounds as well, by means of doorways, loggias, and balconies. In fact, in most of his designs of villas and palaces, he considered the garden to be an integral part of the house. These designs reflect his continual efforts to integrate architecture and nature.

A further extension of Leonardo's organic view of building design and his special focus on its functional integrity is apparent in his pioneering contributions to urban design. When he witnessed the plague in Milan shortly after his arrival in the city in 1482, he realised that its devastating effects were largely due to the city's appalling sanitary conditions. In typical fashion, he responded with a proposal for rebuilding the city in a way that would provide decent housing for people and shelters for animals, and would allow the streets to be cleaned regularly by drenching them.

The Thoroughly Modern Nursery

We start our observations of flows in and around buildings by focusing our attention on the spaces most occupied by infants and young children. While the young are the most sensitive and vulnerable, they are also the potential of our future. Children, like adults with weakened immune systems, are affected more subtly and easily by the dynamics of multiple flows. This means that where flows are inadequate, or lacking, their potential to complicate health and introduce disease is greater.

Imagine a young child asleep for the greater part of the day in a room filled with formaldehyde from the glue in the particle board; with chemically, laden bactericides and fungicides in the flooring and wall paint; with heavy metals from the brightly coloured clothes and toys; and with bromine fire retardants in the mattress, bedding, curtains, and carpets. The windows are triple glazed and UV (ultraviolet) protected, with heavy curtains to keep out light and a thick carpet to dampen sound while the child sleeps. Double insulation and an energy-efficient recirculation of heated or cooled air make for an airtight environment to further block noise. The disposable diapers and infant hygiene products are laden with artificial fragrances and parabenes, and coloured with chemical dyes and optical whiteners. The water is heavily chlorinated and the air conditioner filter contains chemicals to kill bacteria. The electric wires that pass over or around the bed emit electromagnetic charges that launch dust particles into the air to be inhaled. Artificial squeaks from plastic toys and crackling of the radio waves from the baby monitor can be heard, and a WiFi antenna secures that the internet works 24 hours a day, anywhere where our iPad follows us.

Mind you, everything in this room is individually tested and approved. None has a proven track record of causing harm, despite a few exceptions where one toy or another contains toxins that should not be present there. The reality is that the child in this stressful environment is forced to divert too much energy to immune defense. The diversion of energy to process the stress created and accumulated, or to limit damage from the toxic surroundings, diminishes what is available to keep the immune system strong and the child exuberant and healthy. The statistical incidence of respiratory ailments and skin rashes afflicting young children is nowhere close to a comfort zone. To the contrary, we are clearly moving towards an era where more and more problems arise. While there is no one to blame, the system has flaws. The combination of all these broken flows has led to a demonstrable increase in health problems. The National Center for Health Statistics (NCHS) overwhelms you with statistics that underscore this reality.

Thus while all the material conveniences in a thoroughly modern nursery are designed to facilitate the comfort and care of the child, we find that they actually run counter to an environment that would optimise health and comfort. What is needed is to rethink the whole concept, choosing solutions that create a living environment that strengthens rather than stresses the immune system. Innovations, such as glue power of the gecko and the mussel, colouration achieved with the photo-optical means used by butterflies and beetles, pH control available from seashells and seaweeds, food-grade chemical fire retardants, fire sensors modelled after the jewel beetle, UV protection from the edelweiss flower, sound control made possible by the ormia fly, and hygiene products made with natural silk polymers, algae polyesters, and lycopenes from tomato seed waste, are highly imperative. There is more: the bacterial control in water achieved by vortex technology, biofilm disruption from furanones, electrical power generated from body heat or outside sound, or pressure on crystals—all without the need for wires or cables. Johan Gielis, the smart observer of bamboo, designed the antennas using his latest superformula (also called the Gielis Formula) that permits data transmission with only a fraction of the present energy requirements.

Today allergies and respiratory ailments affect more than 25 per cent of the children in urban areas. An immune system that develops normally and naturally, without excessive factors of artificial sound, chemical overload, excessive WiFi exposure, as well as stagnant and dust-laden air, will function to protect and maintain the health and growth of a child. We must consider ways to best promote life with the solutions devised by nature. We cannot risk the health of our children.

The Flow of Air and Light

In earlier times, our dwellings were constructed with thatched roofs and tiny windows having no glass. Airflow through such habitation was the norm. More recently, ostensibly to save energy, many buildings are constructed with super insulation so that hardly any air gets in or out. The aim of saving energy is to be lauded, but eliminating airflow is not at all beneficial. The walls do not breathe, the roofs do not seep. The chemical foams used to insulate building walls and roofs are, with a few exceptions, constantly off-gassing acids into the air we breathe. Fire retardants applied to buildings and their material components are another known problem. The risk of fire is considered substantially dangerous to mandate the use of flame retardant chemicals, even on mattresses and pillows. Of course, each of these chemicals has been approved, one at a time. Each has been tested and although some are deemed as possible carcinogens, the health risk is considered worth reducing that of death by fire. The unfortunate combination of all these chemicals creates an overdose we should avoid. Althoughout night, we inhale a chemical cocktail we did not need in the first place.

When we block the natural flow of air, we are not connecting the facts and are overlooking the reality of a building. Were we to solve building ventilation with the same methodical approach as that of the humble termite, a world of connections would unfold. The flow of air, the composition of household materials, and the pH of the air and walls could all contribute, rather than complicate or obstruct. Utilising insights as to how natural systems succeed at resolving these challenges would allow us to make genuine progress in achieving real sustainability without increasing investment costs.

It is possible to have continuous air flow and save energy at the same time. Ecosystems have been evolving along those lines for millennia. At present, the best way to reduce the chemical load caused by off-gassing, bacterial contamination, and electrically charged dust particles would be to facilitate more air flow through the building. If we design the building so as to thoroughly refresh the air at least once an hour, then exposure to suspected carcinogens in minute amounts will not pose a problem for most people. While opening a modern building to allow the continuous flow of cold, hot, or humid air from the outside would exacerbate energy use, natural systems have reconciled both objectives. What they can teach us will provide multiple benefits.

One of the newer approaches to heating in buildings is radiant floor heating. Hot water circulates through pipes laid in the subfloor, providing heat with greater efficiency than can be achieved by heating the air. A new improvement, less cumbersome as well as less costly, was developed by Korean scientists, Young-Suk Shu and Tae-Sung Oh who were inspired by observations of decomposing plant matter in the soil root zone. Ants and termites transport an estimated 15 per cent of all plant material to the second layer of topsoil. Aeration by earthworms, as well as fungi harvesting by ants and termites, assists further decomposition of the plant matter. The heat from decomposition warms the soil around the root zone, increasing the osmosis between the roots and leaves of the plants, thereby enhancing growth and improving flavour of the harvested crop.

The Korean scientists developed a thin film of nano-sized carbon fibres that could be placed under a wooden floor or a carpet to produce surrounding temperatures of up to 98° F using only 12-volt solar power application. This application was initially tested in Japanese and Korean greenhouses as a method for keeping plant roots warm. On saving over 70 per cent of the previous heating energy expenditure for greenhouse production, it is now making its entry into home heating applications.

While this innovation is just one advancement, it could be used to enhance ecological carpets such as those made by Interface Global. The most advanced versions could be composed of meshed carbon fibres woven throughout a base made from either rubber or PVC

(Polyvinyl chloride). The carpet tiles electrically connect through the micron-size carbon fibres and can even obtain their energy from thin-film dye-sensitised solar cells attached to the windows, generating an ideal comfort-level temperature for bare feet. Heating provided by direct current generated through dye solar cells, which allow passage of light will tackle mite infestation from two angles. First, the UV radiation will directly kill the mites. Second, the temperature in the carpet will be high enough to dry any scraps, crumbs, or morsels dropped on the floor, eliminating possible nutrient sources to keep mite proliferation under control.

Insect Insights Relative to Humidity

Termites are farmers. They have perfected a system that involves bringing biomass into the deeper soil to farm fungi. Delicate control of temperature and humidity is imperative for success. Over millennia, termites have learned that unless the temperature and the humidity are exact, fungi do not proliferate, even when offered an ideal growth medium. Termite nests are always 81°F and the humidity is constant at 61 per cent. Everywhere they live, in every climate, termites have learned to control air circulation by building tunnels and chimneys. Whether in Dallas or Dacca, Oslo or Osaka, and regardless of variation in the outside temperature, termites successfully build their air-regulating infrastructure, maintaining its flow and quality merely by changing the colour, width, length, or height of their infrastructure of tunnels and chimneys.

Chimneys warm the air, which rises as exhaust from the nest and creates a vacuum inside. Whether hot or cold, the incoming exterior air is channeled through tiny tunnels built into the underground nest. If the exterior air is hot and humid, it cools and sheds moisture. If it is cold and dry, it warms and absorbs moisture. This is simply based on the basic laws of physics. Termites know exactly how tall the chimney must be, and how long and deep the underground tubes must be in order to always maintain the nest temperature and humidity, regardless of outside conditions. They acquired this ability over millions of years without a thermostat or the need for energy and pumps.

Humans have been regulating the interior temperature of our dwellings for far less time. Given our much shorter record of experience, we are only beginning to access the mathematical models necessary to construct buildings with a predictable and comfortable air flow. Lacking the tools innate to the termite, we unfortunately chose electricity and fossil fuels as the driving force, neglecting the laws of physics with their wonderful fail-safe characteristics. Nearly all our inventions include moving parts, which in a physical world will sooner or later reach a fail state. The termites designed their lasting solution without any moving parts. It is a solution that we can use too.

A Living Filter

Flowing air in and out of a building is a great first step. We can also orchestrate flows inside the building to thoroughly cleanse and oxygenate the air. Remember, oxygen brings alkalinity. Consequently, we must move beyond physics and acquire an understanding of biology in general, and plants and micro-algae in particular. It is not difficult to recreate an interior environment that precipitates dust and charged particles into the soil. Over two decades ago, a small company named Living Filters (Levande Filter AB), pioneered this concept for air filters inspired by the NASA-funded research aimed at cleansing air in space ships.

Prof Lars Thofelt developed the plant system and since 1998, his Living Filter systems have been installed worldwide. In coordination with the architect, these systems are designed so that air turbulence within the building channels the inside air through a collection of 150 different plants strategically located near the ceiling. The logic of this comes from rainforest ecology, where we observe that these forests are not only a home for biodiversity and a source of oxygen, but are also massive air filters. In the Amazon, floating dust particles from as far away as Africa can be captured by the rainforest plant matter to precipitate into the soil with the rains and replenish topsoil. The collection of plants in a Living Filter is permanently lit with highly efficient LED lamps. Every 15 minutes, a mist of water is sprayed on the leaves. This mist percolates through the illuminated and moistened plants, cleansing the air of dust and airborne toxins. The result is noticeable: air is enriched with oxygen and nicely alkaline.

Fungi in the Basement

When a building is closed and insulated, humidity is trapped inside. Long, humid summers cause the moisture to condense on basement insulation and mold to grow. Dampness in closed areas without air circulation produces the ideal conditions for fungi to invade a home, especially in the basement. Fungi release spores into the air that can cause respiratory diseases. If your house is made of wood, then both building and occupants are at risk. If you have a steel frame building, then only your health is at risk. Expert remediation companies will treat the walls with metal oxides, freeing the building of fungus but emitting chemical gas particulates for a couple of years. These are particles that you should never inhale. This is the superficiality of our 'one cause–one effect' way of thinking. It is reminiscent of core business strategy where we abstract all unintended consequences.

If, on the other hand, we design the building to let air flow through the basement and allow full spectrum light (including UV radiation) to reach the interior, then we eliminate the conditions for fungus growth and actually cleanse the building. Anders Nyquist uses a prisma light to bring natural full-spectrum light into basements. This not only offers free illumination during the day, but also a first response to the onslaught of unwanted fungi. With proper ventilation, the spores that cause respiratory problems are exhausted from the building. This is a good start, with a potential that goes beyond merely resolving a problem. A connected world can achieve multiple benefits for multiple partners. There are opportunities for entrepreneurs to seize.

Now we again make the link to pH. Most materials commonly used for walls and flooring exacerbate the stifling effect of insulation and other flow barriers, creating conditions that allow mold and fungi to proliferate. The fungi growing in dark static conditions such as basements thrive in an acidic environment. Thus, another way to control fungal growth is to change the pH the basement making it more alkaline. If the fungi do not find conditions conducive to their proliferation, they simply remain dormant. Wall and floor coverings can be made from sources of calcium carbonate, such as crushed seashells. If sheetrock were used, the insulation in the wall could be seaweed-based. Both seaweed and seashells are abundant, inexpensive, and highly alkaline. Used as raw material for floor covering and wall insulation, their performance matches the functionality of materials currently available.

A new understanding of environmental conditions such as air flow, light, and alkalinity can help us eliminate the conditions wherein fungus grows as well as lessen exposure to toxins that stress our immune systems. In this manner, we start weaving information together, connecting insulation to fungi, to air quality, to health, and to the design of a healthy building.

Åke Mård, founder of the innovative MRD Construction Company in Sweden, has another approach to controlling mold in basements. Pittsburgh Corning supplies him with glass foam blocks that are manufactured as structural building materials in Belgium and the Czech Republic. The inputs are air (mainly CO_2) and recycled glass, and the output is a multi-functional load-bearing structure. Recycled glass enriched with carbonic gas is lightweight and has the advantage of being resistant to acids and molds while simultaneously insulating. Vermin cannot eat their way through. This is exactly how we imagine the economy of the future: use available resources and obtain multiple benefits. These glass foam blocks replace four products in one prefabricated material. They relieve the pressure on bottle makers to produce bottles from recycled glass. Here again we see how nature cascades nutrients to other partners in a system.

This innovation is strongly along the lines of the goals of Earthstone, a New Mexico (USA) business which emerged separately from the construction initiatives in Sweden. Earthstone was founded in 1993 by Andrew Ungerleider and Gay Dillingham in response to the destructive strip mining they had noticed in their region. Earthstone's patented technology takes glass beverage bottles out of the waste stream and puts them to work by creating abrasion products (for example, substitutes for sandpaper), consumer cleaning products (paint remover), and horticultural products (substituting glass fibre in hydroponics). Their production design emulates natural models cascading nutrients and energy, and has achieved market share over a decade of success. The new factory is located adjacent to the Albuquerque landfill, their source for waste glass, and part of their energy used comes from the methane gas released from decomposing biomass in the landfill. This project is a clear example of an industrial solution that reduces the adverse impact of our excessive waste generation, putting products on the market that perform competitively, while using available resources.

The Challenge of Triple Glazing

There is more to be said about glass. Homeowners invest in double and even triple glazing to save energy. Often, it is even subsidised through government tax incentives. Although expensive, triple-glazed window panes are considered a sure way to save money and the environment. It is part of a sustainability strategy that requires more investment to save the money needed to pay back the same. These energy-saving measures are often combined with a window covering coated with a UV-protection film intended to prevent fading of colourful carpets, wall hangings, and pictures. As we have noted, eliminating the UV light is an open invitation to mites. There is no longer any natural physical inhibitor to their growth.

The Flow of Water

The next flow to consider is water. How do we use water in any building? Without exception, the largest use of water in houses, and definitely in schools and office buildings, is for washing and waste removal. We block the flow of air and light in modern buildings but exaggerate that flow of water through multiple tubes and pipes—some for cold, some for hot, others for gray water and yet again more for black water. Oddly, the first thing we do with digestive waste is to mix it with potable water. Our body's method of acquiring nutrients involves a complex system of stomach, kidneys, liver, bladder, and intestines. We have basically one input pipe with a valve to direct water and solids to the stomach and air to the lungs. There are two output channels—one for liquids and another for solids and gases. It works quite efficiently.

Drinking water is a necessity to life, yet not a commodity amply available to all. When it is used to wash away waste matter, we are not seeing the connections. Water is the most precious substance on earth. In many places, drinking water is expensive, more expensive than petroleum even at US$100 a barrel. When we have the luxury of easy access to clean drinking water, why do we render it unusable by blending it with human digestive waste? In addition, we also add harsh chemicals and chlorinated paper.

You may not think that urine is a remarkable liquid. Yet it is rich in potassium, one of the core nutrients that give our heart the ability to regulate blood flow. Our body cannot accumulate potassium because it is a toxin in our blood stream. Thus, it is discharged as rapidly as it accumulates from consuming a healthy diet. Urine should not be wasted, but requires to be returned to the nutrient cycle. In the era of the Roman Empire, it was the emperor himself who had the unique privilege of collecting urine from the citizens' dwellings to be used as a cleansing agent.

Faeces are a different matter. Few animal species deliberately drop faeces in water, except perhaps birds, such as the flamingo, whose droppings stimulate the growth of algae on which shrimps thrive, and on which the birds in turn depend for nutrients. There are good reasons why our digestive system separates faeces from urine. The combined odour of faeces and urine is unpleasant. In current custom, urine and faeces, along with voluminous quantities of formerly drinkable water, are flushed away and pumped to water treatment systems where the organic matter is expensively devoured by bacteria stimulated by massive amounts of air pumped into the water. If faeces and urine were separately collected, as accomplished by our digestive system, there would be little or no odour, provided there was a flow of air to quickly dry the faeces.

That is the function of the dry-separation toilet designed, operated, and fine-tuned by Dr Matts Wolgast, a Swedish scientist from Uppsala University. Alternatively, a simple vortex set up to take advantage of the power of gravity could quickly separate solids from liquids. Water cleansing systems such as those evolved by clams would also contribute, as would purifying water using the methods devised by pistol shrimp. Yet, even these end-of-pipe solutions go unused in modern buildings. Were we to eliminate the need for water to transport digestive waste to central water treatment plants, where *E. coli* and *Vibrio cholerae* thrive, then we would eliminate not only the risks linked to these potential sources of disease, but also the voluminous, industrial-scale quantities of harsh chemicals required to control these harmful bacteria. Although bactericides reduce the risk of disease, they render the waste water totally useless for any form of consumption, unless subjected to a lengthy and costly recovery process.

At the Laggarberg School in Sweden, designed by Anders Nyquist, the on-site operation that processes all toilet waste, operates with the logic of an ecosystem. Although flushing toilets are the legal requirement, once liquids and solids are flushed they are immediately separated using a simple vortex. Waste heat is used to dry the solid matter. This destroys all pathogens, parasites, and any excreted antibiotics and hormones before they can have a detrimental impact on humans and their environment. Children at Laggarberg who spend their school years in this learning environment innately comprehend, from day-to-day exposure, the common logic of sustainably managed waste systems.

We think of water as the liquid that flows through pipes from a place where it is in abundance to wherever it is needed. Cities have established efficient water distribution networks. Imagine the thousands of miles of pipes that bring water from the Colorado River to Los Angeles. Imagine the huge investment New York is making to install septic tanks upstate so as to preserve its watershed. Now consider what happens to rainwater. It is collected in the sewer pipes buried beneath city roads and simply drained away! Although water is becoming increasingly costly, the State of Colorado even prohibits its urban residents to capture rainwater from their buildings. How is this possible? How can flushing rainwater into the sewage system be permitted in order to dilute the organic load? It is time to think of water as our most precious resource. Prior to birth, we are more than 98 per cent water. Our adult bodies are more than 80 per cent water. Its daily consumption fuels our survival. We treat water the way we do because we do not see the flows. Let us get out of the box (again) and ask the simple question, "Where is the largest quantity of untapped drinking water on Earth?" It is in the air.

The first and foremost solution to meet our needs for water is to capture rainfall. In every building and on every street, there are water catchment areas that could channel water towards its most immediate use, without the need for pumps or chemical treatments, since gravity could do the job. Whether a skyscraper in New York or farm in Colombia, rainfall capture would supply the building occupants' water needs.

Capturing moisture from the air is not seriously considered as a mainstream solution. Yet we would gain fresh insight into rich opportunities to tap water from the air by visiting the driest ecosystems and learn how the local plants and animals survive. The Namibian desert beetle (*Onymacris unguicularis*) catches water from the air through the interplay of hydrophobic and hydrophilic surfaces. The Main's frog (*Cyclorana maini*) from Australia can absorb 30 per cent of its body weight in water and encapsulate it in a cocoon. The Thorny Devil (*Moloch horridus*) accumulates moisture through osmosis into an interior reservoir. The *Welwitschia mirabilis*, a desert plant, shares similar abilities with the desert beetle in condensing water from the air. The cactus thorn sucks water out of the air as do pine trees and the *Guadua angustifolia*, an Andean highland bamboo species. The Garoé (*Ocotea foetens*) laurel tree that grows on ridge of the summit of the El Hierro Island in the Peninsula of the Canary Isles produces such streams of water from the clouds that sometimes looks like a waterfall.

If you have ever observed an air conditioner, you know that it drips water all the time. In a similar fashion, a cooling tower on top of a large office building condenses water vapour that accumulates as sweat along the surface of the tower. To get an idea of how much water is suspended in the atmosphere, consider that if the air expelled every day from the top of a large building were to first flow along a combination of hydrophobic and hydrophilic surfaces, it could funnel as much as 100 cubic metres of water per minute from the roof to the floors below. Interestingly, when we study the flow of air from cooling towers, we are discovering the opportunity to let water flow from top of the building downward. That reduces energy costs. Avoiding pumping by using the force of gravity simultaneously reduces water use. Since water 'on top' requires no pumps, we save capital costs. There is a proposal with considerable appeal in an economic crisis: invest less, get more.

Leonardo da Vinci studied water extensively. He was fascinated with water, the flows of rivers, eddies, spiraling vortices, and other patterns of turbulence. He identified two principal forces operating in flowing water—gravity and internal friction or viscosity. At the centre of Leonardo's investigations of turbulence was the water vortex, or whirlpool. The vortex was creatively approached in the 20th century by Viktor Schauberger, an Austrian scientist and forester. As we have noted, a vortex has the capacity to cleanse water. The relationship to building design is an easy step. Capture water from the cooling towers, flush a toilet, shine the windows and mop the floors, pump it through a vortex-generating pipe, oxygenate and cleanse through the internal pressure, and each floor down it can be used again, then delivered clean to the basement. This is an efficient use of water that makes a difference.

When we then flow water through a vortex, separating solids from liquids, water from the tenth to the first floor could be reused for toilet flushing nine times. Since flushing toilets are one of the largest water guzzlers in office buildings, a vortex system would save both water and energy. If the surface of the building is covered with material inspired by the physics of the lotus flower or ability of the abalone to maintain a clean and shining interior shell, then neither water nor chemicals are needed to cleanse it, saving more water. Costly window-cleaning machines could be eliminated from operational expenses of the building. Are these solutions a reality or a dream? It is up to us. Plants and insects prove they work; many are benchmarked. The water repellent on the legs of water striders is so effective that no moisture ever sticks. It permits these insects to walk on water.

These ingenious solutions have been fine-tuned through millions of years of survival in the desert and pragmatic application of physical laws that work all the time, without exception. Compared to their abilities, our complex systems of pumping water from the mountains through dams, or converting salt water to potable water with the massive energy expenditure required by reverse osmosis, begin to look like archaic technologies.

The combined flow of air and water offers a vast range of opportunities that can be appreciated by understanding the laws of physics and chemistry. Despite being easy to comprehend, these laws are seldom adapted as solutions. Take the example of a checkered surface with hydrophobic and hydrophilic textures. The massive clouds of air that dissipate from cooling towers could instead flow over a sheet of squares. Some squares are hydrophobic; they 'hate water'. Some squares are hydrophilic; they 'love water'. Tiny bubbles of water are rejected from the hydrophobic surfaces before they have time to evaporate. These bubbles collect on the hydrophilic surfaces, forming droplets and flowing downward by gravity alone to fill tanks on the top of a building. This supply may not be enough to satisfy every need. Nonetheless, the idea helps us contemplate vast water resources we have never before considered. If the cooling towers were to expel their saturated air in a swirl, thereby generating a vortex, it could even 'press' the water out of the air without any checkered surfaces. The first such systems have been installed by Watreco on the island of El Hierro.

Once we perfect the design of these innovations, we can combine them with the latest insights into the cleansing capacity of a vortex in water pipes. By redesigning the production and consumption models, and taking the time and effort to rethink the entire system, we have a chance to achieve a solution that could save us from massive worldwide water shortages. These innovations, once applied, can cut costs immediately and relieve the stress on scarce water resources that characterise every megalopolis in the world.

The entire coastal zone of California has suffered from water shortages for decades. If there were access to water from the moist air that is always present because of the temperature inversion between the cold ocean currents and the hot inland deserts, the largest economic benefit would be increased land value. Remember Las Gaviotas, a desolate area once considered worthless and now a regenerated rainforest valued at 3,000 times its original cost. An increase in property value based on the inclusion of a commons, like abundant water resources, would be a welcome reversal to the current trend of property devaluation and speculation. Good land that meets basic needs, starting with drinking water, holds good value.

The Heat Island Effect

In the sweltering summer heat of New York or Boston, Galveston or Chattanooga, building air conditioners are on full blast. Hot outside air is pushed through these cooling systems and water-saturated heated clouds surround the buildings. The air conditioners produce cool air inside. The warm and humid air exhausts to the outside, rendering the exterior air in the immediate vicinity—including that available for the air conditioning uptake system—likewise warm and humid. Thus the energy required to cool hot, moist air increases. With little wind, the area becomes a heat island. In the summer, when such a heat island effect is at its peak, the warm conditions needed for the spread of *Legionella* spp. (the bacteria responsible for Legionnaire's disease) will be at prime. Rising temperatures cause bacterially proliferated biofilms to get thicker, and consequently the health risks heighten. When you enter a building through revolving doors meant to avoid heating or cooling loss, there is no decompression, thus no movement of air. The more people who gather in these airtight buildings, the more heat is captured inside.

Each adult produces about 60 watts of energy every hour. Energy used for heating or cooling adds heat. A meeting room hosting a thousand people can produce 60 kW hours, and such heat requires proportionally more cooling. Anders Nyquist's design of a sporting hall at the Laggarberg School in Sweden uses an ingenious approach. When heat is emitted by excited spectators during a lively school sports event, the naturally occurring air flows actually bring in the cooler outside air. His design demonstrates that as more people enter the hall, greater airflow occurs, keeping the inside air refreshed and comfortable. That is a systemic design that works!

Building designs create sets of unanticipated problems. The solutions are to serve multiple purposes, while producing cost and energy savings and reducing the risks to human health. Healthier buildings that save energy with lower capital and operating costs are the bottom line of this bundling of innovations provided by solutions from the natural whole systems.

The Flow of Sound

Prior to birth, we are composed primarily of water. The sounds that resonate through the amniotic fluid definitely affect us. In fact, some pediatricians have suggested that pregnant women listen to classical music, or to the chanting of Gregorian or Tibetan monks, because they consider that these sounds enhance an infant's mental development. Alexander Lauterwasser's work in the field of cymatics demonstrated that a flow of sound suffusing a body of water achieves a constant and therefore predictable determination of shape. Sound is a wave; waves produce pressure, and sound waves have different levels or frequencies. Lauterwasser placed a drop of water on a metal plate and applied a sound source. He observed that as sound waves vibrated the water, the latter moved. Different waves at different pressures generated different complex patterns of movement. A specific frequency always produced a particular movement and shape of the water at a fixed surface tension. A minimal change in frequency caused alterations in the complex but rhythmic movements.

Each of us knows from experience that pleasant sounds are soothing, and unpleasant sounds can range from mildly annoying to positively unbearable. We can imagine the ambience of living near a babbling brook or within hearing of ocean waves at the seashore. Living or working next to a freeway or a railroad line requires an accommodation that renders noise awareness subliminal, although wearing.

Since even inanimate objects such as buildings produce noise, exploring innovative ideas that channel the flow of undesirable sounds in our daily environments might help us find ways to reduce the effect such sounds on us. Scientists study how the streamlined shape of bottlenose dolphins and whales allows them to convert the pressure from water and wind vortices into efficient power. Perhaps we might similarly capture the energy potential of sound and convert it using minute piezoelectric transformers, gaining sufficient electrical energy to power small battery-driven devices such as cell phones. Instead of just blocking noise from the freeway traffic buzzing around the building, we could devise ways to capture and convert it to energy. Thus, physical solutions to noise amelioration could also achieve energy savings.

The Flow of Energy

The cost of energy delivered to a building depends on two factors: demand and supply. The cases described in this chapter, and throughout the book, demonstrate that a dramatic reduction of energy use can be accomplished by using solutions that require less and provide more. In fact, utilising only the innovations presently described could potentially reduce the need for electricity in any building, from a gymnasium to a child's room, by 75-80 per cent. To this we may add the wonders of the cold light made by squid and fungi, the self-cleaning demonstrated by the lotus flower, and heat conservation accomplished by the tuna. Technologies provided by the sandfish lizard could give us friction reduction, which is an energy saver, because our incapacity to reduce or overcome friction requires additional energy. As noted earlier, all these ways and means to reduce energy consumption are possible and do not compromise our health, as do any number of current materials. That is good, but there are even better possibilities.

If we turn our focus to supply, as we have already noted, a building has tremendous potential to generate its own electricity. While the pressure from sound and noise will not be enough to power everything in a modern building with electronics, security systems, computer networks, elevators, and air conditioning, we might once again emulate natural systems, welcoming the contributions of all, even the smallest numbers and the tiniest volumes.

The largest source of energy must be the most readily available power generator, perhaps the source that subjects the whole building to structural compression and requires the tensile strength that dominates the design. Throughout this book, we have referred to the great power of gravity. Why not use it in building design?

A redesign of the building structure could set the foundations at each floor on crystals like quartz, silk, or even sugar cane. Based on nanoscale crystals and a 10-story building, it has been guesstimated that the total power from gravity-induced piezoelectricity could reach 6,000 kW/hr. That is not bad. If the quartz energy source were precisely located on each floor, typically under each one of the columns, it would be possible to have electricity available throughout the building with a limited need for cabling. Hence, further reducing the need for copper and mining. It would take only one generation to have these building techniques approved and implemented in new structures. If the science can be demonstrated, then the conservative and risk-averse construction industry will shift for the better, and buildings will require less investment and achieve lower operational costs. If bamboo were incorporated with reinforced concrete to erect the structure, the building would not only be energy efficient, but actually sequester carbon dioxide too, since the carbon absorbed by the bamboo would offset emissions from the cement. Now we are talking serious stuff!

The second large potential but unexploited source is to use local gusts of wind, the way a zebra does. Each large building impacts the local climate, generating turbulence. These turbulences could even be enhanced through planned exterior colour choices, not just reflecting the sun but ensuring that the light and dark variations provide surface cooling and generate local airflows. It does not make much sense to place windmills in the centre of town, since these would make too much noise and not catch sufficient wind. However, it would be possible to place a series of mini- and micron-sized windmills that would constantly generate energy—each equipped with the smart surface that nature provided to whale flippers for the purpose of reducing drag and increasing lift.

Each person in the building emits the energy equivalent of 60 watts of electricity per hour and thus should be considered a source of energy. The technology from the Fraunhofer Institute is capable of capturing energy from even just half a degree of temperature difference between the body and the sensor. Once it is commercially available, this innovation will permit us to move building design another step closer to sustainability. The more people inside, the less additional energy needed. A building with a thousand people inside for 8-10 hours per day would generate an estimated 60 kW/hr during working hours. If this is efficiently transformed, it could power every computer in the building. It presently works at laboratory scale. It can work tomorrow in large-scale office buildings, and generate significant quantities of additional local energy for local consumption. The very low distribution costs will convince forward-thinking architects to include sound, pressure, temperature, and micro flows of wind into their designs for optimal energy generation and application. All the scientific confirmation is in place. What is needed next is an entrepreneurial effort to incorporate a portfolio of these innovations into an integrated design.

The Flows of People and Matter

Movement flows of people and product have been studied in considerable detail by systems engineers and city planners and designers. We strive for efficiency and optimal flow in airport or shopping queues, in delivery and removal of goods consumed, in transport of product and people, in consumption of goods and services, entertainment and education. When we link these flows to the other flows we have discussed, we might realise that we could indeed design a building capable of generating nutrients. A bathroom, generally moist and warm, could provide an ideal breeding ground for mushrooms. The starch in our food waste could be converted into bioplastics using only a fungus. Rooftops could become gardens, not only producing locally appropriate fruits and vegetables, but also by reducing the building's surface temperature and energy consumption. Buildings designed to recycle nutrients and augment food security could yield unintended benefits, by providing an energising and relaxing environment where food crops can flourish and healthful exercise can take place. This would be a building worthy of the genius of Friedensreich Hundertwasser, the brilliant Viennese architect.

The Center for Ecoliteracy in Berkeley, California, and Slow Food in Torino, Italy, have both been active in creating school gardens in urban environments. Now we have the opportunity to surpass this accomplishment and create a self-sustaining environment. Brasilia, the capital of Brazil with two million inhabitants, meets 90 per cent of its fruit and vegetable needs within the city boundaries owing to the visionary urban design by Lucio Costa, and the building's architecture by the world famous architect, Oscar Niemeyer. If access and allocation were designed into the flow of the buildings and the surrounding space, with comfort and sustenance as priorities, then water and nutrients can be abundantly available for our needs. Waste generated from consumption is kept locally available and is contributed to the nutrient stream that simply yet remarkably returns to us as sustenance. It is an elegant cascade that cycles and recycles, benefitting and utilising all materials. It is a whole systems model perfected by nature and available to meet diverse needs.

Schools as Sustainability Classrooms

Schools are an ideal testing ground for learning how to work with flows. Between first grade and graduation from high school, children spend an estimated 20,000 hours in classrooms. This is a staggering amount of time, which many feel is inadequately spent. Considering the tremendous investment of time and patience that we require of children, how is it possible that saving money determines ways in which schools and classrooms are designed? Shouldn't the overarching principles be establishing a healthful environment for optimal learning and participation? How much is that worth? We have only touched the surface of these issues. Nonetheless, there are many ready and available options for designing school buildings that are optimally healthy, less costly to maintain, and which avail themselves of the dozens of scientific insights described herein. These are nothing less than shifts in the way we live.

Conditions for good health should not be subject to calculations of financial profit or cost cutting. School buildings are an ideal place to implement principles of health and sustainability and to showcase them in the public domain where they may contribute to the public good. Imagine a school building where over a hundred core concepts in physics, biology, and chemistry are visibly and functionally integrated into the building and operation of the school. Imagine the connections students would make by observing these sciences in manifest display. The children and their teachers would have the opportunity to become familiar with the innovations and to learn the science behind their functioning through daily appreciation and exposure. The school itself becomes a living science laboratory. Living what you learn makes acquiring knowledge effortless. Such a school structure would steer society towards sustainability. The obvious differences between the new and old technologies would inspire many youngsters to become tomorrow's innovators and entrepreneurs. This is the springboard from which imagination becomes reality.

In such a building, simple and pragmatic combinations of meteorology with the basic principles of airflow maintain constant interior temperature and humidity even as the exterior pressure and temperature change. Highly efficient LED lights shine day and night on a hundred varieties of plants, automatically sprinkled every 15 minutes with rainwater collected from the roof. The levels of dust particles and air pollutants entering the building or generated inside are kept low by this misting, decreasing the risk of respiratory diseases. The lights are coated not with mercury but with keratin, inspired by the beetle that creates white without chemicals. Chelating bacteria assist in recycling cast-off metals. The inner walls are composed of crushed seashells and filled with dried seaweed, providing a practical and efficient, highly alkaline, anti-fungal, moisture-wicking sound barrier. Natural airflows in the building pass over these materials, keeping the humidity stable and the pH alkaline. The windows allow passage of UV rays to control mites in the chemical-free carpeting. The carpet tiles electrically connect through the micron-size carbon fibres that obtain their energy from thin-film dye-sensitised solar cells attached to the windows, keeping the floors at an ideal temperature for warmth and dry enough for mite control.

Rather than mastering any one technology, implementing a detailed and definitive design plan based on the innovations and technologies introduced here would naturally require insight into a whole system integrated with the local environment. It is the difference between the regenerative and adaptive capacity of an ecosystem and the genius of a single species. Ecosystems simply cannot be reduced to a set of rules. The whole is more than the sum of individual components.

Housing for All

It is impossible to close this chapter without reflecting on the pioneering design work of Linda Garland, who was based for decades in Bali, Indonesia, and Simon Velez who operates around the world from Bogotá, Colombia. They have done remarkable work with bamboo in designing and constructing affordable, renewable and attractive housing that could be the most sustainable of all.

From the perspective of its composition, the relative strength of bamboo defies logic. Its marvelous adaptation is to use tensile and compression strength to perfect advantage. Even though bamboo is a grass and not a tree, its fibres outperform any other cellulose source in terms of building or paper making. Since we should not speak in absolute terms, we also recognise hemp and flax; however, bamboo is the master for technical functionality. It can demonstrably replace both concrete and steel. With over 2,000 species in the Americas alone, it has qualities that make it capable of effortlessly, ecologically, and inexpensively meeting our growing needs for construction materials. At the end of the 20th century, bamboo was still the preferred building material for more than a billion people around the world, especially in the tropics. Sven Mouton, the Belgian architect who graduated from the Jesuit University of Rio de Janeiro, calculated under the watchful eyes of Prof Khosrow Ghavami that bamboo embodies 60 times less energy (and CO_2) than steel offering flexibility and elegance that steel cannot pretend to have.

After the Kyoto Protocol was signed in 1997, Masatsugu Taniguchi, director of Taiheiyo, Japan's largest cement manufacturer, searched for ways to achieve a low carbon footprint using cement. The materials for reinforced concrete are mined and manufactured at high pressure and temperature and leave the earth's face scarred for centuries. Taiheiyo succeeded by utilising bamboo fibres. Simply pressing bamboo with cement weight for weight (50/50, or 75/25 by volume), without any additive or chemical, they created a cement board with a neutral carbon footprint. The bamboo itself is farmed and sustainably harvested on 5,000 acres of land next to a factory on the outskirts of Jakarta.

Innovative architects Renzo Piano and Shigeru Ban were inspired by bamboo to create architectural wonders based on the beauty and performance of bamboo. Maestro Simon Velez, the grand bamboo architect of our time, demonstrated that bamboo can comply with the most stringent construction engineering rules of modern society—German building codes. Velez designed the Zero Emissions Research Initiative (ZERI) Pavilion, erected in Manizales, Colombia, which was then perhaps the largest bamboo structure in the world (later the most popular pavilion at the 2000 World Expo in Hanover, Germany). Two severe earthquakes since its construction have merely shifted a few tiles on the roof.

The king of all bamboos is the *Guadua angustifolia*. When the Spaniards conquered the highlands of Colombia, Peru and Ecuador, they had to wade through dense bamboo jungles. The life force of bamboo was widely and wildly described by the Spanish colonisers whose letters home told how the native Andean cultures used bamboo defensively in combat, as it would pierce quickly through the body, seemingly without force. These colonisers also quickly learned that their European wood and stone construction techniques did not long survive in the earthquake zones of the southern Americas. They found out the hard way, that "buildings must dance to the rhythms of the earth," as Simon Velez characterises the behaviour of bamboo. That is exactly what bamboo does: dance.

As this 25-metre tall 'grass' was cleared to make space for coffee and cattle farming in the southern Americas, it became the preferred local building material. Two hundred years later, these buildings from colonial times still stand, having survived everything the shaking earth delivered. This Latin American experience is confirmed in Asia. At 3,000 years and counting, the world's oldest bamboo building stands as an open pavilion in Manchuria.

Bamboo does not resist an earthquake but rather moves with it. Neither does a bamboo structure require bracing through cross-links to withstand the chaotic upward and sideward pressures. Curiously, bamboo is hollow. It is flexible enough to stand as long as the building has an inward inclination. The mere reduction of the vertical angle to 85° provides such stability that tiles on the roof don't even move. It is a pity that the domination of CAD/CAM (computer-aided design/manufacture) in the architectural design and construction fields since the late 20th century has demanded 90° angles for all construction, resulting in death and destruction every time the earth trembles.

Achieving affordable and beautiful housing for all in the tropics is a goal that can be met with the use of bamboo. A 1,000 square foot plot of land in the Andean highlands would be sufficient to grow a house. Planted with the giant *Guadua angustifolia* bamboo, some 60 bamboo poles would be harvestable after three years. This is sufficient building material to construct a two-story, 650 square foot house with a magnificent balcony and a staircase in the back that permits airflow. Each subsequent year's bamboo harvest would provide enough poles to construct an additional modest home.

Simon Velez's housing design includes a large staircase in the rear, which acts like a termite mound; a heavy roof structure to stabilise the building; and a wide balcony for comfortable ambience. There are no 90° angles. This prevents a sudden collapse in case of earthquakes, making it an extremely safe design. Instead of trying to build an earthquake-resistant building, the bamboo, and the method of joinery used, move with the erratic powers of the earth. The house is remarkably fresh, with light entering freely. The massive overhanging roof protects the structural bamboo from any deterioration caused due to UV light or rain. The rainwater flows around the house, hardly touching the bamboo's surface, collecting in cisterns for drinking water. Although there is wind play, not even a hurricane could lift the house.

The bamboo unused in house construction, considered by many a waste, can be used to produce charcoal. Charcoal production causes noxious gases. Antonio Giraldo from Armenia, Colombia, has developed a method of curing bamboo in its own charcoal gases, much like the traditional curing systems used in Japan. The flow of the gases is channelled to a huge chamber. Under slight pressure, bamboo poles 24 feet long are cured with the fumes from their own charcoal. Instead of using toxic chemistry to preserve the bamboo against termites and fungi, it is cured by its own chemistry. The negative flow of contaminants is converted into a positive flow that not only preserves the bamboo, but also replaces the pollutants that pose health risks. The way the building materials are made and prepared for use is inspired by natural systems, a cascading of nutrients and energy. This is the same method as that used at the Picuris Pueblo in New Mexico with small-diameter wood slated to be burned and now is converted to window and door frames.

Lucio Ventania, a well-known Brazilian bamboo artisan, explains, "As long as structural bamboo is protected from direct sun and never stands in its own water, it will stand, forever." Hence, the logical design features a large overhang that protects the load-bearing poles from water and sun, the two most destructive atmospheric forces. The experience of Manizales and Hanover with subsequent design give rise to numerous social housing initiatives. While Simon Velez provided the first designs for a two-story low cost housing with a balcony to symbolise middle class for only US$12,000, the Jesuit-supported Hogares de Cristo en Guayaquil, Ecuador, pushes the logic to extremes and established pre-fabricated simple social housing for as little as US$950.

This business model is surprising: a poor family arrives with US$50 cash, applies for a US$900 credit, which is approved quickly provided they have access to a piece of land, and 24 hours later, their house is standing tall. The new home owners pay a monthly quota of less than US$20 lifting people off the streets at low cost. Hogares de Cristo's production system crunches out 42 prefab houses a day for an annual turnover of about US$12 million, and this requires the sustainable supply of bamboo from an estimated 5,000 acres. Who provides the land?

Another Magic of Mines

AngloGold Ashanti, the third largest gold mining company in the world with a market capitalisation in excess of US$6 billion, searched to secure water supply for its mines in the Andean Highlands. It learned from Dr Luis Miguel Álvarez Mejía, a vanguard botanist at the University of Caldas, in Manizales (Colombia) that eliminating exotic species from the mine's land concession, and the replanting of native vegetation dominated by bamboo (*Guadua angustifolia*) drops the surface temperature by 15° F—this increases rainfall and guarantees supply of water—forever. Once planted, bamboo proliferates for 70 years until it flowers and dies. Since bamboo is a grass, it can be harvested and without any need for replanting, it will grow again. The regeneration of the forest in Vichada by the Environmental Research Center at Las Gaviotas is now complemented in size and impact by recovery of the Andean Highlands with its original bamboo forest.

Water is only a first and obvious benefit, for the mine and the communities which are stressed out for potable water. The local bean farmers harvest bamboo to make 3-4 metre posts, and deliver the rest to the valley to produce housing requiring another 5-6 metres. There would still be at least 15 metres left which can be pulped to produce water absorbent paper. Kimberly Clark, the maker of Kleenex tissue paper and owner of the Scott brand, has decided to replace eucalyptus and pine-based pulp with locally supplied bamboo. The business cluster around the mine now evolves into a second income and job-generating cycle after a first one emerged converting rocks and tailings into products and cash. Both cycles around mining dramatically increase resource efficiency, while generating multiple benefits for society and the environment. Who could have imagined these hidden benefits from a mining operation even before the mine is operational?

Bamboo remains undiscovered by those who live outside its tropical growing range. Not a single species of bamboo grows naturally in the northwestern US or Sweden, where the largest forestry research institutes are located. Thus focus of the worldwide forestry industry, even in tropical locales, is on species such as eucalyptus and pine, which grow in temperate climates and have nowhere near the renewable potential of bamboo. As awareness of bamboo's sustainable growth habit and building material qualities becomes more widespread, it will serve as an inspiration for innovative architectural projects around the world. Sven Mouton, who was trained under the Brazilian bamboo guru Dr Khosrow Ghavami, at the Pontificia Universidade Católica do Rio de Janeiro, returned home inspired by the beauty and functionality of bamboo in load-bearing structures. He pursued his academic curiosity and concluded that even the bamboo harvested and treated in Latin America and exported to Europe would only consume one-sixtienth of the energy for the production of one square metre per unit strength of a steel structure.

Even though the Brazilians and Colombians spearheaded this integrated approach, it lead to a transformation of the labour market. Ever since the ZERI Pavilion at the World Expo in Hanover, 2000, demonstrated that bamboo has the flexibility, tensile and compression strength to qualify for a German building permit, 250 new companies and 7,000 jobs have been generated. Now if this is considered a success, then look at Vietnam were an estimated 200,000 jobs have been created since bamboo turned into a key component of their emerging economy. The Republic of Korea realised that next to its prowess in electronics and mobile phone systems, it can also develop this massive new industry based on traditional raw materials that can be harvested renewably, while industrialising tradition and culture.

All Flows Considered

An appreciation of how the flow of air, light, water, energy, sound, people, and matter affect our physical space brings a new understanding of ways to design structures that interweave and utilise these flows. It gives us some very practical insights into ways to build and furnish homes, offices, and schools in order to achieve true functionality, cost and aesthetics. A better understanding of all the material, water and energy flows at the macro-level of a mine, gives us very practical insights regarding how to operate this in a community, and how transformative it can be for our model of society.

Pioneering entrepreneurs have shown us that sustainable buildings need not be more expensive. Practical applications from the world of science, well researched and well documented, are opening new possibilities that can finally steer us towards sustainability. Architects dedicated to green building design have the ability to turn possibilities into actualities. Public demand and common sense will help authorities revise building codes and approve industry standards that allow integration of innovations based on solid science and smart business. When we embrace these innovations as a society, we will be able to support the health of our families, our domiciles, our workplaces, and our environment. We will create the industries of the future inspired by the ingenuity of nature. We too can function as an ecosystem, generating what we need from what is available, finding resource in waste, welcoming the contributions of all, and taking part in a cascade of abundance.

15

Making Affordable Housing Affordable

> How can you make money on money?
> Could you ever make water out of water?
>
> — *G.P.*

The Objectives of Economic Growth

The claim of communists in the 19th century, and today a belief shared by many that 'the rich get richer and poor people get poorer' seems now confirmed. In his much—debated book, Prof Thomas Pikkety demonstrates, based on two centuries of statistics, that the rich, who control capital are getting richer. He argues eloquently that as long as the rate of return on capital is higher than that of economic growth the poor will get poorer. The capital used to be land, then it was mainly equipment to manufacture. Today, it is merely cash that expects to earn money on money.

We know that split-second trading through supercomputers in stocks and currencies is making billions for those who have billions. We know that those who make billions, both individuals and corporations exploit the loopholes of tax laws, and if they do pay taxes it is never more than a few per cent on their profits and wealth. Nearly all profitable corporations and the wealthy, limit their involvement in the social economy to Corporate Social Responsibility (CSR) programs that reach out to so few individuals that pictures in the annual CSR report can capture almost all those who benefitted. In addition, all CSR initiatives are also construed as tax deductible, in other words the community pays! How many corporations really turn CSR into a corporate strategy in line with their products and manufacturing? We know that under these circumstances, it is impossible for the poor to ever get rich—unless they cheat the system. The only option out of the poverty trap seems illegal and illicit trade, ranging from drugs to endangered species.

Of course, the reaction when the establishment is confronted with these facts is to debate the results, question the data, then cast doubt over the sources, and ultimately do what all establishments have done throughout history when a new truth is haunting: discredit the author. This is normal. When the facts are finally accepted and not further subject to heated debates, but rather have become the preferred subject of topical conversations, those who formulated the harshest critiques will pride themselves on claiming that it was their original idea anyway. However, there is a strong and fundamental reaction against the confirmation that 'the rich are getting richer'.

The fiercest critique against the theorem proposed by Prof Pikkety comes from the Anglo-Saxon economists who stand by the trickle down effect, which pretends that as the rich get richer, slowly but steadily money and wealth is transferred to poor people. This is only supported by anecdotes and no statistics. Many forget that the USA and Canada are an exception when it comes to wealth creation: a nation that grew from 3 to 300 million inhabitants in less than two centuries, and appropriated all land and resources as their own, has the capacity to spread wealth. Even under these circumstances, the rich have always got richer, except for the Great Depression and the Second World War.

It cannot be neglected that until recently, growth in the US in absolute numbers of middle class citizens has rightly fueled the notion that the American Dream is possible. Unfortunately, the latest statistics suggest that never before have the American wealthy become so much wealthier. Ample evidence shows that two income families, living in megalopolis like New York, Chicago and Los Angeles, cannot make ends meet, nor put their children through college. Data indicate that in 1964, 23 per cent of all children in the USA lived in poverty. Fifty years later, despite US$16 trillion of investments in poverty alleviation in the wealthiest nation of the world, 22 per cent of all children in America still live in poverty. Children living in poverty is only one parameter, the income gap between the US's richest and poorest metropolitan region has reached in 2014 the widest on record.[1] What happened to the American Dream?

The hard absolute numbers dampen the positive impression created by relative data. Statistics prove, whatever argument you wish to substantiate: sometimes you use absolute numbers, sometimes you use percentages. Reality can be presented either way. However, when it comes to poverty, there is only one number that counts in our assessments: the absolute! It seems that more efforts were directed to reduce pain and discomfort of poor people by providing aid. And while that is appreciated, some argue that this is the very reason for the poverty trap, and aid needs to be transformed into empowerment. The hard reality is that aid programs managed by governments, corporations and foundations have not been successful in securing access to the tools to get out of that trap.

While poor people derive no benefit from enduring low economic growth rates, they have lost wealth, jobs and income, while investors have done very well. Funds will not release the monies under their control, unless there is a high return on capital. Except for government bonds, no capital provider is satisfied with an annual return under 10 per cent. Business plans that do not provide a minimum 20 or even 30 per cent are not considered. It is impossible to expect that even rapidly expanding emerging economies will enjoy a double-digit growth rate, higher than that of return on capital. Now that the numbers are on the table, and that the rich gets richer, what do we do next beyond debating the facts any further?

When I read $r > g$ (r is the rate of return on capital, g is the growth rate of the economy), the question that should immediately be raised is how can this simple equation be inverted and generate the opposite: $r < g$.

---

1. US Commerce and Labour Department data for the 100 metropolitan areas by population as reported in the Financial Times, August 13, 2014, cover page under the title: "Record US wealth gap fuelled by disparities in housing recovery."

It is impossible to ignore the fact that poverty is spreading in absolute numbers. Even worse than poverty, is youth unemployment. This parameter that indicates whether or not the next generation has an opportunity to earn a minimum wage required to take care of a family is increasing at alarming rates. This means that poverty is not only on the rise, but is also likely to stay. Jobless youth is not limited to the developing world. Countries like Spain, Italy and Greece have more than 50 per cent of their most dynamic members of society left idle. Palestine is in a stranglehold that puts 98 per cent of all the young people under 26 out of a job. It is an unacceptable waste of human resources when an increasing number of trained and eager young are told that their willingness to work and skills are not needed. Governments accept this hardship and hide behind the need to pursue austerity, balancing the budget. Corporations and the wealthy from their perspective claim that the growth rate is too low, and that first consumption needs to pick up before funding initiatives that carry a low risk and a very high rate of return.

We need to ask ourselves the question: how much more patience are we expecting from poor people? A mother whose children are going to bed hungry every night, and a father who sees his teenage sons making rockets to shoot them across a fence, cannot be satisfied with a promise that all will improve within a few decades, when corrupt governments have been removed, and when free trade agreements have been agreed to provide access to cheap goods worldwide. The only option is to empower poor people to care for themselves and design solutions with what they have. This requires a redesign of the business models with ability to respond to the basic needs of all, while offering a reasonable return to investors.

Models to Empower the Bottom of the Pyramid

When there is rampant poverty, and billions face unmet basic needs for water, food and nutrition, housing and community, health and health care, energy, waste management, and mobility, education and culture, how is it possible that some claim that there is no demand? How could free world trade ever ensure health care for the newborn? The response is that there is demand, but no money! Prof C.K. Prahalad and Stuart Hart demonstrated in their article first published in 2004 that 3 billion people who survive on US$2.50 per day represent a staggering US$2.7 trillion in cash each year. The bottom of the pyramid does represent a market ready to be integrated into formal economy. The question is how to tap into this vast purchasing power with traditional business models and finance that has high expectations for its minimum rates of return? It is not easy for a traditional corporation to imagine ways to transform themselves.

For example, Unilever was inspired by the *Fortune at the Bottom of the Pyramid* and decided put shampoo into small affordable sachets, instead of the large bottle that is beyond the means of poor people. These micro-portions of shampoo are sold through network marketing and tiny neighbourhood stores. These initiatives do not empower poor people, nor provide access to quality products at competitive prices. On the contrary, the incursions into these emerging markets drain cash out of these marginalised communities, that never used synthetic shampoos with artificial colouring and odours, polluting their scarce waters. Rather this shampoo fuels the enterprise's drive to ever higher economies of scale and better margins. The strategy is to build up consumer acceptance and brand recognition so that the local distributor can soon be approached for selling more from the same vendor, or be replaced by large chains of distribution.

Change the Business Model

Over the past 20 years, I have been looking for better models than the best that we have been able to imagine to date. This is not a critique, this is a search for better. We can lift poor people out of poverty, and reverse the trend of the rich getting richer by changing the business model beyond tweaking of the present one. We need to design something completely new. It is surprising how few are aware that inclusive growth in a sustainable society requires a dramatically better performance at all levels. However, so few are prepared to question the prevailing models that aim to cut costs, and how so few question the drive towards free trade and globalisation, which are myopically considered the only opportunities to ensure growth and therefore are heralded as the panacea for socio-economic problems.

I am surprised that people believe that the market in general, investments in search of high rates of return, would turn the poverty trap around, while aid would soften the sharp corners, and breakthroughs in science like nanotechnologies, genetic manipulation and smart grids will do magic. We have to realise that whatever we attempted with the best of our intentions is not making a fundamental difference for the 3 billion living in poverty on this Earth. Worse, we seem prepared to accept poverty. Instead, we should design and create competitive business models that are adequately capable of responding to the basic needs of all.

We need to focus on the business model and aim to recover the leadership at the entrepreneurial level. Macro-economic trends are the amalgamation of decisions taken and initiatives undertaken at the micro-economic level. So instead of attempting to mainly guide the world from the cockpit of a plane influencing interest rates, tax policies, currency exchanges and trade, we need to turn the economy around on the ground starting where the needs are most urgent, like the shanty towns in Asia, the townships in Africa and favelas in Latin America. Let us call these the Corridors of Growth. How can we create and implement an inclusive growth strategy, where not only basic needs are met, but also where benefits derived from integrating poor people into the economy and into a caring society, include creating wealth for the most needy.

Incapable of Delivering to the Poor

It is critical to look at the reality today: the market economy is not capable of delivering to poor people! If the market is not capable, it is because the present business model is not capable. The result is that poverty and unemployment are the rule. That is hard to accept. The key economic players have adopted the logic of the economies of scale, searching for ever lower marginal costs balancing quality with price in order to stimulate sales, while obtaining higher total margins, thus offering a better return on capital. Since the top priority is to always offer higher returns and lower costs, the economic system turned into a harsh one where laying off people for the sake of productivity is the norm.

In order to create ever higher economies of scale for standardised products, there is a need to eliminate trade barriers. Free trade has been the name of the game, providing for free movement of goods, services and capital, but not of people. Boundaries have never been more difficult to cross, and the issuing of a visa has turned into a business of its own. So when goods, services and capital are expected to move freely across boundaries, then the challenge is to remunerate people sufficiently within that globalised economy, so that they can overcome their poverty trap and the desire to emigrate at whatever cost. Those who see no exit, knowing that their parents and grandparents did not find any either, will find one in violence, drugs, fundamentalism and terrorism.

The globalised economy claims to balance demand and supply through the setting of a market price. The modern economy has subjected everything to a price setting including something as necessary for life as water. Water used to be a Commons, provided for free by nature and society, which now carries a price. Thus there will always be millions who will never be able to access basic goods and services. If we agree that global model of product and service delivery is incapable of reaching poor people (otherwise they would not be poor), then we need to ensure that people in those 'Corridors of Poverty' can respond to their own needs with what they have. This is not in defiance of the globalised economy, this is rather a response to the incapacity of the present globalised economy to be inclusive. So if this delivery process fails by design, we have only one option and that is to change the model and implement a novel market economy.

The immediate reaction to this straightforward conclusion is: this is not possible. The explanation is that if this was possible, then it would have been done a long time before, and would have been scaled up to reach everyone. However, if a new business model is fundamentally different than that practiced before, it is unlikely to have a global acceptance, the first year, or the first decade. It took the free trade economists Adam Smith, the author of *The Wealth of Nations* and David Ricardo, the inspiration for the theory of comparative advantages, neither of whom had access to statistics or empirical data, over a century to see their concepts prevail as a dominant economic logic. So why is it now necessary to deliver proof of concept at worldwide scale immediately? We need to build up the micro-economic case studies before we derive macro-economic conclusions.

Respond to Basic Needs

Business models that respond to people's basic needs with what is locally available could improve livelihoods. However, the money earned cannot be drained out and rather should continue to circle through the communities. If people have their hard-earned US$100 in hand, then this cash is used to alleviate their most urgent needs. The money must be spent locally, and the next need should be sourced locally as well. This creates a catalytic effect in the local growth cycle. As more money circulates, the locally produced portfolio of products and services diversifies further, so that more money moves faster from hand to hand, and more is kept in the community as capital. This is a possible double-digit growth model. If the money is not circulating within, then cash brought back from work will flow out of the community, thereby stunting growth.

So the growth model is: (1) respond to the basic needs; and (2) circulate the hard earned cash locally. This could make double-digit growth viable.

Inclusive Growth

1. Respond to basic needs with what you have;
2. Circulate cash locally.

Of course, one wonders how much human resources, capital, materials and energy is locally available to ensure these transformations at rapid rate. Will this proposed double-digit growth not lead to shortages, price increases and even imports? Of course, there are limitations and there will be challenges. But the present model of standardisation and globalisation based on an unending drive to cut costs keeps poor people poor since all their cash spent on basic consumption is flowing out of the community.

Do we realise that in South Africa, 34 per cent of the purchasing power of poor people who survive on less than US$2,500 per year is reserved for food; and those who survive on US$600 per year spend 47 per cent on food? Also, every food item consumed is supplied from outside the community?

While many questions arise, the main purpose is to develop this inclusive growth concept in more detail and apply to the housing needs in Africa. The development of the case below is not hypothetical, rather it is a reflection of a reality, and a confirmation of an intention to succeed. While each of the programs and initiatives mentioned have been implemented somewhere, the scale of investments and the magnitude of impact has not been achieved anywhere. However, its time has come. It is against the backdrop of a 31 square kilometre real estate and community development project in the City of Cape Town that we run the principles and the logic described above, and put forward a case that will inspire others to join and learn from the process; that is to implement one of the most ambitious inclusive development initiatives.

New Model for Delivery of Homes

Anyone walking through a shanty town senses the lack of dignity in this desolate world. The citizens have the right to be impatient and to be upset. There are many innovative business models to respond to the basic needs. We must make a choice and decide on the direction to follow. Possibly the first business model that requires a fundamental shift is the delivery of affordable housing. South Africa is a young democracy with a young population and a rapidly growing urban lifestyle. It faces a growing demand for shelter. The government has a long list of people waiting to get a house, and recognises that it needs to deliver at least 2.3 million homes so to eradicate poverty.

The South African government is keen to deliver but has failed to live up to the expectations. After a detailed assessment of the situation, it is clear the government is not to blame; we should blame the prevailing business model. Whenever a real estate project is conceived, investors (capital) will extract all capital gains prior to the construction of the first house and leave builders with the task to construct shacks cheap and fast. The business can be summarised as: rezone, resell and cash out. It is necessary to unveil the logic of this money-making machine, that does not share any of its massive financial gains with the people who are in dire need for shelter, and who desire to live in a sustainable community.

How does it work? First investors take control of land through options, preferably options on agricultural estates that have exhausted the soil and have lost all productivity. The option agreement implies that the investors do not buy the land, but only promise to buy on a future date, at a pre-arranged (low) price. The investor pays a fee for having that right, and nothing more. When the property is finally rezoned through a political decision, the land is acquired and more often than not, is instantly resold from the option holder to a property developer. Land that was worth one is now easily worth 4-10 times more. So without investing full amount of the value of the eroded agricultural land, and solely operating with options, billions are made owing to a political decision.

According to the present business model, the bad news for future home owners is that the capital gains are (legitimately) taken out of the project to enrich those who succeeded in assembling the options, and getting the political decision through. None of these gains are used to make housing affordable.

Real Estate for Poor People

1. Agricultural land is rezoned.
   Capital gains are drained out of the project.
2. Unserviced land is developed into serviced land
   Capital gains are drained out of the project
3. Low cost housing is delivered to poor people
   There is no capital to create really affordable housing

The barren land is then serviced, often with public funds and is developed by a new group of investors who will undertake urban planning. When the infrastructure for water, electricity and sewage is in place and construction can start, the project, now ready to deliver houses, is sold again to a housing developer. The sale of serviced land earns those who delivered the rezoned land ready for construction their portion of capital gains. This represents the second profit taking in cash even before the first house is built. Unfortunately, this newly added true value is similar to the first one pulled out of the project and accumulated in bank accounts to earn more money on money speculating on future deals or split-second trades in currencies. An informed guess calculated that 20 years of social real estate development in South Africa has generated sufficient capital gains in the hands of a few, which can reduce the cost of all social housing already delivered by half.

Then comes the housing development company, the one who must now deliver the house. Since all the capital gains have been extracted from the project, there is no capital left. Worse, the exit of capital gains have been made possible by taking on debt into the project. The housing development company is thus leveraged to the edge and depends on mortgage financing of the end consumer to pay off debt and make a profit. It is the consumer financing of the first-time home owner who now have his affordable housing that will pay off the developer's debt and the capital gains paid to speculators, which has already been extracted.

The housing development company makes money on a margin and its profitability depends on the capacity to squeeze out every possible penny from suppliers. The delivered buildings are certainly not cozy homes. These are shelters without the required conditions to build a community. In order to get the lowest possible cost price, materials are sourced from the cheapest offer. This leads to the global sourcing of all building materials, fittings and installations. While this meets the logic of low cost housing, it also drains the total value of such once-in-a-lifetime capital investment out of the community. It is impossible that home building programme implemented along this logic can ever lift people out of poverty? It is impossible, since the poor people carry the debt that serves to pay for the capital gains drained out of the project!

What if the principle of responding to the local needs for a home with is locally available resources was applied, starting with the capital generated by changing the purpose of a land? Imagine that the capital gains are not drained out of the project, but are allowed to be its integral part. As a result, instead of pressing every supplier to the last cent, assets and resources will be available to pay local suppliers at reasonable prices. This ensures that the US$25,000 investment in a first home is also an injection of the same amount into the local economy. That represents a livelihood for 5 breadwinners who can now aspire to buy a house. It is the start of a positive cycle. Better, if the materials are locally supplied, the cash circulates locally, strengthening the financials of this housing initiative since capital gains were kept local. Besides that, houses can be sold at even lower cost to the first-time owner! This is a new business model.

This business model is not against remunerating capital. It is in favour of asking capital providers and speculators the open question: "How much is enough?" Instead of making one billion or more on a hot deal twice, would the investors who signed the options and assembled the land be prepared to only make 300 million on the deal and dedicate the remaining 700 million to the provision of affordable housing and infrastructural services, which are now operated locally with the original investors still as partners? And, most importantly, are the investors who stay on from beginning to the end prepared to earn a multiple of the amount, diverted to affordable housing in additional income generated from the new revenue streams, as described below?

The decision to shift agricultural land outside the city's perimeter to developable land inside the city's urban edge is a political decision. Can we agree that if and when a political decision of this magnitude (and profit) is taken, then the benefits should in the first place go to the people represented by those officials? Can we agree that instead of making 300-500 times the value of the options, that a return of 10 or even 50 times is enough? Would investors be satisfied making 3-5 times the original amount? This powerful argument will not be received with open arms by traditional real estate development companies, that have accumulated wealth for decades. To contain capital gains within reason is only a first component of this new business model. We need to rethink every component, and generate income for investors and poor people at the same time, on every need we can respond to locally.

Buy Local

How much steel and cement is needed to build a house? A representative of the light steel makers and cement mixers would argue that the house cannot stand the test of time without their materials. Sometimes we have to be inspired by the greatest architects of modern times who changed the rules of the game. Frank Gehry, the American architect, certainly belongs to the exceptional creators of form and beauty. Few people realise that foam glass is central to his structures. Foam glass can be virgin material or recycled glass heated up and injected with CO_2, to create carbon neutral building materials that are light, cheap, resistant to acids, fireproof, structural and are part of a prefabricated building system.

These Corridors of Poverty have waste management problems, and there is abundant glass for recycling. Today recycling is not well paid. If the core structure of affordable houses can include glass foam, then this building technique creates value from nothing, whilst diverting glass from the local landfill. This is not the recycling of waste! Glass foam offers higher quality housing at lower cost and generates additional jobs that circulate extra cash. It eliminates the use of fire retardants and introduces insulation that had never been part of affordable housing standards. This is not what Frank Gehry had in mind when he designed the Guggenheim Museum in Bilbao that has attracted one million visitors to the Basque Country, a region that has been plagued by decades of terrorism counting more than 1,000 casualties. The local upcycling[2] of waste to a building material is one of the many industrial initiatives that communities could embark on in order to turn their housing programs into one of the many engines of growth.

Evolving from a Deal to a Flow

Let us compare the amount of money that can be made on the sale of a house and the closure of a mortgage, and then compare this income with the potential revenue generated over the next 25 years; with the sale of water, food, energy, waste management, mobility and so much more that is needed by the same community. If the community buys electricity from a national monopoly, the monies spent on energy leave the community. The alternative would be that of a new local direct current (DC) grid, that can eliminate the transmission losses and theft of power, and ensure that all electricity generated is local and renewable. Excess production is stored in water that is pumped up and locally kept, recovering energy through gravity powered in-pipe turbines and heat pumps that receive water at 90°C and delivers it at 40°C, thus powering the network at low cost. This DC system now circulates power and money through a growing local economy.

The state usually obliges power companies to ensure a minimum power supply to poor people at marginal cost, or even for free.

2. *Upcycling* was the title of my book published in Germany in 1998 by Riemann Verlag demonstrating the we have to go beyond recycling, the end product has to be more valuable that the original one and this can only be achieved if it is used in another sector.

Monopolies, either state controlled or privatised energy companies, have great difficulty making money from these Corridors of Poverty. The non-payment of utility bills is high, and the pirating of electricity from transmission lines makes the delivery of power to the bottom of the pyramid, a loss-making operation. To deliver the minimum power requires subsidies from the government and/or a cross-subsidy from the higher rates charged to industry and homes. Since the present delivery mechanism does not perform, nor makes money, and the poor do not receive any service, the best way to resolve this is that poor people should generate their own power.

While energy is critical, water is of equal importance. Installing and operating each separately is a costly operation. Combining the delivery mechanism of both offers a portfolio of solutions. This combination of water and power is not only a financially viable delivery system, but also an ideal platform for building up a network of emerging micro-, small- and medium-sized companies. Unfortunately, governments and business are organised and operate in silos. Water is dealt with by water experts; power is the fief of power experts. Policymakers have not understood and business strategists cannot imagine that the combination of water and power offers additional growth to the local economy and turns the cluster of basic services profitable beyond the present standard investment returns. In other words, electricity and water are not merely indispensable services, rather these are catalysts, stimulating investments that permit growth in the poverty corridors.

Meeting Basic Needs

Power lines transmitting alternating current (AC) throughout a township are tapped by local citizens who do not pay, worse this drains revenues out of the community and the city, while individuals risk their life. The City of Jozie is losing US$260 million per year due to stolen power. The social conditions are such that any culpability for theft of power is politically unviable. In addition, those who do have meters, often do not pay their bills. No city can afford to lose over one legislature of five years more than one billion in lost electricity revenues. If policymakers or developers wish to improve the situation, then there is a need to imagine a fundamental shift in the business model. Technologies and the business model have to improve, without negating people who need the rightful access to power needed for their livelihood. While the engineers may not appreciate the proposals, we are firmly in favour of creating hundreds or even thousands of smart local DC grids in the Corridors of Poverty. While this smart grid is quite different from the concept promoted at international fora, this energy distribution system based on DC is piracy safe.

Containing piracy and involving the local community in energy economics is not the only reason to shift from AC to DC. Eighty per cent of electric devices used in shanty towns run on DC. DC powered phones and radios, or LED lamps are not only the most energy efficient on the market, but also the cheapest once industry is not obliged anymore to transform power from 220V AC to 12V DC. Once the electronic steering of power is simplified from the energy point of view, then we can improve performance. LED, for example, can be enhanced with the capacity to also be an internet carrier. Light Source Internet, known as LiFi (instead of WiFi), offers broadband access to the Internet at the speed of light. These seem to be the type of innovations that ensure that everyone has cheap access to power and the net at lower cost.

DC power grid skills are widely available in the townships. All cars, with repair shops in every corner of the urban tissue, run on 12V DC. This implies that all appliances, which are presently designed with inverters and transformers, can thus be simplified and produced cheaper, and perhaps even locally manufactured. Driven by local skills and boosted by hands-on manufacturing, a new strategy for power emerges. The lost money due to piracy and non-payment could be partially transformed through an investment in local DC grids, powered by renewables like the Solarus system, uniquely adapted to the multiple needs of poor people. The Solarus power and thermal energy device provides hot water and electricity in one unit. This approach facilitates the building of a local community, based on the energy and cost-efficient delivery of power and water offering economic benefits beyond elimination of the negative like piracy, electrocution and non-payment. It converts the negative spiral into a virtuous growth.

In order to stimulate this double-digit growth postulated as the condition to eradicate poverty, there must be multiple advantages as described briefly in the case of glass foam and Solarus power and water solution. The technology must be converted to a business model that generates multiple cash flows and offers a series of non-financial gains, that are equally important to the community. The case of health comes quickly to the forefront. The additional advantage include the delivery of sanitised water by maintaining temperatures in the geysers above 90 °C at all time. Geysers automatically switch off heating at 55 or 60 °C. At that temperature level, are geysers breeding bacteria? Unfortunately, the safe water temperature of 70 °C would put an excessive demand on the national power grid, resulting in blackouts. It is only through local solutions that these urgent health challenges are overcome.

From Water and Power to Health

The new business model around the smart local DC grids works with the national electric grid as its back-up. The local DC grids are the basis of local delivery, with decentralised production relying in the first place on solar and water storage (gravity and heat exchange) exploiting the abundant sun. For every 10-50 households, there is a trained "DC Lady" as proposed by Harry Stokman, the Dutch expert in the field, supervising the delivery of water and power, and ensuring payment of the bills, while guaranteeing delivery. If one of the small grids breaks down, then the DC grid can immediately provide delivery. Since water will be stored at 90 °C, the heat pumps will make up for any shortfall in power by dropping the temperature to 40 °C generating the additional energy needed, without investing in batteries.

This generates for a community development project a minimum of 4,000 jobs while creating the local social capital needed to build up confidence, thanks to the reliable supply of water, sanitised water and power. The deployment of this delivery mechanism supervised by local citizens empowers them, and generates the income that is otherwise lost. Thus this solution is kickstarted with the 'lost' monies that are in the system, which never reached the power supplier, and could never be deployed for the benefit of the people. There are fortunes at the bottom of the pyramid, there is a need to find out how to tap them.

When cities switch to this smart DC system, the first benefit is the elimination of gastro-intestinal diseases, while it will provide cheap heating in the winter fighting the flu by creating better living conditions. Improved health increases workers' productivity and secures better school grades. In addition, the entire new value chain from Solarus water and power panels, to the DC grids, simplified appliances and lights, complemented by internet at the speed of light could be locally manufactured. This strengthens the local primary and secondary industries and ensures that affordable houses evolve into communities. These components of urban design are basic and easy to implement, yet never factored into the cost-cutting and revenue boosting program of the current power supply company.

Multiple Cash Flow

At least 70 per cent of the Solarus and the DC-system can be manufactured locally, generating jobs. This virtuous cycle of more jobs and more revenue and more local spending in local hands works as follows: the production of the Solarus systems will require a frame made from heat resistant plastics. This supports a new recycling program. Today heat resistant plastics are recycled with all plastics, and scavengers sell it at US$50 per ton to intermediaries, who sell it on to Chinese buyers for US$150. When the Solarus units are locally assembled with locally molded frames, made from locally recycled plastics collected from the regional dump, then waste is (again) turned to value, and cash circulates once more in the economy. Fortunately, today all plastics are correctly labelled and these new components successfully outcompete globally sourced aluminum, generating more jobs and income, strengthening the argument that we can create growth in the Corridors of Poverty.

The creation of new industries from scratch is a mammoth task. These industrial initiatives require a solid but small start, with the vision to scale up when needs expand. The Solarus assembly is simplified to the point that it reaches break-even, producing only 200 units per month. This is in stark contrast to the 1,300 units per day of standardised panels that are required to make a profit on a solar panel. This extremely low volume, which is the result of a simplification of assembly design and the ingenious exploitation of global supply chain concepts, reduces the risk of getting started. Now it is possible to plan for at least one plant in Western Cape alone, distributing wealth and improving the local buy-in. This will spread understanding of the innovations in water and power, using the language that convinces: the experience of the workers who have a job, and that of the users who have power, purified water, hot water and perhaps even heating. Even those who do not read and write fluently can fully understand this new reality and explain it to their neighbours. Apart from health and jobs, this new business model will inspire people, bringing a message of hope in most pragmatic terms.

A potential market of one million units for the Western Cape development alone, and an estimated budget of one billion that was previously pirated can now be earned and plowed back into the community, adding income to the city and the people. This cash flow and benefit should not be handed over to a savvy investor from overseas. These local units deliver multiple benefits, permitting us to offer power at a lower rate than coal or nuclear. This means that the homeowner will have more purchasing power available for key expenses like education, lifting the whole family into middle class. This new decentralised delivery of water and power combined with local production and quality control is all part of the inclusive growth real estate process; underpinning the logic of shifting from a culture of dealmaking, to a participation in the never-ending cash flow. The positive impact in the community will strengthen this emerging vision around a better future. This will reduce violence and the need to revert to illicit trade.

We have only begun to describe a handful of initiatives. The impact, when dozens or even hundreds of comparable opportunities are unfolding in parallel, will be substantial. That is why, any development project committed to inclusive growth should start by building up a portfolio of opportunities and take this as a powerful tool, to mobilise capital beyond real estate, aiming to build affordable housing. It is about growing a new community. If we see the impact discussing power and water, what would the impact be if we extend it to include food, nutrition and health, culture and education, mobility and jobs?

Food, Nutrition, Sanitation and Health

Fruits, vegetables, grains and meat have become global commodities. Seeds and animal semen are controlled by a few, the harvest is traded by a few, it is processed by a few, it is imported by a few, and it benefits a few. While the drive to stamp hunger out of this world must be applauded, and the resolve of many organisations who undertake that merits admiration, it cannot become an opportunity for a few to earn more on the back of poverty. Over the past years, Africa has seen an absolute increase in undernourishment, whereas Asia has seen a slight decrease in the number of families suffering food insecurity. The difference between the two continents, is that poor people in Asia have succeeded in becoming net food suppliers, ensuring their own self sufficiency while trading their excesses on the market.

This is what is needed in Africa. Africa has a fast rising number of urban poor who cram into shanty towns with densities in excess of 20,000 people per hectare, leaving little or no space for local agriculture. The demand for social services from kindergarten to hospitals, sewage, fresh water supply is so high that most municipalities cannot afford the lay-out required. Unless food security is tackled simultaneously with sanitation and health, urban zones will witness the same inefficiencies in this delivery as has been with water and power. Stand-alone strategies to meet stand-alone targets will fail. The solution for the delivery of food, nutrition, sanitation and health to poor people succeeds when integrated business models prevail.

A new real estate development inside the urban boundaries must plan for a 90 per cent food security. This is viable if open spaces are secured with a solid flow of soil enrichment. This is not only a matter of nutrition; this is a strategy to ensure that money circulates and remains in the community, owing to internal delivery of food. The high population density reduces distribution and packaging costs. Established programs to farm edible mushrooms on coffee and tea waste, offers a first platform that guarantees a variety of protein for human and animal consumption. The processing of coffee grounds and used tea leaves into substrates for mushrooms makes use of a tiny stream of biowaste from households. However, it is converted to a catalyst in the local economy. Every kilogram of moist used coffee or tea leaves can produce another kilogram of edible mushrooms, converted into a broad portfolio of essential amino acids, while the leftovers after harvesting the mushrooms are ideal as a chicken, or goat feed.

Mushroom farming is fast and easy, providing results within weeks. Urban vegetables gardens, the edible bushes and parks can all form part of the overall urban planning, the key is the continuous circulation of nutrients and energy. One of the critical resources is human waste. It is considered by many as a cost, requiring an expensive capital lay-out, but for others it is an opportunity. Few realise the business models that could emerge from a waste management process that aims to secure long-term health, food security and jobs, while replenishing the topsoil that is highly dependent on the continuous addition of fertilisers which are beyond the means of majority of the residents in shanty towns.

The modern standard is to use water to flush toilets. Dry toilets are an anachronism for most citizens, even though one-third of drinking water in urban zones is consumed for discharging toilets—probably one of the most inefficient uses of this scarce resource. Infants are the only members of the family exempt from going to the toilet and flushing water. Diapers have become the standard and while this may save some water, it is an increasing problem for the waste management of cities. The landfill authorities around the world predict that as much as 8 per cent of solid waste will be diapers. These artifacts of modern life were invented first in Sweden before the Second World War, and quickly emerged as a symbol of modernity. The problem is not only volume, modern diapers absorb urine effectively. No parent rinses out the liquid to reduce the weight of the 8,000-10,000 diapers a baby uses, before she or he is toilet trained.

Children who are not yet potty trained should never be considered a problem. Plastic diapers that cannot be composted, should be considered the problem. There are biodegradable plastics that could be used. Unlike the expensive plastics ones, locally produced and distributed diapers are much cheaper. On balance, compostable diapers represent the beginning of a process that replenishes the soil, besides generating revenue and jobs. As has been demonstrated by Ms Ayumi Matsuzaka, the experimental scientist who works with the Botanical Gardens of Berlin, a daily service to produce, supply and recover diapers which are subsequently composted in combination with charcoal, producing terra preta allows a fast, sound and safe replenishing of topsoil.

The diaper economy is a cash economy. The 10,000 diapers that an infant soils in its first years of life, produce approximately 3 tons of high quality soil, which supports the planting of fruit trees on depleted soil. Actually, diapers should not be a cost to the family, it should be an investment that is harvested in the form of fruits. When the baby turns a teenager, approximately 1000 fruit trees will bear fruit, offering plentiful harvests for decades to come. Why limit to the planting of one tree at birth since the baby produces enough nutrition for over a thousand trees.

This requires urban planning with urban agriculture and urban edible gardens, combined with urban industries, bringing a market for green plastics that can only become successful if the business model evolves from the selling of locally produced diapers with biodegradable plastics, to a system that generates topsoil on depleted land and provides long-term food security while sequestering carbon dioxide.

When one foresees the size and the scope of activities in the emerging communities and knows that the fruit trees will dot the region at a rate of 1,000 per newborn earmarked for social and economic development, then there is a next opportunity: bread! The baking of bread has become so industrialised that the local bakeries have vanished, or have been reduced to the heating up of pre-baked and pre-mixed frozen dough. There have been various initiatives to revive the local bakery, nearly all of them have failed. The reason: if a small bakery competes with a minute version of the industrial one, it will fail in the competitive game. In order to develop a local bakery that is successfully competitive, it needs to change the business model, starting with the dough.

The recent successes in Mexico and Algeria with local bakeries, demonstrate that bread has to be cheaper and contain more nutrition. This has been accomplished by making agreements with fruit processing companies (for example, guacamole in Mexico or grape seeds in Algeria). All seeds are dried, ground and blended up to 25 per cent into the bread mix. The logic of local economic development is always the same: use what you have and ensure that the money paid daily for bread is now circulating in the local economy. It has been calculated that for every 50-100 households, there could be one bakery that uses the excess energy of the local grid at night, delivering fresh bread every morning. This provides the ideal platform for micro-enterprises.

A housing program that aims to provide homes for 200,000 families like Western Cape must plan for at least 2,000 bakeries, creating an estimated 3,000 jobs. The industrial version of that same supply chain will generate at most 100 jobs, and spend one-third on transport, packaging, marketing and distribution. The replacement of 25 per cent of the dough with ground fruit seed flour and the elimination of associated expenses, make the local bakery competitive, generating employment with a multiple of 30. If on top of that, the housing developments could be located close to wheat or corn production, the generation of value by small bakeries in the community can out compete any industrial factory, while the fortified and mineral rich bread has improved the quality beyond the means of industrial operators.

The number of jobs generated, based on available cash flow, capital, materials, human resources and even waste offers a first insight in how a local economy can outcompete a global economy. This outline of a few opportunities confirm that demand can be met with local supply, generating local value, jobs which permit savings and the build-up of social capital. There are hundreds of additional opportunities, and a few more in the next pages will support the slogan: ... and it has only just begun!.

Waste Management and Energy

The organic component of solid waste streams, is estimated to average 50 per cent. However, the poorer people are, the lower the inorganic part. The biodegradable, renewable and organic waste should never end up in a landfill, neither should they be incinerated. The better approach is to exploit the extra organics from the waste of bottom of the pyramid to generate more value. Health is a core concern and therefore any waste, with the exception of coffee and tea that has been sterilised through its use, needs to be cured. The ideal treatment is anaerobic digestion, in other words, methanogenic bacteria mineralise the content, making it inert producing biogas which is two-third made of methane and one-third of CO_2. This bacterial digestion requires a stable, solid and diverse supply of organic matter that is blended through smart chemistry. Sludge from waste water treatment can be smartly combined with organic waste from households and food markets as well as local small scale argo-industrial processing plants. This smart chemistry generates up to four times more biogas than when sludge or the organic waste is digested separately or mixed without consideration of the enhanced reactions.

If the local economic development considers glass as a raw material for the building industry, as mentioned, then it requires CO_2.

This gas molecule can be extracted from the digesters' biogas. Instead of requiring an external supply, foam glass can now be completely locally produced. Production engineers need to study predictability of the supply chain of good and materials. The digestion process offers great comfort since it serves one of the most secure and permanent deliveries of the raw materials: the day that there is no sludge nor biomass waste, there will be no living community. It is key to build up new industries that rely on secure and predictable material flows so as to predict through mathematical models how much income and how many jobs can be expected, while meeting immediate needs of the local community.

Fast Moving Consumer Goods

Goats and chickens should be reared in and around urban developments. While the avian flu has taught the world a few hygiene lessons, the integration of local production of animal protein provides food security and is yet another catalyst in the local economic growth. Goat farmers on the Canary Islands, small-scale farms with up to 50 animals, enjoy the highest productivity in milk production. Goats' milk is considered healthier than cow's milk since they have less lactose and the chemical structure is similar to that of breast milk. Goats also provide leaner meat. Every small goat farm in the urban environment needs a cluster of businesses, so that the maximum value is generated.

Goat milk has the highest value when it is used in ice cream! If local farmers team up with a chain of local cooperatives to process goats' milk into cheese, yoghurt and ice cream, based on the business model where a farmer receives a 10 per cent participation in the ultimate price paid by the consumer, then local farmers will earn more cash than has ever been viable. When goats and chickens are slaughtered in a local butchery, offal can be converted into protein through the rearing of soldier fly larvae which are the most productive producers of protein. The South African company AgriProtein, based in Cape Town has proven that this is viable in both the urban and peri-urban zones, confirming the earlier experiences of the Songhai Center in Porto Novo, Benin. Hygiene, animal husbandry, food production and nutrition go hand in hand with economic growth aimed at uplifting poor people. The same soldier flies can effectively treat human waste (black water and raw human waste) and in turn help resolve another costly budget item on every city's ledger. This process has passed all sanitary tests to the point that the European Union has approved it.

The portfolio of opportunities for arranging food security within the urban edge is vast. It cannot be ignored that all productive industries require investments. All projects can mobilise funding, provided it can demonstrate demand, a predictable cash flow, a known capital outlay, a transparent break-even point and clarity on the social impact. If we cannot come to a common understanding regarding the advantages of an economic development on a case by case explained and understood method, on the back of an envelop, then we cannot fast-track inclusive growth. The implementation of these initiatives cannot be subject to a rigid plan, nor the play of excel spreadsheets. Rather inclusive growth is driven by a high motivation, a focus on local resources, generating even more added value, responding to the basic needs first and ensuring that the cash generated circulates first and foremost in the local economy. Remember, challenge is that r<g!

Mobility and Jobs

The standard model is that poor people live in shanty towns and every morning start their odyssey to find or go to work. The gravitational centre of poverty provides for no jobs. Millions of people undergo a 2-3 hours journey (one way) spending up to one-third of their meagre income, just on getting to the job. Beside being a waste of time, energy and resources, it does not even make sense. The logic of employment in industrial zones is partly due to the traditional zoning of cities with residential, commercial and industrial zones arbitrarily divided according to a master plan made up by urban designers, who have limited experience with the planning of inclusive growth. The outcome is that poor people invade open space and are forced to organise their own way to work.

The growth potential to lift people out of poverty, is once again demonstrated with the ill-directed financial resources. It is common for a single mother of 4 children, aged between 3 and 12, to live in with her mother. She spends about 5 hours each day commuting to and from work, where she is an office cleaner. The journeys cost nearly 40 per cent of her monthly salary of South African Rand (ZAR) 1,900 (US$190). She leaves home at 05:00 to be at the office at 07:30, starting with a 2 kilometre walk to the taxi stand, which takes her to the train station. After arrival in the main station, she takes another taxi. After leaving work at 16:00, she may not get home until 19:00, as the trains are often late. She spends over ZAR 700 a month on transport and nearly 100 hours on the road. The inefficiencies that a private household economy has to tolerate would be totally unacceptable in industry. Yet, industry in general and employers in particular externalise the cost of mobility and expect the marginalised workers to carry it.

The lowest income earners working in the informal economy spend currently 30 per cent of their income on transport. In the South African context, one-third of the income can be converted into a bond, implying that the cost of transport (ZAR 700/month) equals the value of the bond (ZAR 210,000) against which a house could be acquired. With lesser distance between work and residence, the money spent on going back and forth to work would be converted from a cost into an asset. The total amount of money that can be diverted over 25 years from expenditure to capital for the planned 200,000 homes in Western Cape reaches ZAR 40 billion (approximately US$4 billion). While this demonstrates the 'Fortune at the Bottom of the Pyramid', it also confirms the concept that poor people have the potential to create their 'City of Joy'. It is hard to realise the power of the small numbers, and even more difficult to grasp what this number represents to facilitate the new arrival of members of the middle class, owing to this initiative of affordable housing.

While jobs in the described local economic development model, based on inclusive growth that captures the dynamics of capital gains 'on the table' are increasingly local, there is a need to connect with the region. This requires the provision of 'feeder' transport, i.e., transportation from the new development zone to the main arteries of public transportation. In the 1990s, Mr John Thomas "Jack" Lupton, heir to the Coca-Cola bottling fortune, wished to put his birthplace, Chattanooga on the map. He wished to unlock the run-down inner centre of the city, in an innovative way. Mr Lupton embraced the idea of local electric bus transportation for a city of approximately 170,000 inhabitants. The city forged ahead against the advice of all major experts in public transportation and turned the Chattanooga Area Regional Transport Authority (CARTA) into the first American public authority that offers a free shuttle service with electric buses. There was no expertise in the region, and without the leadership of a few city fathers including David Crocket, the technical, political and organisational obstacles would never have been overcome.

CARTA now has a 20-year history. The electric bus system first saw the quick exchange of batteries in the bus depot and garage, is now improved by wayside induction: a buried coil charges the bus wirelessly in the parking lot, or at a curbside stop. The charge can be regenerated by solar. While traditional charge methods provide battery power to run a bus over 65 kilometres, this induction charge system increases the buses' driving range to 160 kilometres. The energy and maintenance cost is only one-fifth of the cost (with fuel at US prices). Since the minimum partial recharge only takes one minute, the buses can run all day, reducing the capital investment in vehicles. When operational costs decrease to a fraction and the living laboratory has a 20-year track record, the city can transform into a centre of research and of manufacturing cutting-edge transport technology. Mr Lupton achieved what he wished.

The bus system based on batteries provides an additional advantage. Any power grid based on renewable energies requires a back-up. The traditional solution is a pack of batteries. While this is a technically sound option, it is also an expensive one. Batteries have a rather short life and this makes solar and wind energies often uncompetitive—unless one opts for a solution that combines the battery power of public transportation found in the bus batteries as an additional source of electricity when the water is cold and the sun does not shine. While these back-up batteries do not have to supply power for more than few hours, it is a necessary installation when one wishes to avoid the traditional back-up of diesel generators. Now the smart grid of the new inclusive development ensures that the bus batteries, which run on 12V DC, are charged at night with the excess energy that the day offered. At the same time, the bus batteries provide a powerful and cheap component in a resilient community at half the cost.

The built, operation and maintenance of 20-seat passenger buses provides job opportunities. Mass transit busses are managed within the metropolitan area, and feeder busses in the local area. Since the scale is smaller, the window for innovation is larger. This system brings hand-on engineering face to face with new skills that were not available at any of the large educational centres; hence it represents an opportunity to position the academic platform of this new inclusive development. While others pursue information and communication technologies (ICT), nano-technologies, sophisticated sensors and biotechnologies, this new development zone uses the hands-on experiences, bundling dozens of inclusive growth projects with their financial models as the basis for learning to a local and international student audience. As a result, this living laboratory of inclusive growth brings all possible benefits to the community, including learning.

Culture and Education

The creation of a community requires more than water, food, housing, energy, mobility and jobs. One of the most prolific industries is the arts, based on culture and tradition. This must be part of any local economic development since it builds on the skills that people have had for generations. Perhaps some cannot read or write, but over centuries, they have enjoyed the knowledge and the wisdom of their ancestors. It is therefore critical that the emerging community enjoys respect and appreciation for the diversity that characterises human settlements. Unfortunately in the recent past, culture has been viewed as a necessary expense. The inclusive growth model considers it as an opportunity to generate revenue and jobs and celebrate the community.

The African arts and crafts, music and dance are internationally acclaimed. However, just like nature has been considered endangered, and therefore had to be protected, culture is also regarded as endangered, and consequently must be subsidised and protected. Protection costs money and therefore will face many hurdles to succeed. It is important to go beyond preservation and embark on active promotion of the arts, through the creation of master classes inspired by the German apprentice system that has succeeded to identify the innate capabilities of a child at an early age and provide them with technical training, saving many from pursuing an academic path that does not suit their strengths. Exposure to the arts and crafts strengthens the creative, hands-on and technical minds that can find their career paths.

This reflection on culture and arts brings education to the forefront. Any community that wishes to have a better future for the next generations, does not need schools where the children are taught to memorise what the teacher already knows. These communities need a learning environment where the children imagine early on, how they can do better than their parents, and believe they can succeed. If the young bear this attitude to life, then these communities will grow. If community schools emerge in an environment that offers a new approach to urban design and development, and implements a broad range of innovative business models that respond to the needs and facilitates growth in economy that the children can witness in their teenage years, then this living laboratory represents an ideal basis for an educational platform. This learning environment will not only serve the needs of the local community, but will also attract national and international students from high school to university.

As soon as parents have some additional financial resources, spending on education is one of the budgets that increases fastest, from learning English (the biggest spend around the world today) to science. Many parents know all too well that not getting into school, or not finishing school combined with teenage pregnancy, is one of the most predictable ways to remain in poverty. Failure to attain a high school diploma and having a single parent family of three ensure that the next generation stays in poverty too. Parents who have gone through this predictable course of life, are often the most dedicated to guarantee that their children do not fall into the same trap. Therefore, it is key that children sense the progress and imagine their future.

Children need challenges and must be inspired. That is why inclusive growth with all the new models that are proven elsewhere, provide a learning environment that permit children to imagine more than the knowledge of their parents and teachers. This process starts with the design of the school itself. Most educational institutions are designed to meet low cost budgets. Since the early 1960s, Anders Nyquist designs highly ecological and functional buildings. He applied his science, experience and wisdom to schools in order to ensure that children admitted have a healthy and challenging environment. This may cost more on capital and building materials, but will be lower on operational expenses. However, the greatest benefit is that healthy children will study better. Those that go to a local school where natural filters cleanse the air, will not sneeze after someone else sneezed thanks to filters made of broad-leaf plants grown in locally produced terra preta soil derived from the diapers of their siblings. It has been demonstrated that when innovations are all around, they turn into a way of life. The children will first inspire their parents, change their behaviour based on solutions that have been tested in school.

The critical component is the financial one. It is not about cost, rather it is about value. If there is a school, or a network of schools, where children are known to be healthier and perform better academically than elsewhere, what would parents do if this is a public school where one can only register on a first come-first serve basis, with locals getting the absolute priority? Parents generally want to move closer to the school. And what happens when more parents want to live in the immediate vicinity of a school to guarantee them a spot for their child? The land value of the property consequently increases. When assets grow, people who live in that neighbourhood become bankable beyond their job and mortgage. They can enjoy an asset that represents their life investment because the region promotes health and education, which ultimately means local, economic inclusive growth. School fees are local; capital gains are local; community has a chance to evolve from discrimination to inclusion, and the rate of return on capital is outpaced by the rate of social, ecological and economic growth that represents the basis for a future for a whole generation.

This vision turns into reality when real estate and local development aim to achieve inclusive growth, building up assets that in one generation lift people out of poverty. It takes a few years for land speculators to make 500 times the investment. It takes a generation of double-digit growth deploying these funds to lift a whole society, simultaneously providing the investors with a solid return on investment.

16

Cascading a Blue Economy

> The Earth provides enough to satisfy every man's need, though not every man's greed.
>
> — *MAHATMA GANDHI*

Opting Out of a Dead End

Predictability, although considered a prerequisite of economic success, creates an artifice that blinds us to the ramifications of our actions. Adherence to a core competence and reliance on linear calculations and scientific abstractions achieves a monopolistic economic model that leads to more and more transportation and energy consumption so as to reach the consumer waiting at the end of the supply chain. Tighter supply chain management and just-in-time assembly creates a global and interdependent economy that delivers more and cheaper products to consumers. Global free trade is considered the engine of growth, the tool that makes greater efficiency available to everyone in the world. Shipping cookies immersed in preservation gases, air-freighting deep-frozen pralines, or filling tankers with orange juice may be nothing more than excesses of that logic. Yet such methods will never enable the next generation to provide food and livelihood for all players. Unemployment and poverty will be the only enduring outcome.

Traditionally, seasonal foods provided the micro-nutrients needed for a particular time of year. Each fall harvest, Native Americans ate *huitlacoche*, a truffle-like fungus growing on corn, as a boost for their immune system, preparing them for winter's onset. Now *huitlacoche* is a delicacy that can be consumed all year, even though its beneficial effect is primarily seasonal. In reality, our appetites are enticed and trained by the marketers and media outlets of our culture. If this is the basis of marketing as defined by the axiom taught by Philip Kotler, "Supply what the consumer wants," perhaps we might more carefully consider our wishes. Excessive stimulation of demand for products that fulfill desires and ignore basic needs creates a linear goal that focuses on garnering greater share of disposable income. We seem to overlook that it is an unsupportable system advancing along a destructive path. It is a path that leads to a world of carbon emissions, lost biodiversity, profligate use of non-renewable raw materials, and excessive reliance on toxic chemicals. It is a path without a future. What we have may be the best we could imagine to date, but we have to imagine and do much better.

A Curiously Winding Path

Throughout this book, we have reviewed the best inspirations that can be found in natural systems for resolving our present economic and ecologic impasse. We have explored successful benchmarked and implemented models, and have examined the potential of others. We have considered how some might fit linked or bundled applications. Everywhere we have discovered tremendous potential to generate more jobs, while increasing material efficiency and productivity beyond the dreams of many. This is remarkable because we have been led to believe that an increase in productivity is only possible by shedding jobs. Nature knows better, transforming apparent scarcity to sufficiency and ultimately to abundance. The cascading of energy and nutrients among the five kingdoms of nature permits multitudes of human-scale production units to provide for all prevalent needs. While our current focus on maximising one output leads to scarcity on one hand and poverty on the other, ecosystems always have enough for all.

All players within an ecosystem make their modest contributions dependent on the availability of nutrients, energy and the impetus to respond to basic needs. Everything evolves and when crises occur, everyone adapts. In natural systems, no one has a license to remain out-of-step for too long. Natural environments have no big players dominating the field. There is much more room for small contributors. A tree that grows to 100 feet does not decide on the basis of this achievement to further continue to 1,000 feet. Were it to succeed in the attempt, physical forces would destroy it. Business pursues a strategy of ever-lower marginal costs, assuming that the cost of making one more unit will always be less, thus justifying the blind race for size and market control. Growth, based on the consolidation of power, triggers unnoticed collateral damage, and renders the whole system inflexible and resistant to change.

Ecosystems benefit from a renewing cascade of nutrients and energy. These unending flows permit life to adapt and thrive. Conditions of apparent scarcity progress towards visible sufficiency and even abundance. In natural systems, as soon as there is too much food, some species proliferate or new species emerge. Waste removal is handled by passing it forward in the nutrient stream so as to be utilised by other players. For a tree, its fallen leaves are nutrients for soil bacteria, ants, and worms whose output in turn becomes nutrients for the tree.

Natural systems have a different approach to chemistry as well. First, the main solvent is water, which is considerably more benign to the overall system than any of the catalysts that humans have invented. Second, the bonds between two molecules are mainly non-covalent, which means they can be easily taken apart. They degrade, and can be reused and recombined in other molecules. Nature's chemical engineers apply the 'zip-unzip' concept to their methods. It is this ability to degrade, separate, and reintegrate that allows the overall system to have such high material and energy efficiency. To produce a stronger web for its offspring, the spider simply reprocesses the polymers of its old web into the constituent amino acids, and spins it anew.

Non-linear models, often equated with chaos, underpin natural systems. In fact, just about everything in natural systems follows non-linear pathways. In his book, *La Nouvelle Alliance*, Belgian author Ilya Prigogine, the 1977 Nobel Laureate in chemistry, describes these natural relationships as "dissipative structures." It is our desire to squeeze everything into straight lines and right angles that renders most manufactured products energy inefficient. Nature demonstrates that while the shortest distance between two points may be a straight line, the fastest and most energy-efficient pathway follows the swirls of a vortex.

As we adjust our production and consumption system to emulate natural systems, we must indulge the apparent surprises provided by non-linear models. This does not mean that all is unpredictable. Physics still applies in our universe. Then again, it does mean we must seek out the interactive forces and hidden connections that will permit us to gain multiple results with one set of initiatives. This is demonstrated by termites' capacity to control temperature and humidity with great precision by constructing underground micro-tunnels through their mounds. These termites express a deep understanding of ways in which everything interacts. The ultimate result of these complex relationships and seemingly chaotic interactions is that termites have food because an edible fungus thrives in the underground environment they create. Using locally available resources results in a marvelous system that secures basic needs for the termites, while warming the roots of plants that will grow the leaves, well masticated by the termites, on which the fungus thrives.

We will need to understand and appreciate symbiosis—how species work together to achieve the common goals of a whole system. The renewal made possible at Las Gaviotas came from recognition of the symbiosis between pine trees and mycorrhizal fungi. An appreciation of how natural forces always evolve towards the best use of resources within an ecosystem allows us to recognise the regenerative capacity of natural systems to overcome calamities that are often the result of our own ignorance. Nature does not calculate cash flow. While we are obsessed with monetarisation (to our own benefit), natural systems generate multiple benefits best measured in protein and trace minerals, drinking water, energy sources and defense systems. Nature produces betterment through the calculation of an integrated benefit flow. Such synergies lead to common benefits, such as free, abundant and unpolluted water and air, the generation of topsoil, flexibility and adaptability owing to biodiversity. If entrepreneurs in these new competitive businesses were to include such outcomes in their goals, then it would continuously build common benefit (the commons) and realise enormous social capital that have been either neglected or privatised. Perhaps, like the Kingdom of Bhutan, we could monitor our national happiness index, rather than our gross domestic product.

The linear economic model prescribes placing a market value on everything, calculating the costs of each input, allocating overhead for every output, and converting cost centres to profit centres that are made to compete for internal resources through outsourcing. The resulting calculation is derived from the logic of consolidation—basically adding it all up while eliminating double counts. This does not unveil synergies amongst different divisions of the same company, nor identify the commons that are considered free, and thus without economic value. Neither does it put a price on the externalised costs imposed on society, which is located outside the logical framework of the core business; nor disclose the lost opportunities that simply cannot be considered because they are not part of the core business, like the social housing from bamboo or the stone paper from rock waste. Most commonly, we simply impose the costs on future generations who are not made aware nor informed in detail that we are exploiting the Earth beyond easy repair and leaving the problems for them to resolve. As a result, climate change occurs without any real understanding of the urgency to undertake corrective action. There is a disconnect between the available information confirming the dramatic rise in temperature and sea levels, and our strategy to negotiate a global agreement by employing lawyers who debate a few words and decimal points ensuring that no one commits to anything. And this has been going on for 20 years. Hence, we cannot expect political leadership at the global scale anymore.

In business, companies opt to maximise profits and target market share, regardless of social cost to a local community, by producing wherever the cost for a single product is lowest. Industrial and policy decisions never consider prioritising full employment as a viable option. When the largest instant coffee maker in the world can generate at least US$6 billion in additional revenues creating a minimum of 100,000 jobs, while producing millions of tons of cholesterol- and saturated fatty acid free food, the company decides to burn all waste to recover some energy. In the past, we have condemned companies for doing bad, in the future we will condemn companies for refusing to do good.

In contrast, natural systems employ everyone; no one is considered too old or too young. Where ecosystems clearly promote innovation, collaboration, patience and perseverance, the current economic model is rather insensitive to any change not initiated by or not serving the interests of dominant players themselves. Market leaders with their streamlined production and distribution systems fiercely resist any change that risks the existing processes and revenue streams, including of course bonuses.

We often forget that species and ecosystems have coped with numerous disasters in the past and have rapidly evolved to adjust to new and even dramatically changed circumstances. This is the approach we must take towards carbon dioxide emissions and other so-called greenhouse gases. If we isolate CO_2 and do not consider the whole system, then we are likely to overlook the real solutions. The harvesting of CO_2 for the production of biofuels by micro-algae is a simple yet brilliant solution that generates multiple benefits, including continuous harvesting and reuse of carbonic gases in photo-biorefineries and making of polyesters without sulfuric acid. If, on the other hand, we only think about the gas and the resultant problems and decide to formulate engineered solutions for its elimination, then constructs like nuclear energy and the disposal of vast quantities of CO_2 into deep oceans may sound logical and obvious, at whatever cost and paid for by the taxpayer. These expensive choices are only obvious when the capacity of ecosystems to provide for solutions is abridged to a single concept presented in oversimplified targets, such as lowered emission rates. This eliminates the opportunity to balance risks or create new long-term options. It leaves people to scramble for quick-fix solutions that cannot predict long-term collateral effects.

In an evolutionary model where changes are recognised as what is normal, flexibility is also the rule. Risks inherent to inevitable changes are mitigated because a natural system will evolve with a simple yet complex algorithm: always searching for ways to reduce material and energy needs so that more life, and more diverse life, can populate the system and render it resilient. Flexible communities and ecosystems are resilient. Our society has embraced so many rules and regulations, dogmas and untouchables that we have lost resilience.

The opportunities for entrepreneurship inspired by the power of ecosystems mark the goals of a Blue Economy. What we see unfolding before us goes beyond the genius of each species. The total is more than the sum of its parts. A world that is home to these marvelous ecosystems cascading nutrients and energy endlessly is the one that can accept the challenge to resolve poverty and misery, inequality and waste. Focusing merely on a hundred innovations that draw from of nature's remarkable examples, we envision that it is possible to generate as many as 100 million jobs over the next 10 years.

Let us inspire the creativity and determination of entrepreneurs around the world who will find in these innovations multiple opportunities to construct a renewed economy. If we shift our gaze and our focus to find inspiration in the marvelous workings of nature, we can than move from capacity to competency, from scale to scope, creating a Blue Economy for a blue planet.

17

Who is in Favour of GMO? (genetically modified organisms)

If you see barren land and think it is worth nothing.
Think again.
If you think that drought will kill the harvest
Think again.
If you think people need special food to avoid blindness.
Think again.

— *G.P.*

The Rt Hon Anders Wijkman, Member of the Swedish Royal Academy of Sciences, an accomplished environmental activist who served a decade as member of the European Parliament, asked the question: "Should I be against all forms of GMO?"

Actually, the inherently positive approach that characterises the Blue Economy to finding solutions to major challenges faced by humanity always starts by searching for the best ways to achieve a competitive, sustainable, healthy and happy society. While scientists, politicians and business leaders may have found and implemented great social and technological solutions in the past, we can always do better, much better indeed. So, the key message is: do ponder to be 'for or against', find out what is much 'better'.

In our quest to attain a society capable of 'responding to basic needs for water, food, health, housing and energy for all', we cannot leave any opportunity unturned, because 'we do not like it'. We have to look reality in the eye, going beyond notions of good and bad, going beyond what fits our dogmas and what does not. We have to ask ourselves: "Is there better?" Often we find seemingly best solutions at that moment in time, not realising at the outset the unintended consequences that may be caused by our impatient drive toward quick solutions.

I know this dilemma all too well. Back in the early 1990s, I went out of my way to promote biodegradable soaps, outcompeting the market leaders without advertising by distributing an ecological product made in an ecological factory only to realise that this success caused a greater demand for palm oil, which over the next decade led to the destruction of 2.5 million hectares of rainforest, including ruining major tracks of the habitat of the orangutan. Was I, responsible for destruction of the rainforest because I wanted to contribute to cleaning up of the rivers in Europe? It is only then that I realised that biodegradability—even with the best of my intentions—often has nothing to see with sustainability. How could I pretend to clean up the rivers in Europe while undermining the livelihood of the habitat of primates?

I realised the hard way that we need to look at the whole system and not simply pursue one single objective. Every time we focus solely on one problem and find one quick solution, we are most likely to cause these unintentional consequences. It takes years, sometimes decades to realise the adverse effects of our deeds, and then it is often too late. If we decide to ignore the negative impact and side effects of our hasty actions, and fail to dramatically improve, then we tend to cause collateral damage—knowingly causing harm—a strategy condoned by the military. However, it cannot be embraced by civil society.

We need to create the space to look at the hard reality through the eyes of a child, observe all ramifications of the challenges we face without preconceived ideas. We study our options, employ scientific knowledge to the best of our abilities and design a model that advances life on earth.

This is how I pursue the soap and detergents business today. I—and the Zero Emissions Research Initiative (ZERI) Foundation—actively promote the extraction of d-Limonene from citrus peels, which is perhaps one of the most effective, competitive and sustainable cleaning products. We convert waste from the orange juice industry into cleaning agents thereby outcompete palm oil derivatives by using available resources. The waste from the peels after extraction of the active ingredients can serve as an animal feed. Instead of causing damage to the rainforest or simply managing waste, we can generate three revenues and double the number of jobs. This is the Blue Economy.

After pondering over all possible options, I am encouraging companies from Japan to the United States (US), Brazil to South Africa to embrace this better solution. Why would you limit yourself to continue with palm oil-based soaps and detergents when there are now certified sustainable sources? Can someone explain to me how a monoculture can ever be sustainable?

I recognise that the d-Limonene may be the best option today. Improvements, even radical improvements, can emerge anytime. That is the pathway of evolution, building better competitiveness. At least, there is no more need to destroy rain forests.

It is against this background and positive approach that I responded to Anders' question about GMO, drawing from my experience as entrepreneur and innovator, committed to get better results faster, serving this simple purpose: respond to the basic needs of all with what we have, navigating the known and unknown, always prepared to take the risks to do much better than we have been able to do.

The first question we have to answer is: What is the purpose of GMO? If the purpose is to make crops resistant to drought, then the next question is: Why do you want to plant a crop that needs water in an area that does not have water? And if climate change is the cause of the drought (an easy excuse these days) why don't we switch to crops that can grow under these environmental conditions?

Do We Have 5 or 1,000 Choices?

Of course, if options for crops are limited to five varieties (wheat, rice, corn, soy, palm) planted as monocultures, and we have discarded all other 1,000 opportunities that are proven locally, then we have no option: we must genetically modify these crops to resist drought. But, what if in this era of biodiversity we search for the best seeds, the result of millions of years of adaptation, then we can embrace the best option that is readily available and proven to work, without any potential unintended consequences.

We can actually plant these seeds immediately without the need to undertake further research, save the money that now is spent on approvals, media campaigns and lobbyists who all try to get this 'drought resistant' seed endorsed by policymakers.

A quick review of established seed banks confirms that there are hundreds of biota available for any latitude or altitude with proven track records to withstand drought. However, the next argument will be that the "traditional product" cannot produce enough to feed the world. Is that true? We are made to believe that only five main crops and only GMO combined with (owing to GMO reduced) chemical cocktails will save us from famine and starvation. Let me analyse that logic.

If we only consume a fraction of what is produced (0.1% of tea, 0.2% of coffee, 17% of sugar cane, or 20% of a tree destined for paper), and the rest is simply left to rot, generate methane or burn, or to be plowed it back into the soil, then it is true that we will never produce enough. Thus, if we rely on a few monocultures that only extract one ingredient for consumption, then we will turn poverty and hunger into sustainable phenomena. I doubt if appetite of the world's growing population would ever be able to have food security for all, even with the introduction of widespread GMO. Maybe the creation of this permanent scarcity is what the suppliers of GMO need in order to justify their argument that they alleviate hunger in the world.

Monocultures, irrigation, seed selection and fertilisers have boosted output of single crops, no doubt. However, this approach has lost sight of the tremendous opportunities beyond wheat and rice. We should cascade our agricultural resources, just like ecosystems do. Actually, humans are the only species that waste waste. No other living system does that. So, instead of facing the permanent risk of famine, using proven integrated farming techniques combined with the best of modern agriculture, we can progress beyond the concept of scarcity and plan for sufficiency, and even dream of abundance.

Thus if we turn agriculture into a system of production and consumption that uses all local resources, through farming mushrooms on coffee waste as is done in Africa and Latin America, or on rice straw as is the tradition in China, then we will be able to produce 100 times more amino acids for human consumption than is available from export crops today. There is not even one GMO or irrigation plan that can come close to this performance that is proven.

Burn It—Eat It Or Build With It

In the past, agricultural waste from rice straw was used as a building material in Cairo. When concrete and cement began to be used, Cairo faced intolerable air pollution due to the burning of excesses of rice straw. The best option proposed was to genetically modify rice to short straw varieties. Who could be against reducing respiratory illnesses caused by uncontrolled incineration of agricultural waste?

However, in a sprawling megalopolis like Cairo, why was the option of generating more food not retained? The farming of straw mushrooms in an urban area generates jobs, income and converts waste into food, while eliminating air contamination. It is now done in 16 countries. Was the excuse that the Egyptians do not eat mushrooms? They never ate hamburgers either, but cheap hamburgers are recently the rage. So is there a flaw in our economic logic?

The mindset that underpins the drive to GMO is the construct of scarcity. The efficient allocation of scarce resources provides the logic for business. Unfortunately over the past half century, business is reduced to a core business based on a core competence. How often did I hear that one or the other multinational is not into mushrooms, and therefore this option of converting agro-waste to food—however laudable and even competitive—is not even considered? Actually, we have to admit that these companies are not capable of taking up this proposal; management simply does not have the skills needed to introduce this simple innovation; and shareholders are capable of understanding it but need to be exposed to the option.

If we are prepared to embrace integrated farming, cascading nutrients in the field or inner cities, instead of focusing on one and discarding the rest, then we can produce food even on dry farmland or in urban concrete jungles. As a result, we can have 1,000 other sources of vegetable protein known around the world, and 5,000 varieties of edible fungi that combined can one day produce more than we can eat!

If all coffee waste were used to farm mushrooms, we would produce an additional 16 million tons of food—using what we have today! Imagine the impact created if we add tea, straw, cobs, and pruning from orchards. It may surpass the 100-million-ton mark, bypassing food from fish catch and fish farming. While this sets the stage, there is a need to present a second example to clarify my approach towards finding the best solution, and offer a framework for assessing the potential contribution of GMO to a sustainable, healthy and happy world.

Do Not Be Against—Be in Favour of Better

We remember some 15 years ago, the arrival of Golden Rice? This GMO rice was heralded as a definitive solution in the fight against blindness. It was introduced as one of the greatest contributions of science, and probably one of the key reasons why you asked "if I am against all forms of GMO?" If the purpose is to protect children from blindness, we can genetically modify rice to include betacarotene into the rice kernel. How could anyone ever be against this option?

We should not form our opinion on what is good or what is bad, we should choose the best possible option, with the least risks, based on an understanding of all possible unintentional consequences to anyone else with whom we share the planet.

When confronted with such a societal challenge like blindness, we should first ask ourselves why is that blindness is on the rise? Quickly, we realise that there is a shortage of betacarotene—obvious!

Is that enough reason to rush to and genetically modify rice to include betacarotene? I beg everyone to bear with me and think this through.

We should ask ourselves the question: Why is there a shortage of betacarotene in the food supply chain around rice paddies? Studying ecosystems we realise that micro-algae, including the blue green algae, are just about always around. This is one of the first forms of life that emerged on earth. These have been in existence for over a billion of years, and weathered all calamities. Micro-algae are known producers of betacarotene and many other nutrients. So what happened to them around the rice paddies?

We realise that there used to be a scum growing on the irrigated paddies. This scum has been removed due to the chemicals used in rice farming to boost output. That scum is rich in micro-algae, and very rich in betacarotene. In earlier times, Chinese, Vietnamese, Laotian, and Cambodian farmers used to put shrimps and even carps in the rice paddies. These organisms devoured betacarotene-rich algae and secured it into the food chain so that people had enough of it, naturally using all available resources. That cultivation system is not as high in rice productivity as a monoculture, but this traditional system of cultivation generates more nutrients, providing food security, and even improves the necessary defenses against modern illnesses such as blindness. This farming system provides more disposable income, since all basic needs can be covered locally. This puts more money in the pocket to pay for school. Export crops are notorious for generating more output, and an income that fluctuates with the world market prices.

Our modern farming system of rice focuses on maximising output eliminated betacarotene (and much more) from the supply chain! In our drive to increase the output of one component—rice—we lowered the natural cultivation of all the essential amino acids and micronutrients that rice alone cannot supply. How can we accept that the solution to blindness is genetic manipulation?

If we really want to fight blindness, and if that is our genuine purpose, then we should farm rice, let the scum form on the water, and feed it to the ducks, crustaceans and fish. Then we have a balanced intake of protein, and simultaneously have a good supply (again) of betacarotene, while naturally fertilising the ponds with manure. As our research demonstrates, integrated farming system produces more nutrients than intensive rice farming could ever achieve. We are not substituting blindness for famine as some proponents of GMO want us to believe.

Golden Rice does not solve any issue beyond blindness at a premium. Rather, GMOs perpetuate unsustainability in farming, both on the production side (too many inputs depleting topsoil) and the consumption side (too much of the wrong food).

How is it possible that the Swiss company that controls Golden Rice had an exclusive patent (until 2012), exploiting the sale of 'anti-blindness' rice for a profit? If the purpose is to earn money and maximise return to shareholders, then this should be spelled out when waging the campaign to halt blindness.

Let us not say that business is bad. We have to ask ourselves constantly "Is there a better way?" And the answer in this case is that: There is indeed a much better way! This better way addresses our shortcomings without leaving the world in hunger. Time has come to stop patching up the problems with quick fixes, and start implementing lasting solutions that can always evolve to improvise ways over time.

In Brazil, we calculated that the amount of betacarotene that can be naturally produced per hectare per year by the ecosystem that made rice so competitive is 40 times higher than what could ever be genetically engineered into the rice. This can be achieved at a lower cost.

So we cannot be against Golden Rice or GMO, I am always challenged to ask, "What is best to achieve a goal?" If the goal is to fight blindness due to a shortage of betacarotene, then Golden Rice is a poor option. Worse, it is an expensive and a rather ineffective option compared to the integrated farming techniques that have been proven to function. We should ask the next question: Do the farmers earn more money by stamping out blindness? Or, does this rice seed cost more, solely increasing the supplier's profit?

The company that developed Golden Rice requested early on support from the United Nations (UN), and asked governments to grant an exclusive license to operate. Is it ethical for a company to use an exclusive patent to profit from stamping out blindness, especially if it applies for grants and tax breaks in order to guarantee a minimum return?

If the UN pays or governments make up for the difference, then it is tax money that foots the bill! I am fundamentally against the diversion of citizens' earnings to guarantee a profit margin, or to subsidise research programs that do not solve any substantial problem, but only placing patches on the challenges of our time.

Until today every case that has been posed to me justifying GMO, I have found much better solutions that provide—higher output for the whole (not on one crop); contribute to the health and livelihood of all and stamp out hunger once and for all. Also guess what, these solutions are more competitive as well.

18

China will Feed Itself

> The glass is never half full or half empty.
> It is always full with water and air.
>
> — G.P.

If there is one country that knows how to feed itself, then it is China. However, a major shift in diet, an upgrade to meat, wheat, milk and corn combined with a massive urbanisation can cause the world supply system of food to crack on its foundations. Prof Lester Brown rightfully asked already over a decade ago, "Who will feed China?" and lately asked the question: "Can the United States feed China?" As Prof Brown eloquently explains with an overwhelming flow of facts, China's middle class represents a new generation that is growing up with hamburgers, shakes and buns and inturn has caused such a shift in appetite that the new Chinese diet—and the generative capacity of its agriculture—is certain to exert tremendous pressure on prices for all internationally traded food items. We are already witnessing so.

As the publisher of some European editions of the authoritative annual report "State of the World", written by Lester Brown and his team at the World Watch Institute, I was privileged to witness the emerging data on wheat imports and how this equated to a massive import of water. A change in diet combined with that in hydrology seemed to force the Chinese to embrace an import strategy that could quickly stress out the Earth's generative capacity. Although the questions raised by Prof Brown at first caused consternation, over time and with historical statistics confirming the trends, the legitimate question that he had raised over a decade ago, is now everyone's preoccupation.

China has been able to feed itself throughout history, and is a leading innovator in agriculture. The people living in the Central Plains of China introduced farming based on the interrelationship between water conservancy and agriculture. They built the first irrigation system Dujiangyan, a World Heritage in Sichuan around 250 BC. The Great Canal started to be dug in 486 BC in Yangzhou and was completed in the Sui Dynasty (581-618 AD). This vast infrastructural work served during the Yuan Dynasty in 1293 to connect the five major water drainages of China: Hai River, the Yellow River, Huai River, the Yangtze River and Qiantang River, and a series of lakes for its multiple functions of navigation, irrigation, flood and drain control with a total length of 1,794 km.

The Central Plains farmed five cereals—rice, two kinds of millets, wheat and beans. The region raised domestic animals (horses, cattle, sheep, pigs, dogs and chickens), sericulture, cultivated vegetables, oil crops, collected fuel wood, fishing, and was engaged in by-product processing as well. It focused on both agriculture and sericulture, which were the basic features of traditional small-scale peasant economy in ancient China that incessantly replenished topsoil. As a result, China was able to maintain a self-sufficient economy in ancient times. Nowadays, the population of China has reached 1.3 billion. The population projection by 2030 would be 1.5 billion. According to the current average ration of 400 kg of grain per capita per year, the annual demand of grain would be in the order of 600 billion tons (1.5 billion x 400 kg). Today, China can produce 500 million tons of grain in a year. Where to get additional 100 million tons in the future?

The challenge has become even more difficult since the fertility of cropland has decreased. After 30 years of intensive farming, organic matter in the soil is on average only one per cent. The upper limit of chemical fertiliser application is considered to be 225 kg/ha, while the Chinese fertiliser application was nearly twice the upper limit. Soil hardened and turned impervious. The yield response to the additional application of fertiliser is diminishing. At the same time, intensive animal husbandry produces 2.7 billion tons of animal manure a year and only 30-40 per cent is utilised. The arrival of Western farming techniques separated planting from animal husbandry and the unused 60-70 per cent now pollutes soil and contaminates the water table. Traditional Chinese agriculture has been replaced by petro-agriculture with agro-chemicals, fertilisers, herbicides, additives and mulch. This road to Westernisation of food production and consumption has shaken the fundamentals of Chinese agriculture in general and food security in particular.

Building on Tradition or Copying the USA

Although China is free to choose its own options to respond to all the basic needs for water, food, health, housing and energy, a portfolio of innovations provides an insight on how it will be possible for the country to supply all the nutrients needed. It has to be stated early on that it is impossible to ever satisfy demand if the Chinese were to adopt the unhealthy and unsustainable lifestyle of the Western world. As Lester Brown has described in detail, there is simply no way that by emulating the food habits and consumption patterns of the West, especially of the United States (US), can ever warrant meeting the basic needs of everyone in this world, starting with the Chinese. If China were to divert from the Western model, and rely on innovative approaches which are often based on traditional Chinese agricultural practices, then China can feed herself.

If, however, China were to emulate the Western production and consumption model, then the only viable route towards a temporary satisfaction of water and food needs would be massive introduction of genetically modified grains, fruits, vegetables and even animals for consumption, while relying on control mechanisms, such as hormones, enzymes and antibiotics to ensure predictable results. If the biological processes needs to have predictable outcomes, then the only attempt to be made to succeed is to control the growth process with chemistry in general and biochemistry in particular. After all, the ever-changing interplay of the five kingdoms of nature (Monera, Protista, Fungal, Planta and Animalia) will embark on its evolutionary path and elude predictable results. Since natural systems are always ready to adjust to new conditions, and evolve along the never-ending shifts in environmental conditions, outcomes of food production can never be guaranteed. The only way to succeed in securing that output targets are achieved in this technified food production is to control at high cost the fluctuations in environmental conditions and the continuous mutations in the process.

New Science

Whereas the final verdict on GMOs (genetically modified organisms) has not been pronounced, it is clear that going against the evolutionary path of nature is one of the most secured ways of failure. This failure is not due to the fact that hormones and antibiotics combined with genetic modification cannot do the job, it is rather due to the high costs associated with this approach, in conjunction with the business model that is practiced. Although the narrow calculation of the benefits of reducing pesticides by genetically modifying a potato to be indifferent to a bug or fungus may make business sense, the combined cost to the system and the long-term risks entailed by this new variety to the ecosystem, is certainly not understood. When the risks materialise, it will be too late to correct. The approach to GMO should be the same as that towards defense. Since there is no scientific proof that the enemy will attack, can one therefore refrain from armament and civil defense? It is exactly because there is no proof that one has to be prepared. If one waits until there is proof, there will be no time to react to the same when delivered. Hence, I have always proposed to work with what we have, and jointly embark on this evolutionary path to achieve breakthrough results in harmony with nature. Instead of creating your own wave (GMO) against all forces of nature, we should ride the wave benefitting from the forces of nature.

Companies proposing the GMO solution undertake these technological developments only on the basis of proprietary know-how, prohibiting farmers and competitors to access their patented solutions. The logic of these companies is to control the sale of seeds and make a guaranteed high margin in order to justify the investment made in the arduous process to obtain permits, mostly against the will of majority of the people. As the only way to pay for this approach, the companies must opt for economies of scale. However, this is a self-defeating proposition. Indeed, as the monocultures expand their reach around the world, adaptations in the ecosystems surrounding these stereotypes of cultivation will stimulate all other living species to adapt and mutate, not the least the micro-organisms which can genetically modify at will. These changes will undermine the breakthrough solutions based on GMO, and are certain to require additional gene splitting to protect the potatoes and spinach against yet another disease. And once this illness has been championed, another one will emerge. This is the fundamental difference of a cause and effect approach, where mankind (and the companies proposing this model) wishes to be in control and reap the benefits of creating a new strain, and the human intelligence that knows how to harness the inherent forces of life on earth.

Although companies with vested interests and recently trained biotechnology graduates will argue that this command and control approach is the only way forward to save the world from hunger, it neglects the logic and the economics of a different reality towards food security. Of course, those who stand to win from the drive towards command and control of biology will claim the opposite, and discredit these analyses as described below. The verdict will only be out in a few decades. Can China—and India, Brazil, Indonesia and South Africa take that risk—wait until 2040 to see if the chosen pathway of GMO as described above is the best one? And even if GMO controlled farming were to succeed in producing more food in the immediate future, it will be expensive and beyond reach of the large majority of the world population.

Fair and Organic

Does the world have to make a choice between fair trade and organic food carefully farmed in exclusive patches around the world, or GMO mass produced standardised seeds that enrich the patent holders and the seed merchants more than the farmers? The first option is known as the Green Economy and the second one is part and parcel of the Green Revolution 2.0 that has embarked on a charm initiative worldwide since the benefits to the proponent by creating a legal monopoly based on patents is simply too hard to resist. Instead of pursuing the debate between green economy and GMO, we like to put forward as the core challenge as how to deal with the contradiction between using the land and keeping the land fertile.

A Third Way

I like to suggest that there is not an either or, but rather an opportunity to change the rules of the game inspired by the way in which Blue Economy works. Let us be reminded that the Blue Economy proposes to work with what we have, first and foremost locally, and this includes local biodiversity. Inspired by the vision of Vaclac Havel, the playwright and dissident who went on to become the President of Czechoslovakian Republic, who stated that learning is seeing connections we never saw before, I propose that we need to focus on the basics and understand better how we can respond to the challenge of feeding the world in general and China in particular.

The most important key to long-term success in farming, and feeding a population is the continuous rebuilding of a topsoil rich in organic matter. When a society neglects replenishing its farmland with nutrients, poverty and food insecurity will begin dominate. China is the first culture in the world to have deliberately engaged in replenishing the soil, better even, generating topsoil in regions void of that thin layer of life generating substance, which is a precondition for a permanent food supply.

Silk had originated in the times of Huangdi (Yellow Emperor)—a legendary ruler and one of ancestors of the Chinese nation—some 4,000 years ago. Leizu was the Empress, the first wife of Huangdi. It was Leizu that taught the people how to plant mulberry trees in dry land and practice sericulture, to reel silk from cocoons, and spin and weave silk into fabric. Within a decade, it led to the creation of a thin layer of soil. The excrements of silkworms eating about half of mulberry leave catalysed a regenerative process in the soil, now increasingly protected from the sun. When years after starting this regenerative process fruits and vegetables could be planted underneath these trees, it was obvious that this would transform into a way of life, that is found to be surviving even today.

While silk has never lost the favour of the consumers, synthetic fibres such as nylon, rayon and polyamide could be produced at will from petrochemicals. It is the low price and comparative efficiency that has restrained planting of mulberry trees and sericulture, especially in the Pearl River Delta and the Yangtze River Delta. Sericulture is moving to the less developed areas in northern China. However, once we realise that raw silk has the potential to substitute titanium in medical applications, thus representing a value that is a multiple compared to the clothing option, there is a new logic that motivates us to rethink reforestation with mulberry. Millions of hectares of land could be saved from desertification—not just with planted trees to capture carbon dioxide—with the purpose to generate or to replenish topsoil.

This requires a careful choice of tree species that invite animals, fungi, micro-algae and bacteria to repopulate the area in order to create these fertile layers on which life depends. Some varieties of mulberry trees survive on little water in its early life, and are most generous co-habitant of the ecosystem. In order to prevent desertification, China has planted more trees than any other nation in the world, especially in three northern parts of the country. China chooses the species of trees in line with local climate and soil conditions—diversiform-leaved desert poplar (Populars diversifolia)in Xinjiang Autonomous Region; *Paulownia fortunei* along the Yellow River in Henan Province; and gingko (*Gingko biloba*) along the northern bank of the Yangtze River and Chinese yew tree on its southern bank for its great medical value. Although I can imagine China engaging in at least one million square kilometres (100 million hectares) of reforestation with mulberry-like trees to preserve the long-term health of farmlands, a second opportunity emerges elsewhere: the cities.

Regeneration of Topsoil

If we maintain the focus that food security depends first and foremost on the generation of topsoil, as a precondition of 'being able to feed the world', then there is a need to recover all nutrients from the cities. Although the farming culture and tradition in China has been recycling nutrients for over millennia, through a sophisticated combination of anaerobic digesters, algae farming in the slurry, multiple crops, intercropping, earthworm rearing, mushroom cultivation and fish farming with many variations to the same theme depending on the locally available resources, this approach has been sidetracked in the drive towards urbanisation. The Chinese practiced permaculture (eco-agriculture) and its adaptations, hundreds of years before it had even become a concept in the Western societies. The question China should resolve is how to avoid falling into the trap of modernity where all these valuable resources are converted into problems ranging from costly waste water treatment systems, water table contamination smelly waste dumps that emit massive volumes of methane gas with solutions that only cost money.

China is one of countries in the world to have used biogas technology early in its history. By the end of the 19th century, simple biogas digesters had appeared in the coastal areas of southern China. Mr Luo Guorui invented and built an eight cubic metre Guorui biogas tank in 1920, and established the Santou Guorui Biogas Lamp Company; moved the company to Shanghai and established many branches along the Yangtze River and in the southern provinces. *Chinese Guorui Biogas Digester Practical Lecture Notes* was published in 1935, the first monograph on biogas in China and in the world. By the end of 2006, China had built 18.7 million digesters in rural areas, 140,000 sewage digesters, and more than 2,000 livestock, poultry and industrial wastewater biogas engineering facilities, with annual production of 9 billion cubic metres biogas, providing high quality biogas for 80 million people. The annual production of biogas is projected to reach 25 billion m^3 by 2020. An English agronomist had once said that as the Chinese farmers return all decayed organic matter to the soil, China can support a large rural population and maintain soil fertility at the same time, before the end of 1970s.

In addition to animal waste, there are two other major streams of nutrients in any society: night soil and food waste. The Western solutions to night soil are septic tanks connected to sewage networks and water treatment plants, and landfills or incinerators for the second flow of waste created by leftover food. If China were to embrace these two options heavily promoted by World Bank and others as a means to enter the modern world, then the regeneration of topsoil will be in peril. This is not just a matter of tradition or technology; it is a matter of turning the Chinese economy into one that is multiple times more efficient than the Western culture has ever been able to achieve. While Leonardo da Vinci already designed cities where the flow of human waste and left-over food were carefully channelled out of the city centres as a basic tool to preserve the health of its citizens and as a source for further production, this logical insight has never been adopted by Western societies. The recovery of organic waste is a matter of smart economics; it reflects a consciousness of the strategic importance to recover nutrients permanently, and secure that the natural cycles continue uninterrupted. In the process, one can generate energy, especially biogas, carbon dioxide which is a gas required for industrial use, and fertilisers capable of replenishing topsoil, and under some conditions even create topsoil.

Night soil, which has lost its traditionally positive name, has been viewed by Western society as a problem. It is only a problem when urine and faeces are blended together with water, not only ruining the nutritional value, it leads to squandering of the most valuable resource required for food security: water! Chinese farmers have always maintained a policy of water conservation. The first irrigation channels in the world were established in China, where a shortage of water occurred in Chengdu plain and Guanzhong plain. In the parts of China suffering from excess of water, the dyke systems were developed to keep the water into ponds supplying extra capacity for protein production. In both circumstances, China turned the problems of either shortage or excess into opportunities for food generation. It is key to point out that rain water is void of nutrients, and therefore needs to be enriched in order to channel necessary energy providers to the roots, which otherwise would never shoot.

Recovery of Water

The urban societies have one generation to come up with an adapted format of its rural traditions of nutrient cycling. If we assess the existing infrastructure in recently built urban zones, then it seems that a 21st century edition of dykes and ponds are timely for China. The Chinese government has already invested at great expense in newly constructed municipal wastewater treatment plants. At the same time, urban households have no means of composting organic waste in their apartments, which ends up in recently built landfills, and increasingly are channelled to 'waste to energy' plants. China cannot permit these nutrients to be wasted or incinerated in a linear way. It needs to recover it all—indeed all that is water and nutrients. The immediate question is: while taxes are collected to pay for sewage, water treatment and landfill, there is no mechanism to pay for the recovery of topsoil, a process that has always been considered a commons. The provision of water was until recently also a commons; however, cities squander this precious resource that lead to scarcity and the only option that modern society has come up with is the commercialisation and privatisation of water supply.

The Blue Economy would approach the regeneration of topsoil and water with all available resources. The existing water treatment systems produce slurry. Some plants attempt to produce biogas—at great expense and with limited success. However, if the slurry is combined with the organic components of municipal solid waste (MSW), then the gas production can reach surprising proportions. The City of Ulsan in Korea was the first to embark on such a venture combining the best know-how from around the world and built a 14,000 m^3 digester attached to the municipal water treatment plant, which daily generates 30,000 m^3 of gas. If the same were extended to Seoul, solely using the four largest existing water treatment plants, then the total production of biogas has been calculated to reach 400 million m^3 annually. If this logic was applied to metropolis such as Shanghai, it could reach a staggering one billion m^3 of biogas per year. Slurry from the digester is a by-product with 60-70 per cent mineralised matter: an ideal amendment to the farmland. The generation of biogas with a return on investment in excess of 20 per cent, generates in addition one million tons of soil nutrients (1 ton for each 1,000 m^3). Instead of costing money, this approach generates adequate income to finance the investments, and provides soil as a commons.

This example demonstrates that all solutions are connected. In our search for more soil, we found more energy and more water at lower cost. This innovative approach does not only operate at lower cost, but also generates more revenues and reduces dependence on fossil fuels. Instead of taxing citizens for a programme to clean polluted water, and then again to deposit the MSW, now a smart investment strategy permits to take the cost off the city's budget and generates income while securing that there is a link between the city and the rural environment that depends on nutrient cycling in order to maintain and even strengthen its capacity to generate food. This could even lead to reduction of taxes, which is always appreciated by the voters and the policymakers. Additionally, it reduces the impact on climate.

The increased demand for water is partly resolved. However, more is needed. Cities are diverting precious water from farm irrigation to flushing toilets. If the highly efficient toilet flushes that only use one and a half litre per use, and a newly invented toilet even free of water are installed, then it will be possible to cut down water consumption, and that of elements that contributes to the generation of soil nutrients. Unfortunately, too few strategic thinkers make the connection between nutrients, night soil, landfills and energy and irrigation water. However, it is exactly these integrated approaches that will lay the basis for a strategy that warrants that China will be able to feed itself.

Integrated Farming Systems (IFS)

Now, the basis of nutrient cycling and water is established, the two core inputs are safeguarded. A second innovation is required: the rediscovery of integrated farming systems (IFS). China has been the master in cascading of nutrients and energy, which has been copyrighted in modern days as Cradle to Cradle. I remember well my first visit to Wuxi's Asian-Pacific Regional Research and Training Centre for Integrated Fish Farming. This system generates so many nutrients that one needs to add surface aquaponics (floating gardens) to the fish ponds in order to convert this biological matter into food easily absorbed through the roots hanging in the water, an ideal additional feed for fish, further improving the uptake of nutrients into the system.

Prof George Chan, born in Mauritius is very well versed in IFS, after spending five years in his ancestral home. He had earned a degree in sanitary engineering from Imperial College, right after the Second World War. The logic of feeding pigs on food waste is nothing new and has been done for centuries. The channelling of manure into digesters is also broadly known and practiced. The conversion of the slurry from the biogas production into a base nutrient for micro-algae, that provides the core nutrients to plankton feeders and benthos, permits the farming of filter-feeding fish without artificial feed. In China, polyculture is always conducted with seven fish species in the same pond including filter-feeding species, grass feeder, omnivorous fish and carnivorous species, actually it emulates aquatic ecosystem in nature with many species to occupy different ecological niches in trophy.

Redundancy!

This system generates so much nutrients that one needs to add some aquatic macrophytes to the fish ponds in order to convert this biological matter into food (easily absorbed through roots hanging in the water), an ideal additional feed for grass-feeding fish, further improving the uptake of nutrients into the system. One cannot but be impressed with such efficient systems that beat every other farming system ever invented or practiced. This is a low maintenance, high output and low labour input responding to the needs of modern Chinese society that will face the graying of its population in the course of the next two decades, and therefore requires an approach to productivity that outpaces any existing standard.

The initiatives unfolding have to deal with rising sea levels and the 1.2 million hectares of flatland along the coasts that is likely to succumb to salinity and alkalinity of the shores due to climate change. When I travelled the coast line of Java (Indonesia) on the occasion of the 9th World Congress on Zero Emissions and the Blue Economy, organised by the Indonesian Blue Economy Foundation, created by Ibu Dewi Smaragdina and chaired by Ibu Sriworo Harijono in Jakarta, it became clear that China, Indonesia and so many more coastal nations need to embrace the farming of sea rice, or face the hardship of climate change.

Prof Li Kangmin, a member of the ZERI network of scientists since the beginning in 1994 and 'a student' of Prof George Chan, has written extensively on integrated aquaculture. His articles, "Extending Integrated Aquaculture to Mariculture in China—New Trends in Fish Farming" and "New Ideas and Approaches to Sustainable Seafood Products" summarise both his experience and vision. Prof Li Kangmin informed us about a major breakthrough in China. Mr Chen Risheng, a graduate from Zhanjiang Agricultural College (Guangdong), studied with his teacher, Prof LuoWenlie, discovered a wild flowering plant with resemblance to rice nearly 30 years ago. In 1987, Chen Rishen started testing this sea rice and 28 years later, his areal had grown to 133 Ha. He created the International Sea-Rice Biotechnology Company Ltd with a research staff of 80 in Beijing. The Chinese Ministry of Agriculture extended trials on alkaline-saline soils in Lingshui, Hainan; Zhanjiang, Guangdong; and Panjin, Liaoning. These test demonstrated that the rice can grow in a soil with a pH 9.3, where no trees can grow. The sea rice can withstand water logging and has no problems being submerged for 3-4 hours during high tide in plain seawater. Since sea rice does not need fresh water, it saves in the order of 1,000 m^3 of fresh water per ton of rice, without any need of fertilisers.

China has an estimated 100 million hectares of saline-alkaline soil. Indonesia has an estimated 150 million hectares along its coastal zones, which is the longest in the world. If both nations were able to grow rice on saline land with a yield of 2,250 kg/ha, then one can expect an additional production of 225 million tons in China and 337 million tons in Indonesia. The conclusion of this breakthrough level of productivity is that both China and Indonesia can feed themselves adequately. However, if we add the clusters described here and also the mushroom farming on rice straw, and carry out the conversion of the substrate into animal feed after harvesting the fungi, then we can realise that this world is set to create abundance where the majority sees scarcity. We see millions of new jobs, where others worry about terrorism and extremism as the result of high youth unemployment rates, for which the traditional economic model of globalisation does not see any outcome on the basis of all statistical analysis. That is why we refuse to look at the statistics and take it as a reality. We are well aware that we have to create a new reality.

Although one cannot pretend that China can feed herself with a briefing of only a few pages, one can understand that the country has all the basic know-how, tradition and culture to make it happen. Instead of quickly embracing GMOs and chemical controls, we should take more time to deploy highly efficient IFS which has allowed Chinese farmers to successfully feed the whole population over the past 8,000 years. Perhaps, the greatest challenge is to modernise China while embracing and strengthening the practices that are the basis of its greatness throughout history. This holistic approach, interconnected thinking, and careful collective planning with a remarkable capacity to observe and emulate natural processes is not only needed to ensure that China can feed its citizens, but also in order to ensure that the whole world can embark on a production and consumption system that responds to the basic needs of all, where necessities and benefits for human beings and nature are cheap, and the indispensiable commons are free.

Ilya Prigogine, the Belgian Nobel Prize Winner, has indicated that Chinese traditional philosophy emphasises studying harmony and coordination as well as holism and spontaneity. The development of modern science is more in conformity with Chinese philosophical concept. If the Western science reaches an understanding of totality and harmony with Chinese culture, it will lead to new natural philosophy and new natural concepts. A system that can indeed make certain that China can feed itself—as it has been doing for eight millennia.

Snapshot

Photo 1

A real view of the regeneration of the rainforest by Las Gaviotas, with the left-over biodiversity along the rivers, and the savannah

Photo 2

The local processing plant at Las Gaviotas producing biofuels from tree resin

Photo 3

Tapping trees at Las Gaviotas

Photo 4

Paolo Lugari holding mycorrhizal fungi at the Las Gaviotas reforestation in the Vichada (Colombia)

Photo 5

Father Nzamujo, founder of the Songhai Center in Porto Novo, Benin

Photo 6

Maggots at the Elsenberg farm of Agri-Protein in South Africa

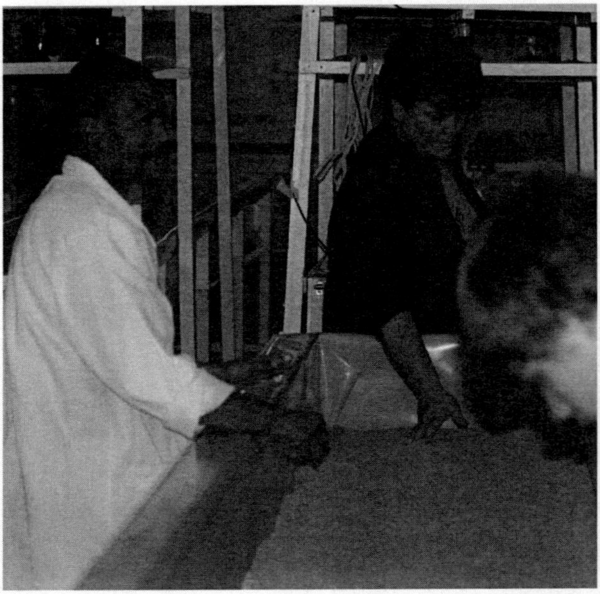

Photo 7

Soldier fly incubation area in preparation for maggot farming at AgriProtein research center in Franshoek, South Africa

Photo 8

ChidoGovera in Obuasi, Ghana, when women learn about the solutions to have food security, then they will sing and dance

Photo 9

Even children can harvest mushrooms, Philipp-Emmanuel at the age of 3

Photo 10

An intense harvest of Pleurotus sp. on coffee waste

Photo 11

Mushroom farming in Colombia (Manizales) on coffee waste

Photo 12

Nikhil Arora, ChidoGovera, Alejandro Velez setting up BTTR Ventures in San Francisco Bay area

Photo 13

Women and children attending ChidoGovera's training course in Obuasi, Ghana

Photo 14

Anders Nyquist mentioned in the chapter on Design with the Flows

Photo 15

The Laggarberg School designed by Anders Nyquist in Timrå, Sweden with the termite ventilation system

Photo 16

The landscape of El Hierro prior to the installation of the energy and water systems

Photo 17

The government of El Hierro (Canary Isles) dedicated to self-sufficiency in water and energy

Photo 18

Porto Torres, Sardinia, Italy: ENI chemical plant before reconversion into a biorefinery by Novamont

Photo 19

Bioitalia: the reconversion of an old chemical plant into a biorefinery by Novamont

Epilogue: Realising a Dream

I see skies of blue, and clouds of white,
The bright blessed day, the dark sacred night.
And I think to myself ... what a wonderful world.

— RECORDED BY LOUIS ARMSTRONG
(COMPOSED BY BOB THIELE AND GEORGE DAVID WEISS)

In 1994, the Zero Emissions Research Initiative (ZERI) pioneered the conversion of coffee pulp waste from the farm into protein by using the waste to grow mushrooms for human consumption and feeding animals the spent substrate. It took nearly a decade of research before each step in the process from farm to consumer was certified. Twenty-two scientific publications provide the backbone of the Pulp-to-Protein program. There are over 10,000 people working with mushrooms in Colombia, along with dozens of villagers in Zimbabwe, who base their livelihood on these simple and sustainable practices. In addition, Indian villages used this technique to become self sufficient in food production, following many years of malnutrition and hunger. By 2014, training programs introduced the systems approach to farmers in Colombia, Ecuador, Brazil, Dominican Republic, Ghana, Tanzania, Congo, South Africa, Cameroon, Mozambique, and launched in inner-cities from the Netherlands, to France, Belgium, Spain, Mexico, South Korea, Australia and the USA. And it only has just begun!

"Coffee waste is an amazing substrate for mushrooms, rich in fibres and caffeine," explains Emilio Echeverri, the former Vice President of the Colombian Coffee Federation. Echeverri supported the Pulp-to-Protein program from its inception and was later elected governor of the coffee-growing state of Caldas. In a caffeine growth medium, mushrooms reach maturity three times faster than when farmed on oak, thus offering the potential to save oak and be competitive owing to a better cash flow.

Carmenza Jaramillo undertook research on farming white button mushrooms (*Agaricus bisporus*) in 1978. After she learned the basics about tropical mushrooms from Prof Shuting Chang, she embarked on six years of research and published peer-reviewed articles in both English and Spanish international journals, she was completely committed to the goals of the initiative. She started her own

The Future of Hope in Zimbabwe

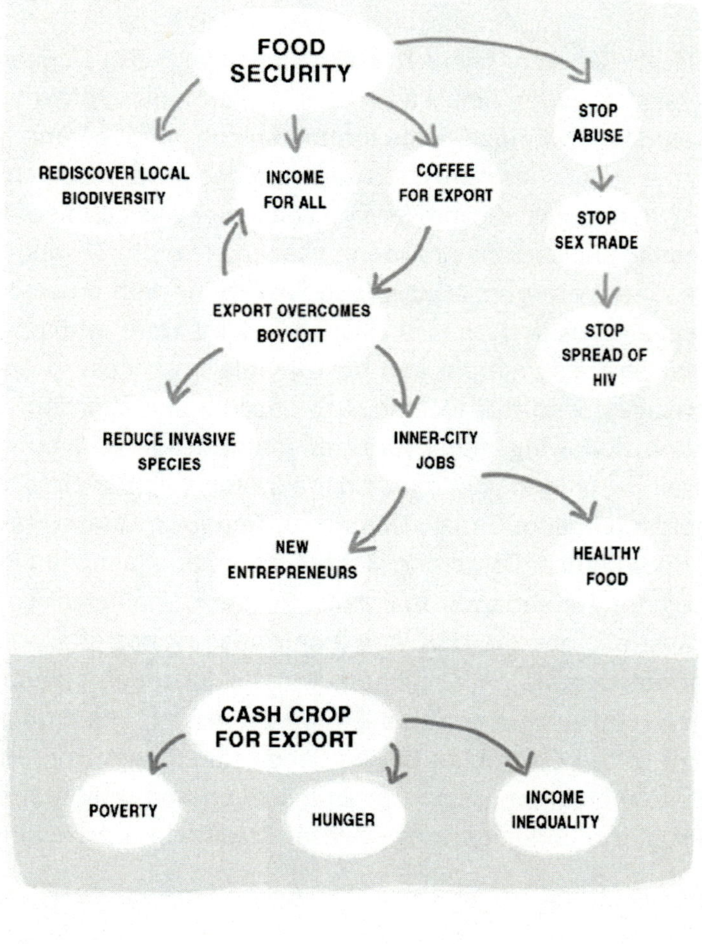

mushroom farm in Manizales, Colombia, and trained many others. By now Carmenza's students, like Francenid Perdomo, have become the experts, generously training others and cascading the knowledge to help many others achieve food security. Sharing this information over open source is the basis of its success.

In parallel, Chido Govera, a Zimbabwe-born orphan who survived for years on a bowl of peanuts a day, learned this method of farming mushrooms at the age of 11. She went from poverty to self-sufficiency over a span of few months. Chido had the unique opportunity to spend two years at science laboratory of Africa University in Mutare, Zimbabwe. Under the guidance of Margaret Tagwira at the University's horticultural laboratory, Chido perfected her knowledge of mushroom tissue culture and complemented her natural talents with science. It is evident that Chido has the proverbial 'green thumb'. What she touches produces food.

Paul Katzeff is a social entrepreneur who created Thanksgiving Coffee in Mendocino, California, and was the first in the US to sell certified Fair Trade coffee. His company was the first in California to become carbon neutral by offsetting emissions through planting 75,000 trees in Ethiopia. Also they were the first to operate their corporate car fleet fueled by biodiesel. Katzeff introduced all his colleagues in the Specialty Coffee Association of America (SCAA) to the Pulp-to-Protein concept developed by the diligent women of the ZERI Network. According to Katzeff:

> We have always been stuck between the cash crop and local development. But now, the waste of the cash crop is providing food security. This is the economic model to follow.

Small Success in California

Following the economic crisis of 2008, the ZERI Foundation proposed the conversion of coffee grounds into mushrooms as one of the many rapid and pragmatic responses. The idea was enthusiastically greeted by Mrs Makini Hassan, director of the Marin City Community Development Corporation. Her statement was emphatic. "We are going to do this!" she exclaimed, after learning the details. "With unemployment reaching 11 per cent in California, we need to create jobs, now!"

Chido Govera and Carmenza Jaramillo were present to speak before the SCAA's conference held in Atlanta, Georgia in April 2009, where ZERI received the Association's 2009 Sustainability Award. It was a first much-appreciated recognition and dozens more followed for the entrepreneurs who rendered this business model mainstream. Subsequently, they traveled to San Francisco to demonstrate how to convert the coffee grounds waste from Peet's Coffee & Tea shops into an ideal mushroom-growing medium. They took their expertise to Marin City, an urban area between Sausalito and Mill Valley. The response from Mrs Makini Hassan was effusive. Seldom is there an opportunity such as this to pursue a social enterprise that provides a creative and meaningful way for youth and young adults to generate revenue, meet a viable market need, and learn from this hands-on entrepreneur, Chido Govera, a brilliant method of providing sustainable produce.

Chido and Carmenza helped Nikhil Arora and Alex Velez—both top students in their class at the UC Berkeley's Haas School of Business—to inoculate the first 500 pounds of coffee grounds with mushroom spore and launch Back To The Roots (BTTR) Ventures, their entrepreneurial effort to achieve sustainable income from sustainable practice. Paul Stamets, the American mushroom guru, donated his best spawn to get the production process in the Bay Area going. "If it works in Zimbabwe and Colombia where the conditions are tough, then it can definitely work here," concluded Arora, who dropped a well-paid consulting job to join Velez and pioneer this business model in the Bay Area. Velez stated:

> The beauty is that coffee grounds have only been touched by steam and boiling water. This means the substrate is sterilised and as such, 80% of the energy cost for preparing the growth substrate for mushrooms is eliminated.

The raw material is free, the energy demand is tiny, and product demand is huge. All these factors mean that these young entrepreneurs can offer quality fresh mushrooms at or even below market price, garnering them a greater market share. In addition, the caffeine causes the mushrooms to fruit faster, which in turn That generates better cash flow and achieves more product than competitive mushroom-growing operations. The substrate that remains after harvest is rich in protein and serves as great fertiliser or as feed for chickens, goats, and even bison, as a pilot project with the Picuris Pueblo in New Mexico has demonstrated. However, in the San Francisco Bay area where livestock is rare, it likely has a better future as a feed for house pets like cats and dogs, or as compost for community gardens.

Coffee, Invasive Species and Local Biodiversity

A third opportunity subsequently emerged. I met with Charles Higgins, the Executive Director of Slide Ranch, an organic farm located within the Golden Gate Recreational Park along the Marin County coast. Almost immediately we began collaboration on an extension of the Pulp-to-Protein project right along the beach. One of the Park Services' goals is to remove non-native invasive species. Such an undertaking requires significant time and money. However, if these invasive species are blended with coffee grounds, which have been generously supplied by Equator Estate Coffees & Teas in nearby San Rafael, they become edible mushrooms. Chido, who was able to successfully farm mushrooms on grass clippings, broken branches, and corncobs in her village back in Africa, looked at the invasive species and concluded, "It is like being in Heaven. We have never had such a wealth of biomass in Zimbabwe."

Having three trial units operational in only two weeks is indicative of the potential of the Pulp-to-Protein model. According to Nikhil, "Only 8-10 coffee shops suffice to create a production unit, each of which can generate about 10 jobs." Realising that the Bay Area has an estimated eight million inhabitants, the potential is such that mushrooms could become a protein source comparable to and as readily available as chicken. At the same time, it generates good income, creates thousands of jobs and offers inexpensive, high quality food. Even though Alex and Nikhil had to struggle to get the business off the ground, they persevered in their ambitious goal for BTTR to create 250 jobs. By 2015, their team had grown to 20. The sky is the limit, but some estimates suggest that coffee grounds alone could generate 50,000 jobs in America. Why wait to try it out?

Arora and Velez were selected by Newsweek in 2009 as one of the Top 25 Entrepreneurs who are younger than 25 and then in 2012 as one of the Top 30 Entrepreneurs younger than 30 published by Forbes. Then they were part of the 100 fastest growing companies in the San Francisco Bay area, beating many of the emerging internet start-ups. They were runners-up in the BBC World Challenge, a global competition aimed at finding projects or small businesses from around the world that have shown enterprise and innovation at a grass-roots level. The business model inspires. Jan Willem Bosmans Jansen who launched a comparable business in the Netherlands in cooperation with La Place, the Dutch restaurant chain, was twice elected as the sustainable entrepreneur. While Nikhil and Alex evolved to home-growing mushroom kits, Jan Willem went on to convert his excess output in croquettes slowly but steadily moving up the value chain, giving a new purpose to the bankrupt greenhouses that dot the farmland of Egmont, North of Amsterdam. Cédric Péchard from France launched mushroom farms in containers downtown Paris. What a challenge to get a permit to take the place of a parked car.

Wild mushrooms that may cost US$25 per pound in season, and are impossible to get out of season, may soon be available year-round, thanks to coffee grounds and invasive species blended with the entrepreneurial approach of Nikhil and Alex. Such an approach reduces landfill, cut down on methane gas production, and increases consumer awareness regarding the solutions to sustainability to be found in their own backyard.

While briefly residing in Mill Valley, I often visited Muir Woods. I was continually amazed by its rich biodiversity evident just in the assortment of fungi I observed. The search for endemic mushrooms in local forestry areas is not a new initiative. It has already been done in New Mexico where the initiatives led to creation of the first ever 'State Mushroom Spore Bank' in the US. The Spore Bank was initiated by Lynda Taylor, one of my first students in America. At a time when Americans are becoming increasingly aware of the need to eat healthy food, mushrooms that are rich in protein and all essential amino acids, and are very low on cholesterol and saturated fatty acids, offer an excellent option. The production scheme proven elsewhere, and now tested by BTTR Ventures in the Bay Area, will provide the basis for nationwide production.

Overcoming a Boycott

Both Chido and Carmenza returned to their native countries, following their contribution to job-generating schemes in America. Both are generous and share their know-how. When Chido attended the local church service during her stay in Marin City, she was asked by one of the parishioners, "Do you like America?" Although she responded in the affirmative, Chido added that she had a mission in Zimbabwe and wished to return. She has made a promise to reach out to the orphan girls, and train them to achieve food security and self-sufficiency with nature as their helpmate. On the last day of her visit in the US, Chido met with Helen Russell and Brooke McDonnell, the co-founders of Equator Estate Coffees & Teas, the women-led coffee wholesaler in San Rafael, California. The idea emerged to create 'Chido's Blend' and for the first time in perhaps a decade to bring premium coffee from Zimbabwe to the US. After years of boycott, farmers from Zimbabwe would have the opportunity to sell their exceptional coffees to US consumers!

Chido hopes that over the next decade, she can reach out to thousands of girls throughout Africa. She will not rest as long as orphans are abused or consider themselves as victims. They are desperate for gaining access to a well with water, an earthen hut, and a small plot of land to tend as a vegetable garden for feeding themselves. The usual price they must pay is that of submitting to abuse, most often by their own relatives. As orphans neither have a living mother, nor a father who will pay a dowry, few can ever get married. However, if these orphans have a skill that enables them to feed their family, then that supersedes the need for a dowry. Chido collected all her life savings and mobilised donations from private individuals and the Rotary Clubs of Belgium, Germany and Zimbabwe to open up in 2015 The Future of Hope Center in Zimbabwe, just outside Harare and will start rescuing the girls one by one. The money that she had earned from teaching communities about ways to farm mushrooms on agro-waste will now serve to build a network of positive change where it needs to happen: in the local community.

From these experiences, we can realise that the world is replete with connections. In natural systems, everything is connected to everything else. We see that in our modern society, we can connect surmounting a trade boycott with the export of a cash crop, the waste of which becomes food security and inturn generates jobs both in Africa and in American inner-cities. Food security makes independence and self-sustenance possible. Over-owing dependence can eliminate the preconditions for abuse, and promote conditions for health and prosperity. All this can be made possible by coffee drinkers in the US who purchase Chido's Blend coffee from Equator Estate Coffees & Teas. It is a profound example of how individual consumer choices can carry us far toward affecting economic outcomes in far away places. In the same way, Chido's work as mentor to Zimbabwean orphans and to ecologically dedicated entrepreneurs is a profound example of how one individual can affect the lives of many.

We may hope that these small successes can inspire others to greater achievements, and that individuals everywhere will realise the meaning and importance of contribution to a Blue Economy in their own lives. A Blue Economy embraces the contributions of all. A Blue Economy cascades in endless innovation and evolution, utilising all contributions and benefitting all participants.

From ZERI to 100

I established the ZERI Foundation in 1996 to explore, imagine and discover strategic levers to development that would promote true sustainability. My ongoing work is to mentor individuals, businesses, and even nation states to become aware of the perfection that nature achieves and to understand that a Blue Economy will lead to an energetic and sustainable success for the people and places of the planet. My current work with smaller communities like the island of El Hierro (Canary Isles, Spain), Nusa Penida (Bali, Indonesia), La Colosa and Gramalote (Colombia), Western Cape (South Africa) and even larger regions like Bhutan, or the City of Johannesburg (South Africa), allows me to mentor in situ economic development with an inclusive growth. We scan for opportunities, screen building up consensus on the projects that everyone agrees on and then we focus on implementation. Using innovations from the growing portfolio of environmental innovations implies that smaller communities can leapfrog over the globalised world's missed opportunities, thereby eliminating the propagation of poverty, pollution and disease.

It is fascinating that when small communities hear about the Blue Economy, there is an immediate urge to sing and dance, celebrating this new vision. Whenever you are sharing this portfolio of breakthroughs in the economic centres, be it a capital city, a multinational corporation or an investment banker, the first request is to submit a feasibility study, followed by an independent technology audit, in order to obtain a small budget for undertaking a pilot project. Of course, no one in the centre of power is prepared to even consider a next step, unless there is a paper report on the table. Never have projects proceeded beyond this trial, and therefore we prefer not to engage along this logic anymore. With passion and science, navigating between fantasy and reality, we can embark on a pervasive strategy to steer society towards sustainability by simply executing the plans. As this updated version goes to press, nearly 200 projects have been implemented, covering nearly every possible sector of the economy and every need in society. It is this capacity of a network of people to pursue their dreams and even go beyond them, that motivates me to maintain by perseverance.

Change Starts in the Periphery

The population of El Hierro has turned down the proposals for installation of a satellite launching platform or a radar monitoring station. They have sought alternatives that could meet their most important criteria: to provide a sustainable future rich with opportunities for future generations. They have opted for innovations described in this book, and invented a few other that are certainly the subject of another book. The public and the private sectors had raised the cash needed to make the entire island of El Hierro self-sufficient in water and energy by the middle of 2014. The farmers have agreed that all agriculture will be produced to organic and sustainable standards within seven years.

All agro-waste will be dedicated to mushroom cultivation. Spent substrate will become compost, or will be cascaded to animal feed. Ivanka Milenkovic has committed her support to this goal. In addition, they intend that within a decade, every single car on the island will be powered with electricity or compressed air from the surplus wind. The original investments required more than US$100 million. How could a small community of 10,500 inhabitants ever raise so much capital? The starting point in the search for funds were the millions that leave the island economy each year to purchase petroleum. The net present value, duly calculated by an MBA (Master of Brilliant Adaptation) who has an MBA (Master of Business Administration) provided an initial fund that covered the start-up requirements.

The security of energy, and the abundance of water stimulates the local economy. Now the *abattoir* operates on the island, increasing the value of animal husbandry for the local farmers. The cheese and yoghurt factory processes goat and sheep milk into delicacies blending herbs and fruits, permitting the local cooperative to pay its members a multiple for their supplies compared to that from the traditional sales to a middlemen who would push it through the distribution channels of supermarkets. The fruit farmers diversify into bananas and pineapples, and the quality grapes are converted into local wines. The islanders of El Hierro never dreamed to compete in a globalised economy. They desired to preserve their community, tradition and ecosystem that are regularly stressed by a shaking earth and underwater volcanic eruptions. Owing to the leadership of islanders of the calibre of Javier Morales, El Hierro has set its mark on the world map as the first island in the industrialised world that is self-sufficient in water and energy, while simultaneously generating jobs at a time when unemployment in Spain tops record levels.

Roald Marth, the Los Angeles-based renewable energy expert who had once dreamt of taking the whole island of Hawaii off the petroleum habit, visited the energy facilities of El Hierro and immediately offered to invest and uphold this to the world. The Herreños, who wanted to safeguard their community, now find an interest from the world in their technologies intermitting wind and water without a battery back-up, while Juan Manuel Quintero, the general manager of Gorona del Viento, the water and energy company only thought of doing a good job. When ordinary people go beyond the obvious, and rise to the occasion, they are able achieve something extraordinary simply by working hard.

Buckwheat in Bhutan

An island that is part of Europe but located off the coast of Africa, is similar to Bhutan, squeezed between China and India, and without the ambition to become a global player in anything else than spreading the word of happiness. The Himalayan Kingdom opened up its borders and was soon advised to become part of the global economy, until it hit home that buckwheat from Ukraine commands a competitive price of US$200 per ton, while the cost price in Bhutan is closer to US$2,000. The Bhutanese, who have farmed their bitter and sweat buckwheat for perhaps 3,000 years, see their millennium traditions evaporate in years with their desire to become part of this global village. At the same time, cheap and genetically modified rice is imported from Thailand, and chemical-rich vegetables and fruits flood the local markets. Buckwheat seems to have no future and farmers wonder who will ever buy their produce.

While trade experts are quick to point out the lack of efficiency and productivity, the benefit of trade based on comparative advantages, and urge Bhutan to join the World Trade Organization (WTO), most citizens realise that free trade based on selling and buying commodities worldwide at the lowest cost does include a future for Bhutan! A new business model imposes itself. A portfolio of opportunities emerged and with enthusiasm and commitment initiatives crystallised one after the other blending the desire to generate jobs for the educated young, to preserve culture and tradition, while maintaining the fragile mountain ecosystems on their evolutionary path.

His Excellency Jigme Yoser Thinley, the first democratically elected Prime Minister of Bhutan suggested that we look into the creation of an alcohol-free beer. It was the start of the creation of a new cluster. Jim Lueders, the creator of the Wildwood Brewery in Montana (USA), proposed to ferment beer with the malt extract from buckwheat. This implies that 92 per cent of the buckwheat is animal feed, and 8 per cent is used to make beer. Animals were never before fed adequately. Then a programme started to harvest wild yeast from the Himalayas to produce beer the way it has always been done. Now the malt extract and the wild yeast, not more then a few bottles, are the core ingredients of a licensing agreement, permitting small scale, high quality breweries to produce the Bhutan blend anywhere in the world. Kinley Tshering, the chief forester of Bhutan who got his degree in Montana, learned how to brew beer when he was a student. He is moving the project from idea to reality with the technical support of Jim. The economics of buckwheat shift overnight. Whereas Bhutanese buckwheat can never compete, the combination of malt extract and wild yeast with a licensing agreement that foresees a 5 per cent royalty on the end price to the consumer implies that each ton of buckwheat is now valued at approximately US$4,000 per ton. Bhutan now has a future for its millennia-old farming tradition, and the majority of nutrients remain within the country. In the process biodiversity (wild yeast) has become a key component in the success story. Would Ukraine ever be able to match this proposal? We are convinced that this is one of the projects that secures a competitive place for Bhutanese beer in the world market, while the locals will be served this healthy brew without the alcohol.

Regenerating the Forest of the Sea

The Caribbean islands suffer. The environment suffers and the people suffer. Unemployment is high, the import of fossil fuels is insatiable and the corals are under stress. The beaches are littered with plastics. Climate change is not helping. While the beauty of these islands is beyond discussion, the reality on the ground is hard. How can paradise be regained? The island of Bonaire, part of the Netherlands with a population of only 17,500 inhabitants, is one of the thousands that is searching for a livelihood; but here a portfolio of initiatives are unfolding that permit us to see a light at the end of the tunnel.

As Fritjof Capra, the systems expert and author, eloquently described—it is a web of life, not just life. Coral are no difference. The damage to the coral reefs is mainly caused by an overpopulation of goats. An estimated 30,000 goats eat all the shrubs they can find, causing soil erosion, and the continuous dust cloud troubles the water and blocks sunlight to the corals. The recovery of ecosystem of the reefs depend on the management of these goats. Now the solutions for soil erosion depends on the provision of feed, that should increasingly come from the sea, and the interface between the sea and the coast.

Mangroves dot the coastal lines and offer protection. The trimming of mangroves stimulates growth of the root system, strengthening carbon sequestration and resilience of the local ecosystem that is highly dependent on this plant species that provides livelihoods to shrimps, bees and flowers. Mangrove twigs and leaves mixed with salicornia, a salt tolerant plant, that grows along the beach and amongst mangroves, provides the ideal nutrition to goats. It is produced with the locally available resources. Now if the goats are well fed, based on readily available feed, then the plant life can recover.

However, if the goats are brought under control, then no further damage is done to the corals. While this is good news, it is insufficient to be content that further destruction has been averted. The key question that needs to be asked: can one restore the errors of the past? Corals have been described as slow growth, but scientific evidence has been accumulating indicating that corals can be stimulated to grow. Based on the experience of Las Gaviotas, the Colombian regeneration of the rainforest on land that had been denuded over two centuries ago, there is a small but growing cluster of scientists that has gathered the experience to plant pioneer species that enable biodiversity to come back. The 8,000 hectares of rainforest at Las Gaviotas started with a simple pine, and today has over 250 local species flourishing side by side and hundreds more are expected to be brought by the birds, bees and wind from the biodiversity that continues to thrive in the Orinoco Basin.

Las Gaviotas was described as "impossible", "a monoculture" and even "a change of ecosystem". Today the successful recuperation of both the ecosystem and the community that operate at full employment and is self-sufficient in water, food and energy, offers an inspiration for the corals. If it was possible to regenerate the forest on land, why not regenerate the forest of the sea? The science has demonstrated on a small scale that it is possible with elkhorn and staghorn corals. Is it possible to regenerate reefs starting with these prolific species? The critique is strong, just like when Las Gaviotas started a quarter of a century ago. However, the only way to discuss the opportunity is to create a new reality.

Martien van der Valk and Paul Coolen, entrepreneurs in tourism with decades of experience, saw the window of opportunity. Building on the available science, they created the Coral Restoration Foundation and started experimenting: is it possible to plant corals? It quickly proved to be possible. Hence, second question: how to manage the coral nursery? Unless one has an outstanding knowledge of the local lay of the land and the sea, it is hard to imagine the location would be the best site. Also, there is a need to adapt to the local conditions in order to build a platform that delivers corals in volume. Las Gaviotas faced the same problem: creating one million treelings per year, capable of resisting the 9-month-long dry summer and the turbulent three months of rain. The solution surfaced only after introduction of the mycorrhizal fungi.

The innovative design of the coral nursery turned out to be a set of plastic pipes, but it can one day also be old television-antennas. When coral are strung in a nutrient current, their growth is not only guaranteed, but also prolific. Three years of experience in nurseries and planting was summarised into a guidebook that became the basis of a diver's course approved by the Professional Association of Drivers (PADI). The confidence grows, and as usual, there is a need to scale up and that requires capital. If all reefs on Bonaire were to be restored to their original splendour, then perhaps as many as 100 million corals would be required. A quick calculation brings the total investment to €500. This is a mammoth task that few are ready to take on. How can this be overcome?

Paul Coolen and his team at BuddyDive see only one option: planting one at a time. Secure that the coral nurseries expand, motivate the tourists to come and learn how to plant, and inspire families to have a holiday with a purpose: regenerating the forests of the sea. After all, 70 per cent of the Earth is covered by water, and at €5 per coral, it only requires a few travel agencies to get the flow of tourists who all will want to return to see what their passion for putting the Earth on a sustainable course has achieved.

It Only Has Just Begun

While successes remain modest, a decade of worldwide effort can achieve major changes. There is no doubt that growing numbers of regions and nation states are becoming aware of and beginning to embrace sensible solutions and innovations that empower people and sustain communities. As initiatives emerge and collaborators share their successes, many will have the confidence to take the next step. Just as Chido Govera in Zimbabwe, Paolo Lugari in Colombia, Father Nzamujo in Benin, Javier Morales in Spain and Kinley Tshering in Bhutan have the vision to enact new ideas and bring them to fruition, thousands of others will step forward with similar vision and strength. We may hope that these ongoing efforts can inspire others to greater achievements, and that individuals everywhere will realise the significance and importance of contribution to a Blue Economy in their own lives. Cascading endless innovation and evolution, a Blue Economy embraces the contributions of all.

The principles of economy are that of a community. The principles of community are that of ecosystems. The success of our economies, of our communities, and of our planetary habitat depends on a collaborative effort to envision and achieve the abundance of a Blue Economy.

I must admit, that I have a hard time convincing policymakers and business leaders to the point that I have nearly given up. Instead, I am diverting more than 50 per cent of my energy and time to translate every successful project that is based on a vision, is driven by science and embarks on a balanced risk into a three-minute long fable. At the time of closing this epilogue, I have 204 fables written and a commitment to produce 365 so as to be able to expose children around the world to the unique opportunities to design and create this world with an inclusive growth. Working with the children offer a fresh approach to life since they never make a distinction between fantasy and reality: everything is reality.

The Blue Economy in Practice in India

The origin of this book, and much of the work described by Gunter Pauli in it relates to technologies inspired by nature—exemplified by the science of biomimetics. Nature has, over the billions of years and successive geological eons and epochs of its existence, developed proven techniques that are based on closed-cycle processes and leave behind neither pollution nor wastes.

As Pauli also shows that technology is not all that matters in determining vitality of the Earth's life support systems or health of our communities and economies. These are equally determined by the behaviour patterns of everyday people, their production systems and the way they make use of the resources present in mother nature.

In this new geological era of the Anthropocene, where one species—homo sapiens—is now in direct competion with the forces of all other natural processes and increasingly, is able to overwhelm some parts of it, all aspects of economic activity need to be realigned in order to regain the balance between society and nature.

This is where the Blue Economy (a worthy successor to the earlier but zero-sum based concept of Green Economy) comes in, bringing together nature-based technologies with humanity-based compassion so as to create new ways to improve human well-being, while keeping the economy within the limits of planetary boundaries.

The fact that the original version of the Blue Economy has been translated and published in more than 38 languages including braille for the blind and sign language for mute and deaf, and in many countries of the world, is testimony to the worldwide thirst for designing a new future.

In this reworked edition, with additional chapter and arguments based on concrete cases and experiences, published in a world premiere in India, Blue Economy 2.0 presents, in addition a few representative case studies from the work of Development Alternatives, which is the Indian counterpart of the Zero Emission Research and Initiatives network, ways by which science can help society in designing meaningful opportunities for creating livelihoods and also the goods and services that enable ordinary people meet their everyday needs.

Ashok Khosla
Chairman, Development Alternatives
Board Member, ZERI

Case Studies

Cascading Like Ecosystems

Ranked innovation	*Potential opportunities*	*Research/ Business Locale*	*Developer*
Eco-friendly urban building design	Low cost, resource and energy conserving, promoting climate change mitigation	India	Development Alternatives
Vertical shaft brick kiln technology	Energy and material efficiency, reduces pollution	India	Development Alternatives
Fly ash brick making technology	Waste recycling, emission free production	India	Technology and Action for Rural Advancement
Compressed earth block making technology	Low cost, eco-friendly and boosting local economy	India	Technology and Action for Rural Advancement
Check dams for water, food and livelihood security in rural India	Environmentally and economically sustainable, increases farmers' incomes, reduces migration	India	Development Alternatives

Substituting Something with Nothing

Ranked innovation	*Potential opportunities*	*Research/ Business Locale*	*Developer*
Chemical free paper technology using recycled materials	Waste recycling, preventing deforestation and pollution, creating sustainable livelihoods for rural producer groups	India	Technology and Action for Rural Advancement,
Tetra pack recycling paper technology	Recycling Tetra Pak cartons, creating wealth from waste	India	Technology and Action for Rural Advancement

contd...

...contd...

Platform Technologies

Ranked innovation	*Potential opportunities*	*Research/ Business Locale*	*Developer*
Water purification technologies for low income households	Providing safe drinking water, promoting good health, low cost, easy to use	India	Development Alternatives
Technologies for point of use (POU) water quality testing	Low cost, easy to use and reliable for promoting awareness on drinking water quality	India	Development Alternatives
Eco-concrete building technologies	Cost effective, environment friendly	India	Technology and Action for Rural Advancement

Innovation: Eco-friendly urban building design

Benefits: Low cost, resource and energy conserving, promoting climate change mitigation

Developer: Development Alternatives, India

Date: 2008

The rapidly growing construction industry accounts for 30–40 per cent of the primary energy consumed globally, one-sixth of the world's fresh water withdrawals and two-thirds of its material flows. It is currently one of the biggest contributors of greenhouse gas emissions responsible for global warming. The silver lining in the dark cloud is that greener alternatives are available that can help the construction sector take the lead in climate change mitigation.

The Development Alternatives world headquarters building, located in New Delhi, is a cutting-edge prototype that showcases environmentally and economically sound solutions for reducing the carbon footprint of construction. The building design optimises the use of local resources, materials and skills through the application of advanced scientific and engineering knowledge; thereby, reducing energy and resource consumption and overall construction costs. Use of virgin construction materials has been reduced by the utilisation of industrial waste materials, such as fly ash and stone dust; thus, creating wealth from waste and also reducing the embodied energy by 30 per cent. The building has re-used materials recovered from demolishing the earlier structure, demonstrating a responsible 'cradle to grave' construction approach. After demolition of the original building, earth removed from the site was recycled into compressed earth blocks that have been used in the building walls. Compressed earth blocks and fly-ash blocks have been used in 90 per cent of the interior and exterior walls. The fly-ash blocks were made using fly ash from a local power plant. As 90 per cent of the materials have been sourced from the regions neighbouring Delhi, CO_2 emissions from the transportation of building materials has been substantially reduced during construction of the Development Alternatives World Headquarters building.

Efficiency in material use is demonstrated in every aspect of this eco-building. Heavy concrete slabs have been replaced by resource efficient building products, such as ferro-cement channels. The stone flooring pattern has been designed to reduce wastage to less than 5 per cent. Teak wood harvested from certified plantations has been used for making the doors and windows. Broken white tiles bought as waste from factory yards have been used to decorate the roof terraces. The architect consciously departed from the use of high energy intensive materials, such as aluminium, steel and glass, generally used in modern urban architecture. This eco-building has incorporated less than half the reinforcing steel used in comparable structures of conventional design, thereby reducing resource consumption and greenhouse gas emissions. The beauty is that the use of these alternate construction technologies and materials has not compromised on the structural stability and quality of the building.

The spatial configuration of the building draws on the principles of passive design and vernacular architecture of the region using balconies, shading grills, terraces and screens that evolved in response to the climate. Innovative approaches, such as curtailing heat gain through the building fabric by ensuring favourable orientation with respect to the sun's trajectory and carefully designing shading and insulation of walls, windows and roofs, has helped save 40 per cent in operational energy consumed. Windows facing east and west, which are subjected to the morning and afternoon sun, have been kept small and shaded by sunscreens. Roof surfaces are finished in white tiles to reflect instead of absorb thermal energy. Micro-climate control is done by the use of features, such as an open central courtyard, a water pond and a water screen that cools the building walls through evaporation. To reduce the ecological footprint of the building and enable lower energy consumption, the Development Alternatives staff have adapted their lifestyle in favour of sustainability by accepting an indoor temperature range of 18-30 degree Celsius. This has substantially reduced the air conditioning load.

Water conservation measures are integral to this eco-building. All rainwater that falls at the site is used to recharge the groundwater, while wastewater is recycled and treated on site in an aerobic-anaerobic digestion tank and used for irrigation and flushing toilets. The cost-effective bio-sand, multilayer gravity filter designed by Development Alternatives is used to purify the drinking water. This costs a fraction of the energy-intensive, reverse osmosis system.

Being efficient in the utilisation of space, materials and energy, the Development Alternatives World Headquarters building exudes the technical sophistication appropriate for contemporary cities and demonstrates eco-friendly and cost-effective building technologies that have the potential to transform the face of the construction industry worldwide.

Innovation: Vertical shaft brick kiln technology

Benefits: Energy and material efficiency, reduces pollution

Developer: Development Alternatives, India

Date: 1998

Job Potential: 30 jobs per enterprise with an investment of US$100,000[1] in 2015

Most of the brick production in developing countries is done through traditional fixed chimney kilns and clamps which are highly polluting. The technologies used are very resource and energy intensive, which exert high pressure on virgin natural resources. In India alone, more than 350 million tons of fertile topsoil and 24 million tons of coal are used in brick production every year. This results in 42 million tons of CO_2 being released into the atmosphere annually; which amounts to 4.5 per cent of the national greenhouse gas emissions.

There are greener alternatives available in the form of the Vertical Shaft Brick Kiln (VSBK) technology. This is an extremely energy and resource efficient brick technology, which was originally developed in China. The VSBK has the lowest specific energy consumption (0.7-0.8 MJ/kg of fired bricks), making it the most energy-efficient brick kiln in the world. High energy efficiency results in reducing the quantum of working capital required for the VSBK operation. This technology uses 25-40 per cent less coal in comparison to the other common brick firing technologies like those used in the Fixed Chimney Bull's Trench Kilns (FC-BTK). Since the cost of coal is one of the major production costs involved in any brick kiln operation, the saving in coal makes the VSBK technology an economically efficient alternative. This technology also reduces pollution by almost 70 per cent, when compared to the traditional fixed chimney kilns, as it has much lower particulate matter (SPM) emissions and minimises the use of coal in its operations. Thus, the VSBK technology provides a cleaner working environment, with lesser dust and smoke, thereby minimising health risks of the workers.

1. The investment cost per enterprise does not include cost of land.

Development Alternatives (DA) pioneered the research and development of the VSBK technology in India to make it suit the Indian sub-continent conditions. DA's affiliate Technology and Action for Rural Advancement (TARA) has commercialised the VSBK technology in the form of the TARA EcoKiln. The construction of a TARA EcoKiln requires very little land. The EcoKiln with two shafts can be set up in just 2000 square metres of land. The four shaft kiln requires double the area i.e., 4000 square metres. The building of multiple shaft production units in the EcoKiln enhances the ratio of land use to production output. TARA has introduced high levels of standardisation in the design of the EcoKiln. The EcoKiln allows the entrepreneur complete control over product quality, unit production cost and pollution emissions. Fuel costs alone are at least 40 per cent lower than those associated with the operation of conventional kilns. Energy efficiency and environmental performance have been further improved through the introduction of refractory lining, fire control, chimney and handling systems. The EcoKiln is amazingly versatile for firing bricks with different qualities of soil. Generally, as a thumb rule if good bricks can be made in a Bull's Trench Kiln (BTK), the same soil can be used in an EcoKiln to make better bricks.

The working principle of the VSBK technology is based on the principle of combustion. The VSBK has a vertical shaft of rectangular or square cross-section. The kiln works as a counter current heat exchanger, with heat transfer taking place between the air moving up (continuous flow) and the bricks moving down (intermittent movement). Green bricks and crushed fuel in the form of coal are stacked into batches and loaded into the shaft from top of the EcoKiln. The combustion of coal takes place in middle of the shaft. Combustion air enters the shaft from the bottom, gets preheated by hot fired bricks in the lower portion of the shaft before reaching the combustion zone. Hot combustion gases preheat green bricks in the upper portion of the shaft, before exiting from the kiln through the shaft or the chimney. Bricks move down the shaft through the pre-heating, firing and cooling zones and are finally unloaded at the bottom of the shaft. The operation requires special skills and training of firemen, fire masters and supervisors. A batch of bricks is loaded and unloaded every 2-3 hours. After the firing process is completed within 24-30 hours, these eco-bricks show a fine, deep red colour and have a good, metallic ring. A compressive strength of up to 200 kg/cm^2 can be achieved using appropriate soil.

TARA EcoKiln uses an inherently fast firing process. Unlike, the conventional firing process of BTKs or clamps, where the firing time is measured in days (14–21 days), the TARA EcoKiln's firing process is completed within 24-36 hours. Thus, the time for uniform heat distribution within the green bricks is short. To ensure uniform heat distribution within the entire cross-section of the mass, there is a need to provide heat from within the green bricks too, apart from the external heat that is given. This heat distribution within the green bricks is achieved through the use of internal fuel. Internal fuel generally comprises medium calorific value materials (1000-2000 Kcal/kg) mixed with the soil during the green brick formation process. The various types of internal fuels recommended for use in the TARA EcoKiln are generally waste materials, such as boiler ash, sponge iron waste, bottom ash from thermal power plants, rice husk ash and other carbon bearing wastes.

The VSBK technology also offers the advantage of uniformity in the quality of production. It is not possible to achieve uniform quality of fired bricks in any other brick firing technology due to heat loss. However, it is possible to achieve 95 per cent uniformity of quality in a VSBK. Compared to traditional clamps, where the brick quality is significantly inconsistent, a VSBK produces mostly first-grade bricks. Breakages and wastage can be limited to less than 5 per cent through stable and well-designed operation of loading and unloading.

Brick production using the VSBK technology is a profitable business for small and medium scale enterprises. Weather factors have minor influence over the VSBK operations. With a roof protection, the eco-kiln can be operated all year round, unlike the traditional ones that do not have this advantage and therefore have to be closed down in the rainy season. The VSBK requires very little maintenance once it is constructed, which contributes to it emerging as an economically viable option. This technology also offers a great deal of flexibility in production as the bricks can be produced according to the market demand. The firing of the shafts is independent from each other, which means it is not necessary to fire or close all the shafts together. A decision on the number of shafts to be operated can be made depending on the availability of dried green bricks and market demand. If the demand is high, all the shafts can be operated and if not, only a limited number can be used to meet the required demand.

The TARA EcoKiln is available in multiple configurations of two, four and six shafts. The most popular model is of the 2-shaft EcoKiln, which produces 10,000 bricks per day and saves up to 50 per cent in energy and fuel cost. A capital investment of US$100,000 can yield a turnover of US$250,000 per annum. The investment made in the eco-kiln is usually recovered within 3 years of operation. Construction of the kiln is completed within 60 days and saleable production is available within 48 hours of the kiln stabilisation. The

EcoKiln technology, thus, provides a quick turnover as bricks are ready for sale within two days of loading.

TARA has a rapidly expanding EcoKiln network currently exceeding 100 enterprises in India. This technology is also transferred to countries in Africa and South Asia such as Malawi, South Africa, Vietnam, Bangladesh, Nepal, Pakistan and Afghanistan.

Innovation: Fly ash brick making technology
Benefits: Waste recycling, emission free production
Developer: Technology and Action for Rural Advancement, India
Date: 2005
Jobs potential: 8-15 direct and 30-40 indirect jobs per enterprise with an investment of USD 70,000[2] in 2015

Most of the electricity produced in India comes from coal-based thermal power plants which generate huge amounts of fly ash, a highly polluting waste. Eco-bricks made out of this industrial waste can have a high compressive strength (up to 350 kg/cm2) and low water absorption capacity (15-20%) when compared to normal bricks. Usually such bricks are made from fly ash, lime and gypsum/cement. They are subjected to a compaction process, followed by curing and drying to produce non-fired bricks. These fly ash bricks are extremely environment friendly as compared to red bricks produced by conventional technologies, given that there are no emissions of greenhouse gases during their production. Also unlike conventional red bricks, fly ash bricks do not use soil as a raw material, thus conserving an important natural resource that is critical for productive farming. Fly ash bricks use up to 60 per cent waste material and hence this brick making technology is an innovative way to recycle industrial waste, improve resource efficiency and mitigate climate change. The use of fly ash bricks for construction is slowly gaining popularity in India.

TARA provides custom-designed solutions and a comprehensive package of services to prospective clients assisting entrepreneurs in the highest

2. The investment cost per enterprise does not include cost of land.

quality of fly ash brick production, commencing with the selection and testing of raw materials (fly ash, sand and lime), determining an optimum mix design, supply of machines and accessories, commissioning and production and quality control training in all aspects of brick production. These services are delivered to the enterprises along with onsite training. TARA operates a Centre of Excellence in brick making technology at Datia in Central India, which has a fully equipped laboratory for testing raw materials and finished products. The technology and machines have been developed based on a scientific analysis and understanding of waste materials, thereby achieving the desired strength of fly ash bricks with optimum utilisation of fly ash, lime, cement and sand.

TARA's fly ash brick technology is a highly profitable business for small scale building material producers, civil contractors and builders. TARA MechRam technology packages with daily production capacities of 5,000 and 10,000 bricks are mostly offered to the entrepreneurs.

Fly Ash Brick Production Equipment

Parameter/ Package	*TARA MechRam-MXV*	*TARA MechRam-MXII*	*TARA MechRam-MX*	*TARA MechRam-MV*
Productivity	1600/hr	1200/hr	1000/hr	650/hr
Personnel	8-9 nos.	6-8 nos.	6-8 nos.	6-8 nos.
Power	31.5 HP	28 HP	24 HP	13.5 HP
Mould size and type available	9"x 4"x 3" and 10"x 5"x 3" plain	9"x 4"x 3"and 10"x5"x3" with plain and chamfered options		
Cost (USD)	37,500	31,000	28,000	16,500

The hydraulically operated TARA MechRam fly ash brick making machines are all simple operating machines that compress the fly-ash mix into the desired brick sizes and optimise manpower requirements while offering an assured productivity. The choice of standard and chamfered brick moulds is available as part of these technology packages. A total investment of US$70,000 (as calculated for 2015) for setting up a mechanised production system assures an annual production of 2 million bricks with a turnover of about US$200,000 per annum. The payback period for the business is around 2–3 years. The benefits of the technology are appreciated by both the public and the private sector.

More than 2 million fly ash bricks using TARA's brick making technology were utilised in a Tsunami re-construction housing project of 1,248 houses in South India. The Development Alternatives World Headquarters building in

Delhi has extensively used the high strength fly ash blocks. TARA has installed fly ash plants at over 100 locations across India. The fly ash technology truly has the potential to clean up the brick sector and transform it into a leader in the area of climate change mitigation.

Innovation: Compressed earth block making technology

Benefits: Low cost, eco-friendly and boosting local economy

Developer: Technology and Action for Rural Advancement, India

Date: 1985-1999

Job Potential: 10 direct and 30 indirect jobs per enterprise with an investment of US$36,000[3] as in 2015

Earth is a construction material that forms the basis of an environmentally sound, economically feasible and socially relevant building technology. The benefits of using earth for construction are its thermal insulation value, easy availability and aesthetic appeal. It is non-polluting, very low in embodied energy and utilises locally available renewable materials and skills, thus benefitting the local economy and promoting self-reliance.

Drawbacks of traditional handmade mud bricks are their limited load-bearing capacity and their high water absorption rates. Compressed earth blocks overcome these limitations by using a mechanical press, which increases the block density through compaction and minimal stabilisation with lime or cement. These blocks have a high density varying between 1800-2000 kg/m^3. This gives them a load-bearing capacity of at least 60 kg/cm^2 and improved water resistance well suited for single and multi-storey construction of up to four storeys.

Compressed earth blocks are low in energy consumption because no fuel is burnt during the brick making process. They are high quality masonry units and are as strong and durable as burnt bricks. When manufactured locally, they are cheaper than burnt bricks and therefore more cost effective. They use non-organic soils and thus do not compete with soils for agriculture. With these advantages, compressed earth blocks can easily be used for construction of simple houses. Greater design care and

3. The investment cost per enterprise does not include cost of land.

stabilisation can ensure construction of more ambitious structures that need less maintenance and are long lasting.

The composition of the soil mix has a great bearing on quality of the blocks produced. So it is very important to test each batch of soil to determine whether it is suitable to make the compressed earth blocks or not. Soils that are classified as clayey-loams soils are excellent for making blocks. Earth blocks are stabilised using chemicals such as lime and cement to achieve better dry and wet compressive strength, enhance cohesion, reduce porosity and improve resistance to erosion by wind and rain. Cement stabilisation is recommended for non-cohesive soils that have low clay content. Cement acts as a binding material improving the cohesion and bulk density of the soil. Lime stabilisation is appropriate for soils that have a clay fraction above 20 per cent.

The compressed earth block press is a very simple mechanical device. A number of such presses have been developed all over the world. These range from simple manual presses to motorised production units. In countries with abundant manpower and low capital investment capability, manual presses are more suitable. TARA manufactures and markets the TARA Balram-MI earth block press, which is manual and is especially suited to Indian conditions.

The design of the TARA Balram-MI earth block press is based on the principle of soil mechanics. Soil exhibits a non-linear response under compression. It is important that the compressing mechanism provides a variable mechanical advantage to match this behaviour. Thus in the development of TARA Balram-MI, there were extensive studies done for using force against compaction of soil. The ramming action of this earth block press is powered by a toggle and crank mechanism. Soil is filled and manufactured blocks are ejected from top of the mould, while ramming takes place from the bottom. The lockable mould is a twin chamber that produces two conventional sized bricks in one ramming cycle. Using the TARA Balram-MI compressed earth block press, five persons can maintain a high production rate of over 150 cycles per hour, i.e., 300 blocks hourly. Including time spent on preparation of soil and stacking of blocks, five people can produce an average of 1200–1500 blocks daily.

The advantage of TARA Balram-MI is that it is very easy to use and reduces cost as no electricity is required for its operation. However, it cannot cater to the ever-growing demands of the construction sector and can only be used for very small, entry-level enterprises. Keeping in mind production at a larger scale, a semi-mechanised machine named TARA MechRam-MV was developed. TARA MechRam-MV has a twin moulding mechanism powered by a single hydraulic power pack.

Making compressed earth blocks can be a highly profitable business for small scale building material producers, civil contractors and builders. A total investment of US$36,000 (as calculated for 2015) for a semi-mechanised production system assures an annual production of 1.5 million bricks with a turnover of US$1,20,000 per year. It is suited for a daily production of 5000 bricks per day. The payback period for the business is around 3 years.

Package Specifications for TARA MechRam-MV

Description	TARA Balram-MV
Production capacity	650 blocks/hour
Roller pan mixer	300 kg/charge
Electrical power (3 Phase)	5+ 7.5 HP
Manpower	8-10 persons
Product transfer mechanism	Pallet trolley

With compressed earth block making technology, bricks can be made at site as per the actual requirements for different applications and this permits optimisation of the total material, cost and energy input.

Innovation: Check dams for water, food and livelihood security in rural India

Benefits: Environmentally and economically sustainable, increase farmers' incomes, reduce migration

Developer: Development Alternatives, India

Date: 1989

Across India, ground water levels have been falling at an unprecedented and alarming rate. This is a result of over-extraction of ground water for intensive agriculture coupled with a reduction in the recharge potential due to deforestation and other land use changes. Crop yields and farmers' incomes have been adversely affected, resulting in stress induced migration from rural areas to cities. With climate change, rainfall patterns are expected to get more erratic, thus, further aggravating the water stress. This is particularly true for semi-arid and drought-prone regions such as Bundelkhand in Central India, which rely on predominantly rainfed agriculture.

The Bundelkhand region comprising 13 districts in the states of Uttar Pradesh and Madhya Pradesh was densely forested, until the late 18th century. After the turn of the century, rising demand for wood and agricultural expansion led to increasing levels of deforestation. Development Alternatives identified water scarcity; augmented by deforestation, soil erosion and increasing extractive pressures stemming from rapid population growth as one of the main factors for poor agricultural production in the region. In 1989, Development Alternatives began promoting check dams as an appropriate intervention to restore the degraded natural resource base in Bundelkhand and to help rural communities escape the prevalent poverty-debt-migration trap.

As opposed to large dams which submerge huge tracts of land and forests and cause in increased water logging and salinity, check dams are an environmentally and economically sustainable option to meet irrigation and drinking water needs of the rural communities. Check dams are small barriers built across the direction of water flow on shallow rivers and streams for the purpose of water harvesting. They slow down the water flow and retain the excess water during monsoon rains in a small area behind the structure. The water stored by the check dam is primarily intended for use in irrigation during the dry season, but can also serve livestock and domestic needs. A major environmental benefit of constructing check dams is recharge of the nearby wells and the underground aquifers in the catchment area, as a result of the water seeping into the ground. Check dams are built in a range of sizes using a variety of materials, including clay, stone and cement. Earthen check dams or embankments can easily be constructed by the farmers themselves.

Through scientific analysis coupled with participatory planning processes, Development Alternatives identifies suitable sites along seasonal streams that can be used to conserve and store rain water. Use of the Geographical Information System (GIS) helps to guide the planning process by scientifically pin-pointing where the check dams should be constructed for maximising the impact. Community participation in the planning and implementation ensures that benefits accrue to all households in the catchment area and that the structure is maintained and managed post construction. Over the last three decades, Development Alternatives has facilitated the construction of more than 200 check dams in the Bundelkhand region.

Check dams provide a sustainable solution for restoring ecological balance and productive potential of the land through water conservation, prevention of soil run-off and regeneration of the vegetative cover, thus contributing to natural resource resilience in rural India. These small dams result in a decreased dependence of the farmers on monsoon rains and enable the availability of water for irrigation as well as drinking water for humans and livestock. Development Alternatives' experience in the semi-arid Bundelkhand region proves that check dams can make agriculture on small farms profitable, which helps farmers break free from the vicious cycle of poor production, poverty and debt. Formerly barren lands have now been brought under irrigation as a direct result of increase in the water availability with the advent of check dams. Lands that earlier only produced a single crop can now be double-cropped, adding an additional season of labour. Water for agricultural and domestic use is now available for more months of the year and in many cases the whole year round.

The average investment required for constructing a check dam (as calculated for 2015) is around INR 10,000 per hectare, which is really less in comparison to a big dam that requires an approximate investment of INR 3,00,000 per hectare. The initial investment made in a check dam can usually be recovered in one or two years through the ensuing increases in agricultural production. Within two years of the intervention, a farmer registers an annual productivity increase of 20-25 per cent, resulting from both enhanced productivity per acre and an increase in cropping intensity. Better market and information linkages and improved produce management leads to an overall increase in income by nearly 30 per cent. Increased yields of staple crops and planting of vegetables and the addition of a second growing season has resulted in greater food security among the beneficiaries. Increase in economic prosperity has brought about reduction in migration rates, which has in turn enabled more children to attend school regularly. Workloads for women in the areas surrounding the check dams have decreased, since they no longer have to walk long distances in order to access water for their domestic needs.

Rainfed agriculture supports about 40 per cent of the country's population. About 85 million hectares or 60 per cent of the net cultivated area in India is classified as rainfed. Rainfed areas can hugely benefit from check dam interventions in terms of enhanced water security, reduced soil erosion, reduced climate vulnerability and improved agricultural productivity. With the global demand for food slated to double by 2050, the need of the hour is to improve per acre productivity without undermining the natural resource base. Compared with large scale, high technology water management approaches, such as constructing expensive big dams, and check dams, are an ideal solution for poor, water scarce rural areas.

Innovation: Chemical free paper technology using recycled materials

Benefits: Waste recycling, preventing deforestation and pollution, creating sustainable livelihoods for rural producer groups

Developer: Technology and Action for Rural Advancement, India

Date: 1996

Jobs Potential: Jobs created for 9 skilled people, 19 semi-skilled people and 32 unskilled people per enterprise with an investment of US$45,000[4] (as calculated for 2015)

World consumption of paper has grown phenomenally over the last few decades. To feed this growing demand, each year billions of trees are cut and highly toxic chemicals are released into the air and water from paper making plants around the world. Clearly, mill-made paper currently in vogue is not a sustainable option.

TARA has pioneered a paper making technology based on the principle of 'creating wealth from waste', which recycles cellulose-rich waste, such as waste paper, cotton rags, denim material and jute rags, to produce high quality handmade paper. Cellulose which has an inherent bonding property is present in natural fibres such as cotton, jute and banana fibres. It is procured primarily in the form of waste cotton available at a large number of cloth factories.

TARA PaperMek technology uses all environment friendly processes such as organic dyeing and bleaching using non-hazardous chemicals. As a result, there is zero pollution. With the elimination of tree wood as the base raw material, this technology prevents deforestation, thereby contributing to climate change mitigation. One ton of TARA paper saves 3 tons of wood and 100 cubic metres of water, giving us:

- 6 trees for life-giving oxygen and carbon sequestration
- 3 years of cooking fuel for one village family
- 25 years' drinking water for one person
- 1 month's income for 60 people

4. The investment cost per enterprise does not include cost of land.

High quality adherence to necessary technical specifications produces high quality and durable handmade paper at competitive rates. TARA handmade paper is available in a wide range of colours, textures and strength. It is used by diverse clients ranging from corporates to testing laboratories, retail stores and academic institutions. Corporates use TARA handmade paper for conference kits, gift items and office stationery, such as letterheads, notepads and envelopes. Academic institutions procure this durable paper for documents that require long life, such as degrees and certificates while testing laboratories use TARA paper as filter paper and bloating paper. Retail stores procure stationery products and home décor products made out of TARA paper for reselling at their retail outlets.

The actual handmade paper making process is quite simple. The raw materials are first sorted to eliminate foreign particles and dust. They are then soaked in water and beaten to a pulp in an electrically powered mini-beater. The pulp is transferred to a univat machine, which lays the pulp out in sheets of even thickness. After squeezing out the excess water by a screw press, the sheets of paper are separated and dried in the sun. The dried sheets are polished with a calendaring machine. Finally, the sheets are cut in required sizes, sorted as per colour, texture, thickness and sent for packaging. On an average, to produce 1 kg of recycled paper, 160 kg of drinking quality water and a 3-phase electrical connection with 50 hp connected load is required.

TARA handmade paper units are available in different sizes. TARA mini paper recycling system is designed for schools, colleges, institutions, hobby shops and vocational training purposes. It is an uncomplicated technology package, which requires a total space of 300 square feet. This mini plant can recycle 25 kg of waste per day to produce 15-18 kg of paper daily. TARA mega handmade paper unit requiring a total space of 930 square feet can recycle 320 kg of waste daily producing 220 kg of paper per day. The equipment used is innovative, low cost and efficient. To set up a handmade production unit with an annual capacity of 24 metric tons, an investment of US$45,000 (as calculated for 2015) is required. TARA has also scaled the TARA PaperMek technology with innovative equipment that can recycle tetra pak cartons to produce good quality paper. On an average, 120 reams of papers can be produced at a TARA mega paper unit.

Approximately 30–40 per cent of the paper is converted into products, such as carry bags, watermark papers and other lifestyle products. TARA paper products, such as lamp shades, gift boxes, carry bags, office files, letter pads, visiting cards, diaries and conference bags, are in high demand due to their eco-friendly attributes, aesthetic appeal and unique designs.

Simple production processes and a semi-mechanised system makes it possible to train unskilled men and women creating green livelihood options for them. TARA's first paper unit was set up in 1996 in a small place called Orchha in Central India to provide sustainable livelihood for Sahariya tribal women. Direct employment benefits go to the people and their families involved at the production units. Indirect and secondary jobs in packaging, printing and logistics are also created for supporting and ensuring the production process. These paper making units have the potential to revolutionise the paper making industry and create millions of green jobs around the world.

> Innovation: Water Purification Technologies for low income households
>
> Benefits: Providing safe drinking water, promoting good health, low cost, easy to use
>
> Developer: Development Alternatives, India
>
> Date: 1998

Across the world, over a billion people lack access to safe drinking water. Over 40 million people, 75 per cent of whom are children, suffer from waterborne diseases every day. A strong focus on low cost treatment technologies is important to provide clean drinking water to the low income households globally.

In India like other developing countries, most of the water-related problems are due to bacterial, physical and chemical contamination. High erosion in streams, less stream flow depth and loose sandy aquifers are major concerns in rural areas as they increase turbidity in community water supply systems. Water filtration systems available in the market, such as Ultraviolet Treatment and Reverse Osmosis, require reliable electricity supply and are not cost effective for the filtration needs of a community water supply system.

Addressing the gap in the reliable and affordable water supply technology space, Development Alternatives, has developed a set of water purification technology packages, targeting the low income household population. These are being marketed by its sister concern, TARA. All these technologies have been thoroughly tested in the laboratory and under different field conditions. The performance claims have been verified and certified by reputed organisations and accredited laboratories periodically.

Jal-TARA Community Water Filter is a revolutionary product designed in 1998 to treat drinking water contaminated with pathogenic bacteria, turbidity and iron using a natural method of slow sand filtration. The fabric disc provided in the filter enhances the physical filtration process by arresting the silt, mud particles and organic matter from passing through. The filter contains specially sized stone aggregates and a fabric disc, which provides extra surface to form a bio-film. It accelerates the biological filtration process by building up the biological community on the fabric disc and sand bed that helps in scavenging and breaking down the pathogens and organic matter in the raw water. The system can be fed under gravity flow or through conventional pumps or operated by solar photo-voltaic.

Jal-TARA filter assures the same level of purity as boiled water. Based on extensive field testing conducted in various parts of the country, it has been found that the filter is capable of removing *Faecal coliform* and *Streptococci* with an efficiency of 99-99.9 per cent. These pathogenic bacteria cause diseases, such as cholera, typhoid, dysentery, amoebic dysentery, diarrhoea and hepatitis. The strength of this filtration system lies in its cost effectiveness, durability and the fact that the process itself requires no chemicals or electricity. Simplicity of installation and operation is another strong feature. The system is designed to have very little maintenance, which can be done easily by an unskilled person. It is very durable and has a long life of about 15 years. It is an ideal filter for institutions, such as schools, community centres and colleges, especially those located in remote areas.

The community level filter, standardised in a 1000-1400 litre water tank (food grade) provides 2000-3000 litres of safe water per day. This amount of water can cater to the drinking water needs of up to 80-100 households. The Jal-TARA filter has been positioned as a water purification solution for institutions and small village communities. More than 250 such filters have been installed successfully all over India.

Jal-TARA filter costs INR 60,000 (without taxes and freight extra). This allows filter entrepreneurs to supply treated water at a cost as low as INR 0.15 per litre of water with a payback period of one year. In comparison, a low cost household filter available in the market supplies treated water at a cost of INR 0.23 per litre and reserve osmosis (RO) purified water costs INR

1 per litre. The safe water supply enterprise business using the Jal-TARA filter is definitely an attractive option for entrepreneurs.

Jal-TARA Arsenic Filter designed in 2012 is an innovative point-of-use water purification system for removing arsenic, iron and turbidity. Long-term exposure to arsenic through drinking water and food can result in adverse health effects, including skin diseases, birth defects, low IQ (intelligence quotient) and cancer. Extensive arsenic pollution of groundwater is found in the Bengal delta plain, covering the state of West Bengal in East India and Bangladesh in South Asia. The problem also extends to the Indian states of Jharkhand, Bihar, Uttar Pradesh, Assam and Chhattisgarh, affecting 5.52 per cent of the Indian population.

The Jal-TARA Arsenic Water Filter is a composite unit, which uses sand bed and zero-valent iron to remove arsenic, bacteria and iron from the contaminated water to provide 15-20 litres of safe drinking water per hour. This filter reduces arsenic levels from 400 ppb to less than 50 ppb, which is the safe limit as per the Bureau of Indian Standards (BIS). The life of this filter is over 5 years.

The operational mechanism is very simple and easy to use. When arsenic containing water is poured into the filter, the arsenic is rapidly absorbed onto the surface of media particles, which contain a special form of iron material. The arsenic-loaded iron particles are then flushed into the sand layer below. Users are cautioned not to dispose of the sludge or washed water ridden with arsenic into the environment, and are advised to safely dispose the same by solidifying into bricks to avoid contamination of soil and water sources.

TARA Aqua+ 'The Magic of Two Drops' is a 50ml bottle of Sodium Hypochlorite Solution (Liquid Chlorine) developed by TARA. Each bottle of Aqua+ can purify 500 litres of water, which is sufficient for a family of 5 members for 1 month. It is affordable, easy to use (add two drops of Aqua+ per litre of water, wait for 30 minutes and it is safe to drink) and aspirational (provides households with 'filter-like' water at an affordable price). Since commercialisation in 2012, TARA has sold over 200,000 bottles of Aqua+ in different states of India, such as Uttar Pradesh, Haryana, Kerala and Tamil Nadu.

Innovation: Technologies for point of use (POU) water quality testing

Benefits: Low cost, easy to use and reliable for promoting awareness on drinking water quality

Developer: Development Alternatives, India

Date: 1994

Globally, waterborne diseases caused by lack of safe drinking water and sanitation facilities kill more young children than AIDS, malaria and measles combined.[5] In India, it is estimated that around 37.7 million people are affected by waterborne diseases annually. Out of this 1.5 million children are estimated to die of diarrhea alone. The annual economic burden of waterborne diseases is estimated at USD 600 million.[6] It is also reported that more than 23 states in India are endemic to fluoride contamination and over 5.52 per cent of the population across 5 states is exposed to excess levels of arsenic in drinking water.

Increasing levels of population without adequate water treatment infrastructure in developing countries has been the key reason for chemical and biological contamination and deterioration of water quality of both the ground water and surface water sources. Unavailability of clean drinking water results in people falling sick with waterborne diseases, which causes long-term health impacts, loss of productivity, time and financial resources.

Based on the felt need for communities and individuals to take control of their water quality, the Development Alternatives has innovated and developed rapid water testing technologies in order to check water quality at source and point of use. TARA Life, a sister concern of Development Alternatives, has launched these revolutionary technologies under the brand name of Jal-TARA. All the water testing products are extremely simple, easy to use and reliable. They are certified by leading laboratories in India. Thousands of children, villagers and professionals across India and other countries have been using these products to verify the water quality of ponds, wells, lakes, rivers and other drinking water sources around their homes and localities.

5. *www.water.org*

6. Drinking Water Quality in Rural India: Issues and Approaches by WaterAid

Jal-TARA Water Testing Kit (Standard) is a mini laboratory that can be carried to any corner of the country. This simple and reliable field kit has been developed using standard laboratory methods. It is designed to test 14 essential drinking and river water quality parameters. These include physical parameters such as pH, temperature, turbidity, hardness; chemical parameters, such as arsenic, chloride, fluoride, iron, nitrate, residual chlorine, dissolved oxygen, phosphorous, ammonia; and biological parameters such as coliform bacteria and benthic diversity. With the reagents supplied in the kit, 100 samples can be tested for each parameter, except for the coliform test in which only 10 samples can be tested. All the tests use only mild acids and reagents and hence are extremely safe for use by children and adults. The price of the standard Jal-TARA water testing kit is about US$250.

Besides the standard Jal-TARA Water Testing Kit, the following customised kits are also available for various pollutants:

TARA Aquacheck Vial is a revolutionary product designed to test the presence of pathogenic bacteria in water, which causes common waterborne diseases. It has been prepared according to the quality control guidelines and improved methods of a United Nations International Children's Agency (UNICEF)-commissioned research study. If a drinking water supply such as a stream or a shallow well becomes polluted with human wastes (faeces and sewage), it may serve as a vehicle of transmission of waterborne diseases, such as typhoid, cholera and dysentery.

TARA Aquacheck Vials are very effective in identifying faecal pollution in water. Pathogenic bacteria present in the contaminated water sample produces hydrogen sulphide gas on coming in contact with the microbial nutrient media present in the vial. If the vial results in visible black colour in about 48 hours, it is then an indication of positive bacterial contamination. In cold climatic conditions, the sample bottle can be kept in the pocket for maintaining the required temperature to achieve better results. Each vial provided in the kit is for one-time testing only. These Aquacheck Vials can be a very useful surveillance tool for identification of bacterial contamination in drinking water sources at offices, schools and houses.

Jal-TARA Arsenic Testing Kit can test arsenic contamination that is often seen in shallow water sources, especially in the Gangetic belt of India and Bangladesh in the South Asian region. The kit has a provision to test 50 samples and the testing range is 10-400 ppb. As per the BIS, the permissible limit for drinking water sources is 50 ppb. The kit can be handy in determining the level of contamination as well as the efficacy of various arsenic water filters prevalent in the region.

Innovation: Eco-concrete building technologies

Benefits: Cost effective, environment friendly

Developer: Technology and Action for Rural Advancement, India

Date: 2008

Jobs Potential: 5-6 direct and 15-20 indirect jobs per enterprise with an investment of US$800,010 as in 2015

Construction sector is one of the most resource- and energy-intensive industries worldwide. With an aim to reduce the carbon footprint of this sector, TARA is promoting a diverse portfolio of eco-concrete technologies that demonstrate an efficient use of energy-intensive building materials, such as cement and steel. Building products, such as doors, window frames, roofs and floors, made using these technologies are cost effective and yet high in quality.

The TARA portfolio of eco-concrete technologies offers business solutions to building material enterprises, contractors and builders. These technologies create easy to produce standardised products that do not require great amount of skill for production. Once the established procedure is properly followed, even an unskilled person can produce these products. All the eco-concrete technologies are designed to yield production within hours of setting up the enterprises, which makes them highly profitable for micro- and small-scale building material producers all over the world.

TARA GreenCast Frames Technology provides a cutting-edge solution for the manufacture of high quality, long lasting and affordable concrete door and window frames using reinforced cement concrete. No wood is used in the production of these frames. Given the current scarcity of good quality timber and the lack of sustainable harvesting practices, wood is not the best available option. Cement-based low energy technologies, such as the GreenCast, form a good alternative. GreenCast frames are highly durable, termite resistant, all-weather proof, easy to assemble and have a universal application as they are applicable for residential and institutional buildings. TARA GreenCast Frames Technology is a good business at small scale in decentralised locations, especially where timber is in short supply or difficult to access.

The GreenCast frames technology package consists of a vibrating table with a choice of moulds, custom-designed accessories and fittings.

The production system consists of specialised rubber moulds, which are placed inside galvanized iron (GI) channels. A series of GI channels are mounted on the vibrating table and fitted with a vibration mechanism to achieve uniform compaction and high quality surface finish. The technology is capable of producing 20 sets of door or window frames in 8 hours shift with 6 operators. With a capital investment of US$8000 (as calculated in 2015), a production value of US$18,000 can be achieved. The technology offers flexibility in production. It can easily be adopted to the production of other building products, such as GreenCast Floors.

TARA GreenCast Floors Technology consists of a flexible production system in which medium and light duty decorative paving blocks are produced with the use of custom-designed PVC moulds. The basic raw materials used are cement, fine aggregate and coarse aggregate. PVC moulds with the concrete mix are placed at one end of the table. The hydraulic compaction gives high quality and strength to the blocks. These concrete pavers are used in driveways, parking areas, fuel stations and rural roads. Acceptability of concrete pavers is very high in urban areas and for rural infrastructure, such as pavements and roads. The joints between the pavers allow for percolation and water recharge into the ground. As a result, these are being promoted as a better alternative as compared to cement or asphalt roads.

This technology offers flexibility in producing other concrete products such as GreenCast Frames. The technology is capable of producing 1000 blocks in a 8 hours shift with 6 operators. A total investment of USD 12,000 for a semi-mechanised production system assures an annual production value of about US$28,000 (2015). The payback period for the business is under 3 years. The ease of application and durability of concrete pavers is very rapidly expanding the market for these products.

Micro-concrete Roofing Tiles (MCR Tiles) Technology provides for low cost roofing needs. MCR tiles are made from cement-based roofing material. These are a high quality alternative to the conventional high energy and low durability options, such as burnt clay country tiles (*khaprail*) and CGI sheets. MCR tiles are also cost effective as compared to other roofing tiles. With an appropriately designed understructure, MCR tiles can be used for a variety of applications in low cost housing, institutional buildings, factories and parking areas.

Considering that large tracts of this country lie in high rainfall and snow fall regions, sloping roofs are traditionally and climatically suitable roofing options. In the mountain regions where slate was traditionally used, state mining cannot be carried out due to ecological concerns. The plains and coastal regions have traditionally used high energy intensive, clay tiles or thatch. The MCR technology provides a viable solution, using stone dust waste and minimal cement. The MCR tiles are securely tied to the understructure with wires and therefore can also efficiently meet the requirements of roofing in regions of high velocity winds like the coastal belt.

The MCR technology promotes skill development, livelihood creation and is a very lucrative small business opportunity for village applications. It is suitable for women to use and therefore promotes women-based enterprises. Business risk for the entrepreneurs is low as the production materials are easily available local materials, such as cement, sand and crushed stone. A total investment for setting up an enterprise is US$8000. This assures an annual production of 75,000 roofing tiles with a turnover of US$15,000 per annum (as calculated in 2015). The business generates over 30 per cent profits per annum. TARA Micron or MCR package is a very versatile machine as it can also be used to produce different types of multi-design decorative pavers.

TARA's *Pre-Cast Roofing Channel Making Machine* provides a cost-effective solution for flat roofs. The pre-cast roofing tiles are made of cement mortar vibrated on a table at a controlled frequency and then set on mould to shape. The mortar used is a mix of concrete, fine sand, coarse sand and fine aggregate. Care is needed at all stages of production to secure quality of the tile. These tiles are water proof, fire proof and insect proof. Hence they are more durable when compared to thatch roofs. They also provide a durable, low cost and thermally more satisfactory option than ACC sheets. These pre-cast roofing tiles can be manufactured locally with low capital investment using local materials and cement and result in a 25 per cent saving in cost when compared to RCC (reinforced cement concrete) flat roof. A total capital investment of US$20,000 is required for a mechanised production system with an annual turnover of US$50,000 (as calculated in 2015). This technology is ideal for use in construction projects, where crushed stone is not available or costs are high.

1) Eco-friendly Urban Building Design

2) Vertical Shaft Brick Kiln Technology

3) Fly Ash Brick Making Technology

3.1 TARA MechRam-MX

3.2 Fly Ash Bricks

3.3 Fly Ash Bricks

4) Compressed Earth Block Making Technology

4.1 Tribal Women Operating TARA Balram-MI

4.2 TARA MechRam-MV

5) Check Dams for Water, Food and Livelihood Security in Rural India

6) Chemical Free Paper Technology Using Recycled Materials

6.1 Paper Recycling Process

6.2 Diaries Made Out of Recycled Paper

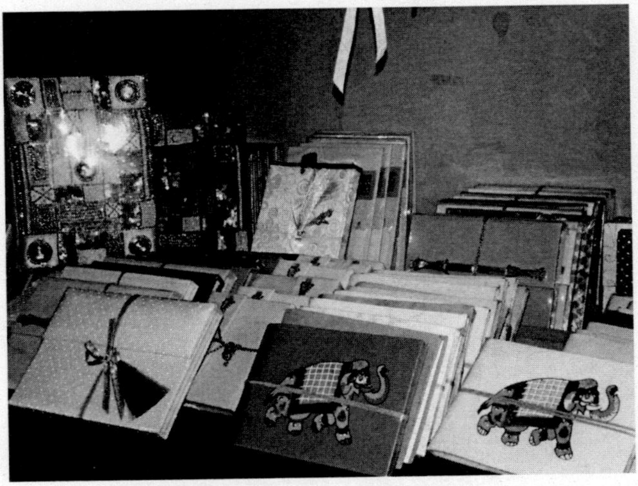

6.3 Products Made Out of Recycled Paper

7) Water Purification Technologies for Low Income Households

7.1 Jal-TARA Arsenic Filter

7.2 Jal-TARA Community Water Filter

7.3 Technologies for Point-of-Use (POU) water quality testing

7.4 Aqua check vial

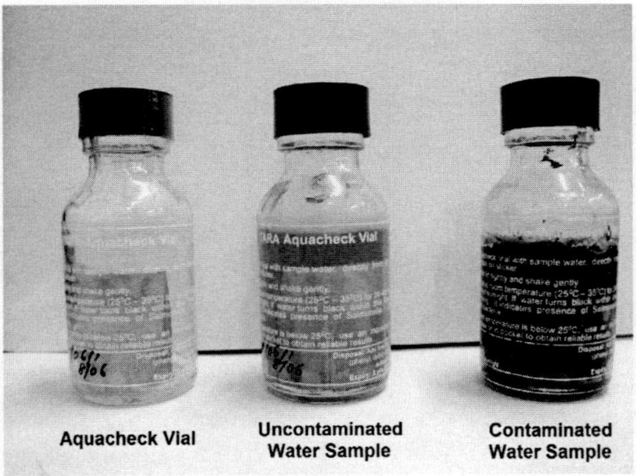

8) Eco Concrete Building Technologies

8.1 Eco Concrete Tiles

Bibliography and References

Books and Journals

Alexandersson, Olaf (2002). *Living Water: Viktor Schauberger and the Secrets of Natural Energy.* Warrington, UK: Newleaf Books.

Appelhof, Mary (2001). *Worms Eat my Garbage: How to Set Up and Mainain a Vermicomposting System.* Kalamazoo, MI, USA: Flower Press.

Ayensu, Edward S. (1998). *Ashanti Gold, African Legacy of the World's Most Precious Metal.* London, UK: Marshall Editions.

Barksdale, Jelks (1968). *Encyclopedia of the Chemical Elements, "Titanium".* New York: Reinhold Book Corporation.

Bartholomew, Alick and David Bellamy (2005). *Hidden Nature: The Startling Insights of Viktor Schauberger.* Kempton, IL: Adventures Unlimited Press.

Benyus, Janine (2002). *Biomimicry; Innovation Inspired By Nature.* New York: Harper Perennial.

Biswas, Asit K., T.N. Khoshoo and Ashok Khosla (1990). *Environmental Modelling for Developing Countries.* Dublin: Tycooly Intl.

Brown, Lester R., Plan B 4.0: Mobilizing to Save Civilization, New York: W.W. Norton, 2009.

Buswell, John (2008). "Development of the World Mushroom Industry: Applied Mushroom Biology and International Mushroom Organizations," *International Journal of Medicinal Mushrooms* X. Redding, CT, Begell House.

Capra, Fritjof (2008). *The Science of Leonardo: Inside the Mind of the Great Genius of the Renaissance.* New York: Anchor Books.

_________. (1995). *Steering Business Towards Sustainability.* Tokyo, Japan: United Nations University Press.

_________. (1997). *The Web of Life: A New Scientific Understanding of Living Systems.* Boston: Shambhala Books.

Chang, S.T. and John Buswell (2000-2009). "Development of the World Mushroom Industry: Applied Mushroom Biology and International Mushroom Organizations," *International Journal of Medicinal Mushrooms.* Redding, CT: Begell House.

Coats, Callum (1999). *Nature As Teacher: How I Discovered New Principles in the Working of Nature* (Eco-Technology Series). Dublin, Ireland: Gateway (Gill & MacMillan).

Coats, Callum (1998). *Water Wizard: The Extraordinary Properties of Natural Water.* Dublin, Ireland: Gateway (Gill & MacMillan).

Donachie, Matthew J. (1988). *Titanium, a Technical Guide.* Metals Park, OH: ASM International.

Fleischmann, Wimm, Martin Grassberger and Ronald Sherman (2004). *Maggot Therapy: A Handbook of Maggot-Assisted Wound Healing.* New York: Thieme Publications.

Fredriksson, Marianne and Bengt Warne (1993). *På akacians villkor. Att Bygga Och Bo I Samklang Med Naturen* (On the Conditions of the Acacia, to Build and Live in Harmony with Nature). Göteborg: Warne förlag AB.

Gabriel, Julie (2008). *Green Beauty Guide: Your Essential Resource to Organic and Natural Skin Care, Hair Care, Makeup, and Fragrances.* Deerfield Beach, FL: HCI Press.

Govera, Chido (2009). *The Future of Hope.* Tokyo, Japan: ZERI Foundation.

Gravitis, Janis (2008). "Biomaterials and Bioenergy from Photosynthesis, within Zero Emissions Framework, in Franco Barbir and Sergio Ulgiati (eds). *Sustainable Energy Production and Consumption: Benefits, Strategies and Environmental Costing.* NATO Science for Peace and Security Series C: Environmental Security. New York: Springer Verlag.

Greatbatch, Wilson (2000). *The Making of the Pacemaker: Celebrating a Lifesaving Invention.* Amherst, NY: Prometheus Books.

Ishida, Emile (2009). *Nature Technology: Channeling the Forces of Nature* (in Japanese) Tokyo: Kagaku Douijin.

Kamm, Birgit, Patrick R. Gruber and Michael Kamm (2006). *Biorefineries: Industrial Processes and Products: Status Quo and Future Directions* (2 Volume Set) (v. 1). Weinheim, Germany: Wiley-VCH.

Lovins, Amory, Paul Hawken and L. Hunter Lovins (2008). *Natural Capitalism: Creating the Next Industrial Revolution.* Boston, MA: Back Bay Books.

Margulis, Lynn (1998). *Five Kingdoms, An Illustrated Guide to the Phyla of Life on Earth.* New York: W.H. Freeman & Company.

Margulis, Lynn and Dorion Sagan (2003). *Acquiring Genomes: The Theory of the Origins of the Species.* New York: Basic Books.

_________, (2000). *What Is Life?* Berkeley: University of California Press.

Margulis, Lynn and Karlene Schwarz (2003). *Five Kingdoms: A Multimedia Guide to the Phyla of Life on Earth.* W.H. Freeman Company.

McDonough, Bill and Michael Braungart (2002). *Cradle to Cradle.* San Francisco, CA: North Point Press.

_________. (2013). *The Upcycle: Beyond Sustainability: Designing for Abundance.* New York: MacMillan.

Meadows, Donella H., Dennis L. Meadows, Jorgen Randers and William W. Behrens III (1972). *Limits to Growth, Report to the Club of Rome.* New York: Universe Books.

Miles, Philip G and Shu-Ting Chang (2004). *Mushrooms: Cultivation, Nutritional Value, Medicinal Effect, and Environmental Impact.* Boca Raton, FL: CRC Press.

Molisson, Bill and Reny Mia Slay (1988). *Permaculture: A Designers' Manual.* Tasmania, Australia: Tagari Publications.

Panati, Charles (1989). *Extraordinary Origins of Everyday Things.* New York, Harper Collins.

Parker, Andrew (2004). *In the Blink of an Eye: How Vision Sparked the Big Bang of Evolution*. New York: Basic Books.

Pikkety, Thomas (2012). *Le Capital au XXIe siècle*. Paris: Seuil. Transalated in 2014 as *Capital in the 21st Century*.

Prahalad, C.K. and Stuart L. Hart (2005). *The Fortune at the Bottom of the Pyramid: Eradicating Poverty through Profits*. Philadelphia, PA: Wharton School of Business.

Posamentier, Alfred and Ingmar Lehmann (2007). *The (Fabulous) Fibonacci Numbers*. Amherst, NY: Prometheus Books.

Priya, Shashank and Daniel Inman (2008). *Energy Harvesting Technologies*. New York: Springer Verlag.

Rangers, Jorgen and Dennis Meadows (2004). *Limits to Growth: The 30-Year Update*. White River Junction, VT: Chelsea Green.

Rau, Thomas and Susan Wyler (2009). *Swiss Secret to Optimal Health: Dr. Rau's Diet for Whole Body Healing*. New York: Berkley Books.

_________. (2003). *Biological Medicine: The Future of Natural Healing*. Marion, MA: Biological Medicine Network.

Rodríguez, Lledó (2009). *Camilo, Bioconstrucción (Spanish Edition)*. Madrid: Ediciones Literarias Mandala.

Rozema, Jelte, Yiannis Manetas and Lars Olof Björn (2001). *Responses of Plant to UV-B Radiation (Advances in Vegetation Science)*. New York: Springer Verlag.

Rubio, Luna (2007). Germán, Arte y Mañas de la Guadua, Una guía sobre el uso productivo de un bambú gigante (Art and Skill of the Bamboo: Guide to the Productive Use of Giant Bamboo). Bogotá: Ino Arte.

Shirai, Yoshihito, Kenji Sakai, Masayuki Taniguchi, Shigenobu Miura, Hitomi Ohara and Toru Matsumoto (2003). "Making Plastics from Garbage: A Novel Process of Poly-L-Lactate Production from Municipal Food Waste", *The Journal of Industrial Ecology* 7(3-4), 65-74 (Summer/Fall).

Stern, Lord Nicholas (2007). *The Economics of Climate Change: The Stern Review*. Cambridge, UK: Cambridge University Press.

Tanner, Michael D. (2014). "War on Poverty at 50: Despite Trillions Spent, War Won", *Foxnews.com*. 8 January.

Todd, Nancy Jack and John Todd (1994). *From Eco-Cities to Living Machines: Principles of Ecological Design*. Berkeley, CA: North Atlantic Press.

van Dieren, Wouter (1995). *Taking Nature into Account: A Report to the Club of Rome*. New York: Springer Verlag.

Vieira Costa, J. Alberto, Luciane Maria Colla, Paulo Fernando Duarte Filho (2004). "Improving Spirulina Platensis Biomass Yield Using a Fed-Batch Process", *Bioresource Technology* 92(3): 237-41. St. Louis, MO: Elsevier.

Vollrath, Fritz (1992). *Spiders Weird and Wonderful*. London, Hodder Children's Books .

von Vegesack, Matteo Kries, Jean Dethier, Klaus Steffens and The Vitra Design Museum (2000). *Grow Your Own House, Simon Velez and Bamboo Architecture* (English and German Edition). Weil am Rhein Germany: VITRA Design Museum.

von Weiszäcker, Ernst and Amory Lovins (1998). *Factor Four: Doubling Wealth.* London, England: Earthscan Ltd.

von Weizsacker, Ernst, Charlie Hargroves, Michael H. Smith, Cheryl Desha, Peter Stasinopoulos (2010). *Factor Five: The Promise of Resource Productivity*. London: Earthscan.

Weisman, Alan, Gaviotas (2008). *A Village to Reinvent the World.* White River Junction, VT: Chelsea Green.

White, Richard E. and Gloria Eugenia Gonzalez Marion (2007). *Las Gaviotas: Sustainability in the Tropics.* Worldwatch Institute. June.

Wiesel, Elie 1982). *Night.* New York: Bantam Books.

Wijkman, Anders (2008). *Unmitigated Disasters: The Victims of Man-made Catastrophes, Bourton on Dunsmore*. UK: Practical Action Publishing.

Wijkman, Anders and Johan Rockström (2012). *Bankrupting Nature: A Report to the Club of Rome*. London: Earthscan.

Wilkes, John (2003). *Flowforms: The Rhythmic Power of Water.* Edinburgh, UK: Floris Books.

Winans, Stephen C. and Bonnie Bassler (2008). *Chemical Communication among Bacteria.* Herndon, VA: ASM Press.

Worldwatch Institute (2008). *State of the World 2008: Toward a Sustainable Global Economy*. Washington, DC: The Worldwatch Institute.

———. (2009). *State of the World.* Washington, DC: Worldwatch Institute.

Yang, Jiashi (2006). *Analysis of Piezoelectric Devices*. Hackensack, NJ: World Scientific Publishers.

Other Works by Gunter Pauli

Pauli, Gunter (1987). *Crusader for the Future: A Portrait of Aurelio Peccei, Founder of the Club of Rome*. Oxfordshire, UK: Pergamon Press.

———. (1995). *Breakthroughs*. Hanslemere, UK: Epsilon Press.

———. (2000). *Upsizing: The Road to Zero Emissions, More Jobs, More Income and No Pollution*. Sheffield, UK: Greenleaf Publishing.

———. (2006). *Gunter's Fables*. Hogares Juveniles Campesinos, Bogotá, Colombia and ZERI.

———. (2007). *Out of the Box: Zeri Management Stories*. Cape Town, South Africa: Future Managers.

———. (2012). *Zen and the Art of Blue.* Taiwan: CommonWealth.

List of the Fables by Gunter Pauli

Inspired by the 188 projects and the science described in the Blue Economy here are 190 titles of fables:

A Fair Price

A Healthy Diet
A Shaky Earth
A Soup of Bacteria
A Throne for All
A Tooth Fairy
A Vegetable Chemical
African Farms
Animal Medicine (Medicina Animal)
Are you Prepared?
Are you Scared?
Attention is Energy
Bacteria on the Run
Bamboo Hangers
Bamboo Miracles
Beautiful Schools
Bees at Home
Better or Cheaper
Big Ears
Biological Batteries
Blowing in the Wind
Bread with Seeds
Breakfast in America
Building a Cathedral
Can Apples Fly? (Manzanas Voladoras?)
Cakes with Wind
Can Plants Sing?
Carbon Pencils
Chimps on Pension
Cold Feet (Pies Frios)
Colombian Mushrooms (Champiñones Colombianos)
Color without Paint
Computing with Light
Coral Care
Cozy Condors
Crabs for Dinner
Cutting Wood while Growing Forests
Crystal Palace
Dams in the Desert
Don't Eat Me Alive! (¡No Me Comas Vivo!)
Don't Leave me Alone (¡No me Dejes Solo!)

Dragons Everywhere
Dressed up in Algae
Dress-up Party
Drink it - Wear it
Ducklings' Breakfast
Edelweiss in the Sun
Edible Forests
Farmers Background
Farmers of the Sea
Farming in the City
Faster than Light
Fast Relief
Fishing without Nets
Floating in the Air
Floating in the Soup
Flour Bombs
Fluttering Flags
Forest Drinking Water (Aqua Potable del Bosque)
Forgive to Forget
Free of Filters
Fresh Air for Free
Fuel from the Trees
Fungi Tea with Music
Generous Geraniums
Getting More
Going Against the Current (Contra la Corriente)
Grandma Bison's Garden (El Jardin de la Abuela Bisonte)
Green Hair and Four Eyes (Cuatro Ojos, Pelo Verde)
Goats for Dinner
Going Round in Circles
Grow a House(Cultiva una Casa)
Himalayan Buckwheat
Holidays for the Body
House Sitting
How much is enough?
How Smart are You?
How to Say Goodbye
How to Swing it Together!
How to Take it Apart (Como des Baratarlo)
Hunting Yeast

Insect Grass
I love to Move it - Move it
Jewelry from Rice
Learning to Share
Learning to Teach
Let us Sleep
Light and Abundant
Light my Fire
Life Cycles
Living with Lice
Looking in the same Direction
Males Only (Solo Machos)
Maggots' Spit
Making Money on Money
Master Copycat
Masters and Grand Masters
Math for Beginners
Metals without Mining
Metals without Moulds
Milk or Cheese
Mine Water
Mite Farm
Mosquito Bites
More than one Earth
Noses and Ears to See (Narices y Oidos que Ven)
Only Healthy Food Please
Oranges from Soap (Jabon de Naranjas)
Oranges against Fire
Palm Oil
Paper from Stone
Planting Forests in the Sea
Plastics from Straw
Plastics in my Tommy
Please Play with Me (¡Por Favor Juega Conmigo!)
Power Forever
Power from a Waterhose
Rabbit Fuel
Rare on Earth
Ready to take the Risk
Red Rice (Arroces Rojos)

Sailing with the Sun
Salt Water to Farm
Scratch my Back (Rasca mi Espalda)
Shake to Charge
Shifting Gears
Shiitake Love Caffeine(Los Shiitake Aman la Caffeine)
Shoes from Silk
Shooting with Air
Slow Food
Smart Monkeys
Solar on both Sides
Solar Power at Night
Speed of Light
Spinach in the Sun
Spinning like a Spider
Stinging Nettles
Strong as Silk
Super Food
Surviving the Cold
Talking Water
The Ant Farmer (La Hormiga Agricoltura)
The Bear and the Fox (El Oso y el Zorro)
The Bearded Dragon
The Body's Oil
The Buzz of Silence
The Cactus Home
The Desert Witch (La Bruja del Disierto)
The Devil in the Detail
The Five Kingdoms of Nature (Los 5 Reinos De La Naturaleza)
The Goddess of the Tropics
The Happy Robot
The Hippo Beauty Parlor (Salon de Belleza del Hipopotamos)
The Incredible Fly
The Intestines of the Earth
The Kelp Dance
The King of Hearts (El Ray del Corazones)
The Magic of Chili
The Magic Hat (Sombrero Majico.)
The Math of Honey
The Mountain Goat (La Cabra Montanera)

The Skin of the Earth
The Smart Grid
The Smart Mushroom (El Hondo Sabiondo)
The Solar Blue Dragon
The Solar Tree
The Strongest Tree (Arbol Mas Fuerte)
The Tallest Tree
The Tree we Forgot
The Zebra Aircon (Ventilador de las Cebras)
Ticks for Life
Tomatoes and Apples for Clean Water
Touching the World
Tree Candy (Dulce del Arbol)
Turn off the Lights
Unlimited Gas
Vitamin Factory
Walking on Water (Caminando Sobre El Agua)
Walking on Hair
Water and Stones
We can Swim
We Love Salt
Whatever comes down goes up
Where did the Lamb go?
Where is Home? (Donde Esta Mi Casa?)
Who is the Sweetest?
Who is the Most Beautiful? (Qien es el mas Bello)
Who Needs You?
Why Can't I Steal Less? (Por Que no Puedo Robar Menos?)
Why Don't They Like Me? (Porque no me Qiere)?